WITHDRAWN
UTSA LIBRARIES

Knowledge Externalities, Innovation Clusters and Regional Development

NEW HORIZONS IN REGIONAL SCIENCE

Series Editor: Philip McCann, *Professor of Economics, University of Waikato, New Zealand and Professor of Urban and Regional Economics, University of Reading, UK*

Regional science analyses important issues surrounding the growth and development of urban and regional systems and is emerging as a major social science discipline. This series provides an invaluable forum for the publication of high-quality scholarly work on urban and regional studies, industrial location economics, transport systems, economic geography and networks.

New Horizons in Regional Science aims to publish the best work by economists, geographers, urban and regional planners and other researchers from throughout the world. It is intended to serve a wide readership including academics, students and policy-makers.

Titles in the series include:

Spatial Dynamics, Networks and Modelling
Edited by Aura Reggiani and Peter Nijkamp

Entrepreneurship, Investment and Spatial Dynamics
Lessons and Implications for an Enlarged EU
Edited by Peter Nijkamp, Ronald L. Moomaw and Iulia Traistaru-Siedschlag

Regional Climate Change and Variability
Impacts and Responses
Edited by Matthias Ruth, Kieran Donaghy and Paul Kirshen

Industrial Agglomeration and New Technologies
A Global Perspective
Edited by Masatsugu Tsuji, Emanuele Giovannetti and Mitsuhiro Kagami

Incentives, Regulations and Plans
The Role of States and Nation-states in Smart Growth Planning
Edited by Gerrit J. Knaap, Huibert A. Haccoû, Kelly J. Clifton and John W. Frece

New Directions in Economic Geography
Edited by Bernard Fingleton

The Management and Measurement of Infrastructure
Performance, Efficiency and Innovation
Edited by Charlie Karlsson, William P. Anderson, Börje Johansson and Kiyoshi Kobayashi

Knowledge Externalities, Innovation Clusters and Regional Development
Edited by Jordi Suriñach, Rosina Moreno and Esther Vayá

Knowledge Externalities, Innovation Clusters and Regional Development

Edited by

Jordi Suriñach, Rosina Moreno and Esther Vayá

AQR Research Group – IREA, University of Barcelona, Spain

NEW HORIZONS IN REGIONAL SCIENCE

Edward Elgar
Cheltenham, UK • Northampton, MA, USA

© Jordi Suriñach, Rosina Moreno and Esther Vayá 2007

All rights reserved. No part of this publication may be reproduced, stored in a retrieval system or transmitted in any form or by any means, electronic, mechanical or photocopying, recording, or otherwise without the prior permission of the publisher.

Published by
Edward Elgar Publishing Limited
Glensanda House
Montpellier Parade
Cheltenham
Glos GL50 1UA
UK

Edward Elgar Publishing, Inc.
William Pratt House
9 Dewey Court
Northampton
Massachusetts 01060
USA

A catalogue record for this book
is available from the British Library

Library
University of Texas
at San Antonio

ISBN 978 1 84720 120 1

Printed and bound in Great Britain by MPG Books Ltd, Bodmin, Cornwall

COST is an intergovernmental European framework for international cooperation between nationally funded research activities. COST creates scientific networks and enables scientists to collaborate in a wide spectrum of activities in research and technology.

COST is supported by the EU RTD Framework Programme.

ESF provides the COST office through an EC contract.

Contents

Contributors	ix
About the editors	xi
Introduction	1
Jordi Suriñach, Rosina Moreno and Esther Vayá	

PART I REGIONAL INNOVATION SYSTEMS, AGGLOMERATION ECONOMIES AND KNOWLEDGE SPILLOVERS: THEORETICAL APPROACHES

1. Theorizing regional knowledge capabilities: economic geography under 'open innovation'   19
   Philip Cooke
2. Knowledge spillovers and organizational heterogeneity: an historical overview of German technology sectors   42
   Mark Lehrer
3. The ambivalent role of mimetic behavior in proximity dynamics: evidence from the French 'Silicon Sentier'   61
   Jérôme Vicente, Yan Dalla Pria and Raphaël Suire
4. IT adoption, industrial structure and agglomeration economies   92
   Flora Bellone

PART II REGIONAL INNOVATION SYSTEMS, AGGLOMERATION ECONOMIES AND KNOWLEDGE SPILLOVERS: EMPIRICAL STUDIES

5. Pecuniary and knowledge externalities as agglomeration forces: empirical evidence from individual French data   111
   Corinne Autant-Bernard and Nadine Massard
6. The adoption of ICTs – why does it differ across regions?   136
   Andrea Bonaccorsi, Lucia Piscitello and Cristina Rossi

7. Novel applications of existing econometric instruments to analyse regional innovation systems: the Spanish case   155
   Mikel Buesa, Mónica Martínez Pellitero, Thomas Baumert and Joost Heijs
8. Over-embeddedness and under-exploration issues in cohesive networks: an application to territorial clusters   176
   Francesc Xavier Molina-Morales and María Teresa Martínez-Fernández
9. The regional dimension of university–industry interaction   198
   Joaquín M. Azagra Caro
10. Which factors underlie public selection of R&D cooperative projects?   219
    Lluís Santamaría Sánchez, Andrés Barge Gil and Aurelia Modrego Rico

PART III REGIONAL ECONOMIC GROWTH AND KNOWLEDGE

11. Convergence clubs and the role of education in Spanish regional growth   241
    Adriana Di Liberto
12. Non-linearities, spatial dependence and regional economic growth in Europe: a semiparametric approach   260
    Roberto Basile
13. Urban heterogeneity in knowledge-related economic growth   280
    Frank G. van Oort and Otto Raspe

Index   *305*

Contributors

Corinne Autant-Bernard, CREUSET, Jean Monnet University, Saint-Etienne, France.

Joaquín M. Azagra Caro, INGENIO (CSIC-UPV), Spain. E-mail: jazagra@ingenio.upv.es.

Andrés Barge Gil, Universidad Carlos III de Madrid, Institute of Economics, Laboratory of Analysis and Evaluation of Technical Change, Spain. E-mail: abarge@eco.uc3m.es.

Roberto Basile, ISAE (Institute for Studies and Economics Analyses), Rome, Italy. E-mail: robertobasile66@yahoo.it.

Thomas Baumert, Instituto de Análisis Industrial y Financiero (IAIF), Complutense University of Madrid, Spain.

Flora Bellone, University of Nice, France. E-mail: bellone@idefi.cnrs.fr.

Andrea Bonaccorsi, Department of Electrical Systems and Automation, University of Pisa, Italy. E-mail: a.bonaccorsi@gmail.com.

Mikel Buesa, Instituto de Análisis Industrial y Financiero (IAIF), Complutense University of Madrid, Spain.

Philip Cooke, Centre for Advanced Studies, Cardiff University, Wales (UK). E-mail: cookepn@Cardiff.ac.uk.

Yan Dalla Pria, Associate Professor, Sociology, CSO – IEP – Paris.

Adriana Di Liberto, Università di Cagliari e Crenos (Centro Ricerche Nord-Sud), Italy. E-mail: diliberto@unica.it.

Joost Heijs, Instituto de Análisis Industrial y Financiero (IAIF), Complutense University of Madrid, Spain. E-mail: joost@ccee.ucm.es.

Mark Lehrer, Associate Professor of Management, Sawyer School of Management, Suffolk University, Boston, USA. E-mail: marklehrer@gmail.com.

Contributors

María Teresa Martínez-Fernández, Universitat Jaume I, Castellón (Spain), Department of Business Administration & Marketing. E-mail: tmartinez@emp.uji.es.

Mónica Martínez Pellitero, Instituto de Análisis Industrial y Financiero (IAIF), Complutense University of Madrid, Spain.

Nadine Massard, CREUSET, Jean Monnet University, Saint-Etienne, France. E-mail: nadine.massard@laposte.net.

Aurelia Modrego Rico, Instituto Flores de Lemus, Universidad Carlos III de Madrid, Spain. E-mail: modrego@eco.uc3m.es.

Francesc Xavier Molina-Morales, Universitat Jaume I, Castellón (Spain), Department of Business Administration & Marketing. E-mail: molina@emp.uji.es.

Lucia Piscitello, Department of Management, Economics and Industrial Engineering, Politecnico di Milano, Italy. E-mail: lucia.piscitello@polimi.it.

Otto Raspe, Department of Economic Geography, The Hague, Netherlands. E-mail: raspe@rpb.nl.

Cristina Rossi, Department of Management, Economics and Industrial Engineering, Politecnico di Milano, Italy. E-mail: cristina1.rossi@polimi.it.

Lluís Santamaría Sánchez, Universidad Carlos III de Madrid, Department of Business Administration, Spain. E-mail: lsantama@emp.uc3m.es.

Raphaël Suire, Associate Professor, Economics, CREM – CNRS – Rennes, France. E-mail: raphael.suire@univ-rennes1.fr.

Frank G. van Oort, Department of Economic Geography, The Hague, Netherlands. E-mail: oort@rpb.nl.

Jérôme Vicente, Associate Professor, Economics, LEREPS/GRES – IEP – Toulouse, France.

About the editors

Jordi Suriñach is Professor of Econometrics at the University of Barcelona and Co-Director of the AQR Research Group. He is also the director of IREA (Regional Institute of Applied Economics). He has been Vice-Rector of Research and Science Policy of the University of Barcelona from 2002 to 2005. He is a member of the European Association of Regional Sciences, and Visiting Scholar at the University of Paris II since 1994. His main research interests are regional growth and convergence, econometrics modelling, and short-term economic analysis. Professor Suriñach has published his research in international journals such as *Annals of Regional Science*, papers in *Regional Science, Regional Studies, Urban Studies* among others. He was the chairman of the COST ACTION A17 European Network: Small and Medium Enterprises, Economics Development and Regional Convergence in Europe. His relationship with international institutions and universities all over Europe and the United States is also remarkable. He has participated in different public projects focused on SMEs and regional development: 'Small and Medium Enterprises and economic development and regional convergence' (CICYT-SEC2002-10471-E), 'Regional system of policy observatories' (CICYT-SEC2002-10470-E), 'Growth and spatial location of economic activity', 'The role of firm size and some methodological advances' (SEC2002-00165) and 'Spain and the EU enlargement: analysis of the regional and sectoral effects' (SEJ2005-04348/ECON (2005–2007).

Rosina Moreno is Assistant Professor of Applied Economics at the University of Barcelona. Her teaching areas are mainly associated with Econometrics. Her current research interests are focused on regional growth, public and human capital impact, sectoral and regional externalities, spatial econometrics and innovation capabilities in SMEs. She has published her research in international journals such as *Regional Science and Urban Economics, International Regional Science Review, Annals of Regional Science and Environment and Planning*, among others. She has also contributed to books published by Springer-Verlag, Cambridge University Press and Edward Elgar Publishing. She has participated in several publicly funded projects at a national level on the topic of SMEs and regional development, such as 'Localization, growth and regional externalities with the European Integration Process' (SEC1999-0700), 'Small and Medium Enterprises and economic development and regional convergence' (SEC2002-10471), 'Human capital, productivity and regional growth: Analysis of the heterogeneity of the effects' (SEJ2005-07814/ECON) in addition to projects funded by Europe, such as 'Forecasting models currently applied to indicators computed on the basis of survey results' (ECFIN/2002/A3-01) and 'Feasibility of a tool to measure the macroeconomic impact of structural reforms' ECFIN-E/2005/001. Rosina Moreno was also a member of the European Network COST ACTION A17 Social Sciences (European Commission).

Esther Vayá is Assistant Professor of Applied Economics at the University of Barcelona. Her teaching areas are mainly associated with Econometrics. Her current research interests are focused on regional growth and convergence, regional externalities, localization of activity, urban indicators, strategic planning, and spatial econometrics. She was a member of the European Network COST ACTION A17 Social Sciences (European Commission). This network of 22 European countries worked together until June 2005 on Small and Medium Enterprises and innovation. She is a habitual referee for the journals of *International Regional Science Review*, *Regional Science and Urban Economics*, *Regional Studies*, *Papers in Regional Science*, and *Oxford Economic Papers*. She has participated in different public projects focused on SMEs and regional development, such as Small and Medium Enterprises and economic development and regional convergence (CICYT-SEC2002-10471-E) and 'Spain and the EU enlargement: analysis of the regional and sectoral effects' (SEJ2005-04348/ECON (2005–2007).

Introduction
Jordi Suriñach, Rosina Moreno and Esther Vayá

Technological change is widely recognized as the primary engine for economic development, a force that can lead to the establishment of a thriving knowledge-based economy. This accumulation of a wide variety of relevant knowledge is essential to ensure innovation. Firms, as individual entities, can play a key role in this development of specific innovations but the process that fosters and disseminates technological change throughout an economy involves a complex network of interactions between different firms as well as other organizations and institutions.

As firms attain an increasingly higher degree of specialization they become more heavily dependent on acquiring complementary knowledge from other organizations. Firms will seldom innovate in isolation, but rather will establish linkages with a range of actors that include, among others, customers, suppliers, universities and technology transfer institutions. Due to the ever-changing competitive environment, innovation is today considered a collective undertaking in a global complex of interactions between business networks.

Analyses of innovation data reveal that it is the large EU agglomerations that tend to be the principal engines of innovation and growth in national economies. Major gaps are still to be found between core and peripheral regions in terms of R&D expenditure and the numbers of R&D personnel employed and patent applications made, all of which has an impact on future development opportunities. Agglomerations are responsible for a high proportion of the outcomes that are considered the accomplishments of national and regional systems of innovation. Such agglomerations provide firms with specific resources, the exploitation of which generates significant externalities. Among others, they offer a supply of factors of production and infrastructure, including the quality of available labour (with specific skills and forms of training), the availability of capital (i.e., venture capital institutions), communications and research infrastructures (including universities and research institutes), and the socio-cultural infrastructures that are often vital for guaranteeing the effective operation of the entire economic system.

In many European countries, labour supply is falling as the population ages and this may have a negative effect on economic growth. A rapid increase in productivity will be required to offset the problems arising from these labour shortages, while production processes will need to become more knowledge-based to permit the necessary increases in productivity.

The situation described above produces high levels of uncertainty and creates what has been termed a 'turbulent environment', leaving companies increasingly vulnerable. European companies and their workers will need to prepare themselves for fierce competition from stronger firms that often emerge elsewhere in this turbulent field, and they must be prepared to respond by implementing more complex and effective strategies. Among other measures, companies will have to specialize and learn to enhance their innovation capacity continuously.

Researchers and policy-makers in this field have devised the notion of the 'innovation system' in discussing this situation. This concept is also concerned with the structuring of the problem, in other words, with the effective coordination and management of the processes of knowledge creation, acquisition, distribution and use. While innovation may be seen as a basic characteristic of market systems in general, the growing popularity of the concept reflects the fact that systemic innovation is a major contributing factor to industrial dynamics.

This book examines all these topics in detail. In fact, the book gathers together studies reported at the Final Open Conference, entitled 'Knowledge and Regional Economic Development', which was held in the Facultat de Ciències Econòmiques i Empresarials in the Universitat de Barcelona between 9 and 11 June 2005. This conference was the last event in the A17 COST Action entitled 'Small and Medium Enterprises, Economic Development and Regional Convergence in Europe'. COST is an intergovernmental European framework for international cooperation between nationally funded research activities. It creates scientific networks and enables scientists to collaborate in a wide spectrum of activities in research and technology. Its activities are administered by the COST Office (www.cost.esf.org).

The main objective of the COST Action was to determine the factors that stimulate the birth of small and medium-sized enterprises, and the factors that attract them to locate in a particular region, together with a discussion of the way in which these two processes might promote regional convergence in the European Union, in particular in the wake of the integration of countries from Eastern Europe.

More than 20 European countries participated in this Action, which was divided into two working groups. The first was concerned with the study of policies to support the development of SMEs and regional growth, with particular attention to regional externalities. The second examined the way in which small and medium-sized firms contribute to regional development in terms of employment, investments and regional product.

The results of the research carried out as part of this COST Action have been presented at various meetings as well as at the Final Open Conference held in Barcelona. Evidence of the quality of this research is the fact that much of it has been accepted for publication. Specifically, two books have been published, *Regional Economic Growth and the Wider Europe*, published in 2004, and *Regional Externalities*, published in 2007, as well as a special issue entitled 'The Knowledge Production–Economic Growth Complex', which appeared as volume 39(4) of the journal, the *Annals of Regional Science* in December 2005.

The Action concluded with the celebration of the aforementioned conference, which enjoyed a high level of interest among COST and non-COST members alike. Some 110 delegates from many European (Spain, Italy, Germany, the Netherlands, France, Sweden, Austria, among others) and non-European countries (United States, Japan, Israel, Malaysia) were able to participate. The presence of David Audretsch, Philip McCann and Gianmarco Ottaviano as keynote speakers provided considerable added value. What is clearly undeniable is the current relevance, both academically and politically, of questions of innovation, knowledge, human capital and agglomeration economies within the wider field of economic development. Furthermore, in a period of increasing delocalization, the studies were able to send out an optimistic message in the belief that Europe can continue to be the reference for future regional growth. Indeed, Europe has the potential for improvement in many of the factors considered crucial for growth and development: flexibility, training, accessibility, logistics, knowledge-based production processes, etc.

The Conference was structured around nine broad topics: (1) firms, innovation and location decisions; (2) public research centres and innovation; (3) regional innovation systems and innovation clusters; (4) knowledge externalities and agglomeration economies; (5) growth and regional convergence; (6) economic development, innovation and regional policy; (7) labour market and human movements; (8) human capital and education; (9) information and communication technology (ICT). A selection of papers from each of these areas makes up this book.

The book is structured in three parts: Part I provides a theoretical examination of regional innovation systems, agglomeration economies and knowledge spillovers; Part II examines the same concepts within an empirical framework; while Part III considers innovation and human capital as determinants of regional economic growth and convergence.

Part I of this volume contains four chapters that analyse the notion of regional innovation systems and that examine the importance of agglomeration economies and spillovers for the creation of knowledge. The concept of knowledge spillovers is used to explain a number of major economic phenomena, including the geographical clustering of inventions and patents; the social returns to R&D that significantly exceed private returns; and the sizeable disproportions that exist between firms in terms of their R&D inputs and outputs, with small firms being responsible for far more product innovations than large firms relative to their measurable knowledge resources.

In Chapter 1, 'Theorizing regional knowledge capabilities: economic geography under "open innovation"', Philip Cooke examines issues related to the management of complexity that arise from increasing rates of globalization, knowledge-dependence and the externalization of the production of goods and services in the modern economy. Unusually, this chapter focuses on the activities of economic governance agencies that design enterprise support mechanisms by brokering 'regional innovation systems'. As the 'knowledge economy' has evolved, making the value of the research knowledge generated by small and medium-sized enterprises and universities, in particular, of far greater value than ever before, governments have begun to promote regional innovation system-building. However, knowledge demands mean heightened complexity in the crossing of boundaries between 'epistemic communities'. Managing knowledgeable interactions in environments that demand greater and greater innovation is eased but not entirely overcome by means of digital knowledge flow platforms (DKFPs). Reference is made to cases of DKFPs evolving in practice in economic governance organizations, but at a later date and in ways that differ from the methods used by firms.

In Chapter 2 on 'Knowledge spillovers and organizational heterogeneity: an historical overview of German technology sectors', Mark Lehrer departs from the mechanisms accounting for the local boundedness of knowledge spillovers. The most frequently cited explanation for why knowledge spills over locally rather than globally pertains to the tacitness and stickiness of knowledge. However, it could also be the case that many knowledge flows are localized for the same reasons that certain types of business transactions remain localized. Thus, Lehrer provides a historical review that tracks the differential nature of knowledge spillovers that were ostensibly important in four German technology sectors during the late 19th and late 20th centuries. The review suggests that in the domains in which Germany was highly successful (organic chemicals and electricity around 1900), and also in those in which German high-tech performance was mediocre (biotechnology and computing during the late 20th century), knowledge spillovers were far from automatic and required special organizational effort on the part of firms and/or policy-makers.

The intersectoral comparisons made by Lehrer also point to why experimentation with ways of managing knowledge spillovers is an important process in the development of technology-based industry. In three of the four sectors discussed (organic chemicals, electricity and biotechnology), key knowledge spillover processes took place within the context of complex contractual arrangements that varied substantially from one industrial setting to another: long-term relations between university professors and firms (organic chemicals), turbulent strategic alliances (e.g., AEG and Siemens in the Berlin electricity cluster), and regional technology start-up incubators (biotechnology). These arrangements and their disparity lend credence to the idea that firms experience a priori difficulty in knowing how to organize activities to capture knowledge spillovers and to the consequent need for organizational innovation. The disappointing results of most post-war German high-technology policies based on more or less automatic knowledge externalities likewise calls into question the notion of local knowledge spillovers as a kind of knowledge leakage across organizational boundaries, suggesting instead the notion of knowledge flowing in tandem with complex transactions and organizational arrangements.

Jérôme Vicente, Yan Dalla Pria and Raphaël Suire deal with the complex link between geographical proximity and innovation in Chapter 3, 'The ambivalent role of mimetic behaviors in proximity dynamics: evidence on the French "Silicon Sentier"'. Their chapter analyses the complex links between proximities and clusters, from empirical monographs investigating the relational aspects of proximity to econometric analyses applied to the study of knowledge spillovers. In their chapter, they choose to focus on just one of these, but perhaps the most original, namely the role of sequential interactions and mimetic behaviours in co-location processes. Their purpose is to understand why firms tend to converge rapidly in their decision to locate near to one another (geographical proximity), and how this convergence process gives rise to other forms of proximity, defined at this stage as socio-economic proximities. First, they show that geographical proximity is not a sufficient condition for the collective performance of clusters. Second, they focus on the convergence of locational choices through the process of mimetic (or herd) behaviours. Their purpose is to show that according to the mimetic process of co-location, the nature of socio-economic proximities can be very different and have a strong influence on the stability and the performance of clusters. They also introduce the notion of mimetic behaviour of location in order to show that co-location processes can be the result of sequentiality, uncertainty, legitimacy and non-market interactions, rather than the outcome of full rational and isolated decisions and pure strategic market interactions.

Vicente, Dalla Pria and Suire show, first, the utility of analysing clustering processes based on the supposition that firms decide to locate sequentially and that they have heterogeneous preferences of location. Second, they demonstrate that this sequentiality provides a firm basis for communication, observation and coordination between companies, which can give rise to rational mimetic interactions and convergence in location decision-making (geographical proximity). Third, they also show that the very nature of socio-economic proximity depends on the mimetic process at work in the aggregation process. If uncertainty and legitimacy dominate, the convergence of location decision-making can give rise to cognitive proximity, while if coordination and innovative interdependences dominate, depending on the degree of competition and of division of labour, the convergence process leads to a relational proximity.

The final theoretical contribution is provided by Flora Bellone in Chapter 4, 'IT adoption, industrial structure and agglomeration economies'. In this chapter, she departs from the idea that information technology (IT) offers large growth potential for peripheral regions suffering from economic backwardness. She argues that the IT revolution has not brought about uniform increases in the growth performance of the European regions. Major regional imbalances have been detected in recent empirical studies of the location of IT-producing sectors and the dispersion of IT investments in user sectors. Bellone shows that economic geography is not only an important component of the incentives to invest in IT-producing sectors, but also that of the incentives to provide IT to user sectors. She applies the theory of circular causation in accounting for the propensity of IT investments to cluster even in user sectors.

The analytical framework adopted by Bellone is centred on a small open economy endowed with a fixed amount of labour and engaged in the competitive production of homogeneous final consumption goods based on that labour and an endogenous variety of IT intermediate inputs. Within this framework, the importance of fixed local entry costs and the existence of pecuniary externalities due to demand complementarities among the local providers of IT goods and services are highlighted. These key features of IT-based production processes are what allow for spatial agglomeration in IT investments and that give rise to localized cumulative causation processes despite the very low level of variable transport costs characterizing trade flows in IT goods and services. In addition, the model explains how technological constraints interact with market failures. In this sense, even if technological constraints are relaxed (as a consequence of a proper investment in infrastructure), coordination failures may still appear, particularly in regions without a sufficiently well-developed industrial base.

Part II once again focuses on the notion of innovation systems, agglomeration economies and knowledge spillovers, but here the studies are conducted within a specifically empirical framework.

Models of economic geography and growth usually make two assumptions: first, externalities result from diversity and, second, that they are geographically bounded. In addition, most empirical studies that analyse agglomeration processes use spatially aggregated data and focus on either pecuniary or knowledge externalities. Within this framework, Chapter 5 by Corinne Autant-Bernard and Nadine Massard, 'Pecuniary and knowledge externalities as agglomeration forces: empirical evidence from individual French data', represents an advance in the study of the mechanisms underlying the agglomeration effects of economic activity given that, using individual data for firms, they propose an empirical framework that jointly models pecuniary and knowledge externalities. The authors, thus, seek to build an econometric model with a unified analytical framework for traditional agglomerating forces and knowledge externalities so as to clarify the degree of localization of these phenomena in both geographical and technological space. Specifically, Autant-Bernard and Massard analyse three potential sources of externalities: pecuniary externalities resulting from a decision to locate close to other firms; pecuniary externalities related to the labour market and to the local area insofar as it provides a market for final goods; and knowledge externalities associated with R&D spillovers. In each case, the authors undertake an evaluation of its geographical and sectoral dimension.

Based on a sample of 822 French firms, the authors test a Griliches production function, where (in its simplest version) the sales of each firm are explained by the workforce employed at the company; purchases of goods, raw materials and other supplies; and the firm's internal R&D expenditure. In order to consider potential pecuniary and knowledge externalities and to evaluate their geographical and sectoral dimension, the Griliches production function is widened (in a more complete version) to include the number of firms and employees in the same sector and in the other sectors in the same French *département* and in neighbouring French *départements*, together with the R&D expenditure of other firms in the same sector and in other sectors present in the same French *département* and in neighbouring French *départements*. In addition, sectoral dummies are included to verify the presence of spatial autocorrelation in the residuals of the regressions.

The preliminary results from this study indicate that proximity to other firms in the sector appears to be an overwhelmingly attractive force. However, their results are inconclusive as to which industrial structure – specialized or diverse – is superior, as their findings point to benefits that can be gained from both types of structure: while specialization seems to favour pecuniary externalities originating from proximity to other firms, diversity facilitates knowledge externalities and pecuniary externalities derived from the labour market and from the proximity to final consumers. The tension between these forces might in part explain the co-existence of specialized towns alongside more diversified areas.

In Chapter 6, 'The adoption of ICTs – why does it differ across regions?', Lucia Piscitello, Andrea Bonaccorsi and Cristina Rossi take up the topic of knowledge diffusion and focus on the existence of disparities in the adoption of information and communication technologies (ICTs). Several studies have reported remarkable disparities in the adoption of ICTs both between developing countries (global digital divide) as well as between regions in the same country (local digital divide). The authors investigate whether such disparities in ICT diffusion are due to heterogeneity in the characteristics of firms (in line with equilibrium models) or whether ICT diffusion is influenced by epidemic effects (non-adopters choose a new technology when they come into contact with adopters in neighbouring areas and learn about it).

Specifically, Piscitello, Bonaccorsi and Rossi propose a spatial econometric framework for analysing disparities in ICT adoption by Italian firms at the province level (Italian NUTS 3), taking into account both the potential existence of spatial heterogeneity and spatial dependence, in a similar approach to that adopted in the previous chapter. The penetration rate is then used as a proxy for the level of ICT adoption in each province, measured by the percentage of firms (located in the province) that had at least one domain name registered in the Registration Authority databases in 2001. In order to account for the differences in ICT adoption, a number of explanatory variables are defined: local absorptive capacity (proxied by means of the number of patents and publications by university researchers in relation to the number of firms in each province), the characteristics of the firms (average firm size), and sectoral composition. The results show that ICT adoptions in a province are positively influenced by its industrial composition and, in particular, by its local absorptive capacity, showing that areas that are poor in general technological activity and research are less likely to make active use of the Internet. By contrast, firm size was not a significant factor. In addition, a significant spatial heterogeneity (North–South duality) and spatial dependence pattern were detected, confirming in the second case the presence of epidemic effects in the diffusion process. Thus, ICT adoption in each province is dependent on ICT adoption in its neighbouring provinces, demonstrating that proximity remains a key factor.

The literature emphasizes the problems involved in using individual indicators including patents, R&D expenditure, percentage of sales related to new products, etc. to measure the global concept of innovation. In this context, Chapter 7 by Mikel Buesa, Mónica Martínez Pellitero, Thomas Baumert and Joost Heijs, 'Novel applications of existing econometric instruments to analyse regional innovation systems: the Spanish case', seeks to get to grips with the measurement of national and regional innovation systems. The authors present novel applications of existing econometric instruments for the measurement and evaluation of regional innovation systems using multivariate analysis.

They seek to develop new ways of measuring innovation (systems), on the understanding that the concept is not directly observable. In creating 'combined' indicators that might reflect different aspects of regional innovation systems, they employ factor analysis. Having obtained the factors, 'standardized factor values' are assigned to each region. They first establish a typology of regional innovation systems by cluster or conglomerate analysis, with the factor scores being used as independent variables. They then create the IAIF index of regional innovation that comprises the weighted sum of four partial indexes and that offers the possibility of summarizing these typologies and quantifying and analysing their development over time. Third, they estimate a knowledge production function using the number of patents as the output variable and the corresponding factorial scores as independent variables. And finally they compare the efficiency of the regions by conducting a data envelopment analysis.

The approaches adopted in analysing Spain's regional innovation systems in this chapter employ existing information for variables and indicators related to science, technology and innovation, from the perspective of resources and results and incorporate aspects of an institutional nature as well as factors of the productive structure. The study considers the period 1994 to 2000 and examines the 17 Autonomous Communities (corresponding to NUTS 2). The study identifies four factors as determinants of regional innovation systems: the first factor is related to the regional and productive environment of innovation, the second to the role of the universities, the third to the role played by the civil service in innovation, and the fourth is concerned with innovating firms. Having identified five regional innovation systems in Spain, a highly heterogeneous structure is detected, with strong asymmetries between the strengths and weaknesses of each region. As for the production function, the authors detect a strong influence of environmental variables in the quantified innovation flows across the weighted sum of patents. Specifically, a large productive structure plays a key role in achieving results related to technological innovation, which ratifies the importance of a certain critical mass and a minimum market size. Other factors (innovating firms, the civil service and the universities), while being shown to play a significant and positive role, are nevertheless reported as being of secondary importance.

In Chapter 8, 'Over-embeddedness and under-exploration issues in cohesive networks. An application to territorial clusters', Francesc Xavier Molina-Morales and María Teresa Martínez Fernández explore the potentially negative effects of social networks on innovation by analysing the territorial agglomerations of firms. It has been argued that industrial districts represent local configurations that are high in social capital, given that they are characterized by mutual trust, cooperation and an entrepreneurial spirit as well as by the existence of a multitude of small local firms with complementary and specialized skills. Thus, proximity provides frequent, repeated, non-marked, informal contacts, all of which facilitate strong ties and the density of the network of ties. These social interactions stimulate exchanges of information about competitors, production technologies, recent developments and so on. In addition, such interactions and the development of trust facilitate the exchange and combination of knowledge resources and as a result improve the innovation capacity of firms. However, these cohesive networks have been criticized in terms of the costs involved in their maintenance, the lack of autonomy that they might constitute, and the obligations derived from prevailing norms and values. In fact, some studies report cases in which excessive interaction between the same actors can undermine the efficiency of economic actions and, on occasions, bring about the economic decline of an industrial district.

In this context, the authors have conceptualized the limitations of the cohesive network in the district using the notions of over-embeddedness and under-exploring. The former might occur when all the firms in a network are connected through embedded ties. When the impact of social capital goes beyond a certain level of social interaction and trust, the result will be parochialism and inertia. Under-exploring, on the other hand, refers to the absence of autonomous relationships in exploring strategies to capture new and exclusive resources, which means there are few or no links to outside members that can potentially contribute innovative ideas. Using information drawn from a questionnaire distributed among 154 firms located in the east coast of Spain (Valencia region), the authors obtain evidence that the effect of social interactions and trust on innovation can be described as an inverted U-shaped curve. In addition, Molina-Morales and Martínez-Fernández verify the effect of local institutions (universities, research institutes, technical assistance centres, professional associations, etc.) on the capacity of a district's firms to innovate. They conclude that the involvement of local institutions has a positive and linear effect on innovation, as such institutions can be considered intermediate agents that allow districts to escape the obligation of exploring restrictions, since they can monitor what is happening outside the district.

Finally, the authors outline the best course of action to be taken by a firm. They encourage firms to interact with local institutions and other cluster participants so as to enhance their environmental conditions. In addition, and as a consequence of the vital role played by the entrepreneur and employees alike as mechanisms of knowledge transmission, the authors encourage the implementation of policies that both improve the quality of local labour and foster the internal mobility of employees and the creation of new ventures. Finally, the authors stress the need for policies to encourage cooperation between the members of a district and to build social capital, since both are important for the innovative capacity of firms.

Following on from this discussion of the need to promote links between local institutions and to encourage interactions between firms so as to increase technological innovation, Chapter 9 by Joaquín M. Azagra Caro, entitled 'The regional dimension of university–industry interaction', examines university–industry interactions (UII) and their regional dimension. More specifically, the study seeks to determine the type of firm manager and faculty member that interacts most frequently and whether these interactions occur within or outside the region. In conducting the analysis, Azagra Caro uses data from the Valencian Community, a Spanish region with a low R&D absorptive capacity. In a survey undertaken in 2001, he gathered data about managers working in the manufacturing and telecommunications sectors (700 observations) and about faculty members at the five public universities in the Valencian Community (380 observations).

Using ordered probit models with a sample selection, the author presents evidence to support the claim that belonging to large firms in science-based sectors has a significant positive effect. This constitutes a limit to UII given the abundance of micro-firms in supplier-dominated sectors in similar regions. However, certain personal characteristics of company managers, such as a higher academic degree, positively influenced their propensity to interact with universities. In addition, it seems that promoting engineering and technology, as well as the exact and natural sciences, has a positive effect on contracts with firms. Similarly, the time devoted to R&D also has a positive effect. But the managers in the survey were found to cooperate only rarely on matters of R&D with universities outside the region; the frequency of contacts depending on whether the manager worked within a group of firms. The frequency of cooperation inside the region, however, depends solely on firm size. In the case of faculty members with a greater propensity to contract, Azagra Caro reports that they do not stand out for the frequency of their interactions, some were even found to interact less frequently than the rest (the case of those holding a managerial position) or to interact more frequently outside the region (men). By contrast, faculty members with less propensity to contract – those who had undertaken research abroad for longer periods, were found to interact as frequently with firms inside the region as with firms outside the region.

Finally, the author concludes that improving a firm's human capital is vital, since it enhances UII, and constitutes a more viable policy than seeking to change the economic structure. However, the propensity of faculty members to interact relies on personal characteristics that do not guarantee they will interact more frequently inside the region than they will outside the region, since firms in regions like the Valencian Community may not be able to absorb academic R&D. This is not necessarily a caveat, because the region may benefit indirectly from the interactions taking place outside it.

Lluís Santamaría Sánchez, Andrés Barge Gil and Aurelia Modrego Rico in Chapter 10, 'Which factors underlie public selection of R&D cooperative projects?', stress the importance of R&D as a factor of economic growth. Here two closely related subjects are pertinent to the discussion: (1) the interrelationship between the public and private sectors as sources for R&D financial backing and (2) the decision-making process that determines which R&D projects should receive financial support and the subsequent assessment of the projects. Specifically, the authors present initial data, which are not altogether positive, about the criteria used by public sector evaluators when deciding which projects to finance. Drawing on data for the period 2000–03, following the issue in Spain of a public notice to finance R&D projects, which required the involvement of universities and/or research centres together with private firms, the authors are able to shed some light on the criteria adopted in the selection of R&D projects by the public sector: that the 'input characteristics' are more important than the 'output characteristics'; that support is given per se to projects with low budgets and those requiring many hours of work; that the results depend on the year in which the public notice is issued or on the research area chosen; that equal support is not given to projects that are already recipients of financial backing. All in all, these indicators are not very positive and seem to demonstrate a certain lack of valour as regards the taking of risks when financing such projects.

The problems discussed in this study concerning the ex ante evaluation of projects submitted, together with the failure to undertake an adequate monitoring and ex post evaluation of the projects, are aspects that require considerable work. And it is probable that greater consideration of these areas would help ensure greater efficiency in the use of the public resources allocated for research.

It should also be stressed that the criteria adopted and the type of projects financed by the public and private sectors do not coincide. Some of these differences may be due to the different time schedules for the two project types, or to the actual nature of the research work. But undoubtedly there must be serious doubts as to whether the selection process in public competitions for grants is the most appropriate and whether the most relevant projects receive financial support.

In Part III, attention shifts to stress the importance of a catch-up mechanism, which sees technological improvement as the combination of two distinct types of activity: innovation and imitation. The former is generally associated with technologically advanced economies or economies that are at the technological frontier, and can be thought of as pure research. The latter involves the identification of a growth mechanism resulting from technology transfers among economies and as such should be of relevance for less developed economies. In this case, stocks of human capital increase the capacity to adopt and implement innovations or new technologies from more advanced countries, which potentially ushers in a process of growth or catch-up between countries. The chapters in this section are all concerned, therefore, with the impact of human capital and other types of knowledge acquisition on economic growth.

In 'Convergence clubs and the role of education in Spanish regional growth', Chapter 11, Adriana Di Liberto investigates the returns on education in the Spanish regions by measuring the stock of regional human capital. The study examines the extent to which these have differed in the country's regional clubs and whether different levels of education have different impacts on growth. In addition, by examining the levels of educational attainment in the labour force disaggregated by sector, Di Liberto is able to estimate whether or not excluding the public sector from the analysis significantly changes results on returns to schooling.

Her findings suggest that in Spain, while primary education seems to contribute to growth in poorly developed areas, more highly skilled human capital has a stronger growth-enhancing effect in more developed economies. This means that there is likely to be heterogeneity in the rates of return on education across economies since the effect of schooling in growth regressions is influenced by an economy's level of development. The failure to take this heterogeneity into account in empirical analyses may produce misleading results. Moreover, her results suggest that educational policies should take into account the link between stages of development and growth and expand human capital coherently by taking into account its composition as much as its level. She also finds that the coefficients of human capital variables do not change significantly when the public sector is taken into account.

In the second chapter of Part III, entitled 'Non-linearities, spatial dependence and regional economic growth in Europe: a semiparametric approach', Chapter 12, Roberto Basile sets out to test the presence of spatial externalities in the economic growth of European regions. In so doing, he maintains the functional form as flexibly as possible so as to detect the existence of heterogeneity in convergence speed and growth behaviour.

The econometric results provide strong evidence of non-linearities in the effect of initial per-capita incomes and school attainment levels. Specifically, the negative marginal effect of initial conditions increases with the level of initial per-capita income while a threshold effect in secondary school enrolment ratio is reported: an increase in the rate of schooling is associated with an increase in the growth rate only when the level of schooling investment is above the EU average. These results confirm that the assumption of a common linear model for a set of very different economies is misleading: non-linearities are important in regional growth in Europe even when spatial dependence is taken into account. Thus, the proxy for human capital investment is only associated with a positive impact on growth if it exceeds the European average rate of schooling.

Moreover, the specification used allows the author to identify the effect of interactions between the characteristics (initial conditions and human capital investment) of each region and those of its neighbours. Thus, regions with schooling rates lower than the EU average also seem to benefit from externalities generated by the accumulation of human capital in nearby regions and have the opportunity to grow faster than other regions. Finally, the effect of the interaction between the initial per capita income and the corresponding spatial lag suggests that regions surrounded by richer regions have higher expected growth rates than regions surrounded by poorer regions. The evidence presented by Basile is in line with the argument that spillovers from nearby regions can compensate the mechanisms of decreasing returns to scale to capital accumulation and allow rich economies to grow.

In the final chapter of Part III, Chapter 13, Frank van Oort and Otto Raspe, under the title 'Urban heterogeneity in knowledge-related economic growth', analyse urban economic growth in the framework of the knowledge economy. Specifically, they seek to verify the hypothesis that larger cities enjoy greater opportunities for economic growth in a knowledge economy, since these cities offer the best opportunities for interaction, variety and specializations.

They enhance the conceptualization and measurement of the knowledge economy and urban heterogeneity by using eight indicators grouped under three main factors (knowledge of workers, innovation and R&D). So as to identify the key elements in urban growth, they then describe how these three factors manifest themselves in the Dutch municipalities. They are now in a position to compare the main spatial interrelations between these three factors, and to identify the characteristics of the municipalities and those that contribute most to economic growth. Their results are to some degree surprising inasmuch as they show that not all the factors contribute equally to growth and that the largest municipalities do not occupy the best positions in this process. Particular attention, therefore, needs to be paid to the dimensions, indicators and factors used to measure the concept of the knowledge economy, and to the results that interrelate the different municipalities (in terms of their size, location within the Netherlands and the type of city) with their contributions to economic growth.

ACKNOWLEDGEMENTS

This volume could not have come to be without the resources provided by the COST Action as well as the technical support given by the Scientific Committee of the Final Open Conference 'Knowledge and Regional Economic Development' held in Barcelona: Manuel Artís, Edward Bergman, Ayda Eraydin, Bernard Fingleton, Henk Folmer, Charlie Karlsson, Enrique López-Bazo, Raffele Paci and Javier Revilla-Diez. We also thank the rest of the members of the AQR Research Group at the Universitat de Barcelona for their support during the Conference.

We gratefully acknowledge the effort of the authors and also the anonymous referees who provided us with very useful advice that resulted in a substantial improvement of the papers. Finally, we are grateful for the secretaries of the AQR Research Group, Berta Ballart and Bibiana Barnadas, for their assistance in relation to the preparation of this book. And we particularly appreciate the work of Anna Giribet who worked with us meticulously towards the final version of the book and who always kept a smile despite the many corrections to be made.

We trust that this volume will provide many interesting insights for further discussion and debate among economists and regional policy-makers alike.

PART I

Regional innovation systems, agglomeration economies and knowledge spillovers: theoretical approaches

1. Theorizing regional knowledge capabilities: economic geography under 'open innovation'

Philip Cooke

1.1 INTRODUCTION

The digital implications for system organization are profound. When the system in question is largely external rather than internal to a firm, as is the case with regional innovation systems (RIS), this is even more the case. However, where they exist as functioning or even aspirational system entities, RIS, being innovation-oriented with creative, knowledge-exploring and knowledge-exploiting intent, increasingly tend, on the whole, to seek to build digital system linkages appropriate and necessary to the demands of innovation (March, 1991). However, where regions have been referred to as 'learning regions' (Florida, 1995) this may be less the case, because of asymmetric knowledge problems that arise not from being innovator but imitator systems (Akerlof, 1970).[1] Reasons why this is likely are explored, and further reasons advanced as to why enthusiasm has waned for the somewhat normative injunction that institutions, organizations or persons should be 'learning' subjects, rather than, say 'sociable', 'knowledgeable' or 'innovative'. It may be suggested that this myopia is implicit in a technological determinism associated with imperatives for market expansion of subjects controllable in desire for, and utilization of, mass consumption goods, including information (Adorno, 2001). Distinctions between knowledge and information are drawn where appropriate.

Somewhat the same can be said of 'innovative' firms versus 'learning' firms because of what Levinthal and March (1993) call the 'myopia of learning', occasioned in part by the problem of learning from samples of one or fewer (March, Sproull and Tamuz, 1991). We shall examine key problems of the myopia of learning and asymmetric knowledge in what follows, showing ultimately that system reorganization is an absolute necessity to get the optimal efficiency gains from introducing digital systems. The emphasis will be far more upon questions of content than hardware, in tune with the comment reported in Beskind (2004) to the effect that narrative cinematic culture is like a clothesline. Independent directors like to look at the different clothes on the line, while Hollywood is interested only in the line itself. Much of the problematic nature of 'being digital' (Negroponte, 1995) lies in the failure of commercial operators to pay attention beforehand to both the limitations and implications of hardware and the primacy of content, organization and social relations.

For the first time in history, practically all the information required to navigate the oceans of a globalizing knowledge economy are embodied in the Internet. Yet the demand for proximity to sources of economically valuable knowledge has never been greater. The rise of knowledge clusters like Oulu in Finland, Kista in Sweden, Cambridge in the United Kingdom and Cambridge, Massachusetts in the United States, let alone Silicon Valley, are testimony to the human desire for face-to-face and handshaking business contact. This paradox is widely commented upon by leading economists and business analysts (Krugman, 1995; Porter, 1998; Chesbrough, 2003) who show that the age of the hierarchical, vertically integrated production function embodied in the fabric of the multinational firm has changed significantly. Ushered in to replace it is a system we have called Globalization 2 (Cooke, 2005b) based on externalized 'node and network' forms of interaction. The Internet and other digital means of managing such informational complexity were said to be essential if we would but learn its rubric and adapt practice accordingly. But, rather like 'e-learning' and 'online learning' as means to do this, much less is heard of their virtues now than hitherto. The reason is that they underplayed and even ignored the important corollary regarding 'learning organizations', which is that good knowledge management also requires 'developing organizations'. By that is meant reconfiguring inherited hierarchies and their associated technologies and incentive systems.

In what follows, a brief analysis will be provided, in the next section, of the nature of key problems induced inside corporations by myopic attempts at inducing learning by digital means (knowledge management systems) in the absence of care about organizational content of the systems being introduced. After that, attention is devoted to the infinitely more complex issues surrounding the introduction of digital systems into the externalized world of interactive innovation and its regional institutional platforms. As with the preceding section, textured case material is advanced for illustrative purposes. These sections, preceding brief conclusions, are both illustrated with some exemplars of organizational practice in embedding digital systems in both 'learning' and 'innovative' environments.

1.2 SEVERAL MYOPIAS OF INTRA-ORGANIZATIONAL LEARNING

In this section the emphasis in the analysis will be on digital interaction regarding intra-organizational relations, which failed because of inadequate understanding that increased efficiency means, changing the organizational form from vertical to horizontal structures. To advertise the reason at this point, failure to recognize this requirement acts as a disincentive to compliance from those assumed by 'management theory' to be latent knowledge resources. Acting otherwise means knowledge capture ends up with elites and the incentive for non-elites to interact diminishes. Naturally, this is an organizational management, not a specifically technological disjuncture. However, rather in the manner that Akerlof (1970) identified the asymmetric information problem as the incapability of a buyer to judge what used car might turn out to be a 'lemon': in other words an expensive mistake, the purchaser of 'recipe knowledge' from the airport bookshelf or management consultant is faced with asymmetric knowledge. This is made doubly problematic when such knowledge asymmetries extend to absence of the requisite technological knowledge to judge claims made for the efficacy of, for example, digital systems.

'Digital systems' have now been mentioned more than once, as have 'asymmetric information' and 'asymmetric knowledge'. These need defining and distinguishing. In the context of this contribution, 'digital systems' are essentially for communication. They integrate communications software solutions for telephony, intelligent networks, Internet, wireless interaction and so on. They are more or less sophisticated tools to facilitate the flow of information, including commands, around any system. In an earlier era, the idea of 'expert systems' used to be promoted as technologies to sit alongside managers within organizations to aid complex systems management (Callon, 1991). At their apogee, we might say that the expert systems involved in spacecraft guidance or computerized aeronautics constitute excellent, effectively indispensable, technological achievements. But the selling of such complex tools adapted to organizational management, except for accounting systems, has perhaps produced less impressive results. Why should this be? Primarily because social systems are infinitely more complex than those analysed in 'rocket science', though that is not to disparage those achievements one iota.

A decade ago, the equivalent for organizational management was 'knowledge management systems' designed to facilitate organizational learning, primarily from within its own internal human resources. However, digital (and non-digital) modes of knowledge capture and transfer were not adequately thought through beforehand. Thus the procedure, presented stylistically, was as follows:

- Knowledge management systems (KMS) technology was designed or purchased.
- KMS were inserted into the corporate hierarchy structure.
- Line workers and middle-management were encouraged to share knowledge.
- Knowledge moved upwards to executive level through use of technology.
- KMS provided no feedback, nor rewards for their implementation.
- Organizational 'silos' prevented lateral knowledge exchange.
- Little evidence emerged revealing positive results from deploying KMS.
- Workers stopped operating KMS.

Clearly, such disappointing results, inside the relatively favourable administrative environment of the single, large business firm, offered plenty of opportunity for knowledge enhancement and potential for organizational learning. In Hansen's (2002) empirical analysis of the complex of problems arising from KMS implementation failures, he drew the fairly obvious, but in fact extremely challenging, conclusions for the modern corporation summarized in the following:

- KMS cannot work if the organization is not changed.
- A key initial requirement is to reduce organizational hierarchy.
- Associated with this is the imperative to remove 'silo' structures.
- This entails the organization of knowledge flows through 'lateral learning'.
- Incentivization of the workforce to exchange knowledge is essential.
- Good knowledge exchangers must be rewarded by a measurable incentive input–output system.
- Digital systems software design facilitates interactive knowledge transfer processes.

For tighter integration of 'information' flow, for example in integrated supply chains, proprietary software clearly exists and is implemented, often by third parties for global clients with complex scheduling. In such circumstances, there is no actual imperative to change organizational structure as radically as Hansen (2002) suggests.

But knowledge and information are not the same thing. We might refer back to the dawning of 'information science' with the famous paper by Shannon (1948). He defined information as messages possessing *meaning* for sender and recipient. As demonstrated in his definition, we would nowadays categorize this as a 'train timetable' theory since Shannon said that communication's 'significant aspect is that the actual message is one *selected from a set* of possible messages' (1948, p. 379, original emphasis). Typical of its time, this was a linear, inscriptive, traditional engineering metaphor. Thus the recipient chose from a menu of provided information with meaning for the next action, as a relatively passive receiver. With such a prescribed menu approach to cognition, learning is made easy, repeatable and efficient.

Knowledge is much more complex, open-ended, negotiated and potentially dissonant in its interpretation than this. At the extreme it is comparable to pinning down quicksilver while herding cats. Its forms are manifold, including *abstract* (mathematical), *synthetic* (engineering) and *symbolic* (aesthetic) (Simon, [1969] 1996). Its organizational processes involve *exploration* (basic research), *examination* (tests/trials and applied research) and *exploitation* (commercialization) as identified in part by March (1991). 'Examination' knowledge, especially in relation to standard compliance and other due diligence to prevent harm to the public from innovation, is introduced by Cooke (2005a). Finally, it is also traditionally divided into *tacit* (internalized, implicit, encoded) and *codified* (open, explicit, decoded), concepts that exercise analysts of *spatial knowledge domains* (Feldman and Florida, 1994; Lo and Schamp, 2002; Asheim and Gertler, 2004) as well as knowledge management systems (Zander and Kogut, 1995; Szulanski, 1996). We may observe how these combinations of sub-concepts assist our understanding of certain process similarities and differences in knowledge management by observing Table 1.1. What this shows, and makes us think about, is that the tacit-codified dyad may no longer be sufficient to denote the knowledge realization process under conditions that stress relational interactivity rather than linear, hierarchical knowledge flow and transfer. Thus, what might such an intermediary concept be?

We gain some insight from consulting Nonaka and Takeuchi (1995) who refer to *externalization* to capture implicit-to-explicit knowledge flow, and *internalization* regarding explicit-to-implicit knowledge flow in the

Table 1.1 Characteristics, forms and stages of knowledge production

	Abstract	Synthetic	Symbolic
Exploration	Mathematical reasoning	e.g., Gene therapy	Experimental artwork
Examination	Theorems to test	Clinical trials	Art exhibition
Exploitation	e.g., Penrose tiles/patterns	Therapeutic treatment	Gallery sale

knowledge production process. The term that captures the interaction between externalization and internalization of knowledge in spatial knowledge domains and knowledge management systems is the *hermeneutic or interpretative* function, which, as an active knowledge form, is referred to as *complicit* knowledge.

This is cognate with research conducted by Haas (1992), Galison (1997) and Brown and Duguid (2000). The connection is that Galison (1997) explains the process of epistemological 'boundary-crossing' among actors acculturated to distinctive disciplines as a process akin to the evolution of 'pidgin' languages among distinctive language groups (see also, Lester and Piore, 2004). Haas (1992) refers to holders of the most professionally internalized sets of epistemological communication codes as 'epistemic communities', of which the scientists that Galison (1997) writes about are paradigm examples. At a lesser level, say among the ICT engineers that Seely, Brown and Duguid (2000) refer to are 'communities of practice' across professional sub-groups. These occupy spatial knowledge domains in specific spatial locations and prefer *transceiving* knowledge with each other than with their professional peers in a different spatial knowledge domain. Solving the interpretative problem interactively is key to translating tacit into codified knowledge. Here the category of complicit knowledge is introjected (Table 1.2).

That, of course implies changing the internal organization along lines adumbrated in Hansen (2002), something Dirckinck-Holmfeld (2002) demonstrated in discovering how e-learning failed when no change was made to the traditional lecture-based pedagogy of traditional learning. However, when e-learning was introduced in higher education institutions established in the 1970s in Denmark, based on a project-focused rather than traditional pedagogy, e-learning functioned highly successfully.

In Table 1.3 this is done by recognizing the importance of identifying *implicit* knowledge domains (e.g., post-genomics in Greater Boston) that are at least knowledge quasi-monopolies, mechanisms for extracting useful knowledge through complicit third party mediation (e.g., incubation, intermediary technology institutes) and appropriation of rents from *explicit* knowledge (patents, licences). Then, the implantation of reproducible

Table 1.2 Knowledge: from implicit domains to digital innovation systems

	Implicit	Complicit	Explicit
Knowledge domain	Invention	Translator	Appropriation
Knowledge capability	Talent	Research	Technique
Innovation system	Institutions	Networks	Digital

knowledge capabilities through the training of talent in the next generations that capably transfer as well as transform and evolve knowledge technically and commercially is a necessity. Finally, innovation systems take institutions and construct regional advantage through institutional networking that, in itself, embodies where appropriate and feasible, digital knowledge flow platforms (DKFPs) that systemically support knowledge exploration, and knowledge examination to knowledge exploitation interactions. The DKFPs thus become complicit in the innovation process in a Callon-like network that integrates people and machines (Callon, 1991).

1.3 OPEN INNOVATION, ASYMMETRIC KNOWLEDGE FLOW AND SPATIAL KNOWLEDGE DOMAINS

The organizational change implied by systemically transforming knowledge domain implicit to digital explicit knowledge is clearly challenging. But that it is being met by some firms in some sectors is testified to in what follows. Of particular interest here is the manner biotechnology and the pharmaceuticals industry pioneered 'open innovation' because of asymmetric knowledge problems, a style that Chesbrough (2003) shows has spread to other sectors of late. Implied in open innovation is the widespread adoption of especially digital explicit knowledge transfer. But in open innovation the fact that this also requires implicit knowledge has been realized, often through complicit third parties operating in small and medium-sized firm networks, also involving research centres of excellence in universities or research institutes. Hence, illustrative of creating *constructed advantage* through enhancing *regional knowledge capabilities* by creating spatial knowledge domains institutionalized as regional innovation systems is the process, described by Chesbrough (2003) of *open innovation*. Here the knowledge asymmetry is in three dimensions: scale, sector and space. Table 1.3 is an attempt to capture the complexities of the knowledge linkage and digital systems interactions necessitated in a process, now widely pursued by large corporate entities in life sciences, ICT, automotive engineering, advertising and even household products according to writers like Chesbrough (2003), Schamp, Rentmeister and Lo (2004) and Van den Biesen (2004). Table 1.3's exemplar sector is biotechnology, but this can be repeated for many other knowledge-intensive and even not so knowledge-intensive sectors like the food industry. Essentially, Boston is known as the world-leading centre for post-genomics biotechnology research (exploration knowledge) while San Francisco and San Diego are better-known respectively for their technological leads in screening (and sequencing)

Table 1.3 *Bioregional knowledge asymmetries, domains, capabilities and innovation systems*

	Scale	Sector	Space
Exploration	'Big pharma'	Biotechnology	Boston
Examination	Screening	Genomics	San Francisco
Exploitation	Drug	HIV/AIDS	San Diego

equipment, and therapeutic treatments in immunology. Accordingly, they may be said to predominate in these 'knowledge domains'. Under 'open innovation' conventions, large corporations have rapidly abdicated basic and even much applied research to such 'knowledge domain' regions and industry clusters. These are composed of knowledgeable research centres of excellence and specialist R&D services firms.

Knowledge institutions evolve asymmetrically, hence particular spatial knowledge domains become expert in 'ahead of the curve' knowledge (tacit, exploration) while others become so in examination and exploitation knowledge, or some specific combination of these knowledges. These regional knowledge capabilities become structurally embedded by specific institutions that facilitate network inter-relationships, supported also by digital systems enabling codified data interchange (but not tacit and possibly not complicit, hence the importance of spatial domain proximity). But the variation in regional knowledge capabilities impels implicit, complicit and explicit exchange among distinctive spatial knowledge domains with specific combinatorial knowledge capabilities.[2] Once structurally and relationally embedded these domains have evolved to the status of regional innovation systems (RIS) capable of supporting more than one distinctive industry cluster (Cooke, 1992; Granovetter, 1992).

Much recent literature enables a reconstruction of how such clusters actually evolve. They are dependent upon both virtual and real-time relational embedding by means of digital software and communication systems. Table 1.4 is an attempt to capture the processes in question conceptually, recognizing a literature on the causes of innovation on whether and at what point knowledge specialization and knowledge diversification are predominant. Table 1.4 also recognizes the interplay in the literature on knowledge secrecy and knowledge openness captured in the economic concept of contractual 'transaction costs' on the one hand, and 'open science' on the other. With the decline of in-house R&D by large corporations and the rise to prominence of universities as leading exploration (but not exploitation) knowledge institutions in the modern world, 'open science' naturally leads to 'open innovation'.

Table 1.4 Characterization of successful spatial knowledge domains

	Specialization	Diversification
Pipeline	1. Embryonic	4. High success
Open science	2. Innovative	3. High potential

To explain what the table shows, it suggests the following. In the early stage (1) of a technology, there will be few firms or researchers with the requisite combination of scientific and commercialization expertise for technology exploitation. However, when the two come together and the market potential of what has been discovered is realized, there will be a 'pipeline' -type transaction to patent knowledge, arrange investment and create a firm. This was exactly the history of Genentech after recombinant DNA Nobel Laureate Herb Boyer and partner Stanley Cohen met Robert Swanson, venture capitalist with Kleiner, Perkins, Caufield & Byers (KPCB) in 1976 before any cluster existed in San Francisco. Thereafter (Stage 2) more firms formed as scientific research evolved and new spinouts sought to emulate Genentech's success. Once this process has begun, the sector remains specialized but employees who retain, as do founders, close affiliation with their host university, open 'channels', and knowledge spillovers are accessed to create a highly innovative environment around 'open science' conventions. Stage 3 is reached when diversification begins and specialist suppliers or new technology research lines and firms form as, for example, after a breakthrough like decoding the human genome. Large research budgets are by now attracted to leading centres and this stimulates further 'open science' communication, cross-fertilization through knowledge spillovers and further firm formation. In Stage 4, after this, many serious entrepreneurial transactions occurring through 'pipeline' relations with big pharma take place, eventually, where trialling proves successful, licensing deals for marketing a healthcare product are struck between big pharma and specialist firms.

Summarizing the key connections discussed so far in regard to the conceptual underpinnings of functioning regional innovation systems, attention to Figure 1.1 reveals the main elements in the framework discussed thus far and elaborated below. At this stage, digital practicalities are not engaged, mainly since they are captured in the linkage vectors between each conceptual network node.

Of key importance as drivers of the processes leading to spatial knowledge domains and specialist knowledge clusters are Krugmanian increasing returns that result in geographical knowledge monopolies. It was shown elsewhere how in bioscientific knowledge clusters, particular city-regions,

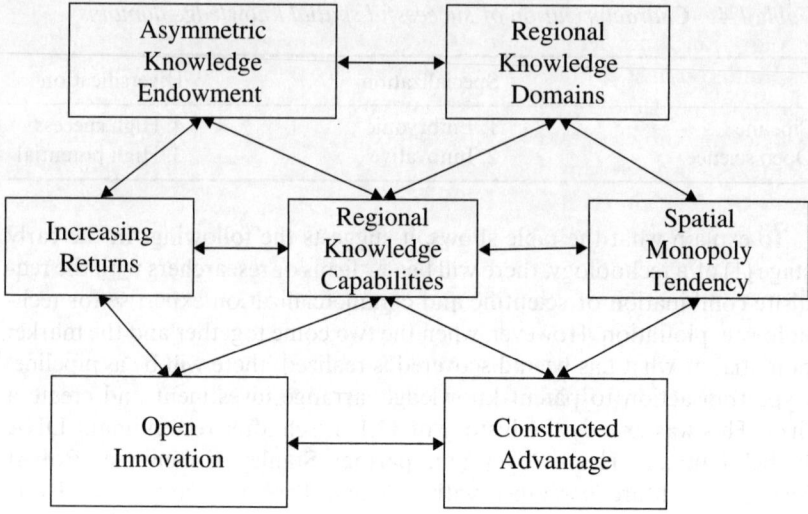

Figure 1.1   Dynamic regional knowledge capabilities

notably in the United States, had evolved recombinant innovation expertises, constructed on evolved advantages, in particular kinds of abstract or synthetic knowledge backgrounds. Thus, medical research in Boston and ICT knowledge monopolies in California gave specificity to those particular knowledge domains:

1. *Asymmetric knowledge*: after Akerlof (1970), whereby specific knowledge expertise is cumulative, path-dependent and attracts increasing returns to scale (Krugman, 1995) tending towards spatial knowledge monopoly.
2. *Knowledge capabilities*: after Penrose [1959] (1995), firms (and their host regions) grow competitively from practising dynamic organizational and knowledge networking expertise (see also Teece and Pisano, 1996).
3. *Open innovation*: after Chesbrough (2003), the practice of contractual R&D outsourcing from corporations to PROs and specialist firms. Locations with asymmetric knowledge capabilities also yield up localized knowledge spillovers from PRO conventions of 'open science' that outweigh possible knowledge 'leakages' but add to regional knowledge monopoly, further benefiting open innovators.
4. *Constructed advantage*: after Foray and Freeman (1993) whereby economic governance raises systemic regional innovation capabilities from attention to the interplay between economic, governance, knowledge and environmental advantages, thereby improving the likelihood of attracting and retaining 'talent' and regional competitiveness.

This explanatory model clearly works for the iterative process of taking exploration knowledge through its examination phases to ultimate exploitation as a commercial product via academic entrepreneurship and 'big pharma' funding. But it is becoming generic, in other words, it also applies to knowledge-to-product processing in the completely different context of a project inside the large firm and in other sectors. Accordingly, with the help of Akerlof (1970) and Chesbrough (2003), armed with a spatial sensibility towards digital systems, we have an explanation of the modern innovation process that satisfies both the exigencies of markets and conventions of 'open innovation'. The interesting thing about research on 'open innovation' is that it begins with pioneering cases from bioscience, the model thereafter migrating to other industries as reported by Chesbrough (2003) who is thus able to broaden the project model of 'open innovation' to other industries.

Regarding innovation, the 'market' perspective is propounded by Zucker, Darby and Armstrong (2002) while a good example of the 'social' perspective is provided by Owen-Smith and Powell (2004). The former show that commercialization of new knowledge such as that involved in biotechnology required the mastery of a very large amount of basic scientific knowledge that was largely non-codified. Thus firms became inordinately dependent on research scientists to *transceive* for them. The latter were well attuned to working with industry, hence receptive to such interaction. Locations with concentrations of such knowledge to transfer thus became magnets for pharmaceuticals corporations. However, the more 'social' perspective of Owen-Smith and Powell (2004) sees that over time the research 'conventions' of 'open science' influence firms in their network interactions with others. Researchers may not remain the main intermediaries among specialist research firms and spinouts as the latter grow in number. As they engage in commercialization of exploration knowledge and exploitation of such knowledge through patenting, they experience greater gains through the combination of proximity and conventions, than through either proximity or conventions alone. This is dynamic knowledge networking capability transformed into a regional capability, which in turn attracts large pharma firms seeking membership of the 'community' or 'domain'.

1.4 FROM LEARNING ORGANIZATIONS TO DIGITAL KNOWLEDGE FLOW PLATFORMS (DKFPs)

We now come to a consideration of digital knowledge management systems challenges faced in entities such as regional innovation systems and even, as second-order phenomena 'learning regions', but more particularly spatial knowledge domains that display *knowledge capabilities*. To highlight, briefly, two known empirical cases of this, let us first consider GlobalScot, a knowledge flows management system designed to enhance regional knowledge capabilities of business and its support agencies in Scotland. By creating a virtual spatial knowledge domain of the Scottish diaspora embedding a transceiver mechanism, this transforms a learning region into a regional innovation system. Learning, by definition, is always asymmetric to knowledge. The initial regional conditions are characterized by Akerlof's (1970) Nobel Laureate work on 'asymmetric information' though the parlance preferred in this narrative is the less passive notion of 'asymmetric knowledge'.

Although 'the myopia of learning' has been condemned since at least Levinthal and March (1993), penetrating critiques came recently, as indicated, from two fairly distinct sources. To recap, the first was Hansen (2002) who showed the failure of organizational learning wrapped up in the language of 'knowledge management' to lie in failure to develop the organization. He showed large firms sought to look into the brains of the workforce to transform its implicit or tacit knowledge (Polanyi, 1966) into explicit or codified knowledge and exploit it. These ideas had been floated in Nonaka and Takeuchi's (1995) influential book on the knowledge-creating company. However, Hansen showed that the 'knowledge management systems' put in place had produced disappointing results. Recall that this was for three reasons. First, the knowledge management system technologies were designed so that knowledge mainly moved upwards to executive level. Second, workers received no feedback or knowledge-sharing opportunities and, crucially, no new incentive structure to reward them for sharing tacit or specific codified knowledge, so they stopped divulging knowledge for obvious reasons. Finally the 'silo' structures of large-firm bureaucracy also prevented lateral movement of knowledge and information. Accordingly, only top management in theory benefited from knowledge transfer, but they were first presented with knowledge overload that could not adequately be absorbed organizationally, then they were confronted with a knowledge drought when the workforce stopped engaging.

Further, recall that Hansen's recommendations required organizational change that could enable digital knowledge management systems to function optimally on the basis of what we are referring to in this chapter as digital knowledge flow platforms (DKFPs). The first step is to reduce organizational hierarchy and remove 'silos'. Then knowledge has to be organized so that it has lateral as well as vertical upwards and downwards vectors, allowing for feedback looping. Next, the workforce must be incentivized to share knowledge, not merely through improved job satisfaction but through pecuniary rewards based on the frequency, quality and impact of knowledge-sharing. Finally, appropriate digital systems software is required so that knowledge-sharing is made technically simple through interaction with computers and mobile telephony. A minimum requirement would be a database entry system and an intranet, possibly extending to an extranet to the extent that, for example, suppliers and customers were to be included in the knowledge management system.

The second illustration of how DKFPs require organizational transformation came from Aalborg University, Denmark where Dirckinck-Holmfeld (2002) showed how e-learning failed when no change was made to the traditional lecture-based pedagogy of traditional learning. This discovery occurred with the introduction of e-learning Internet-based activity in Aalborg University itself, where it worked. But when it was transferred to other Danish universities it was a failure. The reason was that Aalborg, like Roskilde University was one of Denmark's two new universities dating from the 1970s. In those radical times they were organized with an interdisciplinary core curriculum centred upon students engaging in team-based project work rather than lecture-based learning. E-learning in a classroom where a video of a lecturer standing at a lectern with text of the lecture scrolling down the side of the lecturer's image proved actually to be a good cure for insomnia. However interactive, project-based team learning where problem-solving information of relevance to knowledge development by the student team is instantly accessed by Internet is actually efficient, effective and exciting. However, most universities still mainly use lectures rather than projects to teach, especially the much enlarged classes of the 2000s, hence e-learning has failed to make great inroads. That is not to say that lecturing itself cannot be refreshed by DKFPs, as cases show where the lecturer accesses from a console Internet updates to points that are being made verbally. But this requires levels of expenditure and expertise, never mind possible time inefficiencies if technological discontinuities occur, which make it something of a luxury in most public sector pedagogic contexts.

Thus, some important lessons were absorbed about learning and knowledge generation itself during the past decade. For example, many business leaders confronted with the preceding account might emphasize the fact that their businesses have successfully run DKFPs for years if not decades. But these are usually information not knowledge management systems. Hence, as long ago as the early 1990s, IBM utilized a third party to manage its supply chain for items costing then less than DM 50 per unit. At that time, in Germany for example, the media giant Bertelsmann was IBM's favoured third party supply chain manager for small items. IBM's strict internal accounting rules meant that, at that time, more valuable items had to be signed off by the head purchasing manager (Cooke and Morgan, 1998). More recently, it has become common for global supply chain management for all predictable items to be managed even by small, specialist third party supply chain management companies. Hewlett Packard in Scotland, for example, and presumably elsewhere, was, in 2002, contracting this function to such a company that used proprietary IBM Lotus Domino software to replenish consignment stocks as these ran down (OECD, 2004).[3] But such systems are scarcely knowledge management, they are scarcely even artificial intelligence – another digital dream that turned sour in the 1990s – but simple automatic shelf stacking systems based on codified information. Clearly the key lesson learned is how different knowledge is from information.

To dwell on this distinction for a moment, let us consider the nature of the difference. Information theory can be traced back at least to the pioneering research at Bell Laboratories of engineer Claude Shannon (1948, pp. 379–80) who, it will be recalled, defined information as messages possessing *meaning* for sender and recipient. As noted, this is a 'train timetable' theory since Shannon said that communication's 'significant aspect is that the actual message is one *selected from a set* of possible messages' (1948, p. 379, original emphasis). Thus you choose from a menu of provided information that has meaning for your next action as a relatively passive recipient. Typical of its time, this was a linear, inscriptive, traditional engineering metaphor. This approach then fuelled research professing to have identified 'information overload' (Miller, 1978) from the exponential growth in messages, subsequently increasingly diffused by 'information and communication technology' (ICT) (Seely Brown and Duguid, 2000; Lievrouw and Livingstone, 2002). This rather conflated information and knowledge. To return to the train timetable, it is clearly full of information, but it is as Shannon said, only useful when meaningful. But meaning is not supplied by the information but by the knowledgeable actor. In this case the knowledge of where he or she wishes to travel to is what gives the timetable meaning on which action is based. So the distinction is based on interactions between the supply of (codified) information, the application of meaning derived from tacit (but codifiable) knowledge that triggers subsequent *action*.

1.5 DKFPs AND REGIONAL INNOVATION SYSTEMS

Hence we have a glimpse at the cause of a major problem both for firms and other kinds of organization, including whole economies or regional parts of them that must change to confront new pressures to innovate, be creative and implement novel strategies. Digital systems react to information not knowledge, especially not tacit knowledge. Transferring tacit knowledge to the outside world in a meaningful way is not a direct but a mediated process. Thus far, much of the knowledge management literature has been insufficiently appreciative of these considerations. The innovation literature typically refers to the necessity for implicit knowledge to be made explicit and codified as documentation, manuals or software, for example, in order that the potential productivity of new knowledge may be realized (Edquist, 1997). Thereafter such knowledge becomes information that may be configured for digital analysis and application as discussed above. However, organizational knowledge is difficult to translate, especially when the organization is externalized and takes the complex form of an economy or a regional part of it. Hence knowledge transfer is a much more uncertain, indeed, strictly asymmetrical process (Akerlof, 1970; Cooke, 2005b). To improve, become more competitive or innovative, a firm, organization or person may try to learn from the observable information that may be gained from what is perceived to be a superior performer. It might engage in study visits to benchmark 'best practice', another activity that has grown enormously in scale in the past decade or so.

But an organization or person that becomes accustomed to learning from elsewhere in the form of pre-existing (pre-digested) information, cannot cope with novelty. Desultory regional economies and their learning organizations are condemned to a treadmill of absorbing old information. After trying to learn its lessons it may possibly implement them in time to discover that superior intelligence from elsewhere has already set new standards. Learning and innovation are opposites, and innovation, as we have seen, requires organizational change.

This is largely because it is difficult to transform the tacit nature of successful practice into the codified recipe capable of successful emulation. This affects the core thinking about knowledge in many fields. That is because tacit knowledge does not transfer simply into codified, because of 'epistemic communities' and 'cognitive dissonance'. Rather it is mediated, but until now there has not been a word or concept to capture that mediation. The third party must be complicit with the knowledge of the implicit knowledge-holder for that knowledge to be made reasonably explicit to his or her interlocutor. In this way, meaning may be given to the member of the 'other' epistemic community by a process somewhat comparable to that of 'triangulation' in social scientific methodology.[4]

A complex organizational change that numerous regions effected in the 1990s and into the 2000s concerns innovation systems, specifically *regional* innovation systems. Although in the EU over 100 regions have been exposed to regional innovation *strategies* since 1994 (Oughton, Landabaso and Morgan, 2002), Carlsson (2006) has tracked over 200 regional innovation systems *studies* between 1987 and 2002, half of them products of empirical research. These show leading and lagging regions improving innovative performance by re-designing their boundary-crossing mechanisms or 'bridging social capital' (Putnam, 1999) between research (exploration knowledge) and commercialization (*exploitation* knowledge March 1991).[5] Moreover, in Cooke, Heidenreich and Braczyk (2004) the evolution of regional innovation systems worldwide in the face of economic downturn and globalization effects is delineated. These now transcend simplistic knowledge transfer notions like the 'triple helix' (Etzkowitz and Leydesdorff, 1997), which presents the institutional clash of 'epistemic communities' (Haas, 1992) among government, industry and universities as akin to a Holy Trinity. The disequilibriating impulses of the 'knowledge economy' have prompted innovative thinking in lagging regions whereby the Holy Trinity is eschewed and even the 'holy of holies', the university, is looked upon askance in the quest for regional *constructed advantage* (Foray and Freeman, 1993). Solutions arising from these new approaches will be presented below.

The point here is that economic governance agencies, like firms and persons, eventually realize the futility of trying to 'clone' successful cases by learning and copying information – even if mediated by a complicit third party[6] – and are forced to the ominous deduction that they must, fundamentally, devise their own solution tailored to their own conditions, informed by lessons from elsewhere, but interacting with the endogenous knowledge base of their own context. This is what is best termed *recombinant* innovation, contrasted with *incremental* organizational innovation, which as Lindblom (1977) showed, may lead conservatively in the wrong direction or even round in circles, and *radical* organizational innovation, which as Simon (1955) showed produces 'variable overload' and is thus difficult to manage. Recombinant organizational innovation is massively assisted by development of regional innovation systems adapted to contextual specificities as discussed above. And of immense support to well-functioning regional innovation systems is a successful DKFP that circulates and communicates much codified or explicit, complicit and potentially some fragmentary implicit knowledge across the 'epistemic communities' that compose it. For, in a far more complex way than that imagined in the triple helix literature (Etzkowitz and Leydesdorff, 1997) regional innovation systems must integrate complexity in the external environment.

For they are composed of two internal sub-systems each open to interaction with other regional, national and global organizations and institutions.

The first is the knowledge exploration and examination sub-system composed mainly of public bodies like universities, research laboratories, medical schools, testing agencies, standards bodies, knowledge transfer bodies and economic governance agencies and funds. While the second is the knowledge exploitation sub-system, composed of mainly private actors like business firms, private financiers, venture capitalists, patent lawyers, management consultants and technical consultancies and design agencies, each in a knowledge value chain position concerned with knowledge exploitation and innovation, otherwise known as the commercialization of new knowledge on the market. For all members of such a 'trans-epistemic community' to have the best knowledge flows of consequence to their professional innovation activity a DKFP is desirable and necessary, but scarcely any economic governance agencies have them. Two that do are discussed in the final section of this chapter below.

1.6 DKFPs IN PRACTICE AND EXPERIMENTATION

How might internal and external disconnects be moderated? In respect of Scottish Enterprise, the question arose of an enhanced intranet facility within the agency, parts of which would be devoted to internal interactions, whereas it had been designed for external business interactions among the Scottish global business diaspora. Time would be needed to populate it with requisite information, and commitment from field officers and HQ staff to keep it updated. Moreover, job descriptions would need to specify as a requirement that it should be an everyday responsibility to find out what of relevance was posted upon it. To give weight to the importance of intra-organizational 'knowledge of the world' this knowledge management and processing function should be given status through the appointment, presumably at the centre but with networkwide scope, of a senior knowledge manager. TalentScot was the forerunner, having been similarly digitally created to enable Scotland's advanced software research Alba Centre to recruit talent in ICT businesses and research. This model was adapted to that provided by GlobalScot as an extranet, albeit focused on Scots and Scotophiles abroad. It is a suitable one upon which to build such functionality. Ironically, one of the greatest potential value-adding functions of GlobalScot, which would be to tap into the knowledge being communicated by persons with valuable anticipatory or foresight understanding of market signals was not designed in from the outset because, correctly, of confidentiality concerns. But a polling function to access key international knowledge (including tacit perceptual as well as explicit knowledge) flows while maintaining security is needed and is in development at Scottish

Enterprise. Hence intra-organizational learning clearly creates opportunities for developing wider reflexive knowledge competencies within the organization and between it and its customers. In the process that can assist systemic or paradigm knowledge development, making transparent tacit assumptions that may be unreliable (Cooke, 2004).

A different model is under development at VINNOVA in Sweden. There, it is internal 'organizational knowledge' concerns that have stimulated the creation of an intranet that could be transformed into an extranet to regional innovation systems the agency is constructing throughout Sweden. VINNOVA was in 2001 an organizational innovation arising from a former technology transfer agency called NUTEK. The latter was seen politically as having failed Sweden's regional development and to be over-wedded to an engineering culture influenced still by the linear innovation model, itself reflected in over-allocation of technology subsidies in the Stockholm area. VINNOVA's task is to build innovation systems in Sweden's regions. It has begun with cluster-building activities in Skåne, Uppsala and west of Stockholm. However, the new economic governance agency contains two cultures and administrative 'silos'. Hence, different parts of the agency did not necessarily know what other parts were doing. Thus, this author's recommendation that VINNOVA should construct a DKFP along lines advocated in Hansen (2002).

By late 2004 such an intranet system had been constructed and populated using a geographic information systems (GIS) program format. Thus, the system contains locational data on all innovation nodes and networks in Sweden and its regions, with detailed firm data available beneath map-based geographical information. On to these bases are added policy information, types of measures and financing regimes. This database GIS will be accessible by all VINNOVA employees, and if successfully adapted so that knowledge may be added in structured form by any authorized member of the workforce, will act as a policy-based knowledge management system. In time, and subject to data protection standards, it could, in principle be made accessible to actors external to VINNOVA, particularly in the regional innovation systems that are being formed. In further time, management attention will have to be given to an incentivization scheme and knowledge management function to ensure the system attracts both knowledge users and producers.

1.7 CONCLUSIONS

Summarizing these findings for the role of digital systems as vehicles of advanced knowledge management, they may be seen to operate through the *translation* of valued knowledge from domain to domain and across epistemic communities both inside the large corporation and in the much more complex externalized world of 'open innovation' among and within regional innovation sytems. Regarding the first, it was evident that imposing knowledge management systems upon otherwise unchanged organizations is a retrogressive step. Learning and knowledge creation arising from evaluation of such mistakes led to the conclusion that 'flattened hierarchies' and strong lateral networking in silo-free environments are the sine qua non of successful introduction of advanced knowledge flows 'expert systems'. The same is true in spatial knowledge domains that are advanced in knowledge capabilities, displaying structural and relational embeddedness in regional innovation systems. Asymmetric knowledge formation means that spatial domains gain from their *constructed advantage* of global nodal networking to identify and connect advanced expertise as in the cases of GlobalScot and VINNOVA. In all circumstances discussed, digital systems are crucial but they rest on social interactions to generate and exploit useful knowledge.

To conclude, the discussion exposed three main things, showing how lessons learned from evaluation of inadequacies in conceptualization of the nature of knowledge have assisted economic governance agencies to advance digitally in their support services to innovation. It was shown first that business made several early efforts to develop 'knowledge management systems' that did not work due to no accompanying changes being made to the organization in which knowledge management was introduced. The critique of this showed that breaking down of silo mentalities and stimulating feedback within the organizational structure were essential, as indeed was incentivization of the workforce. Other digital system management, as with supply chain management outsourcing to third parties constituted information management – a far simpler task than knowledge management because it lacks the tacit dimension.

Second, organizations that increasingly deal with external complexity, across epistemic community boundaries, and including many different kinds of third party complicit knowledge intermediaries are exemplified well by those that engage in economic governance, particularly that characterized by supporting the design and realization of regional innovation systems. Experience of managing complex interactions of this kind where exploration, examination and exploitation knowledge have to be successfully recombined, revealed that past traditions of imitative learning were insufficient to aid implementation of modern innovation support strategies. Third, interactive learning for knowledge creation endogenized to the specific region is now widely seen as a superior albeit challenging methodology. To ensure that key organizational communities either within or outside the nodal organization in a network-based system can access various kinds of knowledge, from the exploratory to the examination and exploitation through the implicit (partially) and complicit to the explicit, such agencies are experimenting with DKFPs. Early results are promising and practical, with GIS technology proving to be a highly effective digital means of facilitating global knowledge flows animated by economic governance agencies involved in facilitating regional innovation systems.

ACKNOWLEDGEMENTS

This chapter was prepared for the joint European Co-operation in the Field of Scientific and Technical Research (COST), European Science Foundation and AQR research group Open Conference on 'Knowledge and Regional Economic Development', Barcelona, June 2005. I am grateful to the organizers for inviting the original paper and thank, among many, Ed Bergman, Javier Revilla Diez, Bernie Fingleton, Simona Iammarino and Phil McCann for discussion and comments. The usual disclaimer applies.

NOTES

1. Demonstrating how un-innovative 'learning' can be even among the 'learned', Akerlof's (1970) paper, which won the 2001 Nobel Prize for Economics, was written in 1966/67 during his first year as an assistant professor at the University of California, Berkeley. Before publication it was rejected by three journals, in two cases on grounds of 'triviality' (Levitt and Dubner, 2005). It is now widely considered the single most important study in the literature on the economics of information. The 2001 Nobel Prize Award Committee noted it was a truly seminal contribution – it addresses a simple but profound and universal idea, with numerous implications and widespread applications. It gave rise to the important economics sub-field of studies in 'asymmetric information' and dominates research in microeconomics concerned with market failure, transaction costs, adverse selection and principal-agent problems.
2. An analogue rather than digital instance of the importance of complicit knowledge is provided in the following. A Tel Aviv, Israel, medical doctor specializing in gastrointestinal medicine was frequently told by patients that endoscopy (camera in a tube for internal patient diagnosis) was painful to throat and oesophagus. He thus had implicit knowledge of a problem. Research on nano-cameras, for example that led Bogdan Dragnea at Indiana University in Bloomington, United States to get an image of what goes on inside living cells and a greater understanding of how viruses work, is also occurring in Israel, some at the behest of the military. Therefore, implicit and limited explicit knowledge of nano-camera technology exists in Israel. The doctor mentioned the endoscopy problem to an entrepreneur acquaintance formerly in the Israeli army rocketry service, who knew of the existence of nano-cameras for guidance purposes. So he had complicit knowledge. The idea of a camera in a pill arose from the conversation and a commercial product now exists as PillCam from GivenImage, the entrepreneur's firm (author research interview, 6 January 2005).
3. This was related by the owner of the specific business, during an OECD mission to Scotland in November 2002 to examine the economic governance agency Scottish

Enterprise's global knowledge flows strategy response to the rise of the knowledge economy. The published report from OECD is available as OECD (2004).
4. Triangulation is the process whereby in, say, interviewing, the interviewer and interviewee interact and some hidden or tacit knowledge comes forth. This must normally be checked with a third party for accuracy and veracity. Hence the knowledge is triangulated with someone complicit with the knowledge field.
5. Elsewhere (Cooke, 2005a; 2005b) this couplet has been shown to be as inadequate as that referring to a facile implicit–explicit knowledge transfer process. This is because, as regional innovation systems research regularly shows, exploration knowledge and exploitation knowledge are also mediated, increasingly so, by examination knowledge that tests and trials innovations to assess whether they are dangerous to humans and the environment. The exemplar case is, of course, the pharmaceutical industry where such examination knowledge is now, in 2005, having to be made public, since large firms have been caught suppressing it, as a consequence of which treatments have had lethal effects on patients.
6. Such as, for example a consultant, another activity that mushroomed in the 1990s. Consultants are well-known for having stock knowledge that they profit from by offering suitably adapted on the surface, basically a 'one-size fits all' solution. Hence in economic governance 'clusters' consultants make a good living despite absence of evidence that their advice works.

REFERENCES

Adorno, T. (2001), *The Culture Industry*, London, Routledge.
Akerlof, G. (1970), 'The market for "lemons": qualitative uncertainty and the market mechanism', *Quarterly Journal of Economics*, 84, 488–500.
Asheim, B. and M. Gertler (2004), 'The geography of innovation: regional innovation systems', in J. Fagerberg, D. Mowery and R. Nelson (eds), *The Oxford Handbook of Innovation*, Oxford: Oxford University Press.
Beskind, P. (2004), *Down & Dirty Pictures*, London: Bloomsbury.
Brown, J. Seely and P. Duguid (2000), *The Social Life of Information*, Boston: Harvard Business School Press.
Callon, M. (1991), 'Techno-economic networks and irreversibility', in J. Law (ed.), *A Sociology of Monsters: Essays on Power, Technology and Domination*, London: Routledge.
Carlsson, B. (2006), 'Innovation systems: a survey of the literature from a Schumpeterian perspective', in H. Hanusch and A. Pyka (eds), *The Companion to Neo-Schumpeterian Economics*, Cheltenham, UK and Northampton, MA, USA: Edward Elgar.
Chesbrough, H. (2003), *Open Innovation*, Boston: Harvard Business School Press.
Cooke, P. (1992), 'Regional innovation systems: competitive regulation in the new Europe', *Geoforum*, 23, 365–82.
Cooke, P. (2004), 'Integrating global knowledge flows for generative growth in Scotland: life sciences as an exemplar', in OECD (ed.), *Global Knowledge Flows and Economic Development*, Paris: Organisation for Economic Co-operation and Development.
Cooke, P. (2005a), 'Rational drug design, the knowledge value chain and bioscience megacentres', *The Cambridge Journal of Economics*, 29, 325–42.
Cooke, P. (2005b), 'Regionally asymmetric knowledge capabilities and open innovation: exploring "Globalization 2" – a new model of industry organization', *Research Policy*, 34, 1128–49.

Cooke, P. and K. Morgan (1998), *The Associational Economy*, Oxford: Oxford University Press.
Cooke, P., M. Heidenreich and H. Braczyk (eds) (2004), *Regional Innovation Systems* 2nd Edition, London: Routledge.
Dirckinck-Holmfeld, L. (2002), *Problem-oriented project pedagogy*, in L. Dirckinck-Holmfeld and B. Fibiger (eds), *Learning in Virtual Environments*, Frederiksberg: Samfundslitteratur.
Edquist, C. (ed.) (1997), *Systems of Innovation*, London: Pinter.
Etzkowitz, H. and L. Leydesdorff (eds) (1997), *Universities and the Global Knowledge Economy*, London: Pinter.
Feldman, M. and R. Florida (1994), 'The geographic sources of innovation: technological infrastructure and product innovation in the United States', *Annals of the Association of American Geographers*, 84, 210–29.
Florida, R. (1995), 'Toward the learning region', *Futures*, 27, 527–36.
Foray, D. and C. Freeman (1993), *Technology and the Wealth of Nations: The Dynamics of Constructed Advantage*, London: Pinter.
Galison, P. (1997), *Image & Logic: A Material Culture of Microphysics*, Chicago: Chicago University Press.
Granovetter, M. (1992), 'Problems of explanation in economic sociology', in N. Nohria and R. Eccles (eds), *Networks and Organizations: Structure, Form and Action*, Boston: Harvard Business School Press.
Haas, J. (1992), 'Introduction: epistemic communities and international policy coordination', *International Organization*, 46, 1–37.
Hansen, M. (2002), 'Knowledge networks: explaining effective knowledge sharing in multi-unit companies', *Organization Sciences*, 13, 232–48.
Krugman, P. (1995), *Development, Geography and Economic Theory*, Cambridge: MIT Press.
Lester, R. and M. Piore (2004), *Innovation: the Missing Dimension*, Cambridge: Harvard University Press.
Levinthal, D. and J. March (1993), 'The myopia of learning', *Strategic Management Journal*, 14, 95–112.
Levitt, S. and S. Dubner (2005), *Freakonomics*, London: Penguin.
Lievrouw, L. and S. Livingstone (eds) (2002), *The Handbook of New Media*, London: Sage.
Lindblom, C. (1977), *Politics & Markets*, New York: Basic Books.
Lo, V. and E. Schamp (eds) (2002), *Knowledge – the Spatial Dimension*, Münster: Lit-Verlag.
March, J. (1991), 'Exploration and exploitation in organizational learning', *Organization Science*, 2, 71–87.
March, J., L. Sproull and M. Tamuz (1991), 'Learning from samples of one or fewer', *Organization Science*, 2, 1–13.
Miller, J. (1978), *Living Systems*, New York: McGraw-Hill.
Negroponte, N. (1995), *Being Digital*, New York: Knopf.
Nonaka, I. and H. Takeuchi (1995), *The Knowledge-Creating Company*, Oxford: Oxford University Press.
OECD (2004), *Global Knowledge Flows and Economic Development*, Paris: OECD.
Oughton, C., M. Landabaso and K. Morgan (2002), 'The regional innovation paradox: innovation policy and industrial policy', *Journal of Technology Transfer*, 27, 97–110.

Owen-Smith, J. and W. Powell (2004), 'Knowledge networks as channels and conduits: the effects spillovers in the Boston biotechnology community', *Organization Science*, 15, 5–21.
Penrose, E. ([1959] 1995), *The Theory of the Growth of the Firm*, Oxford: Oxford University Press.
Polanyi, M. (1966), *The Tacit Dimension*, New York: Doubleday.
Porter, M. (1998), *On Competition*, Boston: Harvard Business School Press.
Putnam, R. (1999), *Bowling Alone*, New York: Simon & Schuster.
Schamp, E., B. Rentmeister and V. Lo (2004), 'Dimensions of proximity in knowledge-based networks: the cases of banking and automobile design', *European Planning Studies*, 12, 607–24.
Shannon, C. (1948), 'A mathematical theory of communication', *Bell System Technical Journal*, 27, 379–423 and 623–56.
Simon, H. (1955), 'A behavioural model of rational choice', *Quarterly Journal of Economics*, 69, 99–118.
Simon, H. ([1969] 1996), *The Science of the Artificial*, Cambridge: MIT Press.
Szulanski, G. (1996), 'Exploring internal stickiness: impediments to the transfer of best practice within the firm', *Strategic Management Journal*, 17, 27–43.
Teece, D. and G. Pisano (1996), 'The dynamic capabilities of firms: an introduction', *Industrial and Corporate Change*, 3, 537–56.
Van den Biesen, J. (2004), 'University–Industry Relations and Innovation Strategy in Philips Worldwide: an R&D Outsourcing Approach', presentation to EU Conference *The Europe of Knowledge 2020: a Vision for University-based Research and Innovation*, Liège Convention Centre, 25–28 April.
Zander, U. and B. Kogut (1995), 'Knowledge and the speed of transfer and imitation of organizational capabilities: an empirical test', *Organizational Science*, 6, 76–92.
Zucker, L., M. Darby and J. Armstrong (2002), 'Commercializing knowledge; university science, knowledge capture, and firm performance in biotechnology', *Management Science*, 48, 138–53.

2. Knowledge spillovers and organizational heterogeneity: an historical overview of German technology sectors
Mark Lehrer

2.1 INTRODUCTION

The concept of knowledge spillovers is often invoked to explain a number of important economic phenomena. These include the geographical clustering of inventions and patents (Jaffe, Trajtenberg and Henderson, 1993; Almeida and Kogut, 1997), social returns to R&D significantly exceeding private returns (Jaffe, 1986; Bresnahan, 1989); and major disproportions among firms between R&D inputs and R&D outputs, with small firms generating far more product innovations than large firms relative to their measurable knowledge resources (Acs and Audretsch, 1990).

Yet while knowledge spillovers provide an intuitively appealing explanation for the geographical and social effects of knowledge as an economic good, the concept is also controversial. Indeed, both critics (Breschi and Lissoni, 2001) and advocates (Audretsch and Feldman, 2004) of the concept agree that local knowledge spillovers stand in need of more basic phenomenological investigation. A particularly contentious point, and the point of departure for the following study, concerns the mechanisms accounting for the local boundedness of knowledge spillovers. The most frequently cited explanation for why knowledge spills over locally rather than globally pertains to the tacitness and stickiness of knowledge (Polanyi, 1966; von Hippel, 1994). Yet alternative spatially limiting mechanisms have been suggested. Knowledge may circulate in parallel with other resources (money, personnel, etc.) in contractual agreements; pecuniary-based local knowledge flows (Autant-Bernard and Massard, this volume) leave open the possibility that what appear to be knowledge externalities at an aggregated level are simply the outcomes of complex market processes (Breschi and Lissoni, 2001 Caniels and Romijn, 2005). Similarly, information exchanged on the basis of local reciprocity (Kesidou, 2004) is hardly distinguishable at an aggregated level from uncontrolled local knowledge spillovers. In other words, local knowledge flows may not always derive from pure knowledge externalities that are geographically limited by specific characteristics of knowledge (tacitness, stickiness), but rather from a more complex set of inherently local transactions. Many knowledge flows may be localized for the same reasons that certain types of business transactions are localized.

The following historical review tracks the differential nature of knowledge spillovers that were ostensibly important in four German technology sectors of the late 19th and late 20th century. The review suggests that both in domains where Germany was highly successful (organic chemicals and electricity around 1900) and where German high-tech performance was mediocre (biotechnology and computing of the late 20th century), knowledge spillovers were far from automatic and required special organizational effort on the part of firms and/or policy-makers (see also Cooke, this volume). To this extent, the analysis is somewhat consonant with the 'knowledge spillover theory of entrepreneurship' (Audretsch and Lehmann, 2005) according to which the realization of knowledge spillovers frequently depends on special organizational and entrepreneurial effort.

The arduousness of the task of capturing knowledge spillovers is addressed also by the longitudinal aspect to the analysis underlining the important role of trial-and-error in developing the organizational means for creating and absorbing critical technological knowledge (Murmann, 2003); especially in the earlier stages of these sectors, a degree of geographical decentralization was generally conducive to organizational experimentation. Reminiscent of the exploration–exploitation trade-off (March, 1991), the following analysis posits a certain trade-off between geographical decentralization for the sake of experimentation and geographical centralization for the sake of efficiency, notably the familiar Marshall–Arrow–Romer increasing returns (Marshall, 1920; Arrow, 1962; Romer, 1986).

An historical look at these technology sectors suggests that experimentation was important in the early phases, with efficiency gaining increasing prominence subsequently, the resulting general pattern being that these sectors became more geographically concentrated over time. The essentially decentralized political structure of Germany, significantly federalist in both in its imperial (1871–1918) and post-1945 phase in matters relating to education and research, lends itself to study of these contrasting geographic aspects of knowledge spillovers.

The following analysis underlines significant variety in the organizational arrangement of firms and R&D institutions underpinning important knowledge spillover processes. The commercialization of technological knowledge involved relatively complex arrangements and transactions whose nature differed from sector to sector, suggesting that economic agents faced relative a priori difficulty in assessing the requisite arrangements for managing knowledge spillovers. The ability of firms, individually or collectively, to capture knowledge spillovers thus depended on whether they had implemented the needed set of 'organizational innovations', an admittedly catch-all term used previously to examine Europe's post-war high-tech deficit (Andreasen et al., 1995; Coriat and Weinstein, 2002). Although the scope and method of the following historical analysis permit only a very selective view of knowledge spillover processes, taken together they are suggestive of the view that the critical knowledge gaps with regard to the exploitation of new technologies concern not only the underlying science and technology, but also the organizational arrangements needed to transform scientific and technological findings into commercial innovations.

2.2 KNOWLEDGE SPILLOVERS AND SECTORAL DIFFERENCES: A FRAMEWORK OF ANALYSIS

A useful distinction for investigating sectoral differences is that between *science-driven* high-tech sectors on the one hand and *market-pioneering* high-tech sectors on the other (Lehrer, 2005). In science-driven sectors, such as organic chemicals in the 19th century and biotechnology in the 20th, firms engage in scientific discovery to fulfil a recognizable market need (e.g., a synthetic indigo dye or a specific cancer remedy). If market needs are known and the knowledge bottleneck lies in the technology to fulfil the need, then the critical knowledge spillovers are likely to lie in the interface between academic science and firms, that is, academia-to-firm knowledge spillovers. Sometimes, however, the reverse holds: the technology is known, but the appropriate commercial applications are murky (Grupp, 2000). In such market-pioneering sectors including electricity in the 19th century and computers in the 20th, the basic science may be established but the markets are ill-defined, either because the precise applications of the technology are unclear at first (as in computing) and/or because the technology requires construction of a complex infrastructure (e.g., an electrical network). In market-pioneering sectors, critical knowledge gaps concerning markets and business models require that firms learn from the experiences of one another, so that firm-to-firm knowledge spillovers play an essential role. The differences are summarized in Table 2.1.

The analysis is organized chronologically, with discussion of Germany's first 'high-tech' sectors, organic chemicals and electricity, followed by their late 20th-century successor sectors, pharmaceutical biotechnology and

Table 2.1 Science-driven versus market-pioneering sectors

	Science-driven sectors	Market-pioneering sectors
Knowledge gaps in commercialization process	Breakthroughs in basic science to develop technology to fill known market needs	Identification of appropriate applications and business models for commercializing known technologies
Primary types of knowledge spillovers	Academia-to-firm (supply-side knowledge)	Firm-to-firm (supply- and demand-side knowledge)
19th-century example	Organic chemicals	Electricity
20th-century example	Biotechnology	Computing

computing. The selection of sectors is based on prominence. The early high-tech sectors were precisely those industries in which imperial Germany was singularly successful (Clapham, 1961; Landes, 1969), just as biotechnology and computing were sectors that were central in discussions of post-war Germany's high-tech deficits (Seitz, 1990; Lehrer, 2000a).

2.3 THE LATE 19TH CENTURY: ORGANIC CHEMICALS AND ELECTRICITY

Organic chemicals and high-voltage electricity were the first 'high-tech' industries featuring systematic organization of scientific discovery for business application (Rosenberg and Birdzell, 1986). Imperial Germany excelled in both 'high-tech' sectors (Cardwell, 1995). By 1914, five German firms – BASF, Bayer and Hoechst in organic chemicals and Siemens and AEG in electricity – had become the world's largest firms in their respective industries (Haber, 1958; Freeman and Louca, 2001) and the largest exporters in their sectors. In dyestuffs, German firms possessed an 85–90 per cent share of the world market and a 75–95 per cent share of dyestuff patents not just in Germany, but also in the United States and United Kingdom (Murmann, 2003). In electricity, the 'Big Four' – Siemens and AEG of Germany, and General Electric and Westinghouse of the United States – became so dominant as to constitute an informal global cartel after 1900, yet the German firms were far larger in terms of sales and exports.

Nonetheless, this concentrated industry structure evolved out of a broader range of firms in the 19th century. Vertical and horizontal integration was but the final stage in a series of organizational moves by these proto-high-tech firms. The specific moves differed substantially across industries, underscoring in particular the differential nature of local knowledge spillovers in science-based and market-pioneering sectors.

2.3.1 Organic Chemicals: A Science-driven Sector of the 19th Century

In organic chemicals, a key source of knowledge was the university system. Competitive success in organic chemicals depended critically on laboratory R&D and thus on the availability of properly trained organic chemists, much more so than in inorganic chemicals where scale and efficiency were paramount concerns (Haber, 1958). German firms developed an extensive competitive advantage based upon German dominance in the field of organic chemistry and Germany's high supply of organic chemists in the 19th century (Beer, 1959; Murmann, 2003). In the course of the 19th century, Germany built up the world's leading system of research universities (Landes, 1969, pp. 346–7; Ben-David, 1977). A key development was the rise of the team-based, professor-guided research laboratory pioneered by Justus von Liebig in Giessen in the 1820s. After 1850, several German states began to invest specifically in their universities' chemistry departments as a source of both economic development and prestige (Lenoir, 1998).

Despite Germany's superior knowledge base in organic chemistry, knowledge did not automatically spill over from universities to firms. Firms had to undertake organizational innovations to leverage the superiority of the national science base. In surveying German companies that succeeded or failed in the process, Murmann (2003) insists on the key role of firm experimentation in an evolutionary process of variation and selection. One vital, but not-so-simple step was building long-term relationships with leading chemistry professors at the universities. In fairly detailed studies, Beer (1959) and Murmann and Landau (1998) conclude that these relationships were multifaceted, with professors consulting for companies in exchange for multiple forms of recompense, including firm employment of PhD students, laboratory supplies and information exchange in addition to undisclosed fees. These studies confirm, at least in the case of German organic chemicals, that key knowledge flows were not pure externalities but mediated heavily by complex business transactions as suspected on a broad level by Breschi and Lissoni (2001). Such professor–firm arrangements were virtually unprecedented and had to be conducted with substantial discretion, impinging as they did on the reigning norms of academic autonomy.

Another and truly epoch-making organizational innovation was the in-house central laboratory pioneered by German companies in the mid-1870s (Homburg, 1992; Reinhardt, 1998), fully 25 years before comparable developments emerged in the United States. These laboratories largely reproduced the academic laboratory pioneered by Liebig (Beer, 1959), an isomorphism that facilitated academia–industry spillovers by providing freshly minted PhDs with company facilities similar to those they had encountered at the university.

Although impossible to prove, the decentralized nature of science in Germany probably helps to explain why Germany developed a creative variety of larger-scale university research institutes (Lenoir, 1998) and also specifically invested more in chemical research laboratories than other European countries. Germany's considerable federalism even after 1871 meant that there was considerable interregional competition among the different German states for academic scientists (Vereeck, 2001). Decentralized market competition for researchers, whether based on prestige or other considerations, results in higher resources for the best performers (David, 2004). German states like Prussia and Bavaria offered top chemists a level of laboratory support with which other countries could not compete (Beer, 1959).[1] Symptomatically, Germany's top organic chemists moved between not only universities, but also states in the course of their careers (Lehrer, 2007).

Germany's dyestuff industry was relatively decentralized in the early decades, facilitating both experimentation in firms' business strategies (Murmann, 2003) and in government policies for chemical science. Towards the end of the century, however, economies of scale led to increasing concentration of the dyestuff industry. With access to water being a critical resource, the largest German dyestuff firms concentrated their modern production facilities on larger rivers, particularly the Rhine. Concentration was also enhanced by economies of scope across products; the organic chemical firms diversified into the technologically related fields of fertilizers and pharmaceuticals. Bayer and Hoechst produced 44 major pharmaceutical innovations in the years 1880–1930, more than the entire United States (30) and United Kingdom (12) combined during this same period (Achilladelis and Antonakis, 2001).

From a government action perspective, supply-side policies matched the requirements of this science-driven sector. Although organizational innovations by firms were necessary to internalize knowledge spillovers from public institutions (e.g., state universities) to obtain competitive advantages, government policies to promote industry by building the research base in organic chemistry were broadly successful (Lenoir, 1998).

2.3.2 High-voltage Electricity: A Market-pioneering Sector of the 19th Century

Whereas scholars largely agree that knowledge spillovers from academia to industry were paramount in enabling the rise of the German organic chemicals industry (Haber, 1958; Beer, 1959; Murmann, 2003), the reasons for the ascendance of the German electrical industry have been less researched to date. Hughes (1983) underlines the greater flexibility of government regulation in Germany (and Berlin in particular) in comparison to the United Kingdom where gas-friendly regulations hampered the development of a national electrical industry. The following explanation, based on secondary research as well as a summer of archival research at the Kiel Institute of World Economics, looks at two admittedly very narrow historical issues: first, at the national level, in which Germany's federalist structure facilitated experimentation in both entrepreneurship and regulation with regard to how to replicate Edison's central generating station in New York City (1882) on German soil; and second, at a local level in Berlin, in which the key producers AEG and Siemens learned intensively from one another (i.e., firm-to-firm knowledge spillovers).

At both levels, the market-pioneering nature of the electrical sector is crucial for understanding why critical knowledge concerned not only supply conditions (as in organic chemicals, where market needs were largely known) but demand conditions as well. What mattered most in this sector was firm-to-firm knowledge spillovers. Unlike in organic chemicals, the role of academic science was secondary; Germany was not exceptional in this branch of science, and indeed there were no academic curricula in electrical engineering until 1884 (König, 1995), trailing rather than leading the development of Germany's electrical industry. The major source of leading knowledge about electricity was arguably the German firm of Siemens and Halske (called simply Siemens since the 1930s), a producer of telegraphs and other electrical devices since 1847 and Europe's largest electrical company for most of the 19th century.

Concerning, first, the national level, it is highly likely that federalism (political decentralization) encouraged critical experimentation in the early phase of the industry. The critical comparison is with Britain, where a centralized regulatory regime for electricity stifled experimentation (Hughes, 1983). The problem was not only the conscious decision of Britain to protect its gas utilities, but the unintended side-effect of a national framework for electrical utilities that was uniform and rigid at a time when the underlying technology was so in flux that latitude in regulation was most needed. In contrast, Germany had no such national legislation; the various states and large cities essentially vied with each other to introduce the new technology after the heralded opening of Edison's Pearl Street Station in 1882. Germany's industrial base for developing electricity was quite decentralized, with large producers emerging in locations as far apart as Berlin, Nürnberg (Schuckert), Cologne (Helios), Frankfurt (Lahmeyer) and Dresden (Kummer), as noted as late as 1904 by Fasolt (1904).

It is against the background of competition between German cities that one can best comprehend the enlightened and flexible stance of the municipal authorities of Berlin, who were willing at key junctures to renegotiate their basic agreement with AEG on building and operating BEW, the city's electrical utility company.[2] Berlin's planners and politicians constituted not only 'an effective, informed, and strong regulatory authority' (Hughes 1983, p. 184), but, shrewd business partners as well, their city coffers received a windfall once the public–private partnership BEW became profitable from 1887 on. At this point, other German municipalities eager for both electricity and supplementary revenue desired to have similar central utility plants, sparking a nationwide boom in electrical products and applications. Federalism thus provided an impetus both to experimentation and to the diffusion of technical and commercial know-how derived from successful experiments.

Yet concentration of Germany's electrical industry did occur, as Fasolt's largest seven electrical companies in 1904 were whittled down to two, Siemens and AEG in Berlin, just ten years later. Beyond just economies of scale and scope, the two firms benefited from local knowledge agglomeration effects. In particular, previous research leaves little doubt about the central significance of a symbiotic learning relationship between these two firms (Kocka, 1972; Feldenkirchen, 1997a). In the one aspect of the pre-1914 German electrical industry that is fairly well-researched and was famous in its day – namely the fierce cooperative/competitive relationship between Siemens and AEG – knowledge spillovers between the two firms play a major role, with Siemens providing the lion's share of new technical knowledge (e.g., supply-side) and AEG pioneering the organizational innovations to exploit the market idiosyncrasies (e.g., demand-side) of this sector.

AEG was founded as DEG, the Deutsche Edison Gesellschaft, to exploit the Edison patents in Germany. AEG originally engaged in a strategic alliance with Siemens, in which the latter specialized in manufacturing while AEG specialized in starting utility companies (central generating plants, electrical tramways). Yet even before Edison's patents were invalidated by the courts, AEG adopted many technical innovations from Siemens that were improvements over the Edison technologies (Hughes, 1983). Siemens, for its part, watched and later emulated a number of the organizational innovations implemented by AEG.

Three organizational innovations by AEG were noteworthy in this market-pioneering sector. The first involved establishing local companies to coordinate the formation of supply and demand for electrical utility services. AEG founded utility companies in partnership with other investors, banks and government officials. Following American practice, AEG's business model involved holding a partial equity stake until the utility venture became profitable, then selling the stake and investing the proceeds in further ventures elsewhere (Passer, 1953, Ch. 5). In Germany, as in the United States, 'the original technical innovations were followed by innovations in marketing, finance, and business administration' (Passer, 1953, p. 69). That these were truly innovations at the time is documented by the caustic remarks they provoked from the conservative manufacturer Werner Siemens, whose firm produced on the traditional made-to-order basis (Kocka, 1972). However, Siemens did vertically integrate forwards into utilities, just as AEG integrated backwards into manufacturing, ultimately leading to dissolution of the alliance.

The second organizational innovation was in setting up marketing organizations (called 'study organizations' at the time, that is, pilot projects) to stimulate demand (Kocka, 1972). AEG's study organizations systematically promoted electric lighting through exhibitions, press releases and model installations; such techniques likewise drew derogatory remarks from Werner Siemens, accustomed more to government procurement, but whose company ultimately emulated AEG's practices. In fact, both AEG and Siemens participated in large-scale public demonstrations as a key means for stimulating demand.[3] Venues like the 1900 World Exhibition in Paris (David, 1991) provided German exporters with a reputational advantage. Yet the largest showcase for Germany's electric industry came to be the city of Berlin itself: Berlin became by 1900 an international showcase of electrical applications, a model followed by other German cities and admired by foreign visitors (Hughes, 1983). Developments in Berlin (e.g., adopting 220 volts instead of Edison's 110) were readily copied in other German and European cities.

Third, AEG engaged in the familiar organizational innovation of relying on professional managers rather than family members to coordinate large-scale operations (Kocka, 1972; Chandler, 1990), enabling AEG to surpass Siemens in the ability to grow by borrowing from banks in return for outside monitoring. Siemens' recovery in the 1890s depended on emulation of AEG and becoming a joint-stock company with lesser family control. Ultimately, the diversified multidivisional form of organization, which first emerged in the 1920s in the United States, was introduced well before World War I by Siemens of Germany (Kocka, 1978; Chandler, 1990, p. 471).

In sum, the build-up of Berlin into the Silicon Valley of its day was due not only to economies of scale and scope, but to firm-to-firm knowledge spillovers and learning processes. Whereas most large German producers outside of Berlin went bankrupt or were acquired during cyclical downturns, Berlin-based AEG and Siemens consistently resisted the temptation to decentralize manufacturing operations, building ever-larger facilities in the German capital (Hall and Preston, 1988). The culmination of this process was the construction of Siemens' enormous company complex Siemensstadt ('Siemens City'), with well over 20 000 employees before World War I.[4] Beyond just supply-side economies, on the demand side, Germany's 'Elektropolis' (von Weiher, 1974) benefited from proximity to key government users: the Prussian ministries, the imperial government (especially the military) and the municipality of Berlin.

Berlin was the Silicon Valley of its day in terms of knowledge inputs, concentration of key supply and demand factors, showcase role, as well as sheer scale. On the eve of World War I, the Berlin-based electricity industry accounted for nearly half of the world's total electrical exports. Other German locations, while important in stimulating experimentation in earlier stages of the industry, declined in importance as the sector matured and the production of key knowledge became centralized in Berlin.

2.4 THE LATE 20TH CENTURY: COMPUTERS AND PHARMACEUTICAL BIOTECHNOLOGY

The previous sections noted fundamental differences between a science-driven high-tech sector (organic chemicals) in which organizational innovations aimed primarily at capturing supply-side knowledge spillovers and a market-pioneering sector (electricity) in which organizational innovations captured knowledge spillovers on both the supply and demand side. In both cases, geographical decentralization was useful for promoting experimentation in the early phase of the industry but gave way to increasing geographical concentration. In the late 20th-century technology sectors surveyed below, one can detect some broad parallels, though the life cycle pattern is less clear-cut: the science-driven sector of pharmaceutical biotechnology is still in relative infancy and the market-pioneering sector of computing, though of older age, has traversed different stages that only in a loose sense can be seen as a maturation process.

One way of investigating these sectors is to examine the role of public R&D policies. For the most part, German efforts to promote high-technology industry through joint industry–academia programmes to foster academic-to-firm knowledge spillovers have been ineffective (Stucke, 1993; Lehrer, 2000a). That the elusiveness of these spillovers has to do with organizational factors is indicated by the one high-tech area of successful R&D reform, namely innovative policies for biotechnology in the 1990s. Here R&D reforms succeeded precisely because they redrew the organizational boundaries of biotechnology research and commercialization.

2.4.1 Pharmaceutical Biotechnology: A Science-driven Sector of the 20th Century

Despite extensive public funding for basic science as well as for cooperative academia–industry projects, German biotechnology was commercially disappointing, generating far fewer patents, commercial products and, especially, start-up companies than the United States and the United Kingdom (Jasanoff, 1985; Adelberger, 1999). The commercial performance of German biotechnology recovered in the late 1990s, thanks largely to programmes creating incentives and structures for scientists in the public research sector to begin their own companies on the side (Casper, 2000).

These supply-side policies to improve knowledge spillovers from academia to firms essentially redrew the boundaries between the public and private sector (Lehrer and Asakawa, 2004b). Knowledge spillovers from public-sector laboratories to private start-up companies were governed by complex transactions, with the state in essence signing two parallel sets of simultaneous contracts with public-sector scientists, one in which the latter performed public science and the other in which they commercialized this science for private profit, yet with each activity building on the same common knowledge base. Organizational innovation was important, but the source was not firms, but rather federal policy-makers seeking to emulate the organizational ecosystem of biotechnology in the United States and United Kingdom (Casper, 2000).

In this relatively young sector, Germany's relatively decentralized science base and biotechnology sector was not a hindrance. Once policy-makers decided to encourage biotech start-ups by scientists, the policy instrument they chose was precisely that of an interregional competition (Dohse, 2000). The policy spark behind Germany's biotech start-up boom, the BioRegio competition of 1995, awarded prize money to the best regional biotechnology programmes for incubating start-up ventures, ultimately spawning 17 regional biotechnology centres to assist scientists with business plans, financing, marketing and patenting. The BioRegio competition was novel in encouraging policy variation and experimentation to promote knowledge spillovers (Dohse, 2003).

2.4.2 Computing: A Market-pioneering Sector of the 20th Century

Whereas biotechnology is without doubt an industry still in relative infancy (and hence presumably relatively favourable to a fairly high level of geographical decentralization), the computing sector has, in a certain sense, matured since its birth in the 1950s. Yet it has matured differently from the electrical industry of the 19th century, for instead of evolving in the direction of vertical *integration* it has evolved towards increasing vertical *disintegration* (Langlois, 2003). Within this overall pattern, German computer companies fared differentially. German performance was essentially fair to good in earlier segments of computing (mainframes, minicomputers) featuring vertically integrated companies, but disappointing in more recent open-platform segments (microcomputers and network-based computing) featuring complementary components producers.

Unlike in biotechnology, where government initiative was ultimately helpful, state programmes to support the German IT sector have never had much impact (Grande, 2001). This arguably has to do with the market-pioneering nature of the computing sector, in particular the important role played by demand factors (largely beyond state control in countries like Germany with low levels of military expenditure) and not only supply factors.

Since the 1950s, the computing sector has depended on 'killer applications', that is, commercial breakthroughs arising from the identification of specific user needs that computers could satisfy. Although *mainframes* were originally seen as scientific tools with limited market potential, the discovery of their utility in automating organizational bookkeeping sparked the emergence of a large corporate market. The use of *minicomputers* was very different, mainly for specialized scientific and engineering applications. In *microcomputers*, too, killer applications were important for market take-off. Mass demand for PCs depended on the availability of complementary software products, especially spreadsheets (VisiCalc for the Apple, Lotus 1-2-3 for the IBM PC). In *network-based computing*, take-off likewise depended on the discovery of key applications like e-mail and browsers.

The organizational requirements of these segments were heterogeneous (Bresnahan and Malerba, 1999). In the mainframe segment, vertically integrated firms like IBM were appropriate to the task. In this segment, Germany's industrial performance was typical for Europe. Germany's leading producer Siemens essentially shared the domestic market with IBM from the 1960s to the 1980s, enjoyed periodic government subsidies, and had difficulty penetrating other major European markets dominated by their own national champions. Other German entrants into mainframe computers made little headway.

In mid-range systems and minicomputers catering to scientific and engineering uses, German performance was above-average, propelled by the success of Nixdorf. 'Nixdorf, the minicomputer producer, was the only new entrepreneurial firm in Europe to become a major player [in computing]' (Chandler, 1990, p. 611). Yet Nixdorf itself emerged from a geographically decentralized environment of entrepreneurial computer companies: Dietz, Kienzle, Triumph Adler, Konstanz and Krantz (Bresnahan and Malerba,

1999). Indeed, in the 1960s and 1970s, Germany possessed a fairly robust computer industry, aided by the nature of domestic demand, especially the approximately 2000 *Mittelstand* firms, that is technically oriented and likewise geographically dispersed mid-sized enterprises.

However, in the early 1990s, the switch to personal computers, client-server networks, and open platforms led to almost wholesale collapse of Germany's computer industry, with Siemens and Nixdorf ultimately merging and then exiting all but the service business (Lehrer, 2000b). After holding its own in segments where independent large or medium-sized firms produced stand-alone systems, Germany's computing sector failed in the components-based open-platform environment of the 1980s and 1990s. Such an environment, as provided by Silicon Valley, requires knowledge spillovers among complementary components producers with regard to rapidly changing demand and supply conditions (Saxenian, 1994). Among major German IT companies only SAP proved able to keep pace with technological change.

From the account given in Saxenian (1994) the kinds of knowledge spillovers that are important in Silicon Valley are indeed reminiscent of the metaphors of the tacitness and stickiness of knowledge often associated with the spillover concept. In a very broad sense, one can surmise that Germany's failure in computing was coextensive with an organizational inability to develop a competitive cluster of complementary IT firms capable of mastering the requisite knowledge spillovers in open network computing, although the exact chain of cause and effect is not easy to establish. For present purposes the key point to note is that local firm-to-firm knowledge spillovers à la Saxenian differ from those remarked in the three technology sectors discussed previously.

It may seem like a tautology to say that German computing failed for lack of a geographically centralized IT industry location like Silicon Valley. But in Germany's case the statement is less tautological because Germany once did possess a global centre of innovation in electronics: Berlin. The negative long-term effect of World War II on German high-tech, it seems, was that it deprived Germany of the requisite centralized 'learning base' that Chandler (2001) deems necessary in electronics and computing. Comparison with Tokyo is illuminating. While Tokyo was as levelled by war as Berlin it remained an undivided capital and after the war Japan's electrical companies, mainly Tokyo-based, managed the transition into electronics, semiconductors and computing more effectively than German companies did, with the learning region of Tokyo/Osaka as a vital catalyst (Chandler, 2001, pp. 235–7). The need for a centralized learning base is echoed by the greater geographical concentration that generally characterizes computing in contrast to biotechnology (Audretsch and Feldman, 1996; Swann and Prevezer, 1996).

2.5 CONCLUSION

The foregoing retrospective provided a highly selective rather than comprehensive look at the knowledge spillover process in four major German technology sectors. Yet even such a cursory survey can help address an important open question on knowledge spillovers noted by Audretsch and Feldman (2004), namely the 'relatively uncharted area . . . involving the life cycle of spatial units, such as agglomerations, clusters and regions'. The foregoing analysis, though selective and retrospective, is suggestive of a certain trade-off between, on the one hand, geographical *decentralization* facilitating experimentation with ways of generating and capturing knowledge spillovers (in earlier stages of an industry), and, on the other hand, geographical *centralization* facilitating the appropriation of local knowledge externalities (in later stages of an industry) when the industry-specific means of producing and commercializing technological knowledge have been honed. Consistent with arguments from evolutionary economics (Dosi, 2000; Murmann, 2003), the development of systems for capturing knowledge spillovers may require a phase of decentralized experimentation (variation), but once they do emerge, processes of selection and retention tend to facilitate geographic centralization.

Despite obvious methodological limitations, the intersectoral comparisons are also suggestive of why experimentation with ways of managing knowledge spillovers is an important process in the development of technology-based industry. In three of the four sectors covered (organic chemicals, electricity, biotechnology), key knowledge spillover processes took place within the context of complex contractual arrangements that varied substantially from one industrial setting to another: long-term relations between professors and firms (organic chemicals), turbulent strategic alliances (i.e., AEG and Siemens in the Berlin electricity cluster), and regional technology start-up incubators (biotechnology). These arrangements and their disparity lend credence to the thesis of firms experiencing a priori difficulty in knowing how to organize activities to capture knowledge spillovers and the consequent need for organizational innovation. The disappointing results of most post-war German high-technology policies predicated on more or less automatic knowledge externalities likewise calls into question the notion of local knowledge spillovers as a kind of knowledge leakage across organizational boundaries, suggesting instead the notion of knowledge flowing in tandem with complex transactions and organizational arrangements.

Consistent with the entrepreneurship theory of knowledge spillovers (Audretsch and Lehmann, 2005) as well as any number of neo-Schumpeterian perspectives, the foregoing analysis suggests broadly that commercialization outputs depend not only on the knowledge inputs but on the specific details of organization by which inputs are transformed into outputs (see Cooke, this volume). Though hardly controversial in itself, this finding amounts to a vote against the fairly widespread view that attributes the local boundedness of knowledge spillovers to characteristics of knowledge like tacitness and stickiness. The primary cognitive obstacles to capture of knowledge spillovers do not appear to have concerned primarily technological knowledge per se, but also and more broadly, the appropriate organizational and institutional arrangements needed to commercialize such technological knowledge. This is consistent with treatments underlining the general complexity of market and knowledge-sharing processes (Cowan, David and Foray, 2000; Breschi and Lissoni, 2001) as opposed to the much narrower problem of tacitness and stickiness per se.

NOTES

1. Emblematically, the return of A.W. Hoffmann, a major figure in the 19th-century dyestuff industry, from the United Kingdom to Germany in the 1860s, sealed Britain's decline and Germany's ascent in the organic chemical industry (Beer, 1959).
2. This hypothesis (which for the present must be stated simply as a hypothesis) is based on a perusal of historical documents at the Kiel Institute of World Economics during the summer of 2004. The documents revealed fairly clearly that electrical utilities were assumed to be imminent throughout Germany and that Berlin was essentially in a race with other German cities to demonstrate its commitment to technical progress and prowess. In future work I intend to document this more systematically. I should like to extend my thanks to the Department of Regional Economics at the Kiel Institute for hosting me, and to the University of Rhode Island for financing my archival research in 2004.
3. Both Germany and the United States stood out in this respect: state-of-the-art street lighting in Berlin and long-distance power transmissions from hydroelectric generators on rivers to artificial waterfalls in Munich (1882, over 57 km) and Frankfurt (1891, over 175 km) unveiled milestones of electrical achievements to the general public in the manner of Edison's Pearl Street Station (1882) and Westinghouse's exhibition of AC technology at the 1893 World's Fair (Hughes, 1983).
4. 'By 1913 Berlin's Siemensstadt had become the world's most intricate and extensive industrial complex under a single management. There was nothing approaching it in either the United States or Britain' (Chandler, 1990, p. 469).

REFERENCES

Achilladelis, Basil and N. Antonakis (2001), 'The dynamics of technological innovation: the case of the pharmaceutical industry', *Research Policy*, 30, 535–88.

Acs, Zoltan J. and David B. Audretsch (1990), *Innovation and Small Firms*, Cambridge: MIT Press.

Adelberger, Karen (1999), 'A Developmental German State? Explaining Growth in German Biotechnology and Venture Capital', Working Paper No. 134, BRIE.

Almeida, Paul and B. Kogut (1997), 'The exploration of technological diversity and the geographic localization of innovation', *Small Business Economics*, **9**(1), 21–31.
Andreasen, Lars Erik et al. (eds) (1995), *Europe's Next Step: Organizational Innovation, Competition and Employment*, Ilford: Frank Cass.
Arrow, Kenneth J. (1962), 'Economic welfare and the allocation of resources for invention', in Richard R. Nelson (ed.), *The Rate and Direction of Inventive Activity*, Princeton: Princeton University Press, pp. 609–25.
Audretsch, David B. and M.P. Feldman (1996), 'R&D spillovers and the geography of innovation and production', *American Economic Review*, 86, 630–40.
Audretsch, David B. and Maryann P. Feldman (2004), 'Knowledge spillovers and the geography of innovation', in J. Vernon Henderson and Jacques-François Thisse (eds), *Handbook of Regional and Urban Economics*, Amsterdam: Elsevier, pp. 2713–39.
Audretsch, David B. and Erik E. Lehmann (2005), 'Does the knowledge spillover theory of entrepreneurship hold for regions?', *Research Policy*, 1191–202.
Beer, John Joseph (1959), 'The Emergence of the German Dye Industry', PhD dissertation, University of Illinois.
Ben-David, Joseph (1977), *Centers of Learning: Britain, France, Germany, and the United States*, New York: McGraw-Hill.
Breschi, Stefano and Francesco Lissoni (2001), 'Knowledge spillovers and local innovation systems: A critical survey', *Industrial and Corporate Change*, **10**(4), 975–1005.
Bresnahan, Timothy F. (1989), 'Measuring the spillovers from technical advance: mainframe computers in financial services', *American Economic Review*, **76**(4), 742–55.
Bresnahan, Timothy F. and Franco Malerba (1999), 'Industrial dynamics and the evolution of firms' and nations' competitive capabilities in the world computer industry', in David C. Mowery and Richard R. Nelson (eds), *Sources of Industrial Leadership: Studies of Seven Countries*, Cambridge: Cambridge University Press, pp. 79–132.
Caniels, Marjolein C.J. and H.A. Romijn (2005), 'What drives innovativeness in industrial clusters? Transcending the debate', *Cambridge Journal of Economics*, **29**(4), 497–515.
Cardwell, Donald (1995), *Wheels, Clocks, and Rockets: A History of Technology*, New York: W.W. Norton.
Casper, Steven (2000), 'Institutional adaptiveness, technology policy, and the diffusion of new business models: the case of German biotechnology', *Organization Studies*, **21**(5), 887–914.
Chandler, Alfred D. (1990), *Scale and Scope: The Dynamics of Industrial Capitalism*, Cambridge, MA: Belknap Press.
Chandler, Alfred D. (2001), *Inventing the Electronic Century: The Epic Story of the Consumer Electronics and Computer Industries*, New York: Free Press.
Clapham, J.P. (1961), *The Economic Development of France and Germany 1815–1914*, Cambridge: Cambridge University Press.
Coriat, Benjamin and O. Weinstein (2002), 'Organizations, firms and institutions in the generation of innovation', *Industrial and Corporate Change*, 31, 273–90.
Cowan, Robin, A. Paul David and D. Foray (2000), 'The explicit economics of knowledge codification and tacitness', *Industrial and Corporate Change*, **9**(2), 211–53.

David, Paul (1991), 'Computer and dynamo: the modern productivity paradox in a not-too-distant mirror', in OECD (ed.), *Technology and Productivity: The Challenge for Economic Policy*, Paris: pp. 315–37.
David, Paul A. (2004), 'Understanding the emergence of "open science" institutions: functionalist economics in historical context', *Industrial and Corporate Change*, **13**(4), 571–89.
Dohse, Dirk (2000), 'Technology policy and the regions: the case of the BioRegio contest', *Research Policy*, 29, 1111–33.
Dohse, Dirk (2003), 'Taking regions seriously: recent innovations in German technology policy', in Johannes Bröcker, Dirk Dohse and Rüdiger Soltwedel (eds), *Innovation Clusters and Interregional Competition*, Berlin: Springer, pp. 372–94.
Dosi, Giovanni (2000), *Innovation, Organization, and Economic Dynamics*, Cheltenham, UK and Northampton, MA, US: Edward Elgar.
Fasolt, Friedrich (1904), *Die sieben grössten deutschen Elektrizitätsgesellschaften, ihre Entwicklung und Unternehmertätigkeit: Eine volkswirtschaftliche Studie*, Dresden: Böhmert.
Feldenkirchen, Wilfried (1997a), *Siemens: Von der Werkstatt zum Weltunternehmen*, Munich: Piper.
Freeman, Chris and Francisco Louca (2001), *As Time Goes By: From the Industrial Revolution to the Information Revolution*, Oxford: Oxford University Press.
Grande, Edgar (2001), 'The erosion of state capacity and the European innovation policy dilemma: a comparison of German and EU information technology policies', *Research Policy*, 30, 905–21.
Grupp, Hariolf (2000), 'Learning in a science-driven market: the case of lasers', *Industrial and Corporate Change*, **9**(1), 143–72.
Haber, L.F. (1958), *The Chemical Industry During the Nineteenth Century*, Oxford: Clarendon Press.
Hall, Peter and Paschal Preston (1988), *The Carrier Wave: New Information Technology and the Geography of Innovation, 1846–2003*, London: Unwin Hyman.
Homburg, Ernst (1992), 'The emergence of research laboratories in the dyestuffs industry, 1870–1900', *British Journal for the History of Science*, 25, 91–111.
Hughes, Thomas P. (1983), *Networks of Power: Electrification in Western Society*, Baltimore: Johns Hopkins University Press.
Jaffe, Adam B. (1986), 'Technological opportunities and spillovers of R&D', *American Economic Review*, **76**(5), 984–1001.
Jaffe, Adam B., Manuel Trajtenberg and Rebecca Henderson (1993), 'Geographic localization of knowledge spillovers as evidenced by patent citations', *Quarterly Journal of Economics*, 63, 577–98.
Jasanoff, Sheila (1985), 'Technological innovation in a corporatist state: the case of biotechnology in the Federal Republic of Germany', *Research Policy*, 14, 23–38.
Kesidou, Effie (2004), 'Knowledge Spillovers in High-tech Clusters in Developing Countries', PhD dissertation, Globelics Academy, Lisbon.
Kocka, Jürgen (1972), 'Siemens und der aufhaltsame Aufstieg der AEG', *Tradition*, 17, 125–42.
Kocka, Jürgen (1978), 'Entrepreneurs and managers in the German industrial revolution', in P. Mathias and M.M. Postan (eds), *The Cambridge Economic History of Europe*, Cambridge: Cambridge University Press, pp. 769–77.
König, Wolfgang (1995), *Technikwissenschaften: Die Entstehung der Elektrotechnik aus Industrie und Wissenschaft zwischen 1880 und 1914*, Chur: G+B Verlag Fakultas.

Landes, David S. (1969), *The Unbound Prometheus*, Cambridge: Cambridge University Press.
Langlois, Richard N. (2003), 'The vanishing hand: the changing dynamics of industrial capitalism', *Industrial and Corporate Change*, **12**(2), 351–85.
Lehrer, Mark (2000a), 'Has Germany finally fixed its high-tech problem? The recent boom in German technology-based entrepreneurship', *California Management Review*, **42**(4), 89–107.
Lehrer, Mark (2000b), 'From factor of production to autonomous industry: the transformation of Germany's software sector', *Vierteljahrshefte zur Wirtschaftsforschung* (DIW Quarterly Journal of Economic Research), **69**(4), 587–600.
Lehrer, Mark (2005), 'Science-driven vs. market-pioneering high tech: comparative German technology sectors in the late 19th and late 20th century', *Industrial and Corporate Change*, 14, 251–78.
Lehrer, Mark (2007), 'Organizing knowledge spillovers when basic and applied research are independent: German biotechnology policy in historical perspective', *Journal of Technology Transfer*, **32**, (forthcoming).
Lehrer, Mark and Kazuhiro Asakawa (2004b), 'Rethinking the public sector: recent German and Japanese biotechnology policies as motors of institutional reform', *Research Policy*, **33**(6/7), 921–38.
Lenoir, Timothy (1998), 'Revolution from above: the role of the state in creating the German research system, 1810–1910', *American Economic Review*, **88**(2), 22–7.
March, James G. (1991), 'Exploration and exploitation in organizational learning', *Organization Science*, **2**(1), 71–87.
Marshall, Alfred (1920), *Principles of Economics*, London: Macmillan.
Murmann, Johann Peter (2003), *Knowledge and Competitive Advantage: The Coevolution of Firms, Technology, and National Institutions*, Cambridge: Cambridge University Press.
Murmann, Johann Peter and Ralph Landau (1998), 'On the making of competitive advantage: the development of the chemical industries of Britain and Germany since 1850', in Ashish Arora, Ralph Landau and Nathan Rosenberg (eds), *Chemicals and Long-term Economic Growth*, New York: John Wiley, pp. 27–70.
Passer, Harold C. (1953), *The Electrical Manufacturers 1875–1900*, Cambridge, MA: Harvard University Press.
Polanyi, Michael (1966), *The Tacit Dimension*, Garden City, NY: Doubleday Books.
Reinhardt, Carsten (1998), 'An instrument of corporate strategy: the central research laboratory at BASF 1868–1890', in Ernst Homburg, Anthony S. Travis and Harm G. Schröter (eds), *The Chemical Industry in Europe, 1850–1914*, Dordrecht: Kluwer, pp. 239–60.
Romer, Paul M. (1986), 'Increasing returns and long-run growth', *Journal of Political Economy*, **94**(5), 1002–37.
Rosenberg, Nathan and L.E. Birdzell (1986), *How the West Grew Rich: The Economic Transformation of the Industrial World*, New York: Basic Books.
Saxenian, AnnaLee (1994), *Regional Advantage: Culture and Competition in Silicon Valley and Route 128*, Cambridge, MA: Harvard University Press.
Seitz, Konrad (1990), *Die japanisch-amerikanische Herausforderung: Deutschlands Hochtechnologie-Industrien kämpfen ums Überleben*, Munich: Verlag Bonn Aktuell.
Stucke, Andreas (1993), *Institutionalisierung der Forschungspolitik: Entstehung, Entwicklung und Steuerungsprobleme des Bundesforschungsministerium*, Frankfurt: Campus Verlag.

Swann, Peter and Martha Prevezer (1996), 'A comparison of the dynamics of industrial clustering in computing and biotechnology', *Research Policy*, 25, 1139–57.

Vereeck, Lode (2001), *Das deutsche Wissenschaftswunder: eine ökonomische Analyse des Systems Althoff (1882–1907)*, Berlin: Duncker & Humblot.

von Hippel, Eric (1994), ' "Sticky information" and the locus of problem solving: implications for innovation', *Management Science*, **40**(4), 429–39.

von Weiher, Sigfrid (1974), *Berlins Weg zur Elektropolis: Technik- und Industriegeschichte an der Spree*, Berlin: Stapp.

3. The ambivalent role of mimetic behavior in proximity dynamics: evidence from the French 'Silicon Sentier'

Jérôme Vicente, Yan Dalla Pria and Raphaël Suire

3.1 INTRODUCTION: PROXIMITIES AND CLUSTERS

The notion of proximity has been the subject of a growing literature in economic geography and regional science over the past ten years, particularly in Europe around the works of Kirat and Lung (1999), Torre and Gilly (2000) and, more recently, Pecqueur and Zimmermann (2004) and Boschma (2005). Concurrently, the increase of interest in the 'cluster' phenomenon as a new paradigm of local development in the knowledge society (Porter, 1998a, 1998b; Zimmermann, 2002), in spite of critics (Martin and Sunley, 2003), has invited scholars to understand the complex links between geographical proximity and innovation (Zimmermann, 2001; Boschma, 2005). Following Porter (1998b, p. 199), 'a cluster is a geographically proximate group of companies and associated institutions in a particular field, linked by commonalities and complementarities'. This chapter deals with this topic.

There are several ways to analyze the complex links between proximities and clusters, from empirical monographs investigating the relational aspects of proximity to econometric analysis applied to the study of knowledge spillovers. In this chapter, we only focus on one of them, maybe one of the most original, which is the role of sequential interactions and mimetic behaviors in co-location processes. The purpose is to understand how firms converge more or less rapidly in their decision to locate close to each other (geographical proximity), and how this convergence process gives rise to other forms of proximity, defined as socio-economic forms at this stage. First, we will show that geographical proximity is not a sufficient condition for the collective performance of clusters. Some 'ICT clusters' (Quah, 2000) around the world experienced difficulties in overcoming the recent bubble and crash of net-economy values – such as Silicon Sentier in Paris developed upon below – while others pursued their growth and reconverted to other technologies, such as Silicon Valley in the United States and Sophia-Antipolis in France. Other proximities (socio-economic) characterize clusters and their nature is strongly correlated to the stability[1] of cluster.

Second, we will focus on the convergence of locational choices through the process of mimetic (or herd) behaviors. The purpose is to show that according to the mimetic process of co-location, the nature of socio-economic proximities can be very different and have a strong influence on the stability and the performance of clusters. Following these different points, *a cluster is a geographically proximate group of companies and associated institutions in a particular field, linked by socio-economic proximities.*

In Section 3.2, we refer to the above-mentioned literature to explore the definitions of proximity, not in order to refute all of them, but to elaborate on our own typology, which we will refer to in the rest of this chapter.[2] In Section 3.3, we introduce the notion of mimetic behavior of location – associated with the notion of locational norm (Vicente and Suire, 2006) – in order to show that co-location processes can be the result of sequentiality, uncertainty, legitimacy and non-market interactions, rather than full rational and isolated decisions and pure strategic market interactions. In Section 3.4, we try to demonstrate that the basic nature of socio-economic proximity linking firms within clusters can differ according to the kind of mimetic behavior – or the dominant one – in the co-location process. Section 3.5 gives an empirical illustration with the emblematic French case of 'Silicon Sentier', a cluster that gathered together 300 firms of the net-economy (the famous 'dotcom') during the NASDAQ bubble swelling.[3] The rapid success (1998–2000) and the sudden decline (2001–02) of this famous cluster invite us to reflect on the links between collective efficiency of clusters on one hand and the nature of socio-economic proximity on the other. This is the aim of Section 3.6. Section 3.7 provides some concluding remarks and discusses a research agenda on clusters and regional performance.

3.2 PROXIMITIES: SOME PRELIMINARY REMARKS ON DEFINITIONS

The concept of proximity was developed at the beginning of the 1990s by a French research group of economists and sociologists. Their first motivation was to explain industrial agglomeration, such as industrial districts,

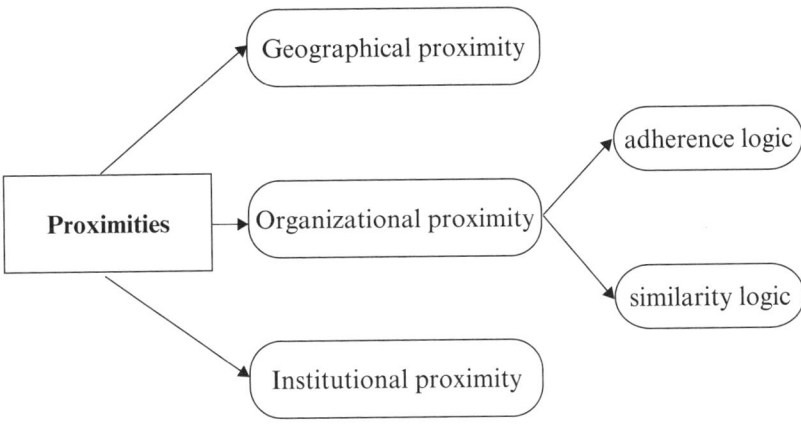

Source: Torre and Gilly (2000).

Figure 3.1   A first typology of proximities

scientific parks or 'innovative milieux' with the aim of going beyond the role of market interactions as the exclusive origins of agglomeration and territorial dynamics. On the contrary, they emphasized the role of non-market interactions through the links between firms or between firms and institutions, such as joint ventures, trust-based cooperation, formal agreements, interpersonal networks, and so on. The second motivation was to propose a tractable analysis grid for the study of economic coordination not only through the local dimension but also through non-territorial coordination means such as transnational networks. The third motivation was to introduce an institutional dimension through the role of informal institutions such as trust, or formal ones such as competition rules or intellectual property rules. Finally, the general motivation, closely linked to all of these specific ones, was to enter into the black box of externalities through the concept of proximities and to develop a detailed analysis of coordination mechanisms at work in the geography of innovation.

Several typologies have been proposed in the literature. The synthesis proposed by Torre and Gilly (2000) is the most convincing and representative. Figure 3.1 summarizes their work. They divide the general concept of proximity into three more specific types.

First, *geographical proximity* can be used to discuss what geographically separates agents (individuals or organizations). The concept of geographical distance is certainly the most appropriate and tractable in order to capture and measure the level of this proximity. But it would sometimes be more relevant to introduce other aspects developed by geographers, such as access times, in order to take into account the social distortion of geographical space due, for instance, to the production of infrastructures.

Second, *organizational proximity* is defined in order to capture the separation or degree of closeness between individuals and/or organizations in a strictly economic sense. According to Torre and Gilly (2000), we can distinguish two logics that govern organizational proximity. On the one side, in *adherence logic*, organizational proximity can be defined as the degree and the intensity of direct interactions between agents. On the other side, in *similarity logic*, organizational proximity can be defined according to criteria that gather agents into classes (capabilities and knowledge for individuals or size and sector for firms). These two logics can be interlinked (although not necessarily) and organizational proximity is not a priori correlated to geographical proximity. Imagine the relations in the economists' community: two researchers can be installed in the same laboratory or university and develop no interactions, whereas two researchers can be located in two separated universities in Europe and have strong interactions through co-publication activities (using travel and e-mail).

Third, *institutional proximity* is generally defined in order to capture what Amin and Thrift (1993) earlier described as the 'institutional thickness'. According to Torre and Gilly (2000) and Kirat and Lung (1999), institutional proximity refers to the fact that agents share the same space of representation, face the same incentives and constraints of their peculiar legal and economic environment in terms of competition rules, managerial culture and so on. Clearly, institutional proximity is introduced in the typology with the aim of adding a collective dimension to the game of interactions, because of the difficulty of individualistic approaches to take into account cultural, political and historical dimensions of economic coordination. Remember our previous story of the economists. Two economists would have less difficulty in co-publishing a paper if they shared the same objective of participating in the 'charisma' (Appold, 2005) and renown of their university and their region. It would be even easier if they faced the same professional constraints in terms of support or valorization for their work. It would be more difficult for two distant economists because they could enter into conflict if they didn't share the same academic and professional incentives for publication (a book in a prestigious collection for one, and well-diffused national reviews for another).

This typology has been already used to develop analysis of regional development, in terms of performance of clusters and innovative regions, and has given robust proof of its relevance to organizational and geographical aspects in the analysis of knowledge creation and diffusion. The value-added of these studies compared with anterior approaches lies in that clusters performance can be deduced from the peculiar combination of all

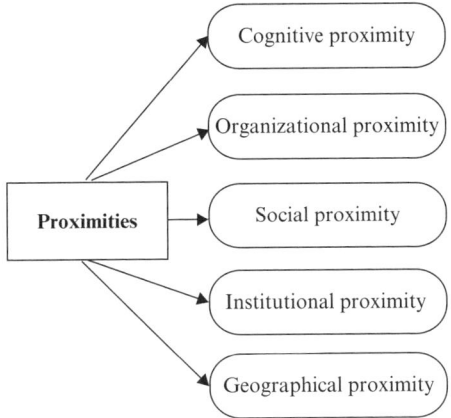

Source: Boschma (2005).

Figure 3.2 A second typology of proximities

of these proximities, and not directly from some presupposed virtues of spatial agglomeration of activities. Nevertheless, some criticisms have been based both on the lack of clarity of the categorization, especially the confusion about the distinction between organizational proximity in its similarity logic and institutional proximity (Boschma, 2005), and on the difficulties of determining some tools to measure and test this typology in empirical micro-analysis (Bouba Olga and Grossetti, 2005).

For Boschma (2005), the concept of proximity has to be reduced into even more categories (five) than the previous typology (see Figure 3.2). In particular, there is a strong necessity to isolate the cognitive dimension from the organizational one, and to dissociate the social dimension (through the embeddedness of individuals in the sense meant by Granovetter, 1985) from the institutional dimension. In this way, the degree of *cognitive proximity* is defined as the 'distance' that separates individuals or organizations in terms of knowledge bases. The introduction of the concept of cognitive proximity in industrial dynamics leads to going beyond the functional and ad hoc distinction between tacit and codified knowledge by focusing on cognitive capabilities of individuals or organizations rather than on the intrinsic nature of knowledge. We can measure a cognitive proximity between agents without referring to notions like organization or economic relations. Hence, *organizational proximity* only refers to the nature of agreements between agents. We could measure a degree of organizational proximity through the relational dimension of a governance matrix or a network organization that ties agents together, and we can deduce that agents are organizationally close to each other from their respective position in this matrix or network.

Organizational proximity also has to be distinguished from *social proximity*. The latter refers to interpersonal links between individuals and can be evaluated according to the degree of friendship (or kinship) and trust between individuals. According to Boschma (2005), social proximity is explicitly linked to the well-known notion of embeddedness (Granovetter, 1985). In that way, social proximity strongly refers to past interactions, for instance through old and durable school or sporting relationships. These relations engender trust and loyalty and can be a source of stability in economic relations. Opportunistic behaviors are not totally excluded, but are statistically reduced by social proximity.

The fourth dimension is related to institutional proximity. It strongly refers to the institutional proximity propounded by Kirat and Lung (1999) and Torre and Gilly (2000), but sets aside the embeddedness dimension of social networks and trust. Two key criteria may allow us to distinguish social from institutional proximity. The first lies in that institutional proximity can be geographically identified in spaces, such as language, cultural habits or legal context of competition, whereas social networks are not easy to identify in a geographical sense (our friends are not necessarily our neighbors and our young economists coming from the same university are nowadays professors in greatly separated universities). Second, social proximity refers to an explicit micro-level of analysis – the identification of relations between individuals – whereas institutional proximity refers to an explicit macro-level of analysis, through the constrained weight of formal and informal rules on individual behaviors.

Finally, *geographical proximity* is defined in a very restrictive sense, which is a direct consequence of the 'lushness' of the other forms of proximity. It only refers to the spatial distance between individuals and/or organizations, and has an importance in the analysis of the performance of clusters only if it is interlinked with the other forms of proximity.

The main merit of this latter typology is to avoid the confusion due to intertwined definitions of proximities in the approach of Torre and Gilly (2000). In Boschma's five-proximities approach, the different levels of analysis are clearly distinguished. Particularly, the cognitive level is well dissociated from the organizational one, and the micro-level (through the definition of social proximity) is clearly dissociated from the macro-level analysis (through the definition of institutional proximity). In real situations, all of them are interlinked to different degrees, but a clear theoretical distinction leads to a better understanding of the weight of each of them in empirical analysis. For instance, too strong a cognitive proximity in technological capabilities linked to geographical proximity can lead to

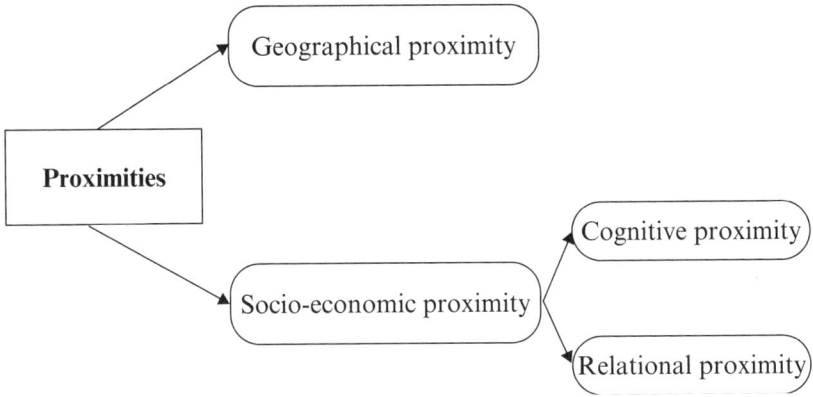

Source: Bouba Olga and Grossetti (2005).

Figure 3.3 A third typology of proximities

unplanned or unintended spillovers when firms compete with each other in the very same product market (see the example of Silicon Sentier below). Too strong social or institutional proximities can lead to collective lock-in by preventing individuals or firms from searching distant information.

In order to develop some measurement tools, Bouba Olga and Grossetti (2005) propose to simplify the typology of proximities by focusing only on the micro-level of analysis (Figure 3.3). Maybe their work is less ambitious than the two former works by Boschma (2005) and Torre and Gilly (2000), because it dismisses the macro-level and the associated institutional proximity, but it remains nevertheless relevant because of the constraint self-imposed by the authors on the association of theoretical definitions to empirical methodologies. In their work, proximities are declined at a first level in only two dimensions: *geographical proximity* and *socio-economic proximity*. Their definition of geographical proximity is close to those of Torre and Gilly (2000) and Boschma (2005). It refers to the distance that separates agents (individuals or organizations) and can be measured with the help of distance and cost indicators, or by supposing binary situations, for example, 'Are we close to each other or not?'.

Socio-economic proximity is intentionally defined in a general way, in order to distinguish clearly the geographical dimension from the other dimensions. But such a definition is too large to be empirically studied and measured, even at a strictly micro-economic level, so it has to be decomposed into categories. Bouba Olga and Grossetti (2005) thus decided to construct two types of socio-economic proximities. The first is *cognitive proximity*. In spite of the analogy with Boschma's concept (2005), Bouba Olga and Grossetti's definition seems to be larger. According to them, cognitive proximity refers to the behaviors and knowledge of agents. Agents are cognitively close to each other when they share the same conventions, common values and representations. This cognitive proximity does not refer only to knowledge and technological capabilities, as in Boschma's approach, but also to managerial practices, discourses, economic actions and so on (see the case of Silicon Sentier below). One of the tools that has to be used to identify cognitive proximity is the analysis of discourses and practices of agents through interviews and an ex post sort of 'pinpointing', which consists of isolating some proximities in behaviors, some routinized behaviors such as the so-called 'taking for granted' that the sociologist Goffman (1973) recognized in the construction of collective identities.[4] The second type is *relational proximity*. It refers to the basic notion of interaction and structure. Individuals or organizations such as firms are close to each other in a relational sense when they share the same interaction structure, make transactions or realize exchanges. The fact that agents are cognitively close to each other does not necessarily signify that they are in interaction, or even that they have the opportunity to communicate. For that, we must identify a communication or an interaction structure. Relational proximity can present several dimensions: agents can be contacted directly or indirectly through intermediaries; interactions can be strong and frequent or weak and scarce, purely cooperative and horizontal or hierarchical and vertical. What does matter is that an intensity of interaction and communication can be identified in order to measure a degree of relational proximity. For that, several qualitative and quantitative tools are available to construct relational databases: not only firm networks, such as in the work of Storper and Harrison (1991) or Markusen (1996), financial relations, patents and co-publications (Audretsch and Feldman, 1996), but also social networks such as friendship, scholarship past relationships, kinship and so on, which can play a major role in industrial and innovative dynamics.

Once again, the first aim of this work is to link definitions to measurement tools. In that way, we have at a micro-level, an integrated (theoretical and empirical) approach at our disposal. Second, we think that it is more relevant to dissociate knowledge and behavioral dimensions from communication and interaction dimensions rather than social, organizational and institutional dimensions from each other – for one reason dissociate at least – because such a typology avoids the recurrent and maybe intractable confusion and intercrossing between these three levels of analysis in the literature.

3.3 THE ROLE OF MIMETIC BEHAVIORS IN LOCATIONAL CHOICES

Relying on the previous theoretical observations, our purpose is now to understand how these forms of proximity emerge. Obviously, literature on this topic is extensive, from new economic geography to regional knowledge economics, or from the weight of market interactions in labor, technology and product spaces and the role of monopolistic competition, to the weight of tacit knowledge, collective learning and inter-firm networks in the clustering processes. All of this literature has led to several papers and robust results. Our aim is not to challenge this literature, but to propose an alternative – and maybe complementary – approach of co-location and clustering process based on mimetic processes of location, along the lines of previous work by Appold (2005), Dalla Pria and Vicente (2006) and Vicente and Suire (2006).

Mimetic behaviors at individual level and mimetic processes at collective level have received little attention in economics and sociology for two main reasons. First, in economics, mimetic behaviors have been until recently associated with irrationality (Kirman, 1992). Second, according to Granovetter (1978), the reason why sociology has historically granted such a minor place to mimetic interactions lies in the sociological tradition in which norms are the result of a strong homogeneity of individual preferences. In this tradition, there is a strong correspondence between the micro- and macro-level, that is to say, that a social or behavioral norm has more chance of diffusing through a population if it corresponds to identical individual anticipations or preferences.

Nevertheless, mimetic interactions are not completely absent in economics and sociology. Some studies in these two disciplines have tried to pass over these respective traditions in order, first, to identify the causes and the individual motivations of imitation, and second, to study the consequences at the aggregate level (see Table 3.1). In order to clarify our position regarding imitation, the rest of this section aims to present these works. The relations between the proximities dynamics and clusters are developed in the following sub-section.

3.3.1 Mimetic Interactions in Economics

In a decentralized system of interacting agents, we can study the individual rationality of mimetic behaviors and their consequences on collective behaviors. In economics, two kinds of work investigated this theoretical opening: models of *informational cascades* (Bikhchandani et al., 1992), also called models of *observational learning* (Manski, 2000), and models of

Table 3.1 Theories and models of mimetic interactions in economics and sociology

	Common Denominators	Uncertainty	Legitimacy	Coordination and Compatibility	Evolving Pay-off
Bikhchandani, Hirshleifer and Welch (1992, 1998) (economic behavior)		Balance between private signal and public information of predecessors	Role of 'fashion leaders'		Fragility, sensitive to external shocks
Arthur (1989) (economic behavior)	Rationality, heterogeneity, sequentiality and cumulation			Network externalities, interaction and cooperation	Increasing return to adoption and stability
DiMaggio and Powell (1983) (sociologic behavior)		Emergence of organizational fields	Following leaders in organizational fields		
Granovetter (1978) (sociologic behavior)			Following leaders in social structure		Increasing utility with collective behavior

increasing returns to adoption (Arthur, 1989), also called models of *interactive learning* (Vicente and Suire, 2006). These models have two strong common denominators. First, agents are heterogeneous according to their preferences and the satisfaction they can obtain from their decisions. Second, social interactions, whatever their nature at this stage, are sequential and cumulative, that is to say, that actions or decisions of predecessors always produce information, which can modify the preferences of others.

Informational cascades have been initially developed by Bikhchandani et al. (1992) in order to explain the emergence, sometimes unexpected, of conformity effects within a population, such as fads or customs, and of all other phenomena in which agents strongly converge towards identical behaviors or decisions. For instance, informational cascades have been theoretically used and empirically tested in financial economics in order to explain speculative bubbles and crashes in financial markets (Orléan, 2001), or the emergence of standards in technological competition (Geroski, 2000). In a formal way, agents are supposed to have a probabilistic private signal on the better-paid action to choose. At this stage, and in this context of uncertainty, it would be rational for agents to choose the action that statistically gives the higher pay-off. Nevertheless, if agents also have the opportunity to observe actions of predecessors, they have to balance their own private signal to the public signal that the actions of others represent. Under specific conditions, it would be rational for agents to imitate others and give up their private signal because they infer that others are better informed (statistically speaking).[5] Therefore, informational cascades can quickly occur and give rise to convergence of individuals' decisions.

We stress the fact that agents decide according to an observational learning process (Manski, 2000), which means that they have the opportunity to reduce the intrinsic uncertainty due to their probabilistic private signal by observing action of others in similar situations. Note also that the weight of informational cascades can be stronger since those entering first in the dynamics are supposed to have such an expertise capacity and reputation that they can influence the trajectory of collective behaviors more easily than is the general case.

So, in economics, the first basis of mimetic behavior we can identify is linked to the fact that agents confronted with uncertainty try to reduce it by imitating others. Such behaviors at individual level can succumb to a strong pressure to conform at a collective level. Nevertheless, uncertainty is not the only source of mimetic interactions. The models of increasing returns to adoption (Arthur, 1989) stress another source, closely linked to social interactions, coordination and compatibility. If sequentiality and accumulation are still observed, the origins of imitation are different and based on another decision process in which networks play a major role.

In a formal way, models of increasing returns to adoption are based on the notions of network externalities and interactive learning. The pay-offs agents can obtain from their connection to a network are positively correlated to the number of previous connected agents. The basic idea is that the higher the number of connected agents, the higher will be the probability of them communicating, exchanging or capturing information, in order to increase their satisfaction[6] (remember our story of economists: if an economist considers connecting to a research group or network in order to exchange empirical data or theoretical ideas, he or she has more chance of improving his or her satisfaction by connecting to a worldwide network than to a small and unrecognized network). However, this increasing satisfaction strongly depends on compatibility criteria governing interactions and communication between connected agents. For Arthur, these problems of compatibility are essentially technological ones. But we can easily show and demonstrate that they could also be cultural or social ones, such as language, capabilities or knowledge (if the economist is a French one and does not speak English, he or she will probably find it difficult to increase his or her satisfaction from his or her connection to the worldwide network of research. He or she could also be in great difficulty in terms of knowledge if he or she wants to connect to, say, an astrophysicists' association).

Network externalities, coordination and compatibility are essential in the growth of networks and in the competition between networks. Joining a network increases the satisfaction of the joiner and of the others who have already joined. In that sense, new connections reinforce the probability of forthcoming connections, in such a way that the network that connects more people than others and reaches a critical mass, through positive feedbacks mechanisms (Arthur, 1990), can progressively and sometimes definitively prevail on the others.[7] Once again, we recognize a mimetic process in the formation of networks, but the learning process that governs individuals' decisions is not (only) an observational one but (also) an interactive one: agents tend to imitate others not because of uncertainty but, in spite of their heterogeneity in initial preferences, because of interactions, communication and exchanges or transactions.

3.3.2 Mimetic Interactions in Sociology

In sociology, literature indeed displays the role of uncertainty but it also stresses the role of legitimacy and recognition (Tarde, 1895). These later dimensions are neglected by economists, developed by sociologists, and present in a lot of situations in which rational mimetic interactions occur.

DiMaggio and Powell (1983) developed a detailed institutional analysis of pressures that force homogeneity in organizational fields, that is to say, in classes of organizations that operate in similar economic environments. According to them, the well-designed concept that captures such homogeneity is the concept of isomorphism, which can be defined as a dynamical process driving each organization to resemble the ones that face the same environment. Of course, market pressure is certainly one of the main forces that lead to homogeneity (and monopoly), because market dynamics and power only select firms and organizational practices that perform. Nevertheless, it would also be possible to observe the diffusion of practices in an organizational field without the possibility of considering that they are better than others. For instance, Strang and Macy (2001) showed, using the conceptual categories of DiMaggio and Powell (1983), that the rapid diffusion of 'quality circles' in a majority of US firms in the 1980s, and their following rapid decline, stems from a search for legitimacy and recognition more than from the effective efficiency of such practices.

So DiMaggio and Powell (1983) identified three categories of institutional isomorphism. Only one of them can be considered as a pure mimetic process. According to them, mimetic processes can be defined as a rational response of agents to uncertainty in emergent contexts (see, for instance, the peculiar context of 'dotcom' in the late 1990s in the following sections). In emergent contexts, it would be more rational to imitate agents perceived as having strong legitimacy than to waste time and money in searching for and experimenting with solutions (for instance, organizational practices).

Similarly, Granovetter (1978) has developed an approach of mimetic interactions based on legitimation, but with a different theoretical scope. For him, there is a strong necessity to go beyond the explanation of collective behaviors as a simple aggregation process of agents endowed with homogeneous preferences. On the contrary, Granovetter, in his threshold model of collective behavior, tries to show that norms can emerge from a sequential interaction dynamics between heterogeneous agents. For that, he has to suppose a form of interdependency between interacting agents, which turns out to be close to the observational learning process developed in the models of informational cascades, and to the idea of legitimacy of DiMaggio and Powell (1983). All of these considerations are captured by the concept of threshold: each agent is endowed with an individual threshold, which can be defined as the number of agents in a fixed population who have already participated in a collective action (a riot or a strike, for instance), and above which he or she decides to participate also. So each agent decides according to whether a sufficient proportion of the population – his or her threshold – has already decided to participate in a collective action. The individual threshold, which is different for each agent, is a sort of legitimacy signal for individual decisions, which can lead under specific conditions to surprising outcomes.

If we try to sum up this short survey on mimetic interactions in economics and sociology, one has to keep in mind that uncertainty, legitimacy, coordination and evolving pay-offs or utilities are strong bases of imitative behaviors. To show such individual driving forces, one has first to suppose that agents are rational, heterogeneous, and that they sequentially and cumulatively interact. Second, one has to consider that agents are not homogeneous either regarding their respective influence on others (fashion leaders), even if this crucial aspect has not been the subject of recent attention in formal analysis and has to be gone into more deeply in the future.

3.4 THE COMPLEX LINKS BETWEEN MIMETIC INTERACTIONS AND PROXIMITIES

In this section, our goal is to show how mimetic interactions are particularly relevant in the explanations we can provide on differentiated proximity dynamics. We propose an analysis grid of clusters formation based on the complex links between geographical and socio-economic proximities and the nature of mimetic interactions working in the co-location processes.

3.4.1 The Role of Uncertainty and Legitimacy in Geographical and Cognitive Proximity Dynamics

First, we can try to demonstrate that uncertainty and legitimacy are strong foundations of geographical and cognitive proximities giving rise to economic agglomerations or clusters, sometimes with a high degree of 'geographic charisma' (Appold, 2005) or collective identity (Dalla Pria and Vicente, 2006), and a correlative and surprising weakness of local interdependences. For *geographical proximity*, we have to imagine that firms decide to locate somewhere sequentially, have in their possession (incomplete) information on the intrinsic features of each alternative of location, and can observe the predecessors they judge relevant in their location decision-making. Generally, these relevant predecessors can be supposed to be other firms of the sector that are in competition or sharing a segmented demand and having a strong reputation in markets. Moreover, this dynamics can be self-reinforcing because the more convergence in locations is obvious, the more uncertainty decreases and legitimacy of location decision-making increases (at least in a short-term period). This increase in legitimacy can be illustrated easily. For instance, firms are better placed to attract external financial resources when they are located in a successful territory. They are also well-placed to attract dynamic and skilled workers in a competitive labor market as 'fashionable' places are in great demand for scientists or engineers. They reduce uncertainty and increase legitimacy by a sort of collective and symbolic capital, sometimes labeled ('Silicon . . .' or '. . . Valley'), which gives rise to and increases individual reputation, even if local interdependences – that is, relational proximity – remain very weak.

In the literature, some papers have explicitly or implicitly displayed this role of mimetic interactions in the formation of clusters and geographical proximity. For instance, Appold (2005) recently studied the locational patterns of US industrial research through the development of research parks. According to him, one of the main reasons for the co-location process of research units lies in the role of mimetic behaviors in decision-making, even if operational conditions for dispersion exist. In a context of uncertainty, decision-makers search for signals to help them to choose suitably. Appold writes that 'the powerful signal, indicating that a location is an "appropriate" choice, might be the presence of other, similar, firms' (p. 20), and defends the assumption that in some several situations, the growth of clusters is more a sort of symbolic representation rather than some collective functional interdependences. Longhi (1999) stressed the successive stages of development of Sophia-Antipolis in France. According to him, the first stage of development of this cluster is more the result of an attraction process of plants of multinational firms, based on an active policy of marketing, than an endogenous process of growth based on knowledge transfers and strong local interdependences. Following Longhi, we could infer that the early location of firms such as IBM and Texas Instrument within Sophia-Antipolis played a strong signaling role for multinational firms that wanted to locate plants in a fashionable and well-reputed European location.

Uncertainty and legitimacy are deep roots of geographical proximity and they can also be deep roots of *cognitive proximity*. Remember that cognitive proximity can be defined according to distance in knowledge and capabilities between agents (Boschma approach) or distance in managerial practices, discourses and routinized behaviors (Bouba Olga and Grossetti approach). This general notion of cognitive proximity can be well-depicted through the sociological notion of 'collective identity' (Dalla Pria and Vicente, 2006). Once again, uncertainty and legitimacy play a major role in this cognitive convergence process. For instance, Geroski (2000) showed that technological standards not only arise from compatibility and network externalities in technological choices, as in most papers on competing technologies. Mimetic behaviors also play a major role in technological adoption and in the so-called S-shaped curve of diffusion because of legitimacy and bandwagon effect induced by social imitation. Such a collective behavior can arise when the uncertainty about features of each technological alternative is so strong that agents prefer to observe others, peculiarly well-reputed others. Lastly, we can recall the example of Strang and Macy (2001) on the surprising success and the rapid decline of 'quality circles' as managerial practices in the 1980s. According to them, and following DiMaggio and Powell (1983), such a phenomenon is mainly due to the uncertainty of the beginning of the post-Fordist period. To explain this strong collective identity and cognitive proximity based on quality circles, they propose a model of mimetic behavior and adaptive emulation in which the role of pioneering adopters (big US firms that explored this Japanese managerial practice) is fundamental in the convergence process and the wide diffusion of this practice in US firms.

3.4.2 The Role of Coordination and Compatibility in Geographical and Relational Proximity Dynamics

We can also try to demonstrate that coordination and compatibility in location decision-making between agents are strong foundations of geographical and relational proximities giving rise to clusters. Opposite to the previous case (uncertainty, legitimacy and cognitive proximity), these clusters exhibit strong local interdependences and firms networks. If *collective identity* can play a role in these clusters, *relational assets* remain their key feature. Uncertainty and legitimacy are not the one and only motivations that lead to convergence in location decision-making and so geographical proximity. Firms can also locate close to each other for more strategic and well-informed reasons. In that sense, this convergence process is based on externalities that differ from the informational externalities of models of locational cascade models. Here, geographical proximity is the result of a sequential process in which firms try intentionally to take advantage of proximity through the weight of knowledge and technological externalities (Torre and Gilly, 2000; Boschma, 2005). Such a process is close to Arthur's (1989; 1990) model of increasing returns to adoption: firms sequentially locate, and for that, compare the benefits of each place according to both their own preferences and the location of predecessors they consider relevant in their production and innovation process. If we suppose that knowledge and technological externalities have a strong local and geographical dimension, as theoretical and econometrical literatures say (Audretsch and Feldman, 1996), but sometimes in contradictory ways (Breschi and Lissoni, 2001), we can infer that geographical proximity is the result of a cumulative process of mimetic interactions based on coordination between firms and compatibility in their location decision-making.

So, innovative clusters can progressively reinforce their attraction according to a convergence process of location decision-making. This convergence process gives rise to a relational proximity because of the weight of the local interdependences the collective process of innovation engenders. Overall, the literature on clusters associates the links between geographical and relational proximity to the weight of tacit knowledge and face-to-face interactions. That is certainly generally the case, but more as a result of interaction dynamics than as an irrefutable assumption regarding economic coordination (Breschi and Lissoni, 2001). We think that mimetic processes of location based on network externalities are more relevant to explaining such a result. In opened innovation processes in which technological convergence is crucial to compete in monopolistic markets, compatibility in 'system products' is strongly correlated to compatibility in location decision-making, as Quah (2000) showed in the case of ICT clusters. And network externalities playing at the technological level also play at the social level, through the development of knowledge-based social networks.

For instance, Longhi (1999), in his paper on the evolving structure of Sophia-Antipolis, noticed that the cluster went through a phase of endogenous growth in the 1990s due to the emergence of social networks in telecommunications and health industries. These social networks were developed thanks to a voluntarist policy of regional planners to invest in public research centers, which progressively gave rise to start-ups and spin-offs in the cluster. So after the location process in the 1980s, based on an exogenous process of attraction of firms directed from outside and with weak internal relations – we interpret this process as a mimetic one based on uncertainty and legitimacy – the cluster overcame the crisis phase thanks to a mimetic process based on technological complementarities, compatibility and network externalities, in which social networks and relational proximity played a major role. We recognized in this cluster history one of the essential dimensions of relational proximity that Saxenian (1994) previously noticed in the Silicon Valley when she said that 'Silicon Valley is a regional network-based industrial system that promotes collective learning and flexible adjustment among specialist producers of a complex of related technologies', adding the weight of social networks in this collective learning and flexible adjustment.

3.4.3 Recapitulative Synthesis

Figure 3.4 tries to propose a recapitulative synthesis of the complex links between proximities and mimetic processes of location decision-making. The main result is that the key features of clusters depend on the combination

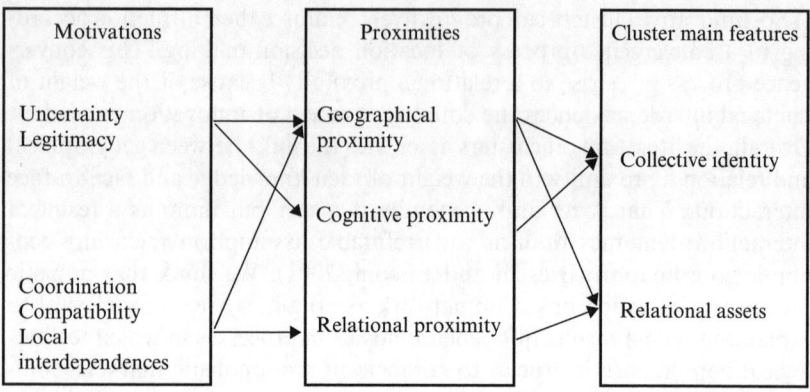

Figure 3.4 Mimetic interactions and proximities

of cognitive, relational and geographical proximities. On the one hand, in clusters where the uncertainty of the pay-offs related to each location alternative and the necessity to be better identified and legitimated by consumers or financiers are strong, clusters can exhibit geographical and cognitive proximity. These interrelated proximities foster the emergence of a strong collective identity because firms converge on location decision-making but also on managerial or organizational practices, above all in a context of emergent activities or sectors. Most of the time, firms in these clusters compete with each other in less differentiated markets.

On the other hand, when technological complementarities and convergence imply coordination in the innovation process, clustering processes give rise to geographical and relational proximities. Collective identity of clusters can be strong, but what insures the performance and the attractiveness of these clusters is that they exhibit a sort of collective relational (and specific) asset, and local interdependences, generally in monopolistic markets.

Of course, the reality of clusters is more intricate than the 'discrete case' of this typology. Each cluster can certainly be considered as a peculiar combination and degree (a continuum case) of collective identity and relational asset in space and time. Nevertheless, such a typology is well-suited to the analysis of not only the socio-economic nature of proximity, but also the location process giving rise to proximity. In the following section, we propose an empirical study of an extreme case of mimetic process of location based on uncertainty and legitimacy. The purpose is, first, to test and illustrate our typology and second to study the collective efficiency of clusters according to the mimetic location decision-making governing the clustering process.

3.5 SUCCESS AND DECLINE OF THE FRENCH 'SILICON SENTIER' (1998–2002)

Silicon Sentier[8] can be considered as the main agglomeration of Internet firms in France during the period 1998–2002. This cluster gathered together around 300 firms of the net-economy (the famous 'dotcoms') during the NASDAQ bubble swelling. The rapid success (1998–2000) and the sudden decline (2001–02) of this emblematic French cluster invite us to reflect on the links between the collective efficiency of clusters and the nature of socio-economic proximity. One can refer to objective initial conditions. But one can also explain the emergence of Silicon Sentier as the result of a collective mimetic behavior based on individual and sequential strategies that confer some peculiar structural properties to the district. To be precise, different kinds of proximity dynamics played a crucial role in the explanation of the success and decline of this ICT cluster.

Initially, the cluster emergence was clearly supported by the favorable real estate situation in this location in the middle of the 1990s, because of the crisis of textile activities. The existence of vast buildings made it possible to rent 'open spaces' at very low costs and represented the first incentive for the Internet pioneers to locate there:

> There were many spaces to rent because the Sentier was in crisis at the end of the 1990s. Since 1992–93, there is a crisis of representation and thus less business in the Sentier: thus the rents were not expensive at the beginning. (Start-up leader)

> In fact the very low rental fees especially attracted us. (Yahoo, *Libération*, December 1998)

The second argument favouring the arrival of the first start-up is related to the high quality of connection to the large international backbones. France Telecom opened in the spring 1998 its principal global information exchange (GIX) named PARIX, which is located in the heart of the Sentier district:

> It was the best district connected to international Internet backbones. (Yahoo, Agence-France Presse, March 2000)

> If all the start-ups are installed in this district, it is because it was historically the first cabled district. (Start-up founder)

The last argument favoring the location in the district over other start-up locations, relates to the specificity of the labor market in the ICT sector, at least during the time of the Internet bubble swelling. Indeed, if one follows

Suire's analysis (2003), the creative labor characteristic of the start-up is looking for urban amenities. Located in Paris center, the district benefits from the fact that it is easily accessible by public transportation and physically located in the economic activity center. In addition, the district is animated at any time. Thus, it was possible to organize meetings in cafés or to go and have a drink after leaving the office. For all these reasons, many people underlined the specific atmosphere that emerged from this district by comparing it to the traditional business districts of Paris (in particular La Défense):

> The advantage is that you walk to your appointment in five minutes. And you can have a beer after work. The district also corresponds to types of people (young people...). (Start-up founder)

> There is the 'hype' side which comes to a specific district... There is also opportunism, the will to create a new relationship between people, a new link with the city (to use public transport more than cars). There was also a reaction towards the not very convivial tower blocks [separation between work and personal life districts]. There is in the Sentier an idea of urban mixing: one works where one lives. When we started, many young people had their flat next to the office. (Start-up founder)

Underlying these economic factors, one has to explain why, between the beginning of 1999 to the middle of 2000, around 300 start-ups from the Internet sector were located in this district, either foreign subsidiary companies (Lycos, Spray, Boo.com, AOL), French start-ups, such as Alafolie.com, Monte Cristo, Multimania, Caramail, Nomade, Liberty Surf, Lastminute.com, Buycentral.fr, Magic Emilie, Net2one, or others, more anonymous. As we will see, mimetic interactions and proximity played a major role and quickly overran these economic factors.

3.5.1 Geographical and Cognitive Proximities...

Uncertainty prevailed, in particular in the context of the Internet-based economy in which business models were not stabilized and in which the need for being identified was rather strong. The convergence of start-up location decision-making can thus be regarded as the result of an informational cascade, resulting from the aggregation of the individual locational choices of these start-ups. These strategies are closely related to a process of observational learning:

> At Nomade, one of the French-speaking Internet search directories, we admit we have been attracted by this reputation of 'Web district': the company will move from Vincennes to the rue Réaumur in January. (*Libération*, December 1998)

There was a fashion effect which consisted in saying that you were in the Sentier (Start-up founder)

'My name is Blabla.com, I belong to the Silicon Sentier' should help us to be identified more than 'My name is Blabla.com, I belong to Paris'. (Person in charge of new technologies, Department of Industry and Finance, *Libération*, January 2000)

In the Sentier, there were mythical places: Free, Spray head offices. . . We did the same: we took rotted buildings in rue de Turenne. (Start-up founder)

This convergence of locational choices created legitimacy and a collective identity for this cluster during the period before the bubble crash. This collective identity engendered positive feedback effects on the individual reputation of local start-ups. In particular, the Silicon Sentier label facilitated the work of the start-up belonging to the community, in particular when they were searching for external funds (venture capital), on which start-up business models are based:

The Silicon Sentier, that remains a joke, but who knows: if we speak about it, perhaps it will end up becoming a reality. (Médiangles, *Libération*, December 1998)

That will facilitate the work of the start-up leaders when they present their projects to venture capitalists. They will be considered as located within a lucky territory. (Jean Ferré, for Creascope, January 2001)

Geographical proximity is a key characteristic of this cluster and both the convergence of location choices and the sequentiality of interactions have strongly driven its path development. One can think that if the leaders of the first net-economy companies had not been located in the center of Paris, in spite of the few advantages of this specific area, such a process would not have emerged so quickly and other districts could have been candidates for such success. This norm of location has been simply built on a mimetic dynamics, which 'cumulatively leads to the idea that to be elsewhere could be an error' (Suire, 2003, p. 387). Young and talented people who belonged to those start-ups shared a common adventure, in a way there was very little cognitive dissonance between them. Many of them were well-educated, shared the same organizational design principle, the same management rules, the same ways of life, close technological skills etc... To put it in a different way, cognitive proximity was very strong:

There are fashion effects: for example, we dress as we like, we live it up, we do business at parties. There is a lot of imitation. There were about 80–100 young managers who tried to combine business and festivity: it is the funky business with its parties and its buzzwords . . . The use of the 'tu' had to be adopted, and you had to be open-minded. (Start-up founder)

The start-up microcosm creates many rules for itself: to work during the night, to do everything together. . . It is a lot of responsibilities put on too weak shoulders but nevertheless, it is good. I also like the flat hierarchy concept (I do not have to play the chief at 26). The only thing which is different here is my armchair. But I do not have the higher wages in the enterprise. We will not reconsider the flat hierarchy, the responsibilities entrusted to young people. . . The only complicated trick is to make the difference between professional life and personal life: there are many start-ups where people lived together, had sex together. . . It is not good. (Start-up founder)

3.5.2 . . . But No Relational Proximity

The analysis could be stopped at this point if the objective was to analyze the success story of an e-business district. However, one cannot disregard the crisis of the net-economy that followed the crash of the Internet bubble at the end of 2000, and its consequences on the attractiveness of Silicon Sentier. One of the first consequences of this crisis lies in the recognition that the Silicon Sentier developed very few local relations and local productive and innovative interdependences. With the early economic arguments gradually disappearing (real estate situation and backbones access), Yahoo was the first firm to relocate out of the Sentier, and after that, many others relocated to different places. Concurrently, the district lost the essence of what we identified as a collective identity: the 'funky business'. This institutional isomorphism had broken up, and the managerial practices and speeches were quickly replaced by more traditional methods, characteristic of small businesses. In Silicon Sentier, the wave of rationalization experienced by the Internet pioneers also spread over the whole community:

We are mainly a publishing firm which developed an Internet activity. (Start-up founder)

In the end, we are a software firm which makes games. (Start-up leader)

At the beginning, to be called start-up was an advantage, but today, it is a disadvantage: the term start-up is denigrated and I do not define my firm as a start-up but as a small business. And I am not the only one. People realized that Internet was not the goose that lays the golden eggs. Today, it is old-fashioned to say that you are a start-up: people think 'it is still wind and it will file for bankruptcy'. We simply do something very traditional: we earn money. (Start-up founder)

Step by step, the label 'Silicon Sentier' lost all the legitimacy it had acquired during the NASDAQ euphoria:

> For me, there was no Silicon Sentier religion. It is just practical and not expansive... But today, it gives a very bad image: it is better not to be located within this district. Many firms went away because the real estate became more expensive and because there were bankruptcies. (Start-up founder)

> We are in Silicon Sentier but I do not feel it because I do not have enough time to try on my suits at the 'pouet-pouet' lunches: I have to manage my business. (Start-up leader)

> 'Silicon Sentier' became 'Silicon Desert'. (Start-up founder)

> [The Sentier], it was enjoyable. But for our public image, we preferred to move in to the 8th district, it is more serious. (Streampower leader, Paris Obs., 2003)

If cognitive proximity can be considered as a strong characteristic of people inside the cluster, the sharing of common values is not a sufficient condition to stimulate constructive social interactions and relations. While exchange of information or networking activities that support the diffusion of tacit knowledge are a key factor of success of Silicon Valley or Sophia-Antipolis, the social mechanisms that we brought to light inside the Sentier did not play such a role. Because of the absence of productive partnerships and of the climate of mistrust, relational proximity was not exactly stimulated in a right and efficient way:

> We developed Internet partnerships with Lycos, Caramail, Chez.com: we remunerate these sites according to the purchases they make in our firms. But we were mistaken because these partnerships do not work. (Start-up founder)

> It is very true in the Sentier: when a venture capitalist shows up at the corner of the street, there are no friends any longer. (Lawyer)

> At the beginning, there was an extraordinary boom in the creation of start-ups, and thus, a strong need for qualified labor whereas the labor force was weak. At that time, the start-ups competed with each other for talented and qualified people. Collaborations could only be limited. On 'First Tuesdays,' the chairmen did not want to send their employees to represent the company because they were debauched by other chairmen. (Journalist).

A strong geographical and cognitive proximity, built on mimetic and sequential decisions of location, but a lack of relational proximity are key to understanding the speed of the (de)clustering process of Internet firms inside the Silicon Sentier. As summarized in Table 3.2, the dialectic of

Table 3.2 Cluster life cycle and proximity dynamics

Phase	Proximities		
	Geographical	Cognitive	Relational
Growth (1998–2000)	+++	+++	+
Decline (2001–02)	+++	+	−

different forms of proximities outlined above and tested in the case of the Sentier is also key to understanding both the performance and the evolutionary stability of a cluster.

3.6 PROXIMITIES, COLLECTIVE EFFICIENCY AND STABILITY

If clusters as areas of regional growth and knowledge creation have been the subject of a growing literature during the last decade, few studies have been devoted to their stability properties. In this final section, we stress the stability properties of clusters in a dynamical sense, that is to say, their capacities to resist to exogenous shocks and to exhibit a continuous growth, rather than the neoclassical notion of stability linked to equilibrium. For that, remember that in the survey of models and theories of mimetic interactions, we identified three motives for mimetic interactions and convergence in behaviors (Table 3.1). We have already underlined two: uncertainty and legitimacy on the one hand, coordination and compatibility in the other. Now, our aim is to show that the third, pay-offs, is essential to understanding the intrinsic stability of clusters, and in that way, to show that geographical and cognitive proximity, as in the Silicon Sentier, are not a sufficient condition for this purpose.

First, in the model of locational cascade, firms tend to converge in location decision-making because mimetic behavior is a rational way to reduce uncertainty and increase legitimacy. If we look closely at the pay-offs of firms (Vicente and Suire, 2006), we can see that individual pay-offs do not increase when individual behaviors converge. The only thing that increases is the probability to obtain a fixed pay-off, but not the pay-off itself. In other words, the structure of pay-offs does not evolve and firms do not gain from their proximity. In that way, the non-deformation of the pay-off structure can thus be a major source of instability of clusters, and it is always possible for an exogenous shock or a succession of informational shocks to break the locational cascade. Empirically, we saw such a breaking in the

Silicon Sentier after the Internet bubble crash and the relocation of Yahoo that engendered the fast decline of the cluster. So we can say that cognitive proximity and geographical proximity coupled together are not a sufficient condition for stability and continuous attractiveness of clusters. Our analysis is closely akin to Boschma's (2005) who shows that cognitive proximity can be a strong source of unintended spillovers when firms compete in the same markets and are closely co-located.

Second, in the model of increasing returns to adoption, individual pay-offs evolve as soon as location decision-making converges, so that the process is strongly path-dependent and the opportunities for a reversal are reduced as soon as the clustering process grows. Local interdependences, formalized by network externalities, reinforce the attractiveness of clusters and their relational asset. Once again, if we look at Arthur's model (1989: 90) in detail, we can associate this path-dependence process to the fact that Arthur introduces an endogenous evolving pay-off system to formalize the benefits that firms gain from their proximity. In contrast with Silicon Sentier, Sophia-Antipolis and the emblematic Silicon Valley have shown their capacity to survive the Internet bubble crash and maintain their attractiveness, due to technological complementarities and variety in the innovation process. Relational proximity is a strong source of stability because of the interdependency of the individual pay-offs in the collective structure, which makes individual relocation strategies very costly.

Behind the analogy of the 'Silicon' label of most ICT clusters, different forms of learning process and mimetic interactions are hidden (Vicente, 2003). Hedström (1998) already identified such a difference in the general case of rational and mimetic behaviors. According to him, mimetic interactions can exhibit different patterns of aggregate behaviors, which depend on the nature of the evolving system of individual pay-offs in the aggregate dynamics. On the one hand, we can suppose that convergence of behaviors (location decision-making for our purpose) is a pure self-fulfilling process, that is to say that firms, as in Arthur's model (1989: 90), face a situation in which the value of a particular decision is an increasing function of the number and proportion of agents who have already taken the same decision. Such a self-fulfilling process, generally interpreted as a prophecy, can be easily explained by collective learning, innovation, trust and finally success on monopolistic markets. On the other hand, we can also suppose that this convergence process is a self-defeating process, that is to say, that firms, as in informational cascade models, face a situation in which the value of a particular decision is a decreasing function of the number and proportion of agents who have already taken the same decision. Such a self-defeating process can be explained in the literature by the fact that firms compete strongly and distrustingly, do not cooperate and can also be affected by spatial congestion effects.

Using these assumptions in a 'spatial version' of the general Hedström model of rational imitation, we can show that the nature of the evolving pay-offs system is the critical feature of the stability of the aggregate behavior (see appendix 3.1 at the end of this chapter). If a self-fulfilling process dominates the mimetic interactions dynamics, a sort of reinforcement process of beliefs occurs and firms converge to a lasting locational norm. In contrast, if a self-defeating process dominates, an erratic and cyclical aggregate behavior occurs, as in the fads and success stories phenomenon. In that way, if geographical and cognitive proximities coupled together do not represent a sufficient condition for the increase of individual's pay-offs, clusters suffer from chronic instability. In contrast again, relational proximity, because of its increasing pay-offs potentialities, appears a strong basis of stability and attractiveness of clusters.

3.7 CONCLUDING REMARKS

In this chapter, we have tried to link recent and stimulating work on proximity dynamics to the advances in mimetic interactions that govern co-location processes, in order to obtain results on the emergence of clusters in knowledge-based economies and on their dynamical stability. In that way, we showed first that it would be relevant to analyze clustering processes by supposing that firms decide to locate sequentially and that they have heterogeneous preferences of location. Second, we demonstrated that this sequentiality is a strong basis of communication, observation and coordination between firms, which can give rise to rational mimetic interactions and convergence in location decision-making (geographical proximity). Third, we also showed that the very nature of socio-economic proximity depends on the mimetic process at work in the aggregation process. If uncertainty and legitimacy dominate, the convergence of location decision-making can give rise to cognitive proximity, while if coordination and innovative interdependences dominate, depending on the degree of competition and of division of labor, the convergence process leads to a relational proximity. Finally, we tried to go beyond the emergence of clusters to explore their economic properties of stability. The key result is that according to the mimetic process at work and to the nature of socio-economic proximity, clusters can exhibit different stability properties, as we tried to show in the emblematic French case of Silicon Sentier (compared with others). We believe that such a result has to be theoretically and empirically improved in the future.

Note that clusters are not the only category of network that exhibit socio-economic proximity, innovation and economic growth. In this chapter, we only focused on clusters in order to study the ambivalent links between geographical and socio-economic proximity. Nevertheless, we are convinced that innovation, growth and performance are not totally and exclusively affected by geographical proximity. Following Simmie (2003) and Zimmermann (2001), the key feature of performance of clusters also lies in the intensity of interactions outside clusters, and we have to invest this question in future research.

ACKNOWLEDGEMENT

We thank the anonymous referee for useful and fruitful comments. Usual caveats apply.

NOTES

1. We define stability in a dynamical and evolutionary sense, that is, a stability in performance and growth, and not the neoclassical stability property, strongly associated to a notion of equilibrium (Boschma and Lambooy, 1999).
2. The typology proposed in the chapter has been discussed with Michel Grossetti, Olivier Bouba Olga and Christophe Carrincazeaux. The former two have compiled a brief research note of these discussions (Bouba Olga and Grossetti, 2005).
3. The empirical illustration has been constructed from both 70 interviews in the cluster (managers essentially) and a review of newspapers in the period 1998–2002.
4. We would like to thank Michel Grossetti for this remark.
5. It is very important to note for the following sections that pay-offs do not evolve. The only thing that evolves is the probability for agents to obtain this fixed pay-off.
6. As in the previous note, it is important to note that in models of increasing returns to adoption, contrary to models of informational cascades, pay-offs evolve. They are an increasing function of the number of members who have already joined the network.
7. Note, once again, contrary to models of informational cascades, that the collective efficiency grows with the number of connected agents, because of the evolving pay-off structure.
8. At the end of 1990s, we find in this small area of Paris some pioneer firms with strong legitimacy like Yahoo, Nomade, Lycos, Spray, etc. During two years, more than 300 Internet start-ups located in the Sentier district as well as incubators and venture capitalists before the rapid decline of cluster at the beginning of 2000.

REFERENCES

Amin, A. and N. Thrift (1993), 'Globalization, institutional thickness and local prospects', *Revue d'Economie Régionale et Urbaine*, 3, 405–27.

Appold, S. (2005), 'The location patterns of U.S. industrial research: mimetic isomorphism, and the emergence of geographic charisma', *Regional Studies*, 31, 17–39.
Arthur, W.B. (1989), 'Competing technologies, increasing returns and lock-in by historical events', *The Economic Journal*, 99, 116–31.
Arthur, W.B. (1990), 'Silicon Valley locational clusters, why do increasing returns imply monopoly', *Mathematical Social Sciences*, 19, 235–51.
Audretsch, A. and M.P. Feldman (1996), 'R&D spillovers and the geography of innovation and production', *American Economic Review*, 86, 630–40.
Bikhchandani, S., D. Hirshleifer and I. Welch (1992), 'A theory of fads, fashion, custom, and cultural change as informational cascades', *Journal of Political Economy*, 100, 992–1026.
Bikhchandani, S., D. Hirshleifer and I. Welch (1998), 'Learning from the behavior of others: conformity, fads, and informational cascades', *Journal of Economic Perspectives*, 12, 151–70.
Boschma, R.A. (2005), 'Proximity and innovation: a critical assessment', *Regional Studies*, 39, 61–74.
Boschma, R.A. and J.G. Lambooy (1999), 'Evolutionary economics and economic geography', *Journal of Evolutionary Economics*, 9, 411–29.
Bouba Olga, O. and M. Grossetti (2005), 'Une (re)définition des notions de proximité', unpublished research note.
Breschi, S. and Lissoni F. (2001), 'Knowledge spillovers and local innovation systems: a critical survey', *Industrial and Corporate Change*, 10, 975–1005.
Dalla Pria, Y. and J. Vicente (2006), 'Processus mimetiques et identité collective: gloire et déclin du Silicon Sentier', *Revue Française de Sociologie*, 47, 293–317.
DiMaggio, P.J. and W.W. Powell (1983), 'The Iron Cage revisited: institutional isomorphism and collective rationality in organizational fields', *American Sociological Review*, 48, 147–60.
Goffman, E. (1973), *La mise en scéne de la vie quotidieme, Volume 1, La présentation de soi*, Paris: Les Éditions de Minuit.
Geroski, P.A. (2000), 'Models of technology diffusion', *Research Policy*, 29, 603–25.
Granovetter, M. (1978), 'Threshold models of collective behavior', *American Journal of Sociology*, 83, 1420–43.
Granovetter, M. (1985), 'Economic action and social structure: the problem of embeddedness', *American Journal of Sociology*, 91, 481–510.
Hedström, P. (1998), 'Rational imitation', in R. Swedberg (ed.), *Social Mechanisms: an Analytical Approach to Social Theory*, Cambridge: Cambridge University Press, pp. 306–27.
Kirat, T. and Y. Lung (1999), 'Innovation and proximity. Territories as loci of collective learning processes', *European Urban and Regional Studies*, 6, 27–38.
Kirman, A. (1992), 'Whom or what does the representative individual represent?', *Journal of Economic Perspectives*, 6, 117–36.
Longhi, C. (1999), 'Networks, collective learning and technology development in innovative high technology regions: the case of Sophia-Antipolis', *Regional Studies*, 33, 333–42.
Manski, C.F. (2000), 'Economic analysis of social interactions', *Journal of Economic Perspectives*, 14, 115–36.
Markusen, A. (1996), 'Sticky places in slippery space: a typology of industrial districts', *Economic Geography*, 72, 293–313.

Martin, R. and P. Sunley (2003), 'Deconstructing clusters: chaotic concept or policy panacea?', *Journal of Economic Geography*, 3, 5–35.

Orléan, A. (2001), 'Comprendre les foules spéculatives: mimétismes informationnel, autoréférentiel et normatif', in J. Gravereau and J. Trauman (eds), *Crises financières*, Paris: Economica.

Pecqueur, B. and J.B. Zimmermann (2004), *Economies de proximité*, Paris: Hermès.

Porter, M.E. (1998a), 'Clusters and the new economics of competition', *Harvard Business Review*, 76, 77–90.

Porter, M.E. (1998b), *On Competition*, Harvard Business School Press.

Quah, D. (2000), 'Internet cluster emergence', *European Economic Review*, 44, 1032–44.

Saxenian, A. (1994), *Regional Advantages: Culture and Competition in Silicon Valley and Route 128*, Cambridge, MA: Harvard University Press.

Schelling, T. (1978), *Micromotives and Macrobehavior*, New York: W.W. Norton & Company.

Simmie, J. (2003), 'Innovation and Urban Regions as National and International Nodes for the Transfer and Sharing of Knowledge', *RSA Congress*, Pisa, March.

Storper, M. and B. Harrison (1991), 'Flexibility, hierarchy and regional development: the changing structures of production systems and their forms of governance in the 1990s', *Research Policy*, 28, 241–56.

Strang, D. and M.W. Macy (2001), 'In search of excellence: fads, success stories, and adaptive emulation', *American Journal of Sociology*, 107, 147–82.

Suire, R. (2003), 'Stratégies de localisation des firmes du secteur TIC: du cyberdistrict au district lisière', *Géographie, Economie, Société*, 5, 379–97.

Tarde, G. (1895), *Les Lois de L'Imitation*, Paris: Les empêcheurs de Penser en Rond.

Torre, A. and J.P. Gilly (2000), 'On the analytical dimension of proximity dynamics', *Regional Studies*, 34, 169–80.

Vicente, J. (2003), 'The Ambivalence of Silicon Label: network Externalities vs. Informational Externalities in Location Dynamics', *RSA Congress*, Pisa, March.

Vicente, J. and R. Suire (2006), 'Informational cascade vs. network externalities in locational choice: evidences on ICT clusters formation and stability', *Regional Studies*, 40, forthcoming.

Zimmermann, J.B. (2001), 'The firm/territory relationships in the globalisation: towards a new rationale', *European Journal of Economic and Social Sciences*, 15, 57–76.

Zimmermann, J.B. (2002), 'Des clusters aux small-worlds: une approche en termes de proximités', *Géographie, Economie, Société*, 4, 3–17.

APPENDIX 3.1:

A Model of Rational Imitation in Location Decision-making: Convergence (in) and Stability (of) Aggregate Outcomes (from Hedström, 1998)

Assume that each firm assigns a unique value β to each alternative of location, and that the probability for a firm to locate in a particular place is equal to its β-value divided by the sum of the β-values of all alternative places. The probability of firm j to choose place i at time t is then equal to:

$$P_{ijt} = \frac{\beta_{ijt}}{\sum_{i=1}^{k} \beta_{ijt}}$$

The β-values are assumed to be influenced by the firm's own assessment of the likely utility value of the various places and by the past location choices of others. Moreover, it will be assumed that the β-values are weighted according to a linear combination of these two sources of influence:

$$\beta_{ijt} = w_j S_{it} + (1 - w_j) V_{ijt}$$

where,

$w_j \in [0, 1]$ describes the relative weight the firm attaches to the past location of others;
S_{it} describes alternative's share of cumulative location made until $t - 1$;
V_{ijt} describes the assessment of firm j on the likely value of each location i at time t.
These values are chosen according to a *self-fulfilling* or a *self-defeating* process (Schelling, 1978), describing the respective weight of network externalities and informational externalities.

Simulation results give an interpretation of the convergence (in) and of the stability (of) aggregates outcomes.

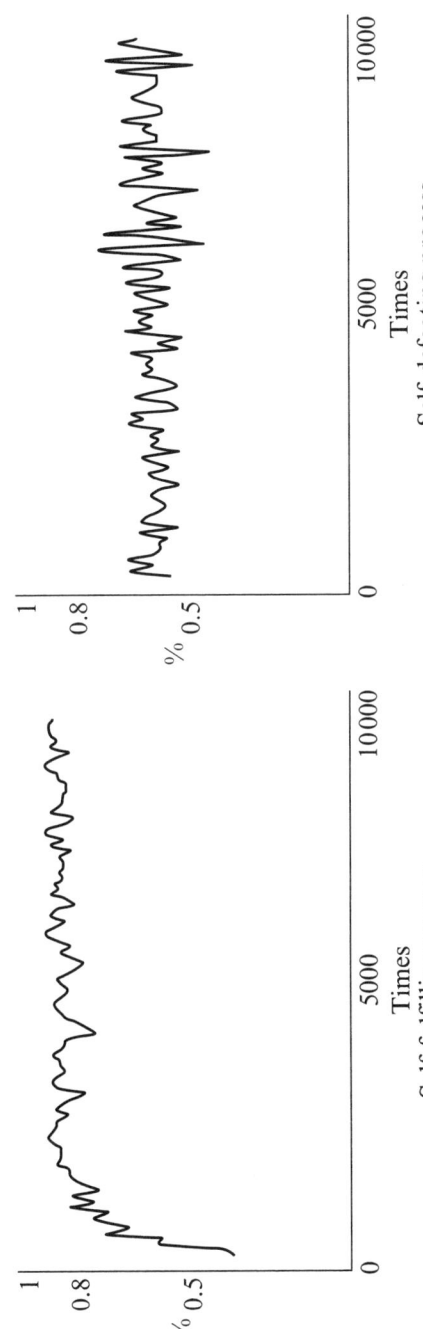

Figure A3.1 Self-fulfilling and self-defeating process

4. IT adoption, industrial structure and agglomeration economies
Flora Bellone

4.1 INTRODUCTION

The information technology (IT) revolution has not induced uniform increases in growth performance in the European regions and recent evidence on the location of IT-producing sectors and the dispersion of IT investments in user sectors, shows strong regional unbalances (Koski, Rouvinen and Yla-Anttilla, 2002). These facts support the idea that economic geography matters in determining IT investments. However, considering that IT is a generic technology and mostly embodied in immaterial goods, it is far from obvious why investment should be concentrated in only certain locations.

I would point to coordination failures rather than technological determinants as the explanation of this paradox.[1] My starting point is recognition that strong microeconomic imbalances characterize IT adoption processes: increasing returns due to fixed local entry costs and pecuniary externalities due to demand complementarities[2] among the providers of different IT goods and services. Such features have been emphasized in the microeconomic literature on innovation (Katz and Shapiro, 1985; Arthur, 1990; Shapiro and Varian, 1999), but are rather overlooked in the macroeconomic issues literature. The aim of this chapter is to show that coordination failures at macro-level – specifically low-growth traps – can emerge as a consequence of such microeconomic imbalances.

The chapter develops a small open economy framework to analyse the difficulties of coordinating the incentives for adopting IT-intermediate goods and services in a local economy, which is not initially involved in production of a large range of those goods. Analytically, our model applies Ciccone and Matsuyama's (1996; 1999) circular causation theory. This theory is well suited to an investigation of the macroeconomic implications of non-convexities arising out of demand complementarities between individual inputs. More specifically, Ciccone and Matsuyama emphasize the structural changes that involve an increase in the roundaboutness of production processes. In this chapter, I argue that the adoption of IT involves this type of structural change as firms adopting IT replace direct labour with a large range of sophisticated intermediate goods (computers, terminals, software, printers, etc.) and an ever larger set of specialized producer services (financial services, legal services, information system management, advertising, accounting, insurance, personal training, management consultancy, etc).[3]

This key feature – that is, the increase in the roundaboutness of production – gives birth to a circularity between the choice of technology by consumer goods producers and the variety of IT-intermediate goods and services available in the local economy. In this chapter, we argue that this circularity can be strong enough at the local level such that a regional economy that inherits a narrow range of IT inputs will be trapped into a low growth path. Consequently, the typical growth dynamics for any small open regional economy will be characterized by multiple equilibria with the possible occurrence of both virtuous circles, that is, when the economy makes intensive use of IT, and vicious circles, that is, when the economy becomes trapped into traditional production technologies.

4.2 THE CONTRIBUTION OF IT TO REGIONAL GROWTH: SOME STYLIZED FACTS ON EUROPE

Two main types of empirical works attempt to evaluate the impact of IT on productivity growth. Growth accounting exercises based on aggregate and industry-level datasets evaluate the contributions of the production and the diffusion of IT in different countries (Jorgenson, 2006 is one of the most recent contributions), while studies based on firm-level data attempt to demonstrate a relationship between IT investment and the distribution of firms' productivity. Both approaches shed light on the issue of regional growth disparities and will be discussed further.

4.2.1 Evidence from Macro- and Industry-level Datasets

Growth accounting exercises based on aggregate or industry-level datasets can help to identify regional disparities from two points of view: first, if European countries exhibit very dissimilar performance in terms of IT-induced growth, this may indicate that there are strong regional disparities;[4] second, if specific patterns of IT production and adoption are revealed at industry level, this may explain why regions with different industrial structures exhibit dissimilar performance in terms of IT-induced growth.

The first evaluations of the impact of IT on aggregate productivity indexes were based on the US economy, where there was a sharp increase in labour productivity and total factor productivity (TFP) growth trends in the mid-1990s. This pioneering literature provoked debate over whether these increased productivity growth rates were restricted to the small number of IT-producing sectors or occurred as a result of the diffusion of IT throughout the whole economy.[5] This debate tended to defend the more general view that TPF productivity gains are not equally distributed among sectors, or that, at least, they should be higher in those industries that relied heavily on IT.[6] Baily and Laurence (2001) confirm this view in part. They ranked the most dynamic sectors in the United States for the late 1990s period as wholesale trade, durable goods industries, finance, retail trade and the airline industry respectively. They also pointed out that productivity in the business and personal services sectors increased sharply during that period.

Concerning Europe,[7] the first stylized fact relates to the low average growth performance of European countries compared with the United States during the 1990s.[8] The second important fact is the increase in the dispersion of intra-European performance during the same period. Hence, while some Northern European countries have matched or even surpassed US performance, the below-average performance of France, Germany, Belgium and the Southern European countries (Italy, Spain) have resulted in Europe being positioned well behind the United States.

The causes of this diversity in growth performances across Europe are multiple.[9] Most empirical studies, however, agree about the significant role played by intra-European differences in IT investments (see Colecchia and Schreyer, 2002; Daveri, 2002; Oulton, 2002; Van Ark, 2002). In addition, these studies report that the contribution of IT to economic growth has been substantial in the United Kingdom and the Netherlands and is rapidly increasing in Denmark, Norway and Finland although it has been less relevant quantitatively in France, Germany, Belgium, Sweden and marginal in Spain and Italy.

In Europe, the main controversy is over how much of the performance gap relative to the US economy is due to an 'IT production gap' and how much is due to an 'IT diffusion gap'. The former argument finds support in a study by Van Ark (2002), which reports that the relative shares of the IT-producing sectors are significantly lower in almost all the European countries. The author points out that these differences are less pronounced in heavy IT-using sectors, specifically in IT services.[10] Similarly, evidence on the spatial repartition of IT investments reveals that IT-producing sectors are far more concentrated than IT-using sectors (Koski et al., 2002).

On the other hand, Daveri (2002) argues that lags in the adoption and diffusion of IT are the main cause of the relative performance gap between the European countries and the United States. Boyer (2001) also points out that the Scandinavian countries are better characterized by their common above-average performance in terms of IT adoption and diffusion rates than by their specialization patterns in their IT-producing sectors. In particular, in these countries the diffusion of IT has been strongly favoured by the decrease in telecommunications prices. Colecchia and Schreyer (2002), in a comparative analysis of nine OECD countries including five European countries,[11] conclude that IT diffusion and usage play a key role in shaping Europe's growth performance disparities. They also emphasize that IT diffusion is favoured by the 'right' microeconomic framework conditions, that is, liberalized and flexible markets, and not necessarily by the existence of a large IT-producing sector.

Thus, studies based on macro- and industry-level datasets support the idea that interregional disparities in IT investments are strong in Europe. They indicate that a significant part of these disparities is linked to differences in specialization patterns across the European regions. However, IT diffusion gaps and inequalities in the intensity of IT use across regions are also important.

4.2.2 Evidence From Firm-level Databases

The empirical works based on firm-level data provide useful insights in relation to the above statements. First, micro-level datasets offer an interesting alternative way to address the macroeconomic issue of the contribution of IT to aggregate productivity growth (see, for instance, Crépon and Heckel, 2001 using French firm-level data). Second, they enable the hypothesis that localization variables are key determinants of firms' decisions to adopt IT and of the firms' ability to realize the productivity gains potentially associated to this technology to be tested. Along these lines, Fisher and Johanson (1994) and Karlsson (1995) emphasize the influence of population density on the propensity for IT adoption by US firms. Karlsson (1995) shows that the influence is stronger the more complex the domain of application in which the firms use the IT. In others words, the localization bias towards large cities is stronger for innovative firms.

Using French data, Galliano and Roux (2003) tested the impact of geographical factors on firms' decisions to adopt IT. Their working assumption was twofold. First, they assumed that urban concentration increases the probability of adopting IT. Second, they assumed that a high concentration of services linked to IT reinforces that probability. While this methodology does not allow the productive impact of IT adoption to be measured directly,[12] the results of their study are quite promising. They found that, when sectoral composition and firm-specific effects and size were controlled for, geographical factors still had a significant impact on both the dimensions mentioned above.

Finally, Atzeni and Carboni (2004) worked on two sub-samples of Northern and Southern Italian firms. Their study confirms that there is a large asymmetry in the IT adoption behaviour and the productivity performance of these two sub-samples. Not surprisingly, Northern firms exhibited higher IT investment rates and higher productivity than Southern firms. More interesting was the fact that the dispersion of productivity growth rates among Southern Italian firms was high. For instance, when they control for human capital, the catching-up dynamics of Southern Italian firms compared with Northern Italian firms in terms of IT investments and total factor productivity growth was similar.

Therefore, micro-based studies further support the idea of large IT diffusion gaps across regions. They point to the relative advantage of regions with large initial industry and innovation bases. They also support the idea that both local endowments in human capital and localized cumulative effects may be explanatory variables.

4.3 A MODEL OF CUMULATIVE ADOPTION OF IT

The evidence presented above suggests that differences in technology and endowments are not a sufficient explanation of regional disparities in IT diffusion and adoption rates. Some circular cumulative phenomena seem to be at work as well. In this section, I describe a model of cumulative adoption of IT, which allows similar regions to experience different IT adoption and growth patterns depending on their history and/or expectations. In this model, I assume that IT firms generally face considerable entry barriers in local markets. This assumption is supported by Melchior and Oi (2002) who show that IT firms have to face small traditional trade barriers, such as tariffs or transport costs, but invest significant amounts in establishing sales channels or adapting products to local markets. Once the existence of those fixed costs in the local supply of IT specialized inputs is acknowledged, the model shows how central they can be in explaining the existence of large disparities in IT investment and induced growth across regional economies. A similar argument is developed in Bellone and Maupertuis (2003).

4.3.1 An Analytical Framework, Borrowed from Ciccone and Matsuyama (1996)

The regional economy is a small open economy (SOE) endowed with a fixed amount of labour (L) and engaged in competitive production of homogeneous final consumption goods based on that labour and an endogenous variety of IT-intermediate-inputs.

The consumption goods technology is generally expressed as:

$$C = F(m_C^i : i \geq 0, L_C)$$

where L_C denotes the quantity of labour and m_C^i the quantity of intermediate input i employed in the production of consumption goods.[13] It is assumed that the consumption goods technology can be rewritten as:

$$C = F(M_C, L_C) \qquad (4.1)$$

where $F(.)$ is a linear homogeneous concave, and twice continuously differentiable function, and:

$$M_C = \left[\int_0^n (m_C^i)^\beta di \right]^{1/\beta} \quad \text{with } 0 < \beta < 1 \qquad (4.2)$$

where $[0, n]$ is the continuum of differentiated IT input available at any moment in time in the local economy. Note that the range n depends both on time and on geographical space. Indeed, over time this range can be increased in a given locality by allocating a fixed amount of resources to local start-up operations. I refer to M_C as IT-intermediate-input composites.

This specification implies weak separability between differentiated inputs and labour. The assumption $\beta > 0$ ensures that no single input is essential for producing IT-intermediate-input composites. All differentiated input enters symmetrically into the intermediate-input composite, and the elasticity of substitution between any pair of inputs in the production of intermediate-input composites is constant and equal to $\sigma = 1/1 - \beta$.

Specification (4.2), widely used in the new growth and New Economic Geography literature, was first introduced by Dixit and Stiglitz (1977) and Ethier (1982) to formalize the idea that the greater the specialization of tasks in the upstream sector, the stronger the productive contribution of intermediate inputs in the downstream sector. In other words, TFP increases with the variety of intermediate inputs available and with an elasticity of substitution higher than 1, the price index of the intermediate-input composite decreases with the number of intermediate goods offered in the economy. Moreover, the weaker the elasticity σ, the stronger this effect. To demonstrate this, let us assume that all inputs are charged at a common price. Then, the cost of the IT-intensive-input composite can be written as:

$$P_M = \left[\int_0^n [p_m(i)]^{1-\sigma} di \right]^{1/(1-\sigma)} = n^{1/(1-\sigma)} p_m \qquad (4.3)$$

Specification (4.2) does not, however, imply that the production process becomes more roundabout when the range of intermediate inputs increases. In order to reproduce this second key feature of IT-based production processes, specification (4.1) needs to be further constrained.

Let us assume that the consumption goods technology combines L and M_C with the following specification:

$$C = F(M_C, L_C) = [M_C^{\beta'} + L_C^{\beta'}]^{1/\beta'} \text{ with } 0 < \beta' < 1 \qquad (4.4)$$

This implies that the elasticity of substitution between M_C and L_C, ε, is greater than 1. In turn, the relative share of intermediate inputs used in technology (4.1) increases more than proportionally as the relative price of intermediate-input composites decreases.[14] In other words, M_C and L_C are strongly substitutable.[15] This means that when the price of M_C decreases, the share of the value-added by the upstream industries relative to the value-added by the downstream industries increases. In other words, the intensive use of IT-intermediate goods and services increases the roundaboutness of production processes. This evolution causes the quantity of direct labour used in the final goods industry to decrease and, reciprocally, the quantity of labour used in the intermediate goods industry to increase.[16]

Formally, this implies a positive relationship between, n, the range of IT goods locally available and the relative share of intermediate inputs in the global output. Indeed, the larger the range of intermediate goods supplied in the economy, the weaker the relative cost of the intermediate-input composite, that is, P_M/w.

If we note α_t the relative share of intermediate inputs in the global output, we have:

$$\alpha_t = \alpha(n_t^{1/1-\sigma} p_m/w) \equiv A(n_t) \text{ with } A'(.) > 0. \qquad (4.5)$$

This property explains the possible occurrence of a circularity between the choice of technology made by the local producers of the final consumption goods, and the incentives to supply locally new IT goods and services to upstream industries. In order to understand this mechanism, let us consider the optimal choice of the suppliers of IT-intermediate-inputs.

Each supplier of IT-intermediate-inputs faces increasing returns in the sense that it can supply the local economy only if it is willing to accept some local fixed costs alongside other variable costs. We note that F and a are the amount of labour necessary to cover the fixed local entry costs and the variable costs for each specialized input respectively.

Under monopolistic competition, each intermediary good is supplied by a unique firm, which benefits from monopoly power in its market niche.

Then, each supplier sets the price applying a mark-up on its marginal cost of production $w_t a$. Normalizing[17] units such that $a = \beta$, this price can be written:

$$p_m(i) = p_m = \frac{aw}{\beta} = w \qquad (4.6)$$

The IT input supplier's immediate profit is given by:

$$\pi = (p_m - aw)m(i) = \frac{p_m m(i)}{\sigma} = \frac{\alpha Y}{\sigma n}$$

which can be re-written taking (4.6) into account, as:

$$\pi_t = \frac{A(n_t) Y_t}{\sigma n_t} \qquad (4.7)$$

Equation (4.7) highlights the double effect of an increase in n, the range of IT inputs locally available or, in other words, the double impact of the entry of a new supplier of IT-intermediate-inputs on the profit of the incumbents. On the one side, this new entry means more competition, which reduces the profit by variety given the level of expenses devoted to these production factors. On the other side, this new entry positively affects the global level of expenses devoted to IT-intermediate-inputs as the share of production costs devoted to IT inputs increases relative to the share devoted to labour. This second effect increases the profit by variety. The net impact of an increase in the range of IT inputs on the profit per variety is then ambiguous. When income effects are stronger than substitution effects, specialized inputs become strategic complements. In this case, pecuniary externalities appear in the provision of IT goods and services.

Finally, let us present the equilibrium conditions. First, the free entry condition in the monopolistic sector is sketched as follows:

$$w_t F \geq v_t, \dot{n}_t \geq 0 \text{ with strict equality holds if } \dot{n}_t > 0 \qquad (4.8)$$

where $w_t F$ is the fixed cost required to enter the intermediate goods sector and v_t is the present value of the new entrant. Second, the no arbitrage condition between the financial markets and the goods markets holds if v_t is equal to the present discounted value of profits[18], which leads to the usual:

$$\pi_t + \dot{v}_t = \dot{r}_t v_t \qquad (4.9)$$

The last equilibrium condition is a labour market clearing condition. Labour supply in the economy must equal the sum of labour used by the final goods producers and labour used by the IT firms:

$$L = L_{BF} + L_{BI} \qquad (4.10)$$

with $L_{BFt} = \dfrac{(1-\alpha)}{w_t} Y_t$ and $L_{BIt} = n_t am(i) + F\dot{n}_t = \left(1 - \dfrac{1}{\sigma}\right)\alpha_t \left(\dfrac{Y_t}{w_t}\right) + F\dot{n}_t.$

According to (4.10), productivity increases are driven by:

$$F\dot{n}_t = L - \left(1 - \dfrac{A(n_t)}{\sigma}\right)\dfrac{Y_t}{F(n_t^{1/(\sigma-1)}A(n_t), 1 - A(n_t))} \qquad (4.11)$$

Equation (4.11) shows that the productivity gains associated with the increase in the roundaboutness of production processes – that is, the increase in the division of labour – can only be obtained through a re-allocation of labour from the final goods sector to the IT sector.

4.3.2 The Evolution of the Economy and the Occurrence of No-growth Traps

In the modelled economy, growth opportunities for the SOE are bounded in the long run by the market size.[19] Indeed, the presence of a constant fixed cost, limits the number of viable competitors in a monopolistic competition market. Consequently, there will be a time when the productivity gains from a new entry will not be sufficient to compensate for the cost of this entry. Regional growth dynamics in this model are transitory. Nonetheless, for some key parameter values, the economy can be locked into a low equilibrium (that is, characterized by a small number of IT firms) or instead follow a transitory dynamic towards a high equilibrium (that is, characterized by intensive IT use and a large monopolistic competition market for those inputs). These different configurations can be described using the evolution of two key variables: n, the number of differentiated IT inputs in the economy and $V = v/Y$, the value of an IT firm measured in terms of its utility.

Using (4.1), (4.7) and (4.9) the evolution of the value of an IT firm through time is given by:

$$\dot{V}_t = \rho V_t - \dfrac{A(n_t)}{\sigma n_t} \qquad (4.12)$$

Simultaneously, (4.8) and (4.10) allow the evolution through time of the number of IT suppliers to be written as:

$$\dot{n}_t = \max\left\{\frac{L}{F} - \left(1 - \frac{A(n_t)}{\sigma}\right)\frac{1}{V_t}, 0\right\} \quad (4.13)$$

which, considering (4.1) and (4.12), leads to:

$$\lim V_t n_t e^{-\rho t} = 0 \quad (4.14)$$

as t tends to the infinite.

The equilibrium conditions require that incentives to enter or exit the IT sector no longer exist ($\dot{V} = 0$) and, consequently, that the number of IT suppliers active in the local market is constant ($\dot{n}=0$). From (4.12), we get:

$$V = \frac{A(n)}{\rho \sigma n} \quad \text{(AA)}$$

and then using (4.13)

$$V = \frac{F}{L}\left(1 - \frac{A(n)}{\sigma}\right) \quad \text{(BB)}$$

The last two equations describe the geometrical locus in which the value of an IT firm and the number of IT suppliers are both constant. A number n^* of suppliers exists such that (AA)=(BB) that can be defined as follows:

$$\Omega(n^*) \equiv n^*\left(\frac{\sigma}{A(n^*)} - 1\right) = \frac{L}{\rho F} \quad (4.15)$$

This shows that the set of IT inputs offered in the economy is a function of market size, that is, the size of the workforce. Then, the division of labour also depends on the size of the market. Reciprocally, the division of labour increases the extent of the market. This circularity is what induces a multiplicity of equilibria when the substitution of direct labour by IT inputs is sufficiently large in the process of technological change. Specifically, Ciccone and Matsuyama (1996) show that multiple equilibria actually occur as soon as the condition $\varepsilon > \sigma > 1$ holds.[20]

Under this condition, $\alpha = A(n) = 1 + wL_{BF}/P_K$ and the equilibrium condition can be written as:

$$\frac{1}{A(n)} = 1 + n^{(\varepsilon-1)/(\sigma-1)} \Leftrightarrow \frac{n}{A(n)} = n + n^{(\sigma-\varepsilon)/(\sigma-1)}$$

such that the value V (given by 4.12) is maximal for a number of suppliers $\check{n}$ given by:

$$\check{n} = \left[\frac{(\varepsilon - \sigma)}{\sigma - 1}\right]^{(\sigma-1)/(\varepsilon-1)}$$

This number is a discriminating value characterizing the nature of IT inputs: as long as $n<\check{n}$, IT goods and services are strategic complements, that is, the demand for one IT input decreases when the price of other IT inputs increases. As soon as $n>\check{n}$, IT goods and services are substitutes, that is, the demand for one IT input increases when the price of other IT inputs increases.[21]

This property means that the evolution of the value of the IT firm when the number of IT inputs increases in the economy can adopt different trajectories as these goods are strategic complements or strategic substitutes. The actual path of the IT firm value will depend on three key parameters: the level of fixed costs, the number of IT inputs available in the economy (that is, initial conditions) and finally the nature of the expectations regarding the entry of IT suppliers.

The level of fixed costs is of primary concern for the SOE. Too high fixed costs (at the extreme, prohibitive costs linked to a shortage of IT infrastructures) are an insurmountable constraint for the economy. Indeed, in conditions of high fixed costs, entry of new suppliers is never profitable even if the initial number of suppliers is low enough that investments could be strategic complements. In this case, each initial condition is a trivial equilibrium as the region is never incited to enlarge the range of IT inputs initially provided to it. This result is explained by the global resource constraint that weighs on an SOE. The region does not dispose internally of enough resources to allow labour to be efficiently reallocated from downstream to upperstream sectors. Foreign help[22] is a necessary (even if not sufficient) condition to reach a high equilibrium characterized by intensive use of IT inputs.

For intermediate levels of fixed costs, the long-run equilibrium depends on initial conditions, that is, the number of IT inputs initially provided to the local economy. In this case, one can identify a low equilibrium (with n_1 suppliers) and a high equilibrium (with n_2 suppliers and $n_1<n_2$). If the

economy is characterized initially by a narrow industrial base (less than n_1),[23] final goods producers have no incentive to use IT. The demand for IT inputs remains low and there is no incentive to evolve towards the high equilibrium. The economy is trapped into traditional production methods.

However, for an initial number of IT suppliers above n_1, the incentives are strong enough to produce a virtuous circle: producers of final goods are prompted to adopt IT and producers of IT inputs are prompted to enter the market. The increase in the roundaboutness of production processes in the final goods sector extends the market size. This increase in market size further increases the incentives for new IT providers to pay the fixed local costs of entering the regional market. This cumulative causation process plays until the degree of competition in the IT sector eventually reduces the incentive to enter the sector. The economy reaches high equilibrium (n_2 suppliers) characterized by a modernized productive system that relies intensively on IT inputs.

For even lower levels of fixed costs, two new effects appear: first, high equilibrium is more easily reached even if the initial industrial basis is relatively narrow ($n_1 < \tilde{n}$). Second, a period of initial conditions exists during which the occurrence or non-occurrence of a virtuous circle will be conditioned by the nature of the IT suppliers' expectations.

In the case that they are optimistic, that is, IT providers anticipate that many of them will enter the local market simultaneously, strategic complementarities are set in motion even if the initial number of IT firms is small. With a self-fulfilling prophecy, the high equilibrium is reached, that is, the positive feedback between entry and increase of the share of intermediate goods in the final goods sector induces the virtuous circle expected along this path. On the contrary, if IT suppliers are pessimistic, a narrow initial industrial base becomes a key barrier to development. In this case, the incentives to provide and to adopt IT inputs within the SOE are non-existent and the economy is trapped into a low growth path.

In this case, coordination failures explain why initially backward regions, despite appropriate infrastructure, endowments and potential needs, may not invest heavily in IT. A corollary of this result is that actions designed to reduce fixed costs may produce miraculous results for a peripheral region. Indeed as local fixed costs decrease, optimistic expectations alone[24] can produce a stimulating impact on the adoption entry process described above.

4.4 CONCLUSION

IT may offer large growth potential for peripheral regions suffering from economic backwardness. However, growth dynamics induced by intensive use of these technologies is not a pattern that is common to all European regions. The literature has emphasized technology-based explanations. For instance, the lack of infrastructure or the low level of human capital has been suggested as being an important constraint to the diffusion of IT and the modernization of production processes. In this chapter, I have shown that economic coordination constraints can also play an important role if the decisions to invest in IT inputs give rise to demand complementarities in a decentralized economy.

It is notable that the pecuniary externalities that give rise to cumulative causation dynamics in the model are not of the same kind as those that enable agglomeration processes in the New Economic Geography approach (Fujita, Krugman and Venables 1999). In the New Economic Geography approach, these are seen as the opportunities to save on variable transport costs, which produce the incentives for consumers and providers to locate in proximity to one another. In this chapter, we consider these to be fixed costs combined with demand complementarities, which give rise to localized cumulative causation processes.

The analysis also explains how technological constraints interact with market failures. In the model presented in this chapter, very high fixed costs act as an insurmountable barrier. In this case, even an ex ante coordination of IT investments is not profitable and consequently the high equilibrium does not exist. If technological constraints are relaxed (for instance with appropriate investment in infrastructure), coordination failures may still appear, particularly in regions that do not have a sufficiently well developed industrial basis.

NOTES

1. Quah (2000) summarizes interesting alternative explanations. For instance, it has been argued that some IT-producing industries are characterized by strong internal and external scale economies, a property that favours the spatial concentration of firms. It has also been argued that efficient IT adoption requires infrastructures and complementary investments in human capital that are not equally distributed across regions.
2. My emphasis on strategic rather than technological or organizational complementarities does not mean that the latter are not important in IT adoption processes (see Brynjolfsson and Hitt, 2003 for supporting evidence).
3. Fujita and Hamaguchi (2001) use a similar argument to explain the increasing use of externally provided intermediate goods and services by manufacturing firms.
4. Note that the reverse implication (i.e., inferring low regional disparities based on similar performance at country level) could be extremely misleading as IT productivity gains are likely to be concentrated within countries.
5. Some authors argued that this growth acceleration was mainly due to improved productivity growth in the IT-producing sectors (Jorgenson and Stiroh, 2000) or, even more specifically, in the computer industry (Gordon, 2000). Other evaluations, however,

6. It is notable that the IT-producing sectors are the intensive users of IT.
7. Comparative analyses of the contribution of IT to the growth performance of European countries are more difficult to implement because of the heterogeneity of the data sources. Most of the existing literature relies on the OECD databases. More recently, the GGDC (Groningen Growth & Development Centre) databases compiled from national, European and OCED sources have also been used (see O'Mahony and Van Ark, 2003).
8. Van Ark (2002) evaluates the gap between the European Union (EU) and the US GDP growth trend as one percentage point per year during the 1990s.
9. They range from slow growth in investment, rigidities in the labour, product and capital markets, to sluggish demand and lack of technological progress (Ahn and Hemmings, 2000; Scarpetta et al., 2000).
10. The criterion used by Van Ark (2002) to distinguish between heavy and light IT users is IT intensity, that is, the share of IT investment in industry output, and the industry share in IT capital stock. According to this criterion, heavy users include some IT-producing sectors particularly printing and publishing, the chemical industry, electrical and electronic machinery and equipment, medical and measurement appliances (together, IT-using industries), wholesale trade, post and telecommunications, finance, machinery rental, computer services, research and development and some business-service-using sectors (accountants, architectural firms, legal offices, consultants and marketing agencies).
11. Finland, France, Germany, United Kingdom and Italy.
12. IT adoption is measured as the intensity of Internet and intranet usage. The ability of firms to translate these uses into productivity gains is not controlled for. This ability may also differ across regions.
13. All endogenous variables depend on time, but time subscripts are generally omitted, that is, unless it would be confusing to do so.
14. For a more general specification see Ciccone and Matsuyama (1999).
15. We should underline that M_C does not correspond here to capital stock, but rather to a set of intermediate goods and services.
16. Note that the underlying hypothesis is not of strong substitutability between labour and capital, but rather of a modification to the vertical structure of production.
17. This normalization is usual within the New Economic Geography approach (cf. Fujita, Krugman and Venables 1999). It does not imply a loss of generality in the equilibrium conditions even if it could be troublesome when implementing static comparative analysis (cf. Neary, 2001).
18. $v_t \equiv \int_t^0 e^{-(r_\tau - r_t)} \pi_\tau d\tau$
19. This feature is a normal artifact of monopolistic competition models à la Dixit-Stiglitz. It would have been more realistic to introduce into the model sources of long-run growth. However, the main objective of the model is to explain the lock-in that prevents IT from being adopted, and not to explain the limits to growth induced by the IT revolution.
20. For more details, see Ciccone and Matsuyama's (1996, p. 43) demonstration.
21. It is noteworthy that if $1 < \varepsilon < \sigma$, the geometric locus described by V does not have a maximum. In this case, the system evolves towards a unique solution.
22. In the case of European regions, this help can be in the form of allocation of EU structural funds for the improvement of IT infrastructures.
23. Note that the number of suppliers n_1 corresponds to $ñ$, that is, the threshold value under which IT inputs are strategic complements.
24. That is, independently of initial conditions.

REFERENCES

Ahn, S. and P. Hemmings (2000), 'Policy influences on economic growth in OECD countries, an evaluation of the evidence', *Discussion Paper Series*, No. 246, Paris: OECD.
Arthur, B. (1990), ' "Silicon Valley" locational clusters: when do increasing returns imply monopoly', *Mathematical Social Science*, 19, 116–31.
Atzeni, G.E. and O.A. Carboni (2004), 'ICT productivity and human capital: the Italian North–South duality', *International Review of Economics and Business*, **51**(2), 265–84.
Baily, M. and R. Laurence (2001), 'Do we have a New Economy?', *American Economic Review, Papers and Proceedings*, **91**(2), 308–12.
Bellone, F. and M.A. Maupertuis (2003), 'Diffusion des technologies de l'information et de la communication et croissance dans les région périphériques', *Economies et Societés*, série **W**(7) 557–87.
Boyer, R. (2001), 'La Nouvelle Économie au Futur Antérieur: histoire, Théorie, Géographie', mimeo, CEPREMAP.
Brynjolfsson, E. and L.M. Hitt (2003), 'Computing productivity: firm-level evidence', *Review of Economics and Statistics*, **85**(4), 793–808.
Ciccone, A. and K. Matsuyama (1996), 'Fixed costs, pecuniary externalities and barriers to economic development', *Journal of Development Economics*, 49, 33–59.
Ciccone, A. and K. Matsuyama (1999), 'Efficieny and equilibrium with dynamic increasing aggregate returns due to demand complementarities', *Econometrica*, **67**(3), 499–528.
Colecchia, A. and P. Schreyer (2002), 'IT investment and economic growth in the 1990s: is the United States a unique case?', *Review of Economic Dynamics*, 5, 408–42.
Crépon, B. and T. Heckel (2001), 'Computerization in France: an evaluation based on individual company data', *Review of Income and Wealth*, **48**(1), 77–98.
Daveri, F. (2002), 'The New Economy in Europe, 1992–2001', *Oxford Review of Economic Policy*, **18**(3), 345–62.
Dixit, A.K. and J.E. Stiglitz (1977), 'Monopolistic competition and optimum product diversity', *American Economic Review*, **67**(3), 297–308.
Ethier, W. (1982), 'National and international returns to scale in the theory of international trade', *American Economic Review*, **72**(3), 386–405.
Fisher, M.M. and B. Johanson (1994), 'Networks for process innovation by firms: conjectures from observations in three countries', in B. Johansson, C. Karlsson and L. Westin. (eds), *Patterns of a Network Economy*, Springer-Verlag, pp. 261–72.
Fujita, M. and N. Hamaguchi (2001), 'Intermediate goods and the spatial structure of an economy', *Regional Science and Urban Economics*, 31, 79–109.
Fujita, M., P. Krugman and A. Venables (1999), *The Spatial Economy, Cities, Regions and International Trade*, Harvard, MA: MIT Press.
Galliano, D. and P. Roux (2003), 'Spatial externalities, organization of the firm and ICT adoption: the specificities of French food firms', coedition of *International Journal of Biotechnology and the International Journal of Technology and Management*, **5**(3/4).
Gordon, R.J. (2000), 'Does the New Economy measure up to the great inventions of the past', *Journal of Economic Perspective*, **14**(4), 49–75.
Jorgenson, D. (2006), 'Information technology and the G7 economies', *Revue de l'OFCE*, Special Issue, *Industrial Dynamics, Productivity and Growth*, 189–216.

Jorgenson, D. and K.J. Stiroh (2000), 'Raising the speed limit: US economic growth in the information age', *Brookings Papers on Economic Activity*, **0**(1), 125–211.

Karlsson, C. (1995), 'Innovation, adoption innovation networks and agglomerations economies', in C.S. Bertuglia, M.M. Fischer and G. Petro (eds), *Technological Change, Economic Development and Space*, Springer, pp. 184–206.

Katz, M.L. and C. Shapiro (1985), 'Network externalities, competition and compatibility', *American Economic Review*, **75**(3), 424–40.

Koski, H., P. Rouvinen and P. Yla-Anttilla (2002), 'IT clusters in Europe: the great central banana and the small Nordic potato', *Information Economics and Policy*, **14**(2), 145–65.

Melchior, A. and V. Oi (2002), *Technology and Market Structure in the Information Technology Industries: Evidence from Norwegian Data*, NUPI report, Oslo.

Neary, P. (2001), 'Of hype and hyperbolas: introducing the New Economic Geography', *Journal of Economic Literature*, **39**(2), 536–61.

Oliner, S.D. and D.E. Sichel (2000), 'The resurgence of growth in the late 1990s: is information technology the story?', *The Journal of Economic Perspectives*, **14**(4), 3–22.

O'Mahony, M. and B. Van Ark (eds) (2003), *EU Productivity and Competitiveness: An Industry Perspective. Can Europe Resume the Catching-up Process?*, Luxembourg: DG Enterprise, European Union.

Oulton, N. (2002), 'ICT and productivity growth in the United Kingdom', *Oxford Review of Economic Policy*, **18**(3), 363–79.

Quah, D. (2000), 'Internet cluster emergence', *CEP Discussion Papers* 0441, Centre for Economic Performance, London School of Economics and Political Science.

Scarpetta, S., S.A. Bassanini, D. Pilat and P. Schreyer (2000), 'Economic growth in the OECD area: recent trends at the aggregate and sectoral level', *OECD Discussion Paper Series*, No. 248, Paris: OECD.

Shapiro, C. and Varian, H.R. (1999), *Economie de l'information*, De Boeck University.

Van Ark, B. (2002), 'Measuring the new economy: an international comparative perspective', *The Review of Income and Wealth*, **48**(1), 1–14.

Whelan, K. (2002), 'Computers, obsolescence, and productivity', *The Review of Economics and Statistics*, **84**(3), 445–61.

PART II

Regional innovation systems, agglomeration economies and knowledge spillovers: empirical studies

5. Pecuniary and knowledge externalities as agglomeration forces: empirical evidence from individual French data

**Corinne Autant-Bernard and
Nadine Massard**

5.1 INTRODUCTION

The two key stylized facts in economic location are the overall unequal geographical distribution of economic activities and their unequal sectoral distribution. The new economic geography singles out three main agglomerating forces: human capital externalities (Marshall [1890] 1971), technological externalities (*knowledge flows that result from non-market interactions*) and externalities based on market interactions (*pecuniary externalities*) (Krugman, 1991).

This chapter aims to propose an econometric model with a unified analytical framework for the traditional agglomerating forces and knowledge externalities, in order to clarify the degree of localization of these phenomena in both geographical and technological space. Specifically, this chapter seeks to expand upon existing empirical results on two levels. First, by introducing knowledge externalities in a production function – more usually applied in relation to pecuniary externalities – and second through the use of individual data.

The following section reviews the basic theories behind location dynamics and localized growth whilst pinpointing the role of pecuniary and knowledge externalities together with the importance of the spatial and sectoral dimensions of these phenomena. In Section 5.3 the econometric model is put forward, as is the data used to assess these phenomena in the French case. In Section 5.4 we will consider the results whilst Section 5.5 concludes the chapter.

5.2 THEORETICAL BACKGROUND

5.2.1 Pecuniary and Knowledge Externalities

Until recently the new economic geography models (Krugman, 1991; Krugman and Venables, 1995; Fujita, Krugman and Venables, 1999) confined themselves to analysing the interplay of imperfect competition, increasing output and pecuniary externalities,[1] largely overlooking any knowledge spillovers. It is only with the crossover between the economic geography models and the endogenous growth models (Englmann and Walz, 1995; Martin and Ottaviano, 1999) that the latter have been taken into account. This synthesis of geography and growth, which combines the traditional agglomeration forces in economic geography models with the phenomena of knowledge externalities, gives an accurate picture of the dynamics of agglomeration and localized growth.

From an empirical point of view however, the assessment of agglomeration forces emanating from these two types of interaction is not unanimously treated by the relevant literature. In their review, Rosenthal and Strange (2005) present a series of estimations that seek to evaluate the importance of the various agglomeration forces found in the economic geography theories. They do note though that these are only separate evaluations where each of the studies is only assessing one or two distinct forces at most. Generally speaking, we can identify a first series of works focusing essentially on pecuniary externalities by means of location models (Mion, 2004) and economic geography models. Such approaches assess the effects of local industrial structures on an agglomeration growth that is studied in terms of employment (Glaeser et al., 1992; Henderson, Kuncoro and Turner, 1995), wages (Lamorgese, 1997) or productivity (Henderson, 2003).

Non-market relationships are better identified in the studies of the 'geography of innovation'.[2] This second approach has the benefit of explicitly taking knowledge externalities into account, by estimating the relationship between the innovation of a whole group of firms in a geographical area and the proximity within this area between the knowledge producers, or the proximity with other areas that are active in both research and innovation. Nevertheless, an analysis of the more traditional determinants in the effects of concentration is often neglected.[3] The economic size of the zone is introduced only as a control or standardization variable, without testing the effects of the economic activities on the agglomeration itself. Consequently, there is no evaluation of the impact of knowledge externalities relative to the more traditional agglomeration determinants.

The first objective of our study therefore, is to estimate a productivity model that allows us to confront the various forces:[4]

H1: The production capability of a firm depends both on the pecuniary externalities and knowledge externalities produced by its environment.

5.2.2 Inside the Black Box of Externalities

The second objective, deriving from the first, is to define the mechanisms supporting these phenomena. As Audretsch and Feldman (2005) point out, two major elements clarify how externalities affect economic geography: these phenomena would be positively affected by the degree of geographical proximity as well as by the level of technological diversity.

Table 5.1 summarizes these basic assumptions presented in the new economic geography models.

Predictions drawn from these models depend on the externality location hypothesis. In the economic geography models, the interdependence between the location of firms and the location of consumers is directly due to the location of pecuniary externalities. Consequently, the presence of a large amount of final and intermediary consumers is an attractive force for firms. This downstream attractive force is enhanced by a force affecting economic agents upstream. By locating close to suppliers, firms can limit the transport cost of inputs. For employees, locating in agglomerations is justified by higher wages and/or more job opportunities. This self-reinforcement in the location of both firms and consumers is therefore directly dependent on the local character of pecuniary externalities. Similarly, in the geography and growth models where spillovers are local, innovation, and hence growth, will be enhanced by the spatial polarization of economic activities. Conversely, if economic agents benefit from externalities carried out locally as well as at a distance, dispersion forces will win and economic activities will be pulled towards dispersion (Baldwin and Forslid, 2000; Baldwin, Martin and Ottaviano, 2001).

Table 5.1 Basic assumptions of the economic geography models

Hypotheses	Pecuniary externalities	Knowledge externalities
Diversity versus specialization	Diversity increases consumers' utility and the number of intermediary goods	Diversity favours innovation
Local versus global externalities	The local dimension explains the agglomeration process	The local dimension explains both the agglomeration process and its impact on growth

Because of these theoretical implications in terms of agglomeration and growth, evaluating the geographical dimension of externalities is a major challenge.

Here is the second set of hypotheses we will attempt to test:

H2a: The effects of pecuniary externalities on the productivity of firms are geographically limited.

H2b: The effects of knowledge externalities on the productivity of firms are geographically limited.

In economic geography models, supported by a Dixit-Stiglitz monopolistic competition framework and a function of a constant elasticity of substitution (CES) utility function, diversity is also an agglomeration factor, either through consumer preference or through available intermediary goods. Geography–growth synthesis models have the same bases – hence a similar focus on the diversity factor. As such, this functions then not only at the level of consumer preferences but also at the level of knowledge externalities because research productivity depends directly on the number of varieties already present in the economy.

In this context, the specialization/diversity debate, initiated by Jacobs, is no longer confined to the role of local structures in growth and moves towards a discussion of the orientation and dynamic efficiency of knowledge flows within or across the borders of industries. Do externalities related to knowledge diffusion tend to develop within a sector between agents with similar abilities (MAR – Marshall-Arrow-Romer – externalities), or between diverse sectors in order to encourage cross-fertilization and to develop new opportunities (Jacobs externalities)? Here is the third set of hypotheses:

H3a: Pecuniary externalities rely on a diversified industrial structure.

H3b: Knowledge externalities rely on a diversified industrial structure.

Until now, the partial nature of the empirical studies has led to an irregular focus on these two dimensions: geographical and sectoral (see Table 5.2). The debate between specialization and diversity has been widely explored for pecuniary externalities. Several studies evaluate the respective roles of location externalities (*intra-sectoral*) and urbanization externalities (*inter-sectoral*), by estimating the effect of local industrial structure on the growth of urban areas. Works assessing pecuniary externalities however, focus purely on the sectoral dimension. The geographically delineated

Table 5.2   Empirical literature on pecuniary and knowledge externalities

Hypotheses	Pecuniary externalities	Knowledge externalities
Diversity versus specialization	Glaeser et al. (1992) Henderson et al. (1995) Lamorgese (1997) Henderson (2003)	Audretsch and Feldman (1999) Greunz (2004) Van der Panne (2004)
Local versus global externalities	Rosenthal and Strange (2001) Henderson (2003)	Jaffe (1989) Jaffe et al. (1993) Feldman (1994) Anselin et al. (1997) Autant-Bernard (2001) Bottazi and Peri (2003) Van der Panne (2004)

nature of these phenomena is postulated as only the internal characteristics of a zone, deemed pertinent a priori, are considered. Only Henderson (2003) and Rosenthal and Strange (2001) provide an evaluation through the productivity survey of a panel of firms. Both studies remark that the effects of neighbouring employment impact positively on the firm productivity and that this impact decreases rapidly with distance, confirming the hypothesis of the location of externalities.

By contrast, in the perspective of the geography of innovation, empirical studies on knowledge externalities have primarily focused on the spatial dimension.[5] The sectoral dimension however, is usually considered as secondary and is not the subject of an evaluation. The sectoral scope of spillovers is postulated,[6] based on the supposition that in the majority of cases the effects of public research have a wider sectoral spread when compared with the effects of private research. Hence, we still have only very little evidence of the impact of diversity on knowledge spillovers. The first attempts to understand whether or not the industrial structure shapes innovation appeared only recently (Audretsch and Feldman, 1999; Greunz, 2004; Van der Panne, 2004).

Consequently, there are as few elements available in the geographical dimension of pecuniary externalities as there are in the sectoral dimension of knowledge externalities. Only Van der Panne's (2004) recent study allows a simultaneous testing of both the geographical and sectoral scope of knowledge spillovers, while only Henderson (2003) evaluates both the geographical and the sectoral scope of pecuniary externalities. No joint evaluation of each of the four hypotheses mentioned in Table 5.1 is available. The geographical and sectoral scope of pecuniary and knowledge externalities is therefore hardly studied. Now, these are central hypotheses in economic geography models; a unified framework, bringing all these dimensions together is therefore required.

5.3 MODEL AND DATA

5.3.1 The Model

The equation tested is a Griliches (1979)[7] production function.[8] The output of firm i is linked both to its traditional production factors, capital (K) and labour (L), but also to the internal R&D (RD_i), and to the spillovers stemming from the features of its local environment (Z):

$$Q_i = \alpha + \beta_1 K_i + \beta_2 L_i + \beta_3 RD_i + \beta_4 Z + \varepsilon_i \tag{5.1}$$

where α designates the constant term and ε_i a random disturbance. The model is specified in logarithms.

Local features comprise factors likely to generate pecuniary externalities: the number of firms already present locally and the size of the employment market; there is also a measure of knowledge externalities through the intensity of private research in establishments located close by. Many authors notice that specifying pecuniary externalities by way of numbering either the plants or the employees can be misleading. Actually these variables are also likely to reflect knowledge externalities circulating, for instance, through skilled workers. By adding R&D variables we wish to clearly distinguish specific knowledge phenomena even if the other variables can not easily isolate the pecuniary externalities.

This first model specification corresponds to hypothesis H1. Estimations of this model will enable a preliminary evaluation of the relative weight of pecuniary and knowledge externalities.

The second specification considered seeks to account for the impact of distance on such externality phenomena. To do this, the features of the local environment are measured according to different geographical levels: the knowledge produced within the agglomeration (here, the French *département*) and the knowledge produced on the periphery of the agglomeration:

$$Q_i = \alpha + \beta_1 K_i + \beta_2 L_i + \beta_3 RD_i + \beta_4 Z + \beta_5 WZ + \varepsilon_i \tag{5.2}$$

where W is a contiguity matrix of order n. Spatial econometric techniques (Anselin's tests [1988] for spatial auto-correlation) will enable us to determine the pertinent geographical level to define the periphery (contiguity of order 1 or higher).

Finally, the third specification will allow us to test the sectoral dimension of these phenomena of externalities. The latter is estimated by distinguishing for each local characteristic, those phenomena that derive from the same sector as the firm i under consideration, and which derive from all the other sectors put together:

$$Q_i = \alpha + \beta_1 K_i + \beta_2 L_i + \beta_3 RD_i + \beta_4 Z_s + \beta_5 \sum_k Z_k + \varepsilon_i \qquad (5.3)$$

where s designates the industry to which company i belongs and k all the other industries present locally. The aim is to provide an estimation of the role of intersectoral exchanges by distinguishing whether they are a source of pecuniary externalities and a means of weakening the competition weight, or sources of knowledge externalities improving the innovation capacity.

5.3.2 The Data

The study relies on the cross-mapping of two national surveys: the French Annual Company Survey (EAE) produced jointly by the Ministry of Industry and INSEE (the French Central Statistical Office), and the R&D survey by the French Ministry of Research. Both surveys are available at plant level. The EAE data used to estimate a Griliches production function however, is only collected at firm level and is not available for plants, whereas studying the geographical dimension requires a view at plant level. Estimations have therefore been carried out as a first approach on firms with just one plant.[9]

The incidence of this restriction in terms of geographical and sectoral distribution seems fairly minimal, as the sample's regional and sectoral proportions were obviously those observed for all establishments carrying out research (see Tables 5.3 and 5.4). The bias would seem greater in terms of size. The employed workforce for all establishments carrying out research is 1179 compared with just 412 in our sample. Apart from this bias in terms of size of the establishments studied, restricting oneself to single-plant firms would probably lead to over-estimation of the role of the geographical dimension. In fact Henderson (2003) does point out that single-plant enterprises rely more heavily on local resources than those establishments belonging to groups.

This cross-mapping produced a sample of 822 firms with their sales, workforce, purchases of raw materials and intermediary consumptions and their internal R&D expenditure (IRDE). The sales, workforce and

Table 5.3 Plant distribution by region

Region	Selected Sample (%)	Total Sample (%)
Ile-de-France	19.23	23.28
Champagne-Ardenne	2.55	2.66
Picardie	3.28	5.20
Haute-Normandie	2.92	3.99
Centre	4.99	5.78
Basse-Normandie	0.61	1.27
Bourgogne	3.77	4.10
Nord-Pas-de-Calais	7.55	5.43
Lorraine	3.65	2.77
Alsace	6.08	3.99
Franche-Comté	2.43	2.14
Pays de la Loire	5.11	4.04
Bretagne	3.16	2.66
Poitou-Charentes	1.82	2.14
Aquitaine	2.80	3.00
Midi-Pyrénées	3.77	3.58
Limousin	1.34	0.98
Rhône-Alpes	18.74	15.42
Auvergne	1.70	1.56
Languedoc-Roussillon	1.09	1.79
Provence-Alpes – Côte d'Azur	3.41	4.22
Total	100	100

purchases were taken from 1999. R&D is the combined IRDE figure for 1997 and 1998.

The local environment features are measured according to the three following variables: the number of companies present locally (*PLANT*), the number of employees present locally as a proxy of the labour market size but also of the final demand (*EMPL*), and the local knowledge production intensity, measured by other companies' R&D expenditure (*RD*). The full set of variables used is summarized in Table 5.5. Descriptive statistics (for the sample of 822 observations) are included in Table 5.6.[10]

In order to evaluate the impact of distance on knowledge and pecuniary externalities, these variables are measured for two geographic scales. The first level is the *département* (NUTS 3)[11] and the second is given by the bordering *départements*[12] (*W* is thus the first order contiguity matrix).

Table 5.4 Plant distribution by industry

Industry	Selected Sample (%)	Total Sample (%)
Agriculture	0	0.06
Food	0	0
Energy (including mining)	0.49	2.02
Other mining and metallurgy	2.07	4.04
Textile, clothes	3.65	3.06
Wood, paper, cardboard	3.04	2.37
Chemicals	12.41	15.08
Pharmaceuticals	5.60	7.68
Rubber, plastics	5.47	5.31
Glass	0.97	1.21
Building materials and ceramics	1.58	2.48
Metal working	8.03	6.18
Machines and electrical equipment	20.31	14.79
Office and data processing machines	1.95	1.44
Electricity	8.15	8.43
Radio, TV and communications equipment	4.50	6.59
Instruments	12.17	8.90
Automobiles	4.50	4.51
Shipbuilding	1.22	1.44
Aerospace	1.22	2.95
Building and civil engineering	0.12	0.12
Transport and communication	0	0
Computer services	0.12	0.06
Engineering services	0.24	0.12
Total	100	100

This gives us individual data, which is a step forward particularly in the assessment of the geographical dimension of externalities. Indeed, a major problem with most studies in this field comes from the geographical level of observations. The unit is the metropolitan area or county for the United States and the region (NUTS 2 or 3) in Europe. By focusing on an aggregated level, these studies are limited by the administrative segmentation of a geographical scale, which is often quite large, and therefore fail to quantify the spillovers enjoyed by each of these firms. Indeed they are measuring inter-agglomeration spillovers, whereas the major factors lie undoubtedly in the relationship between the firm and the agglomeration it belongs to.

Table 5.5 List of variables

Name	Definition
SALES	Dependent variable: SALES
LABOUR	Employed workforce at the company
CAPITAL	Purchases of goods, raw materials and other supplies
IRDE	Firm's internal R&D expenditure
PLANT	Number of firms in the same sector present in the *département*
PLANTK	No. of firms from other sectors present in the *département*
W1PLANT	No. of firms from the same sector present in neighbouring *départements*
W1PLANTK	No. of firms from other sectors present in neighbouring *départements*
EMPL	No. of employees in the sector in the *département*
EMPLK	No. of employees from other sectors in the *département*
W1EMPL	No. of employees in the sector in neighbouring *départements*
W1EMPLK	No. of employees from other sectors in neighbouring *départements*
RD	R&D expenditure in the sector by other firms in the *département*
RDK	R&D expenditure in other sectors by other firms in the *département*
W1RD	R&D expenditure in the sector by firms in neighbouring *départements*
W1RDK	R&D expenditure in other sectors by firms in neighbouring *départements*

5.4 RESULTS

The results of the estimations obtained on this basis are given in the three tables that follow. Table 5.7 presents the estimated coefficients for equation (5.1) and provide Lagrange multiplier (LM) tests for spatial dependence. Table 5.8 estimates different specifications of equation (5.2), focusing on the industry to which each plant belongs. It gives information about location economies. Table 5.9 introduces the sectoral dimension as specified in equation (5.3). It allows us to consider urbanization economies. In each case, we use robust OLS estimations. As we suspected problems of multicollinearity, we systematically computed the mean of variance inflation factors (VIF).

Table 5.6 Descriptives statistics

	Mean	Std-error	Minimum	Maximum	No. of Obs.
Ln(SALES)	12.16	1.29	8.88	17.06	822
Ln(CAPITAL)	11.02	1.69	0.00	16.17	822
Ln(LABOUR)	5.29	1.14	2.94	10.26	822
Ln(IRDE)	9.39	1.16	6.21	15.12	822
Ln(RD)	11.65	1.74	6.95	15.92	822
Ln(RDK)	14.49	1.50	10.14	17.57	822
Ln(EMPL)	7.98	1.16	0.00	10.16	822
Ln(EMPLK)	10.58	0.80	7.38	11.97	822
Ln(PLANT)	3.66	1.03	0.00	6.13	822
Ln(PLANTK)	6.33	0.73	3.91	7.93	822
Ln(WIRD)	12.54	2.25	0.00	16.65	822
Ln(WIRDK)	15.92	1.34	12.97	18.32	822
Ln(WIEMPL)	9.10	1.17	0.00	10.85	822
Ln(WIEMPLK)	11.91	0.74	9.08	12.98	822
Ln(WIPLANT)	4.80	1.12	0.00	7.18	822
Ln(WIPLANTK)	7.69	0.67	5.68	8.85	822

5.4.1 Pecuniary and Knowledge Externalities as Location Economies

Columns (1) and (2) present the results concerning the variables internal to the company. They allow us to observe the positive and significant impact of the labour and capital factors. R&D expenditure from the firm also has a positive and significant effect on the sales. The estimated elasticity indicates that a 1 per cent rise in the R&D expenditure leads to a 0.13 per cent rise in the total sales of the company. Such a result is consistent with most analyses in that field (Mairesse and Sassenou, 1991).

A significant spatial autocorrelation of the errors appears however. So, it would seem that the production of a firm is not independent from that of other firms situated in the same area. Such a spatial dependence proves the existence of pecuniary and/or knowledge externalities between firms.

In column (3), variables external to the firm are introduced. Thus the spatial autocorrelation internal to the *département* disappears. Moreover, the LM-ERRW1 test shows that there is no spatial autocorrelation in the error terms beyond the immediate vicinity. Taking into account the characteristics of the *département* therefore seems sufficient to address the problem of the spatial autocorrelation in the perturbation.

We also introduced sectoral dummies in order to take into account the heterogeneity of the industrial sectors. As indicated through the LR-test (1), these variables are jointly significant. More specifically, we notice the

Table 5.7 Pecuniary and knowledge externalities as location economies

Variables	(1)	(2)	(3)
Constant	4.60*	4.33*	4.16*
	(0.23)	(0.21)	(0.21)
Ln(LABOUR)	0.68*	0.67*	0.67*
	(0.05)	(0.05)	(0.05)
Ln(CAPITAL)	0.26*	0.26*	0.26*
	(0.04)	(0.04)	(0.04)
Ln(IRDE)	0.11*	0.13*	0.12*
	(0.02)	(0.02)	(0.02)
Ln(PLANT)	–	–	0.89^{E-01}*
			(0.25^{E-01})
Ln(EMPL)	–	–	-0.24^{E-03}
			(0.21^{E-01})
Ln(RD)	–	–	0.13^{E-02}
			(0.12^{E-01})
Sectoral dummies	No	Yes	Yes
R^2	0.900	0.920	0.923
Adjusted R^2	0.899	0.918	0.921
LnL	−429.03	−334.91	−317.21
AIC	1.054	0.876	0.840
LR-test (1)	–	188.24*	193.42*
LR-test (2)	–	–	35.40*
Obs.	822	822	822
LM-ERRW0	35.77*	23.55*	1.87
LM-ERRW1	–	–	0.17

Notes:
Dependent variable: log(*SALES*). Robust OLS estimations.
* Significant at 1% level. Numbers in brackets are standard errors.
LR-test (1) indicates whether the sectoral dummies are significant or not.
LR-test (2) indicates whether the external variables are jointly significant or not.
LM-ERR indicates when spatial dependence is observed in the error term. W0 is a weight matrix that takes the value 1 if firms are localized in the same *département* and 0 where otherwise. W1 is a weight matrix that takes the value 1 if firms are localized in contiguous *départements* and 0 where otherwise.

significant positive effect of sectors such as chemicals, pharmaceuticals, the glass industry, building and civil engineering, whereas the machines and electrical equipment sector reveals a systematic negative effect.

It is however, necessary to analyse these first results intensively, on the one hand by estimating more precisely the spatial dimension of these location economies and, on the other, by introducing the possibility of urbanization economies based on the variety of the industrial and technological tissue.

5.4.2 The Spatial Dimension of Location Economies

Evidence of a high correlation between the variables relative to the local characteristics is revealed by the VIF indicator. Indeed, the VIF mean is about 7.91, which is much higher than 3, the value above which it is traditionally considered that multicollinearity can raise problems. This has led us to test several specifications and to calculate for each of them the global significance of the external variables introduced. Table 5.8 then, indicates the LR-test value that has the benefit of being less sensitive to the multicollinearity problem than the 'Student's t-test'.

Estimation (1) evaluates the effect of neighbouring firms. The results are very close to Henderson's estimations (2003). The productive activity of one firm is enhanced by its location in an area where there are many firms in the same industry. The estimated parameters are not far from those obtained when using American data. Henderson observes a coefficient of 0.13 for the nearest periphery (the county), and a coefficient of 0.04 for farther plants (located in the remainder of the metropolitan area). Here, the elasticity of production relative to the local number of plants is 0.08 for the nearest periphery and 0.04 for more distant areas respectively. Consequently, the spatial dimension highlighted by Henderson for such externalities is confirmed.

The second estimation (column 2) evaluates the home market effect, approximated by the number of workers. This effect is significant at the *département* scale. At a distance, the parameter is 10 per cent significant only, which prevents any definite conclusion concerning the impact of workers on a scale larger than the *département*. Again, this tends to validate the hypothesis of a local diffusion of pecuniary externalities (H2a validated).

Knowledge externalities are introduced in the third estimation. R&D carried out in a specific area enhances the production of local plants (with an elasticity of 0.03 inside that area). The impact of distance seems quite strong since outside R&D expenditure is not significant. This confirms the results obtained by the American and European studies on the 'geography of innovation'[13] and supports H2b. It also supports the idea that the effects of proximity differ depending on the nature of the externalities (with a stronger geographical effect for knowledge externalities).

In order to evaluate the relative effect of each of these forces, estimations (4) to (6) bring together these different features of the industrial environment. The results highlight the strong predominance of agglomeration effects due to proximity between plants. The presence of other plants is the main attraction force. This latter, once accounted for the local R&D and the number of workers are no longer significant.

Table 5.8 The geographical dimension of the location economies

Variables	(1)	(2)	(3)	(4)	(5)	(6)
Constant	4.06***	3.79***	3.99***	4.23***	4.11***	4.23***
	(0.20)	(0.22)	(0.22)	(0.25)	(0.22)	(0.25)
Ln($LABOUR$)	0.67***	0.68***	0.68***	0.67***	0.67***	0.67***
	(0.04)	(0.04)	(0.05)	(0.05)	(0.04)	(0.04)
Ln($CAPITAL$)	0.26***	0.26***	0.26***	0.26***	0.26***	0.26***
	(0.04)	(0.04)	(0.04)	(0.04)	(0.04)	(0.04)
Ln($IRDE$)	0.12***	0.12***	0.11***	0.12***	0.12***	0.12***
	(0.02)	(0.02)	(0.02)	(0.02)	(0.02)	(0.02)
Ln($PLANT$)	0.78^{E-01}***	–	–	0.75^{E-01}***	0.79^{E-01}***	0.75^{E-01}***
	(0.16^{E-01})			(0.26^{E-01})	(0.20^{E-01})	(0.26^{E-01})
Ln($W1PLANT$)	0.37^{E-01}**	–	–	0.82^{E-01}**	0.47^{E-01}**	0.82^{E-01}**
	(0.17^{E-01})			(0.41^{E-01})	(0.23^{E-01})	(0.41^{E-01})
Ln($EMPL$)	–	0.55^{E-01}***	–	0.45^{E-02}	–	0.68^{E-02}
		(0.13^{E-01})		(0.21^{E-01})		(0.22^{E-01})
Ln($W1EMPL$)	–	0.26^{E-01}*	–	–0.41^{E-01}	–	–0.39^{E-01}
		(0.15^{E-01})		(0.35^{E-01})		(0.38^{E-01})
Ln(RD)	–	–	0.31^{E-01}***	–	–0.20^{E-02}	–0.28^{E-02}
			(0.09^{E-01})		(0.11^{E-01})	(0.12^{E-01})
Ln($W1RD$)	–	–	0.10^{E-01}	–	–0.58^{E-02}	–0.12^{E-02}
			(0.06^{E-01})		(0.91^{E-02})	(0.95^{E-02})
Sectoral dummies	Yes	Yes	Yes	Yes	Yes	Yes
R^2	0.924	0.923	0.922	0.924	0.924	0.924
Adjusted R^2	0.921	0.920	0.919	0.921	0.921	0.921
LnL	–314.69	–319.97	–326.26	–314.03	–314.47	–314.00

AIC	0.831	0.844	0.860	0.835	0.836	0.839
LR-test (1)	206.98***	204.44***	185.90***	209.54***	200.50***	198.76***
LR-test (2)	40.42***	29.86***	17.28***	41.74***	40.86***	41.80***
Obs.	822	822	822	822	822	822
LM-ERRW0	–	–	–	–	–	0.64
LM-ERRW1	–	–	–	–	–	0.65

Notes:
Dependent variable: log(*SALES*). Robust OLS estimations.
* Significant at 10% level; ** significant at 5% level; *** significant at 1% level. Numbers in brackets are standard errors.
LR-test (1) indicates whether the sectoral dummies are significant or not.
LR-test (2) indicates whether the external variables are jointly significant or not.
Multicollinearity diagnostic: Mean VIF = 7.91.
LM-ERR indicates when spatial dependence is observed in the error term. W0 is a weight matrix that takes the value 1 if firms are localized in the same *département* and 0 where otherwise. W1 is a weight matrix that takes the value 1 if firms are localized in contiguous *départements* and 0 where otherwise.

For the workers, such a result is not surprising. This variable accounts for the positive externalities associated with both a large labour market (Marshall [1890] 1971), and a wide final goods market. Whereas there is very little doubt concerning the local dimension of the labour market, the local dimension of demand, on the other hand, is much more dubious.

The absence of influence due to local R&D is more confusing. It means that the main agglomeration force relies on the presence of other plants, whatever their R&D spending. If knowledge spillovers occur, they result from productive activities rather than from specific means devoted to knowledge production.

Moreover, the local dimension seems less obvious than in our original estimation (1). The confidence interval is higher for the number of plants in the bordering areas, but the parameter is no different from that of the plants localized within the area. Conclusions drawn from studies made separately to test the hypotheses of the economic geography or the geography and growth models should be considered carefully. By focusing on so few specific effects, these works neglect other attraction forces. The effects highlighted by these studies are likely to result from underlying forces, omitted in the models estimated previously. In particular, in the 'geography of innovation' studies, we can guess that the weight of R&D in the knowledge production function would perhaps be significantly lower if the presence of local firms were accounted for together with the presence of local R&D activities.

5.4.3 Urbanization Economies

A second important issue concerns the sectoral dimension of the externalities governing agglomeration. As mentioned above, economic geography models assume that Jacobs externalities occur, stemming from the variety of local goods. Tables 5.9 and 5.10 focus on such urbanization economies by introducing the variables observed for other industries together with the spatial dimension.[14]

The local dimension of each of these externalities is supported by the coefficients of the variables relative to neighbouring areas: none of them are significant. Only the variables internal to the *département* have a positive impact. We must however, be very careful on this point since on the scale of the neighbouring *départements*, the variables characterizing the industry to which the plant belongs and the variables characterizing all the other industries display very high levels of correlation.

Compared with the estimations of Table 5.7, the current results allow us to pinpoint the impact of either the specialization or the diversity of the local industrial structure. For pecuniary externalities, the sectoral dimension seems to depend on the sources of the externalities. The number of

Table 5.9 Urbanization economies

Variables	(1)	(2)	(3)	(4)	(5)	(6)
Constant	3.98***	3.35***	3.56***	4.05***	3.90***	3.87***
	(0.28)	(0.26)	(0.25)	(0.35)	(0.31)	(0.39)
Ln(LABOUR)	0.67***	0.67***	0.68***	0.67***	0.68***	0.67***
	(0.04)	(0.04)	(0.05)	(0.05)	(0.04)	(0.05)
Ln(CAPITAL)	0.26***	0.26***	0.26***	0.26***	0.26***	0.26***
	(0.04)	(0.04)	(0.04)	(0.04)	(0.04)	(0.04)
Ln(IRDE)	0.12***	0.12***	0.11***	0.12***	0.12***	0.12***
	(0.02)	(0.02)	(0.02)	(0.02)	(0.02)	(0.02)
Ln(PLANT)	0.65$^{\text{E-01}}$**	–	–	0.60$^{\text{E-01}}$	0.66$^{\text{E-01}}$**	0.61$^{\text{E-01}}$
	(0.26$^{\text{E-01}}$)			(0.38$^{\text{E-01}}$)	(0.31$^{\text{E-01}}$)	(0.39$^{\text{E-01}}$)
Ln(PLANTK)	0.19$^{\text{E-01}}$	–	–	−0.61$^{\text{E-01}}$	0.19$^{\text{E-01}}$	−0.84$^{\text{E-01}}$
	(0.31$^{\text{E-01}}$)			(0.69$^{\text{E-01}}$)	(0.36$^{\text{E-01}}$)	(0.69$^{\text{E-01}}$)
Ln(EMPL)	–	0.31$^{\text{E-01}}$*	–	0.16$^{\text{E-02}}$	–	0.81$^{\text{E-02}}$
		(0.13$^{\text{E-01}}$)		(0.21$^{\text{E-01}}$)		(0.24$^{\text{E-01}}$)
Ln(EMPLK)	–	0.51$^{\text{E-01}}$**	–	0.84$^{\text{E-01}}$	–	0.13$^{\text{E-01}}$*
		(0.22$^{\text{E-01}}$)		(0.64$^{\text{E-01}}$)		(0.69$^{\text{E-01}}$)
Ln(RD)	–	–	0.11$^{\text{E-01}}$	–	−0.52$^{\text{E-02}}$	−0.72$^{\text{E-02}}$
			(0.10$^{\text{E-01}}$)		(0.11$^{\text{E-01}}$)	(0.13$^{\text{E-01}}$)
Ln(RDK)	–	–	0.32$^{\text{E-01}}$***	–	0.64$^{\text{E-02}}$	−0.13$^{\text{E-01}}$
			(0.10$^{\text{E-01}}$)		(0.16$^{\text{E-01}}$)	(0.17$^{\text{E-01}}$)
Sectoral dummies	Yes	Yes	Yes	Yes	Yes	Yes
R^2	0.924	0.923	0.923	0.924	0.924	0.924
Adjusted R^2	0.921	0.920	0.920	0.921	0.921	0.921
LnL	−316.88	−317.78	−321.81	−315.77	−316.36	−319.90

Table 5.9 (continued)

Variables	(1)	(2)	(3)	(4)	(5)	(6)
AIC	0.837	0.839	0.849	0.839	0.840	0.843
LR-test (1)	191.02***	188.42***	185.68***	190.26***	188.52***	176.78***
LR-test (2)	36.04***	34.24***	26.18***	38.26***	37.08***	30.00***
Obs.	822	822	822	822	822	822
LM-ERRW0	–	–	–	–	–	0.31
LM-ERRW1	–	–	–	–	–	0.22

Notes:
Dependent variable: log(*SALES*). Robust OLS estimations.
* Significant at 10% level; ** significant at 5% level; *** significant at 1% level. Numbers in brackets are standard errors.
LR-test (1) indicates whether the sectoral dummies are significant or not.
LR-test (2) indicates whether the external variables are jointly significant or not.
Multicollinearity diagnostic: Mean VIF = 7.56.
LM-ERR indicates when spatial dependence is observed in the error term. W0 is a weight matrix that takes the value 1 if firms are localized in the same *département* and 0 where otherwise. W1 is a weight matrix that takes the value 1 if firms are localized in contiguous *départements* and 0 where otherwise.

Table 5.10 Urbanization and location economies

Variables	(1)	(2)	(3)	(4)	(5)	(6)
Constant	3.98***	3.35***	3.56***	4.05***	3.90***	3.87***
	(0.28)	(0.26)	(0.25)	(0.35)	(0.31)	(0.39)
Ln(LABOUR)	0.67***	0.67***	0.68***	0.67***	0.68***	0.67***
	(0.04)	(0.04)	(0.05)	(0.05)	(0.04)	(0.05)
Ln(CAPITAL)	0.26***	0.26***	0.26***	0.26***	0.26***	0.26***
	(0.04)	(0.04)	(0.04)	(0.04)	(0.04)	(0.04)
Ln(IRDE)	0.12***	0.12***	0.11***	0.12***	0.12***	0.12***
	(0.02)	(0.02)	(0.02)	(0.02)	(0.02)	(0.02)
Ln(PLANT)	$0.65^{\text{E-01}}$**			$0.60^{\text{E-01}}$	$0.66^{\text{E-01}}$**	$0.61^{\text{E-01}}$
	$(0.26^{\text{E-01}})$			$(0.38^{\text{E-01}})$	$(0.31^{\text{E-01}})$	$(0.39^{\text{E-01}})$
Ln(W1PLANT)	$0.36^{\text{E-01}}$			$0.96^{\text{E-01}}$	$0.41^{\text{E-01}}$	$0.73^{\text{E-01}}$
	$(0.41^{\text{E-01}})$			$(0.59^{\text{E-01}})$	$(0.44^{\text{E-01}})$	$(0.61^{\text{E-01}})$
Ln(PLANTK)	$0.19^{\text{E-01}}$			$-0.61^{\text{E-01}}$	$0.19^{\text{E-01}}$	$-0.84^{\text{E-01}}$
	$(0.31^{\text{E-01}})$			$(0.69^{\text{E-01}})$	$(0.36^{\text{E-01}})$	$(0.69^{\text{E-01}})$
Ln(W1PLANTK)	$0.69^{\text{E-03}}$			$0.23^{\text{E-01}}$	$-0.40^{\text{E-01}}$	$0.17^{\text{E-01}}$
	$(0.49^{\text{E-01}})$			(0.11)	$(0.56^{\text{E-01}})$	(0.12)
Ln(EMPL)		$0.31^{\text{E-01}}$*		$0.16^{\text{E-02}}$		$0.81^{\text{E-02}}$
		$(0.13^{\text{E-01}})$		$(0.21^{\text{E-01}})$		$(0.24^{\text{E-01}})$
Ln(W1EMPL)		$0.92^{\text{E-02}}$		$-0.46^{\text{E-01}}$		$-0.34^{\text{E-01}}$
		$(0.24^{\text{E-01}})$		$(0.36^{\text{E-01}})$		$(0.40^{\text{E-01}})$
Ln(EMPLK)		$0.51^{\text{E-01}}$**		$0.84^{\text{E-01}}$		$0.13^{\text{E-01}}$*
		$(0.22^{\text{E-01}})$		$(0.64^{\text{E-01}})$		$(0.69^{\text{E-01}})$
Ln(W1EMPLK)		$0.19^{\text{E-01}}$		$-0.40^{\text{E-01}}$		$-0.91^{\text{E-01}}$
		$(0.28^{\text{E-01}})$		$(0.87^{\text{E-01}})$		$(0.95^{\text{E-01}})$
Ln(RD)			$0.11^{\text{E-01}}$		$-0.52^{\text{E-02}}$	$-0.72^{\text{E-02}}$
			$(0.10^{\text{E-01}})$		$(0.11^{\text{E-01}})$	$(0.13^{\text{E-01}})$

Table 5.10 (continued)

Variables	(1)	(2)	(3)	(4)	(5)	(6)
Ln($W1RD$)	–	–	-0.16^{E-02}	–	-0.77^{E-02}	-0.41^{E-02}
			(0.86^{E-02})		(0.93^{E-02})	(0.10^{E-01})
Ln(RDK)	–	–	0.32^{E-01}***	–	0.64^{E-02}	-0.13^{E-01}
			(0.10^{E-01})		(0.16^{E-01})	(0.17^{E-01})
Ln($W1RDK$)	–	–	0.21^{E-01}	–	0.26^{E-01}	0.48^{E-01}**
			(0.13^{E-01})		(0.22^{E-01})	(0.23^{E-01})
Sectoral dummies	Yes	Yes	Yes	Yes	Yes	Yes
R^2	0.924	0.924	0.923	0.924	0.924	0.925
Adjusted R^2	0.921	0.921	0.920	0.921	0.921	0.921
LnL	-314.48	-316.51	-320.07	-312.60	-313.29	-310.87
AIC	0.836	0.841	0.849	0.841	0.843	0.846
LR-test (1)	193.32***	190.68***	188.44***	190.80***	192.46***	187.08***
LR-test (2)	40.84***	36.78***	29.66***	44.60***	43.22***	48.06***
Obs.	822	822	822	822	822	822
LM-ERRW0	–	–	–	–	–	0.001
LM-ERRW1	–	–	–	–	–	1.076

Notes:
Dependent variable: log($SALES$). Robust OLS estimations
* Significant at 10% level; ** significant at 5% level; *** significant at 1% level. Numbers in brackets are standard errors.
LR-test (1) indicates whether the sectoral dummies are significant or not.
LR-test (2) indicates whether the external variables are jointly significant or not.
Multicollinearity diagnostic: Mean VIF = 14.41.
LM-ERR indicates when spatial dependence is observed in the error term. W0 is a weight matrix that takes the value 1 if firms are localized in the same *département* and 0 where otherwise. W1 is a weight matrix that takes the value 1 if firms are localized in contiguous *départements* and 0 where otherwise.

plants is significant only when considering the industry to which the plant belongs, whereas the number of workers in the other industries has a stronger effect than the number of workers in this specific industry. This result is almost intuitive. Pecuniary externalities between firms require market relationships such as supplier–customer interactions. It is not surprising that they mainly implicate firms belonging to the same industry. The externalities stemming from the local labour market or from the size of the final goods market are more diffused across the various industries. Even if externalities associated to the labour market may partly result from specific skills, they seem to be dominated by the global dynamism of this market (H3a is partly validated).

The analysis of knowledge spillovers (column 3) also indicates the importance of diversity as a source of economic agglomeration (H3b validated). Indeed, when introducing the local R&D carried out in other industries (RDK), the R&D carried out in this specific industry (RD) becomes insignificant. This reinforces the results previously obtained in the French case (Autant-Bernard, 2003). Cross-fertilization effects tend to prevail over intra-industrial knowledge flows. Competition effects between R&D plants in the same field may explain this result. The specification used here does not allow it to be tested.

5.5 CONCLUSION

The concentration of economic activities may result from a better performing labour market, from better access to suppliers or from a wider goods and services market, but also from the presence of knowledge externalities. Empirical studies are even less likely to quantify the different forces at play. Without claiming to quantify each of these forces, this chapter seeks to identify some of the mechanisms behind economic activity agglomeration effects. Namely three potential sources of externalities are analysed: pecuniary externalities resulting from location close to other firms, pecuniary externalities related to the labour market and to the local area for the market in final goods and lastly, knowledge externalities associated with R&D spillovers. We aim to submit an evaluation of the geographical and sectoral dimensions in each case.

Our preliminary results indicate that the proximity to other firms in the sector would be an overwhelmingly attractive force. The conclusions from the 'geography of innovation' studies on knowledge externalities are questioned when the estimations combine variables representing pecuniary externalities alongside R&D variables. It is also possible to identify some elements concerning the highly variable degrees of specialization or diversity in agglomerations. Our preliminary results seem to indicate not a superiority of one over the other, but rather diverse assets produced by these two types of industrial structures: whereas specialization would favour pecuniary externalities originating from the proximity to other firms, diversity would facilitate knowledge externalities and pecuniary externalities emanating from the labour market and from the proximity to final consumers. The tension between these forces may explain the co-existence of specialized towns alongside diversified areas.

In spite of these encouraging results, this study is only a first stage in the evaluation of the different forces driving the dynamics of agglomeration. Several points need to be improved upon, concerning both the data and the model specification.

First, the current sample excludes firms with several plants, which may lead us to overestimate the impact of the local dimension. Henderson (2003) observes that single-plant firms are more reliant on local resources than corporate plants. Such a restriction corresponded to an initial phase in our study. The objective is to broaden the sample to multi-plant firms carrying out research. The bias related to the focus on single-plant firms can then be assessed, by contrasting our current results with those obtained by allocating to each plant, according to its size, a share of the firm sales and capital.

Second, the results reached from this sample bring out multicollinearity and show potential endogeneity problems. The number of plants, employees, or research laboratories in a given geographical area probably varies according to local wages, property costs, tax levels, infrastructure and so on. These local specificities may also explain the different production and productivity levels between plants. Such mechanisms may generate endogeneity in our model. Since several years of surveys are available for both the EAE and the R&D survey, a new version will use this panel data. This will enable us to increase the number of observations and also to better distinguish the effect of each of the local characteristics as well as to use the GMM (generalized method of moments), as proposed by Henderson (2003), to address the endogeneity issue.

Finally, by focusing on the incidence of the current local industrial environment, this chapter deals with static externalities. The analysis should be extended to dynamic externalities, in order to study how transformations in the economic structures impact on production. The introduction of the temporal dimension is also crucial in order to account for the evolution of the location strategy throughout the industrial life cycle. Since the need for specialization or diversity can change during the industrial life cycle (Duranton and Puga, 2001), the nature of the agglomeration forces is also likely to differ through time.[15]

NOTES

1. See Ottaviano and Thisse (2005) for a review.
2. See Audretsch and Feldman (2005) for a review.
3. Indeed, these works are drawn from technological change theories more than from economic geography models. So their intention is not to take agglomeration phenomena as a whole into account.
4. Apparently there is only one study of this type in existence at the moment: Rigby and Essletzbichler (2002) estimate a productivity model on the basis of individual data permitting the confrontation of three Marshall agglomeration forces ('labour market pooling', 'pecuniary externalities' and 'knowledge externalities'). They consider that these three agglomeration forces have empirical foundations.
5. Considerable progress has been made in this field. Tested initially using a geographical coincidence index (Jaffe, 1989), today the geographical extent of knowledge spillovers is the subject of a far more accurate evaluation by virtue of contrasting different influential geographical levels through use of spatial econometric tools.
6. Some attempted evaluations of sectoral dimension of knowledge spillovers are worthy of mention within this framework. Both Autant-Bernard's (2001) study of the French case and Bottazzi and Peri's (2003) of the European case, estimate knowledge production functions incorporating an indicator of technological proximity. Autant-Bernard (2003) also confronts more explicitly the effect of spillovers emanating from the same sector and those emanating from others.
7. Though studies in the economics of innovation testing a knowledge production function, refer explicitly to Griliches' analysis, this is only a partial basis, as they consider aggregated data and do not directly introduce traditional production factors.
8. This method, envisaged by Anselin, Varga and Acs (1997), Autant-Bernard (2001) or Bottazzi and Peri (2003), does indeed seem preferable to that initially suggested by Jaffe (1989), which was founded on a geographic coincidence indicator. It enables a more rigorous analysis of geographical knowledge externalities. With Jaffe's method, one studies the effect of the spatial research *concentration* within a state on the innovation output of that state. On the other hand, the method of Anselin et al. (1997), Autant-Bernard (2001) and Bottazzi and Peri (2003) allows us to go beyond the mere agglomeration effect. Spillovers, that is, internal repercussions (innovation output variation within a metropolitan district) related to external behaviours (the research expenditure level in surrounding counties), are thus measured in a more direct way.
9. In all, 1731 companies listed in the Annual Company Survey conducted research in 1997 and 1998. The sample of 822 companies was taken after excluding multi-plant firms. From the total companies conducting research in those two years, the average number of sites is 1.4.
10. As zero value variables cannot be transformed into logarithms, 1 has been added to the observations throughout.
11. The French territory includes 94 *départements*.
12. Another specification has been tested including data for region (NUTS 2). It gives similar results, but with a lower explanatory capacity. Results are available on request.
13. See Autant-Bernard and Massard (2003) for a review of the main results in this field.
14. As we can observe, these estimations face a multicollinearity problem arising from the high level of correlation between the different kinds of externalities. The introduction of the whole set of variables barely allows us to identify the effect of each one. For this reason, we introduced successively the externalities associated to the presence of other firms (column 1), the labour market and demand (column 2) and knowledge externalities (column 3) (Tables 5.9 and 5.10).
15. For instance, Vertova (2002) observes different structures of location depending on the maturity degree of the technology.

REFERENCES

Anselin, L. (1988), *Spatial Econometrics, Methods and Models*, Boston: Kluwer Academic Publishers.

Anselin, Luc Attila Varga and Zoltan Acs (1997), 'Local geographic spillovers between university research and high technology innovations', *Journal of Urban Economics*, 42, 422–48.

Audretsch, David B. and Maryann P. Feldman (1999), 'Innovation in cities: science-based diversity, specialization and localized competition', *European Economic Review*, 43, 409–29.

Audretsch, David B. and Maryann P. Feldman (2005), 'Knowledge spillovers and the geography of innovation', in V. Henderson and J. Thisse (eds), *Handbook of Urban and Regional Economics: Cities and Geography*, North-Holland.

Autant-Bernard, Corinne (2001), 'Science and knowledge flows: evidence from the French case', *Research Policy*, **30**(7), 1069–78.

Autant-Bernard, Corinne (2003), 'Specialization, Diversity and Geographical Diffusion of Knowledges', *DRUID Summer Conference 2003: Creating, Sharing and Transferring Knowledge: the Role of Geography, Institutions, Organization*, Copenhagen, 12–14 June.

Autant-Bernard, Corinne and Nadine Massard (2003), 'Innovation and Local Externalities: Evidence and Ambiguities drawn from the Geography of Innovation', working paper CREUSET.

Baldwin, R. and R. Forslid (2000), 'The core-periphery model and endogenous growth: stabilising and de-stabilising integration', *Economica*, **67**(3), 307–24.

Baldwin, R., P. Martin and G. Ottaviano (2001), 'Global economic divergence, trade and industrialization: the geography of growth take-offs', *Journal of Economic Growth*, 6, 5–37.

Botazzi, Laura and Giovanni Peri (2003), 'Innovation and spillovers in regions: evidence from European patent data', *European Economic Review*, **47**(4), 687–710.

Duranton, Gilles and Diego Puga (2001), 'Nursery cities: urban diversity, process innovation, and the life cycle of product', *American Economic Review*, **91**(5), 1454–77.

Englmann, F.C. and U. Walz (1995), 'Industrial centers and regional growth in the presence of local inputs', *Journal of Regional Science*, **35**(1), 389–405.

Feldman, M.P. (1994), *The Geography of Innovation, Economics of Science, Technology and Innovation*, vol. 2, Dordrecht and London: Kluwer Academic Publishers, p. 155.

Fujita, M., P. Krugman and A. Venables (1999), *The Spatial Economy: Cities, Regions and International Trade*, Cambridge and London: MIT Press.

Glaeser, E., H. Kallal, J. Scheinkman and A. Shleifer (1992), 'Growth in cities', *Journal of Political Economy*, **100**(6), 1126–52.

Greunz, L. (2004), 'Industrial structure and innovation – evidence from European regions', *Journal of Evolutionary Economics*, **14**(5), 563–92.

Griliches, Zvi (1979), 'Issues in assessing the contribution of research and development to productivity growth', *The Bell Journal of Economics*, **10**(1), 92–116.

Henderson, J. Vernon (2003), 'Marshall's scale economies', *Journal of Urban Economy*, **53**(1), 1–28.

Henderson, V., A. Kuncoro and M. Turner (1995), 'Industrial development in cities', *Journal of Political Economy*, **103**(5), 1067–90.

Jaffe, Adam B. (1989), 'Real effects of academic research', *The American Economic Review*, **79**(5), 957–70.
Jaffe, A.B., M. Trajtenberg and R. Henderson (1993), 'Geographic localization of knowledge spillovers as evidenced by patent citations', *The Quarterly Journal of Economics*, 577–98.
Krugman, Paul (1991), 'Increasing returns and economic geography', *Journal of Political Economy*, **99**(3), 483–99.
Krugman, Paul and A.J. Venables (1995), 'Globalization and the inequality of nations', *Quarterly Journal of Economics*, **CX**(4), 857–80.
Lamorgese, A. (1997), 'Externalities, Economic Geography and Growth: A Cross-section Analysis', working paper.
Mairesse, Jacques and M. Sassenou (1991), 'Recherche-développement et productivité: un panorama des études économétriques sur données d'entreprises', in J. de Bandt and D. Foray (eds), *L'évaluation économique de la recherche et du changement technique*, Editions du CNRS.
Marshall, Alfred [1890] (1971), *Principes D'économie Politique* Vol. 2, Paris, London, New York: Gordon & Breach.
Martin, Philippe and G. Ottaviano (1999), 'Growing location: industry location in a model of endogenous growth', *European Economic Review*, **43**(2), 281–302.
Mion, G. (2004), 'Spatial externalities and empirical analysis: the case of Italy', *Journal of Urban Economics*, 56, 97–118.
Ottaviano, G. and J.F. Thisse (2005), 'Agglomeration and economic geography', in V. Henderson and J. Thisse (eds), *Handbook of Urban and Regional Economics: Cities and Geography*, North-Holland.
Rigby, D.L. and J. Essletzbichler (2002), 'Agglomeration economies and productivity differences in U.S. Cities', *Journal of Economic Geography*, 2, 407–32.
Rosenthal, S.S. and W.C. Strange (2001), 'The determinants of agglomeration', *Journal of Urban Economics*, 50, 191–229.
Rosenthal, S.S. and W.C. Strange (2005), 'Evidence on the nature and sources of agglomeration economies', in V. Henderson and J. Thisse (eds), *Handbook of Urban and Regional Economics: Cities and Geography*, North-Holland.
Van der Panne, G. (2004), 'Agglomeration externalities: Marshall versus Jacobs', *Journal of Evolutionary Economics*, **14**(5), 593–604.
Vertova, G. (2002), 'A historical investigation of innovative activities', *Structural Change and Economic Dynamics*, 13, 259–83.

6. The adoption of ICTs – why does it differ across regions?
Andrea Bonaccorsi, Lucia Piscitello and Cristina Rossi

6.1 INTRODUCTION

Information and communication technologies (ICTs) are creating new opportunities and challenges for both individuals and firms in many geographical areas all over the world, but their diffusion is still uneven. Empirical investigations show that ICTs are fairly widespread in the North America and Europe, while they are still scantily diffused in most developing countries. At the same time, substantial differences do also exist within industrialized countries. The wide literature on innovation diffusion (Rogers, 1995; Stoneman, 2002) offers a rich framework for understanding disparities in ICTs adoption, referring mainly to two types of model. On the one hand, *epidemic models* liken diffusion to an infectious disease, so that non-adopters choose a new technology when they come into contact with adopters and learn about it. Thus, information spillovers, imitation processes, herd behaviours, and bandwagon effects have been acknowledged to play a crucial role (see Mahajan, Muller and Bass, 1990, for a comprehensive survey of this literature). On the other hand, the so-called *equilibrium models* interpret adoption decisions as resulting from a cost–benefit analysis by individuals or firms, so that the expected pay-off of choosing a technology crucially depends on agents' characteristics. Recent studies have acknowledged the importance of both the approaches in explaining geographical disparities in ICTs adoption (Forman and Goldfarb, 2007).

Along this line, this chapter proposes a spatial econometric framework that allows us to take into account the role played by both the heterogeneity in agents' characteristics, and the epidemic effects stemming from the proximity between adopters and potential adopters. Our empirical analysis focuses on the disparities in ICTs adoption by Italian firms at the sub-regional level (Italian NUTS 3). Specifically, it aims at investigating whether disparities in ICTs diffusion are entirely due to heterogeneity in firms' characteristics or whether diffusion is also influenced by epidemic effects, that is, by the presence of firms adopting ICTs in neighbouring areas.

6.2 ICTs AND THE 'DEATH OF THE DISTANCE': A WIDELY DEBATED ISSUE

Information and communications technologies (ICTs) have been conceived by economic scholars as general purpose technologies, which provide generic functions, and are therefore suitable to be used in a multitude of ways in many sectors (Bresnahan and Trajtenberg, 1996; Javanovic and Rousseau, 2005). Like electricity or steam engines (Rosenberg and Trajtenberg, 2004), ICTs are used in miscellaneous productive activities, but they also present a distinctive feature, as they enable communications and exchanges of immaterial goods over distance. Thus, in the mid-1990s, while the Internet was diffusing across Europe and the United States at an impressive pace, ICTs were declared to be the determinant of the 'death of the distance' (Cairncross, 1997), making space less significant for human activities (Dodge and Kitchin, 2006). Specifically, since ICTs are mostly based on immaterial and human capital investments, they might offer real chances of growth to those areas that have historically suffered from isolation, high transport costs, and/or a lack of public and private physical infrastructures.

The de-materialization of information and communication might make physical location irrelevant for where economic activity happens (Quah, 1996), thus allowing leapfrogging regions to overcome peripherality. Unlike traditional heavy and light manufacturing investment, ICTs may allow firms to relocate productive activities in remote areas (Forman, 2005), increasing regional attractiveness as a strategic location factor, and enhancing territorial competitiveness (Steinmuller, 2001).

The relationship between economic development and ICTs, rooted in the so-called knowledge-based economy, is a widely researched issue in economic literature. In particular, empirical evidence has been provided in order to corroborate the 'death of distance' hypothesis, mainly through the investigation of the effects of ICTs on the time–space patterns of demand and supply by individuals and firms. Ellison and Ellison (2005) highlighted that the online auction market has been experiencing an impressive growth since the late 1990s, while Addison and Rahman (2005) have suggested that economies that successfully implement new ICTs might be able to overcome barriers that have long held back their contribution to global trade (namely, the limitation of a remote geography, and an unfavourable climate). In this line, Gholami, Sang-Yong and Heshmati (2006) found that ICTs increase inflows of FDI to developing countries by lowering transaction and production costs of foreign investors.

Conversely, a wide empirical literature has also shown ICTs diffusion to be unequally distributed spatially, so that their role for the development of peripheral areas should be put into perspective (Khiabany, 2003). Significant spatial disparities still persist in the intensity of ICTs adoption and use (vanDijk, 2005), not only between developed and developing countries, but even within industrialized countries (Rallet and Rochelandet, 2006). Indeed, it has been acknowledged that digital inequalities exist among regions within the same country (local digital divide) and, in some cases, they are larger and more persistent than differences among countries.[1] Recent evidence has been provided, for instance, with reference to the United States (Greenstein and Prince, 2006), Australia (Tranter and Willis, 2006), and Greece (Demoussis and Giannakopoulos, 2006).

Within this context, a widely investigated issue deals with the open question of whether ICTs lead to more or less concentration in economic activities, and specifically with the so-called *urban/rural gap* (Forman and Goldfarb, 2007). Most studies agree with the idea that ICTs favour agglomeration processes. Exploring differences in Internet adoption by US firms depending on their location, Forman, Goldfarb and Greenstein (2005) have found that the Internet enhances the economic centrality of major cities in comparison to geographically isolated areas, even if differences tend to disappear after controlling for sectoral composition. Evidence showing the backwardness of the rural areas with respect to ICTs adoption has been provided also by Mills and Whitacre (2003); Galliano and Roux (2003, 2005); Charlot and Duraton (2006); Kvasny and Keil (2006); Labrianidis and Kalogeressis (2006).

It is worth observing that the empirical literature on the effects of ICTs on labour productivity has also shown considerable lags and heterogeneity across firms, sectors, and geographical areas (Atzeni and Carboni, 2006; Edquist, 2005; Hughes and Morton, 2005); likewise, analyses on e-commerce transactions in the United States have confirmed that geography still matters in e-retail (Ellison and Ellison, 2006).

As far as the determinants of digital disparities across space, studies investigating differences between developed and developing countries have highlighted the role of disparities in income (Pohjola, 2003), in human capital (Dewan, Ganley and Kraemer, 2005), telecommunication infrastructures (Antonelli, 2003; Kenney, 2003), regulatory (Guillen, 2005) and socio-political features (Beilok and Dimitrova, 2003).

Likewise, empirical works on the determinants of local inequalities in the spatial diffusion of ICTs have not only highlighted the role of economic, social, demographic, and technological aspects, but also of factors more directly related to epidemic effects (a comprehensive survey of this literature is in Forman and Goldfarb, 2007). Indeed, the decision to adopt a new technology often depends on the availability of information about the technology itself. The idea is that the larger the number of the adopters, the larger the information spillovers received by potential adopters, and the lower the risk associated with adoption (Rogers, 1995). Thus, with regard to ICTs diffusion at the local level, it is possible to assume that the higher the number of firms adopting ICTs in a geographical area, the larger the information spillovers received by the non-adopting surrounding companies, and the higher the probability of further adoptions. Several empirical analyses have provided evidence corroborating this hypothesis. Bell and Song (2004), for instance, have observed strong neighbourhood effects in the adoption of online grocery services; likewise, using a sample of over 6000 firms, Forman (2005) has shown that imitation processes influence the adoption of advanced ICTs business applications.

Particularly, it has also been observed that the level of ICTs adoption and diffusion within a geographical area depends closely on the absorptive capacity of the firms sited in that area, which refers to their ability to assess technological opportunities and to understand and make use of the new technologies (Cohen and Levinthal, 1989). Indeed, the adoption of ICTs systems requires complementary organizational innovations (Hughes and Morton, 2005) asking for specific skills that are not always available, and it also determines the need for additional personnel training (Bresnahan, Brynjofsson and Hitt, 2002). Learning effects also matter; they may arise from previous adoption of ICTs equipment or of prior technologies (let's think of the EDI – Electronic Data Interchange) (Zhu et al., 2006).

6.3. METHODOLOGY AND DATA

6.3.1 Domain Names as a Proxy for ICTs Adoption

A number of alternative methods for measuring the diffusion of ICTs across geographical areas have been proposed in the literature (for a comprehensive survey, see Greenstein and Prince, 2006). However, most of the studies have identified ICTs with the Internet, referring to the number of Internet hosts (Kiiski and Pohjola, 2002) and users (Norris, 2002), although restricting the problem of differences in ICTs diffusion simply to Internet access is misleading. Indeed, data on Internet hosts are easily available and highly reliable (Wolcott et al., 2001),[2] but they are gathered only at a national level.

Recently, the use of domain names as a proxy of Internet diffusion has been proposed (Kolko, 2002; Zook et al., 2004). Indeed, domains may be a valid proxy for ICTs adoption, mainly because they operationalize the intention to actively supply content through the Net. In general, the registration of a domain name by a firm is the first step towards setting up a website through which to present its goods or to undertake electronic business activities. However, domains provide an underestimation of ICTs diffusion,[3] because: (1) ICTs adoption does not necessarily involve registering a domain, and (2) Internet service providers (ISPs) often offer their users room (on their servers) for adding new content. Thus, domains constitute a lower bound as any registrant is unquestionably an ICTs adopter. Additionally, every domain name is uniquely associated with a registrant whose geographical location and nature are unambiguously recorded in the databases of the organizations that manage the different ccTLDs (country code top level domains) (Grubesic, 2002). The availability of information at the sub-national level makes domains a valid metric to explore the territorial dimension of ICTs adoption.

In this chapter, we refer to the Italian administrative units called provinces, corresponding to level 3 in the Eurostat NUTS (Nomenclature of Territorial Units for Statistics) classification.

Data come from a database containing domain name registrations by different categories of actors (individuals, business firms, universities and research centres, third-sector associations, and public administration bodies), built by the Institute for Informatics and Telematics (IIT) of the National Research Council in Italy (CNR) and the Sant'Anna School of Advanced Studies (Pisa) during 2002–03. These data have been extracted from the databases of the registrations under the ccTLD '.it' that are managed by the Italian Registration Authority (RA) hosted by IIT. A total of 500 000 domain names have been inspected for classification; multiple names registered by the same registrant have been carefully checked and eliminated.

Therefore, as a proxy for the level of ICTs adoption in each province, we used the penetration rate, measured by the percentage of firms (located in the province) that had at least one domain name registered in the Registration Authority databases, as in July 2001. Table 6.1 and Table 6.2 summarize the descriptive statistics and the correlations of our dependent variable *ICT_ADOPTION* and other indicators for the ICTs endowment in the province. More specifically, *IT_EXPENDITURE* is the ratio of IT expenditure to the number of firms (the source is Assinform-Net Consulting, see Table A6.1 in the Appendix to this chapter). The index

Table 6.1 ICTs adoption proxies, descriptive statistics

Variable	Description	No.	Min	Max	Mean	Std. Dev.
ICT_ADOPTION	Percentage of firms in a province that have registered at least a domain name as in 2001	103	1.2	9.1	3.8	1.7
INFRASTRUCTURE	Index summarizing the availability within an area of the facilities for communications through telematic and computer networks	103	17.3	345.0	87.0	51.2
IT_EXPENDITURE	Ratio of IT expenditure by firms in a province to the number of firms in that province	103	1092.3	266 667.1	4049.5	33 204.3

Table 6.2   ICTs adoption proxies, correlation

Variable	ICT_ADOPTION	INFRASTRUCTURE	IT_EXPENDITURE
ICT_ADOPTION	1.000		
INFRASTRUCTURE	0.692***	1.000	
IT_EXPENDITURE	0.488**	0.589***	1.000

Notes: ***: p value < 0.01, **: p value < 0.05.

INFRASTRUCTURE needs further explanation. As it summarizes the availability within an area of the facilities that allow communications through telematic and computer networks, it measures both the quantity and the quality of these facilities (the source is Istituto Guglielmo Tagliacarne, see Table A6.1 in the Appendix). It is worth noting that this indicator encompasses the endowment of broadband access, still poorly diffused in Italy in 2003. A divide in high-speed Internet access existed not only between Northern and Southern regions, but also between rural and urban areas.[4] On the one side, only 25 per cent of the Italian population, mostly resident in metropolitan areas, could have access to a wide range of broadband technologies supplied within a competitive environment; on the other side, 25 per cent of the inhabitants could not benefit from any fixed broadband network.

6.4   SPATIAL HETEROGENEITY AND SPATIAL DEPENDENCE ANALYSIS

As anticipated, we use a spatial econometric framework as it allows us to take into account the role played by both heterogeneity in the agents' behaviours and the proximity effects associated to the epidemic model. Indeed, spatial effects include spatial heterogeneity and spatial dependence, both of which relate to the first law of geography (Tobler, 1979) stating that 'everything is related to everything else, but near things are more related than distant things'.

Spatial heterogeneity refers to structural relations that vary over space, that is, what matters is the location of a particular point in space. Spatial dependence, on the other hand, occurs when the observations at one location depend on the values of observations at other locations.[5]

More specifically, the idea of spatial heterogeneity is linked to spatial or regional differentiation, meaning that there are certain specific characteristics

Table 6.3   ICTs adoption in macro-areas

Area	No.	Mean	Std. Dev.
North	46	4.76	1.31
Centre	21	4.40	1.29
South	36	2.11	0.66
Total	103	3.76	1.65

Note: Kruskall-Wallis test is significant at $p < 0.01$.

in each region that affect economic behaviours within the region itself. In our case, the concept of spatial heterogeneity points to the fact that the level of ICTs adoption in a geographical area depends on the specificities of the area, and of the firms sited there. In short, such a concept might be framed within the above-cited equilibrium models.

As far as Italy is concerned, regions are highly differentiated from social, cultural, demographic, and economic viewpoints, and ICTs adoption is no exception. Figure 6.1 shows the severe geographical disparities in ICTs adoption, which mirror the strong duality in economic development between the Southern regions and the rest of the country. Figures in Table 6.3 highlight that the level of ICTs adoption in Italy is quite low, with an average penetration rate lower than 4 per cent, and that differences between macro-areas are highly significant (the Kruskall-Wallis test is significant at $p<0.01$).

No Southern province ranks in the top 50, the best-performing province in the South ranks 55th and only eight Northern provinces rank below that position. Conversely, all the 20 worst-performing provinces are located in the South. This evidence is in line with Atzeni and Carboni (2005), who have found a consolidated and persistent gap in the rate of adoption of almost all the ICTs systems, for firms located in the South vs. those in North and Centre of Italy.

With regard to spatial dependence, this refers to the fact that one observation associated with a location, which we might label i, depends on other observations at locations $j \neq i$ (LeSage, 1998, p. 3), so that we could interpret this relationship as an indication of the epidemic effects spreading from one local area to another nearby one. In order to assess this point, we calculated the Moran's I statistic.[6] The proximity matrix employed has the generic element w_{ij} equal to the geographical distance between the provinces i and j, measured in kilometres.[7] The results clearly show the presence of spatial dependence: Moran's I is 0.60, significant at $p<0.01$.

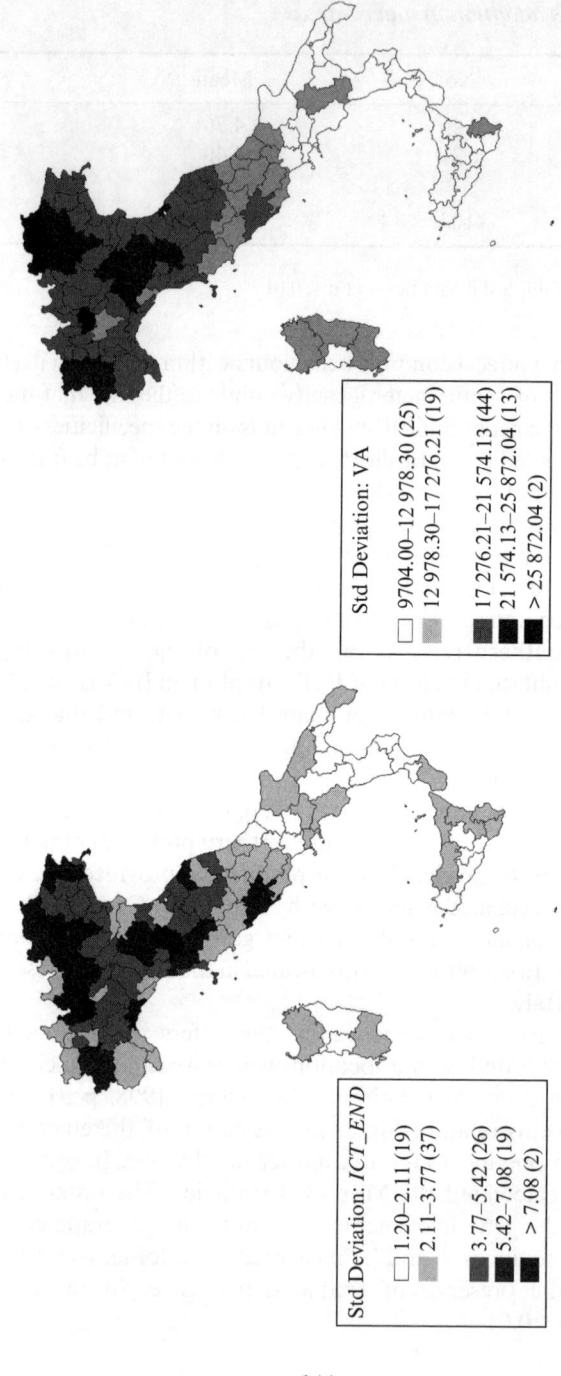

Figure 6.1 Distribution of ICTs endowment (ICT_END) and value-added (VA) per inhabitant across Italian provinces

6.5 EXPLANATORY VARIABLES

In accordance with the literature reviewed in Section 6.2, ICTs adoption is considered to be dependent on:

- *Local absorptive capacity.* A positive relation has been postulated between the absorptive capacity at the local level, and the adoption (and effective use) of ICTs (OECD, 2004). Traditionally, absorptive capacity has been proxied by the output of private and public research, namely patents and publications. Therefore, the variable *PATENTS* is the ratio of the number of patents granted by the United States Patent and Trademark Office (USPTO) in each province, in the period 1991–99, to the number of firms in that province. We also used the variable *PUBLICATIONS*, measured by the ratio between the number of scientific publications by university researchers in each province and the number of firms in that province.
- *Characteristics of firms.* In order to take into account the heterogeneity of firms in each province, in accordance with most studies on new technology adoption and diffusion, we considered the dimensional aspect of firms. Larger organizations benefit from economies of scale, easier access to outside resources and ability to manage adoption risks (for a comprehensive survey of this literature see Karshenas and Stoneman, 1995). Empirical analyses generally confirmed the positive relationship between firms' size and ICTs adoption (Astebro, 2004; Forman and Goldfarb, 2007). Our variable *SIZE* is measured by the average size of firms in each province (calculated as the ratio of the number of employees to the number of firms, in each province).
- *Sectoral composition.* It has been amply demonstrated that the sectoral specialization of a region impacts significantly upon ICTs diffusion in the region itself (Forman, 2005). Specifically, rural market activities (agribusiness, textiles, tobacco, etc.) tend to have lower technological intensity, as they require relatively little equipment in terms of information and/or knowledge transmission facilities (Mitchell and Clark, 1999). Therefore, we adopted a dummy variable, *STRUCTURE*, which equals 1 if the percentage of firms in agriculture in each province is greater than the national average, and 0 otherwise.

The proxies employed are reported in Table A6.1 in the Appendix to this chapter, while Table 6.4 summarizes their statistical description and correlations.

Table 6.4 Descriptive statistics of the explanatory variables and correlation matrix

Variable	PATENTS	PUBLICATIONS	SIZE	STRUCTURE (dummy variable)
Min	0.00	0.00	0.31	0
Max	2.43	4.17	103.46	1
Mean	0.26	0.39	6.20	0.49
Std. Dev.	0.36	0.74	11.15	0.50
Obs.	103	103	103	103
PATENTS	1.000			
PUBLICATIONS	0.305	1.000		
SIZE	0.078	0.185	1.000	
STRUCTURE	−0.305	−0.228	−0.149	1.000

6.6 EMPIRICAL FINDINGS

Empirical findings are reported in Table 6.5 and Table 6.6. According to our conceptual model developed in Section 6.2, ICTs adoption has been modelled as a function of the province's absorptive capacity, the characteristics of firms, and the sectoral composition of the province. Therefore, the model can be expressed as follows:

$$ICT\_ADOPTION = \alpha + X\beta + \varepsilon$$

Additionally, in order to better capture local disparities, we inserted a regional dummy, *NORTH*, that takes value 1 for the Northern provinces, and 0 otherwise (Eq. 1, Table 6.5).

As expected, the estimates show that ICTs adoption of a province is positively influenced by its local absorptive capacity (*PATENTS* and *PUBLICATIONS* are both positive and significantly different from zero at $p < 0.01$); the industrial composition of the province (proxied by the variable *STRUCTURE*) is also highly significant (at $p < 0.05$), while the average firm size did not come out as being significantly different from 0. Importantly, the dummy *NORTH* reveals the existence of two highly different spatial regimes (it comes out positive and significant at $p < 0.01$). The model fits quite well, as it explains 66 per cent of the variance.

Moreover, as spatial heterogeneity could also reflect heterogeneity in the causal effects, we also tested the slope effects for each relevant explanatory variable. Specifically, Eq. 2 and Eq. 3 confirm the strong North–South difference, even with reference to the crucial explanatory variables

Table 6.5 Results from econometric models

Variable	Model		
	Eq. 1 Coefficient	Eq. 2 Coefficient	Eq. 3 Coefficient
CONSTANT	1.834**	1.623*	1.911**
	(2.511)	(1.698)	(2.030)
PATENTS	0.892***	−6.119*	1.273***
	(2.725)	(−1.927)	(3.266)
PUBLICATIONS	0.414***	0.511***	−1.986**
	(2.985)	(3.003)	(−2.440)
SIZE	0.159	0.559**	0.511**
	(0.756)	(2.202)	(2.080)
STRUCTURE	0.465**	0.543*	0.675**
	(2.064)	(1.892)	(2.336)
NORTH	1.870***		
	(7.703)		
NORTH*PATENTS		7.543**	
		(2.393)	
NORTH*PUBLICATIONS			2.540***
			(3.144)
Adj. R-squared:	0.659	0.481	0.511
F-statistic	40.420***	19.908***	21.499***
Log likelihood	−139.551	−161.176	−159.132
Akaike info criterion	291.101	334.353	330.264
Schwarz criterion	306.91	350.161	346.072
Moran's I (error)	1.988**	4.589***	3.958***
Robust LM (lag)	0.308	13.857***	14.359***
Robust LM (error)	2.644	0.468	0.710

Note: Standard errors in brackets; ***: p value < 0.01; **: p value < 0.05; *: p value < 0.10; obs. = 103.

Table 6.6 Results from spatial lag econometric models

Variable	Model	
	Eq. 4 Coefficient	Eq. 5 Coefficient
CONSTANT	1.487*	1.672**
	(1.877)	(2.102)
WICT_ADOPTION	0.521***	0.502***
	(6.470)	(6.201)
PATENTS	−1.732	0.887***
	(−0.664)	(2.711)
PUBLICATIONS	0.489***	−0.607
	(3.558)	(−0.880)
SIZE	0.056	0.043
	(0.270)	(0.210)
STRUCTURE	0.584**	0.651***
	(2.504)	(2.714)
NORTH*PATENTS	2.668	
	(1.024)	
NORTH*PUBLICATIONS		1.114*
		(1.627)
R-squared:	0.659	0.662
Log likelihood	−146.212	−145.458
Akaike info criterion	306.424	304.915
Schwarz criterion	324.867	323.359
LR Test	29.929***	27.349***

Note: Standard errors in brackets; ***: p value < 0.01; **: p value < 0.05; *: p value < 0.10; obs. = 103.

(*PATENTS* and *PUBLICATIONS* proved to be significantly positive only when multiplied by the *NORTH* dummy).

Furthermore, in order to take into account the proximity effect, that is, the possible contagions between contiguous provinces, we estimated a so-called spatial lag model where the ICTs adoption in each province depends on the ICTs adoption in its neighbouring provinces. The equation becomes the following:

$$ICT\_ADOPTION = \rho WICT\_ADOPTION + \alpha + X\beta + \varepsilon$$

and results are reported in Table 6.6.

The estimated coefficients confirm the relevance of ICTs adoption in the neighbouring provinces, showing that proximity (and therefore contagion) does matter (*WICT_ADOPTION* is highly significant in both Eq. 4 and Eq. 5 at $p<0.01$). The role of variables dealing with the local absorptive capacity is maintained.

6.7 CONCLUSIONS

This work contributes to the empirical literature on the North–South divide in ICTs adoption in several ways. First, it corroborates the notion that the spatial diffusion of ICTs seems to follow the existing geography of development, rather than dramatically changing it. In particular, the North–South divide emerges as the major driver for the adoption of ICTs by Italian firms, as captured by the crucial role played by spatial heterogeneity in the econometric analysis.

However, having checked for such heterogeneity, we have found that variables traditionally employed to explain technology diffusion are also significant with regard to the adoption of ICTs at the local level. Specifically, the level of absorptive capacity, measured by the knowledge available at each province level, is crucially important, representing a clear analogy with the idea that only firms that invest in in-house R&D are able to capture externally created knowledge. In other words, areas that are poor in general technological activity and research are less likely to make active use of the Internet, thus suggesting that, in turn, ICTs benefit from local accumulation of human capital. While this effect may be intuitive with regard to *production* activities, due to input pooling and knowledge spillovers (Ellison and Glaeser, 1997), it is interesting to observe how important it is for the adoption of new technologies as well.

Introducing a spatial econometric approach in the analysis of the relationship between the digital divide and the adoption of new technologies also made it possible to detect the existence of epidemic effects in the diffusion process. In other words, spatial proximity proved to be important, as ICTs adoption in one province is significantly influenced by adoption in the provinces nearby.

ACKNOWLEDGEMENTS

The authors wish to thank Giuseppe Arbia, Florence Goffette, the participants at the 45th European Congress of the Regional Science Association Conference and two anonymous referees for helpful comments and suggestions for previous versions of this chapter.

NOTES

1. Large-scale researches have revealed astonishing differences in Internet and computer penetration between North America and Europe on the one hand, and African and Asian countries on the other (Keller, 2002; Mariscal, 2006; UNCTAD, 2006).
2. For instance, every six months, Network Wizard publishes the results regarding all the top level domains (TLDs) on its website, whereas the RIPE Network Coordination Centre (http://www.ripe.net) publishes the data about the ccTLDs (country code TLDs) in its area (Europe, North Africa, Middle East) on a monthly basis. Hosts belong to the so-called endogenous metrics, which are obtained in an automatic or semi-automatic way from the Internet itself. The organizations that manage the different ccTLDs and gTLDs (generic TLDs) perform the hostcount under their TLDs on a regular basis and provide these data on the Web or by FTP (file transfer protocol).
3. It is worth observing that hosts suffer from the same drawback. Indeed, hostcount programs do not reach machines protected by firewalls and private networks (intranets). The use of dynamic IP (Internet protocol) addresses by ISPs (Internet service providers) should also be taken into account. In addition, hosts are prone to overestimation due to a number of factors, for instance the association of multiple IP addresses with the same computer.
4. Source: Osservatorio Banda Larga, http://www.osservatoriobandalarga.it.
5. This classification has been related to the distinction between models of absolute and relative location (see Abreu, de Groot and Florax, 2005 for a comprehensive survey on 'space and growth').
6. Moran's I is a test statistic for spatial autocorrelation; it determines the extent of linear association between the value that a variable assumes in a given location with values of the same variable in neighbouring locations.
7. It is worth noting that the specification of spatial weights is a major point of contention in literature (Driffield, 2006). Hence, we also use a Queen contiguity matrix, whose generic element w_{ij} assumes value 1 if province i and province j have a common border and 0 otherwise. The results of these alternative specifications did not vary substantially, hence they have not been reported here, but they are available on request.

REFERENCES

Abreu, M., H.L.F. de Groot and R.J.G.M. Florax (2005), 'Space and growth', *Tinbergen Institute Discussion Paper*, TI 2004-129/3.

Addison, T. and A. Rahman (2005), 'Capacity to globalize: why are some countries more globalized than others?', in G.W. Kolodko (ed.), *Globalization and Social Stress*, Hauppauge, NY: Nova Science Publishers, Inc.

Antonelli, C. (2003), 'The digital divide: understanding the economics of new information and communication technology in the global economy', *Information Economics and Policy*, **15**(2), 173–99.

Astebro, T. (2004), 'Sunk costs and the depth and probability of technology adoption', *Journal of Industrial Economics*, **52**(3), 381–99.

Atzeni, G.E. and O.A. Carboni (2005), 'North–South disparity in ICTs adoption in Italy: an empirical evaluation of the effects of subsidies', *CRENOS Working Paper*.

Atzeni, G.E. and O.A. Carboni (2006), 'ICTs productivity and firm propensity to innovative investment: evidence from Italian microdata', *Information Economics and Policy*, **18**(2), 139–56.

Beilok, R. and D.V. Dimitrova (2003), 'An exploratory model of inter-country Internet diffusion', *Telecommunications Policy*, **27**(3–4), 237–52.
Bell, D.R. and S. Song (2004), 'Neighbourhood effects and trial on the internet: evidence from online grocery retailing', *Wharton University Working Paper*, http://marketing.wharton.upenn.edu/ideas/pdf/Bell/neighborhood_effects_trial_on_internet_2004.pdf, accessed 10 July 2004.
Bresnahan, T. and M. Trajtenberg (1996), 'General purpose technologies: engines of growth?', *Journal of Econometrics*, **65**(1), 83–108.
Bresnahan, T.E., E. Brynjofsson and L. Hitt (2002), 'Information technology, workplace organization, and demand for skilled labour: firm-level evidence', *Quarterly Journal of Economics*, **177**(1), 339–76.
Cairncross, Frances (1997), *The Death of the Distance: How the New Communications Revolution will Change Our Lives*, London, UK: Orion.
Charlot, S. and G. Duraton (2006), 'Cities and workplace communication. Some French evidence', *Urban Studies*, **43**(8), 1365–94.
Cohen, W.M. and D.A. Levinthal (1989), 'Innovation and learning: the two faces of R&D', *Economic Journal*, **99**(397), 569–96.
Demoussis, M. and M. Giannakopoulos (2006), 'The dynamics of home computer ownership in Greece', *Information Economics and Policy*, **18**(1), 73–86.
Dewan, S.D., D. Ganley and K.L. Kraemer (2005), 'Across the digital divide: a cross-country analysis of the determinants of IT penetration', *Journal of the Association of Information Systems*, Volume 6, Article 10.
Dodge, Martin and Rob Kitchin (2006), 'Net: geography fieldwork frequently asked questions', in Joel Weiss, Jason Nolan, Jeremy Hunsinger and Peter Trifonas (eds), *The International Handbook of Virtual Learning Environments*, Amsterdam: Springer, pp. 1143–72.
Driffield, N. (2006), 'On the search for spillovers from foreign direct investment (FDI) with spatial dependency', *Regional Studies*, **40**(1), 107–19.
Edquist, H. (2005), 'The Swedish ICTs miracle – myth or reality?', *Information Economics and Policy*, **17**(3), 275–301.
Ellison, G. and S.F. Ellison (2005), 'Lessons about markets from the Internet', *Journal of Economic Perspectives*, **19**(2), 139–58.
Ellison, G. and S.F. Ellison (2006), 'Internet retail demand: taxes, geography, and online–offline competition', *NBER Working Paper*, No. 12242.
Ellison, G. and E.L. Glaeser (1997), 'Geographic concentration in U.S. manufacturing industries. A dartboard approach', *Journal of Political Economy*, **105**(5), 889–927.
Forman, C. (2005), 'The corporate digital divide: determinants of Internet adoption', *Management Science*, **51**(4), 641–53.
Forman, Chris and Avi Goldfarb (2007), 'Diffusion of information and communication technologies to businesses', in Terry Hedershott (ed.), *Economics and Information Systems, Volume I, Handbooks of Economics and Information Systems*, Amsterdam: Elsevier, Science.
Forman, C., A. Goldfarb and S. Greenstein (2005), 'How did location affect adoption of the Internet by commercial establishments? Urban density versus global village', *Journal of Urban Economics*, **58**(3), 389–420.
Galliano, D. and P. Roux (2003), 'Spatial externalities, organisation of the firm and ICTs adoption: the specificities of French agri-food firms', *International Journal of Biotechnology*, **5**(3–4), 269–96.

Galliano, D. and P. Roux (2005), 'Spatial inequalities in the adoption of information and communication technologies', *Cahier du GRES*, No. 2005-25.
Gholami R., T.L. Sang-Yong and A. Heshmati (2006), 'The causal relationship between information and communication technology and foreign direct investment', *The World Economy*, **29**(1), 43–62.
Greenstein, S. and J. Prince (2006), 'The diffusion of the Internet and the geography of the digital divide in the United States', *NBER Working Paper*, No. 12182.
Grubesic, T.H. (2002), 'Spatial dimensions of Internet activity', *Telecommunications Policy*, **26**(7–8), 363–87.
Guillen, M.F. (2005), 'Explaining the global digital divide: economic, political and sociological drivers of cross-national Internet use', *Social Forces*, **84**(2), 681–708.
Hughes, A. and M.S. Morton (2005), 'ICTs and productivity growth – the paradox resolved', *MIT Sloan School Working Paper*, No. 4579-05.
Javanovic, B. and P.L. Rousseau (2005), 'General purpose technologies', *NBER Working Paper*, No. 11093.
Karshenas, Massoud and Paul Stoneman (1995), 'Technological diffusion', in Paul Stoneman (ed.), *Handbook of the Economics of Innovation and Technological Change*, Oxford, UK: Blackwell Publishers, pp. 265–97.
Keller, W. (2002), 'Geographical localization of international technology diffusion', *American Economic Review*, **92**(1), 120–42.
Kenney, Martin (2003), 'The growth and development of the Internet in the United States', in Bruce Kogut (ed.), *The Global Internet Economy*, Cambridge, MA: MIT Press.
Khiabany, G. (2003), 'Globalization and the Internet: myths and realities', *Trends in Communication*, **11**(2), 137–53.
Kiiski, S. and M. Pohjola (2002), 'Cross-country diffusion of the Internet', *Information Economics and Policy*, **14**(2), 297–310.
Kolko, J. (2002), 'Silicon mountains, silicon molehills, geographic concentration and convergence of Internet industries in the US', *Information Economic and Policy*, **14**(2), 211–32.
Kvasny, L. and M. Keil (2006), 'The challenges of redressing the digital divide: a tale of two US cities', *Information Systems Journal*, **16**(1), 23–53.
Labrianidis, L. and T. Kalogeressis (2006), 'The digital divide in Europe's rural enterprises', *European Planning Studies*, **4**(1), 23–39.
LeSage, James P. (1998) *Econometrics Toolbox*, www.spatial-econometrics.com, accessed 17 November 2004.
Mahajan, V., E. Muller and F. Bass (1990), 'New product diffusion models in marketing: a review and directions for research', *Journal of Marketing*, **54**(1), 1–26.
Mariscal, J. (2006), 'Digital divide in a developing country', *Telecommunications Policy*, **29**(5–6), 409–28.
Mills, B.F. and B.E. Whitacre (2003), 'Understanding the non-metropolitan-metropolitan digital divide', *Growth and Change*, **34**(2), 219–43.
Mitchell, S. and D. Clark (1999), 'Business adoption of information and communications technologies in the two-tier rural economy: some evidence from the South Midlands', *Journal of Rural Studies*, 15, 447–55.
Norris, Pippa (2002), *Digital Divide: Civic Engagement, Information Poverty, and the Internet Worldwide*, Cambridge, UK: Cambridge University Press.
OECD (2004), *The Economic Impact of ICTs. Measurement, Evidence and Implications*, www1.oecd.org/publications/e-book/9204051E.PDF, accessed 1 October 2004.

Pohjola, Matti (2003), 'The adoption and diffusion of ICTs across countries: patterns and determinants', in Derek C. Jones (ed.), *New Economy Handbook*, San Diego, CA: Elsevier Academic Press, pp. 77–100.

Quah, D.T. (1996), 'Regional convergence clusters across Europe', *European Economic Review*, **40**(4): 951–8.

Rallet, Alain and Fabrice Rochelandet (2006), 'ICTs and inequalities: the digital divide', in Eric Brousseau and Nicholas Curien (eds), *Internet and Digital Economics*, Cambridge, UK: Cambridge University Press.

Rogers, Everett M. (1995), *Diffusion of Innovations*, Fourth Edition, New York, NY: Free Press.

Rosenberg, N. and M. Trajtenberg (2004), 'A general purpose technology at work: the Corliss steam engine in the late nineteenth-century United States', *Journal of Economic History*, **64**(1), 61–99.

Steinmuller, W.E. (2001), 'ICTs and the possibilities of leapfrogging by developing countries', *International Labour Review*, **140**(2), 193–210.

Stoneman, Paul (2002), *The Economics of Technological Diffusion*, Oxford, UK: Blackwell Publishers.

Tobler, Waldo (1979), 'Cellular geography', in Stephen Gale and Gunnar Olsson (eds), *Philosophy in Geography*, Dordrecht: Reidel, pp. 379–86.

Tranter, B. and B. Willis (2006), 'Beyond the "digital divide": Internet diffusion and inequality in Australia', *Journal of Sociology*, **42**(1), 43–59.

UNCTAD (United Nations Conference on Trade and Development) (2006), *The Digital Divide: ICTs Development Indices 2005*, New York and Geneva: United Nations.

vanDijk, Jan A.G.M. (2005), *The Deepening Digital Divide: Inequality in the Information Society*, Thousand Oaks, CA: Sage Publications.

Wolcott, P., L. Press, W. McHenry, S. Goodman and W. Foster (2001), 'A framework for assessing the global diffusion of the Internet', *Journal of the AIS*, Volume 2, Article 6.

Zhu, K., K.L. Kraemer, V. Gurbaxani and S. Xu (2006), 'Migration to open-standard interorganizational systems: network effects, switching costs, and path dependency', *MIS Quarterly*, **30**(2), 515–39.

Zook, Matthew, Martin Dodge, Yuko Aoyama and Anthony Townsend (2004), 'New digital geographies: information, communication, and place', in Stanley D. Brunn, Susan L. Cutter and J.W. Harrington Jr. (eds), *Geography and Technology*, Dordrecht: Kluwer Academic Publisher, pp. 155–76.

APPENDIX 6.1

Table A6.1 Specification of dependent and independent variables

Variables	Description	Source	Expected sign
Dependent variables			
ICT_ADOPTION	Percentage of firms that have registered at least a domain name	Registration Authority for the ccTLD 'it' – Elaboration	
Independent variables			
Absorptive capacity			
PATENTS	Ratio of the number of patents granted by the USPTO in each province in the period 1991–99 and the number of firms in that province	USPTO – Elaboration	+
PUBLICATIONS	Ratio between the number of scientific publications by university researchers in each province and the number of firms in that province	ISI Citation Index databases – Elaboration	+
Characteristics of firms			
SIZE	Ratio of the number of employees and the number of firms in manufacturing	ISTAT	+
Sectoral Composition			
STRUCTURE	Percentage of firms in agriculture. This is a dummy variable that assumes value 0 if the province is below the national average, 1 otherwise	InfoCamere – Elaboration	+

7. Novel applications of existing econometric instruments to analyse regional innovation systems: the Spanish case

Mikel Buesa, Mónica Martínez Pellitero, Thomas Baumert and Joost Heijs

7.1 INTRODUCTION

This chapter tries to get to grips with the measurement of the national and regional innovation systems.[1] We present novel applications of existing econometric instruments for the measurement and evaluation of regional innovation systems using multivariate analysis methods.[2] On the one hand, the evolutionary theory underpins the heterogeneity of the innovative performance, which has to be considered as a multidimensional activity. On the other, the literature emphasizes the difficulty and the weakness of the use of individual indicators to measure the global concept of innovation, as well as patents, R&D expenditures, percentage of sales related to new products, etc. Each of those indicators – although highly correlated – gives a different view of apparently the same subject.[3] Therefore, in this chapter we try to develop some new ways to measure innovation (systems) considering this concept as not directly observable. To create 'combined' indicators that reflect different aspects of the regional innovation systems we used *factor analysis*. This technique, from a set of quantitative variables, allows us to reduce the set of existing variables to a lower set of non-observable hypothetical variables, called factors, which summarize practically all the information contained in the original set. This procedure, as well as allowing us to overcome statistical problems, enables us to register and reflect more efficiently the system as a whole (the agents, the institutions and the relationship between them), whilst making it easier to interpret the findings.

Anyway, the results of the factor analysis by themselves are not the principal objective of this study. Rather, our main aim is their use in follow-up studies. Once we have obtained the factors, for each region 'standardized factor values' are assigned, which will be used for further research. First we establish a *typology* of regional innovation systems. Second, we create the *IAIF-index of regional innovation*. Third, we estimate a *knowledge production function*. And fourth we compare the *efficiency* of the regions through a data envelopment analysis.

These four analyses are highly complementary because they correspond to each of the perspectives of an economic analysis that tries to evaluate the innovation system. The typology of regional innovation systems describes the structure and configuration of the regional innovation system, the IAIF-index summarizes these typologies and offers the possibility of analysing their development over time. The knowledge production function establishes the relationship between the 'structural aspects' indicating the determinants of the knowledge creation, while the data envelopment analysis (DEA) evaluates the efficiency of the innovative activities on a regional level. We did not detect any study that analyses the efficiency of the regional innovation systems, therefore it can be stated that this latter aspect of this study aims to close one of the gaps of the studies on innovation systems.

We consider that the combination of these applications in one sole study is important, as the results of the four analyses do confirm each other reciprocally. Also, the techniques are complementary because we use a multidimensional approach to analyse more or less the same subject – the quality and capacity of the Spanish regional innovation systems – from different points of view using complementary econometric approaches.

7.2 FACTOR ANALYSIS AS A MULTIDIMENSIONAL WAY OF MEASURING REGIONAL INNOVATION SYSTEMS

The different approaches to analysing the Spanish regional innovation systems used in this chapter are based on the use of existing information on variables and indicators related to science, technology and innovation, from the viewpoint of resources and results, as well as certain aspects of an institutional nature and the productive structure. The years studied range from 1994 to 2000, both inclusive, and as a regional study unit we have worked with the 17 Autonomous Communities (corresponding to the NUTS 2 level).

7.2.1 Variables and Indicators

According to the outline presented by Heijs,[4] the variables we have worked with stand for the following aspects: firms and their relationship with the regional innovation system; support infrastructure for innovation; Civil

Service innovation-linked performance; and the regional and national environment for innovation.[5] It should be noted that the border between these sub-systems is at times not very clear-cut and there is a certain overlap between the different areas, so it is not always easy to classify each of the factors, actors or elements according to the four sub-systems. Nonetheless, this classification is useful as an analytical outline to establish the indicators, and point out the aspects they represent within this study, as well as to indicate the influence of the evolutionary viewpoint that propounds the existence of interdependence relationships between the parts or elements of the system.

In the case of firms, we start from the hypothesis that these are the most important elements in innovation systems, not just as instruments for generating knowledge, which materializes in products and processes, but also as sources of internal learning, and as linking elements between the productive system and that of innovation in the case of innovating firms. Therefore, our database also includes several variables related to human and financial resources devoted to R&D, as well as the stock of firms' technological capital.

Regarding the support infrastructure for innovation, understood as the group of bodies conceived to facilitate firms' innovatory activity, we make a distinction between a private part and a public one. The private part refers to the wide range of services among which are found technological centres and parks. Within the public domain, we consider the Public Research Bodies (OPI in Spain) and the universities with their resources and findings. To these are added human resources in science and technology.

In the case of the Civil Service we also use as a base the idea that this institution plays a very important part in the development of systems. On the one hand, the public sector manages an important part of regions' scientific apparatus, while exerting an important role as a financing agent for innovation. On the other, it also has an outstanding role as an agent linked to the development of technological policies. The research has tried to include those aspects via the indicators that reflect the human and financial resources used in R&D, the stock of scientific capital deriving from the latter, as well as part of technological policy, by means of the projects approved by the Centre for the Development of Industrial Technology (CDTI)[6] in the different Autonomous Communities.

Finally, the regional innovation environment is a broad concept including aspects that indirectly impinge on regions' technological and innovation capacities. Five aspects have been incorporated in this research: the productive structure as quantified via added value, employment and exports in industries with varying technological content; accessibility to venture capital systems; accumulated knowledge,[7] as quantified by means of an indicator of the quality of the universities; the size of the regional market represented by GDP value.[8]

7.2.2 Factor Analysis of Main Components

From the above-mentioned variables and indicators, a factor analysis has been applied with the object of determining implicit factors in Spanish regional innovation systems. This technique,[9] from a set of quantitative variables, allows us to determine a lower set of non-observable hypothetical variables – factors – which summarize practically all the information contained in the original set.

In this study we have started out from a total of 35 variables in determining the implicit factors of the Spanish regional innovation systems. Using as a base *the factor loading of a variable* – which is defined as the proportion of the total variability recorded by the factors preserved – the variables and indicators have been established that form part of the final model via a process of trial and error; if the variable is found to be associated with a small community it will be reasonable to include another factor, provided that it is of better use to explain the model, or, rather, to eliminate the variable, if, on the contrary, it did not provide the model with a significant value. The factorial method of data reduction that we have worked with is that of *main components*, and the final solution chosen was the one that was made up of four factors, where 85 per cent of the variance of the model was preserved, and where the communalities take satisfactory values.[10]

7.2.3 Factors Determining Regional Innovation Systems

In Figure 7.1 a synthesis of the information provided by the *rotated components matrix*, is presented, aimed at facilitating a correct view of the indicators classified by factors. Moreover, arrows have been included, to show the relationships between the variables and indicators linked to more than one factor.[11] Each factor records a series of indicators with a high degree of saturation in them. The allocation of a name has been based on their composition, and corresponds to the elements considered essential by theory in innovation systems.

The first factor – Regional and Productive Environment for Innovation (*Environment* for short) – registers a 28.67 per cent variability, and is organized around three aspects: productive structure (including exports according to their technology level and employment), support institutions for innovation and the size of the regional market. All the variables are found to be highly saturated, with values higher than 0.8, except for the one representing medium-low-technology exports. This variable was in turn also found to be correlated with the fourth factor, which registers elements linked to the area of Innovating Firms.[12]

Novel applications of existing econometric instruments 159

FACTOR 1: REGIONAL AND PRODUCTIVE ENVIRONMENT FOR INNOVATION

1) Productive structure
- NAV High- and medium-technology industry in million 1999 € **(0.859)**
- NAV Low-technology industry in million 1999 € **(0.968)**
- Employees high- and medium-technology industry **(0.890)**
- Employees in low-technology industry **(0.975)**
- Export. High- and medium-high-technology industry in million 1999 € **(0.870)**
- Export. Medium-low-technology industry in million 1999 € **(0.666)**
- Export. Low-technology industry in million 1999 € **(0.978)**

2) Support institutions for innovation
- National projects approved by the CDTI in million 1999 € **(0.882)**

3) Size of the regional market
- GDP in million 1999 € **(0.860)**

FACTOR 2: UNIVERSITY

- Internal university R&D expenditure, % of GDP **(0.686)**
- Internal university staff (FTE) in R&D, % of active population **(0.931)**
- University researchers (FTE) in R&D, % of active population **(0.917)**
- Students enrolled in first and/or second part of degree course compared with population aged 16 and over (each 100 000 inhabitants) **(0.631)**
- Students who have finished 1st and /or 2nd part of degree course compared with population aged 16 and over (each 100 000 inhabitants) **(0.694)**
- Students registered in postgraduate courses compared with population (each 100 000 inhabitants) **(0.892)**
- Students who have read their thesis compared with population aged 16 and over (each 100 000 inhabitants) **(0.916)**
- Research quality indicator of university **(0.854)**

FACTOR 3: CIVIL SERVICE

1) Civil Service
- Internal Civil Service expenditure on R&D, % of GDP **(0.908)**
- Internal Civil Service staff (FTE) in R&D, % of active population **(0.899)**
- Civil Service R&D researchers, % of active population **(0.928)**
- Scientific capital stock in R&D (1999 € per inhabitant) **(0.791)**

2) Others
- Venture capital investment (million 1999 €) **(0.533)**

FACTOR 4: INNOVATING FIRMS

0.533

- Firms internal R&D expenditure (percentage of GDP) **(0.809)**
- Internal staff (FTE) of firms in R&D, % of active population **(0.801)**
- R&D researchers (FTE) of firms, % of active population **(0.755)**
- Firms' technological capital stock in R&D (1999 € per inhabitant) **(0.693)**
- Regional distribution of technological centres **(0.703)**
- Annual income of technological centres **(0.701)**

0.500

Source: Own elaboration with the IAIF-RIS (Spain) Database

Figure 7.1 Factors of Spanish regional innovation systems

The second factor clearly reflects the role of the University. It records a 21.58 per cent variability. Particularly noteworthy is the fact that the variables with a higher degree of saturation are those referring to the research environment in its strictest sense – postgraduate students, staff and researchers. Regarding the indicators related to University results in the first and final part of the degree course, there is a lower degree of correlation.

The third factorial axis registers 18.19 per cent variability and basically records variables referring to the Civil Service regarding innovation. To these can be added the variable referring to the venture capital system, which, during the period studied, was largely channelled through the Civil Service.

Finally, the fourth and ultimate factor, which records 16.89 per cent variability, shows those elements alluding to knowledge creation activity in Innovating Firms. Moreover, variables referring to technological centres are saturated in the factor, due to being support units for firms in research, absorption and diffusion of technology activities.

7.3 TYPOLOGY OF REGIONAL INNOVATION SYSTEMS

The factors – or, more specifically, the factor scores – obtained in the previous section have been used in building up a typology of regional innovation systems. The technique used for this purpose has been the *cluster or conglomerate analysis* using the factor scores as independent variables. The cluster analysis is a multivariate technique, which enables 'individuals' to be classified in groups, without the sets constituting them or their number being known a priori. In this case the individuals are the selfsame Autonomous Communities in the different years of study and the grouping methods are both the one considering the proximity between units of each group and the one constructed from the separation between those units.[13]

Bearing in mind the findings, and on examining the variables closely, the solution chosen is the one that establishes five clusters or groups, as this result coincides in the two procedures carried out, which adds an element of confidence regarding the choice opted for. Consequently, the regional innovation system typology set up on the basis of the factors identified in the previous section defines five systems types, four of which comprise just one Autonomous Community – Madrid, Catalonia, Basque Country and Navarre – and another that groups together the remaining regions, regardless of the year of study. In order to show that there exists a significant differentiation among the five previously defined groups, as well as to highlight the factors that, in each case, characterize innovating activities, a variance analysis has been made via the factor classifying the Autonomous Communities in each of those systems. Given a quantitative dependent variable (four identified latent factors) and a qualitative independent variable (a variable or factor identifying each region with a relevance cluster), the *variance analysis with one factor* consists of determining the behaviour of the

Novel applications of existing econometric instruments 161

dependent variable in the established groups by the values of the independent one. Using a 99 per cent level of significance the null hypothesis was rejected, so it can be stated that the types of regional innovation systems that have been detected register different behaviour in the four factors. Figure 7.2 shows the solution obtained by means of the factorial scores of the variables charged with summarizing the statistical information regarding the mean.

As is clearly seen, Madrid is the region with the most complete innovation system, as verified by its factorial scores, which are always positive, and thus above average. Catalonia, the Basque Country and Navarre take what could be considered as an 'assymetrical' system, since only one of the four factors is found in a developed form. The remaining regions have weak innovation systems, and have not achieved important development in any of their components. They are, therefore, regions that still have important weaknesses that

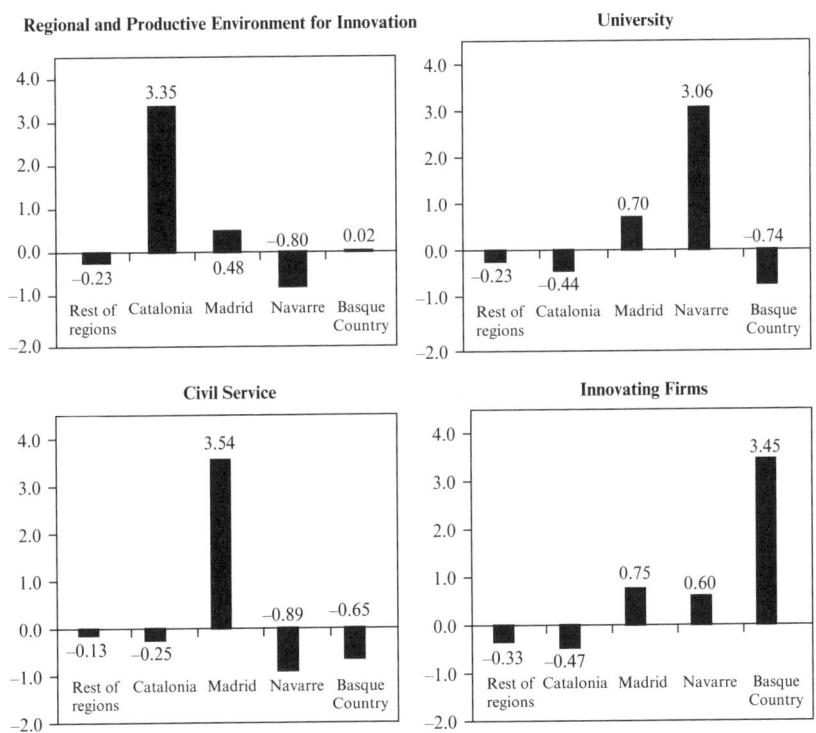

Source: Own elaboration with the IAIF-RIS (Spain) Database.

Figure 7.2 Results of the cluster analysis: mean factor values for each cluster (mean = 0)

should receive preferential treatment in comparison with the other above-mentioned ones as far as scientific and technological policies are concerned.

7.4 THE IAIF-INDEX OF REGIONAL INNOVATION CAPACITY: HOW HAS THE INNOVATIVE CAPACITY OF THE REGIONS CHANGED OVER TIME?

The regional typology obtained by cluster analysis, which has been described in the previous section, has pointed out the heterogeneity that characterizes the Spanish innovation system. Nevertheless, it gives us only a static view of the situation for the whole period studied. In order to complement these findings by a dynamic perspective, we have developed an innovation index, which allows us to observe the evolution of the relative innovative capacity of each region between 1994 and 2000.

7.4.1 Development and Composition of the Index Between 1994 and 2000

The so-called *IAIF-index of regional innovation* is composed of the weighted sum of four partial indexes, which match with the four factors previously calculated. Each of these partial indexes is composed, in turn, by the weighted sum of standardized variables that form each factor. Differing from previous studies we decided not to do the weighting of the variables and partial indexes discretionally but objectively, using multivariable statistical instruments.[14] This allows us to overcome most of the disadvantages pointed out by Grupp,[15] who affirms, that in calculating scoreboards 'the space for manipulation . . . by selection, weighting and aggregation is great'.[16] In doing so we have to cope with two methodological problems. First, it is necessary to calibrate the variables that form the partial indexes. Second, we have to find the proper weighting for each of these partial indexes in forming the IAIF-index of regional innovation. Starting with the second objective, the weighting of each partial index has been calculated as the percentage of the variability explained by each factor with respect to the total retained variability.

In turn, the weighting of the variables that form the partial indexes is calculated as the degree of saturation of the variables in the corresponding factor. Specifically it is the correlation coefficient between the variables and the factor, expressed as the percentage with regard to the total correlation, obtained from the coefficient matrix for calculating points in the components, and corresponds to the inverse of the component matrix.[17] The values obtained are presented in Table 7.1. Finally,

Table 7.1   Composition and weightings of the IAIF-index of regional innovation

Partial Indexes And their Weighting	Variables	Weight of the variable (%)
Partial index 1: Regional and Productive Environment for Innovation (weighting: 37%)	Medium-tech exports	4
	Spanish patents	8
	European patents	8
	Number R&D projects supported by public policies	9
	High- and medium-tech industrial value-added	9
	High- and medium-tech industrial employment	9
	Gross regional product	10
	High-tech exports	9
	Low-tech industrial employment	11
	Low-tech industrial value-added	11
	Low-tech exports	12
Partial index 2: University (weighting: 24%)	Registrations secondary education*	7
	Number of persons that finished secondary education*	8
	Internal R&D expenditures of universities	14
	Registrations tertiary education*	13
	Quality of research in universities	14
	Number of persons that finished tertiary education*	14
	Number of researchers in the universities**	15
	Total employment at the universities**	15
Partial index 3: Civil Service (weighting 20%)	Risk capital	11
	Stock of scientific capital per person***	17
	Internal R&D expenditures of the CS (% GDP)	24
	R&D employment of the CS**	24
	Researchers of the CS**	24
Partial index 4: Innovating Firms (weighting: 19%)	R&D employment in firms**	15
	R&D expenditures in firms (% GDP)	16
	Number of regional technology centres	15
	Income of the technology centres	16
	Number of researchers in firms**	16
	Stock of technological capital	12
	Expenditure in innovation per inhabitant	10

Notes:
* Population above 16 years (for each 100 000 inhabitants).
** Full dedication equivalent by each 1000 persons of the active population.
*** Accumulated amortized R&D expenditures.

Source: Own elaboration with the IAIF-RIS (Spain) Database.

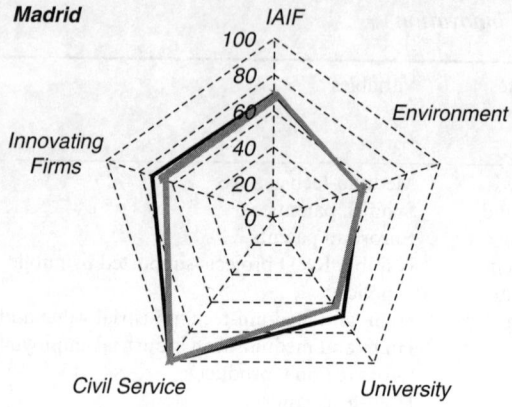

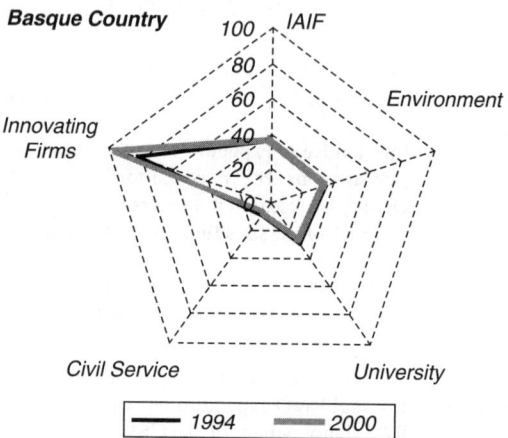

Source: Own elaboration with the IAIF-RIS (Spain) Database.

Figure 7.3 Index points of the four leading regions

each index-punctuation is normalized according to the year's maximum and minimum value, so that they score between 0 (minimum) and 1 (maximum).

As we have already explained, the weighted sum of the partial indexes makes up the (composite) IAIF-index of regional innovation capacity.[18] As we see in Table 7.2, none of the regions obtains values above 70, from which we may conclude that there is still enough 'innovation potential' to be developed. In turn, it is possible to distinguish clearly three types of regions. The

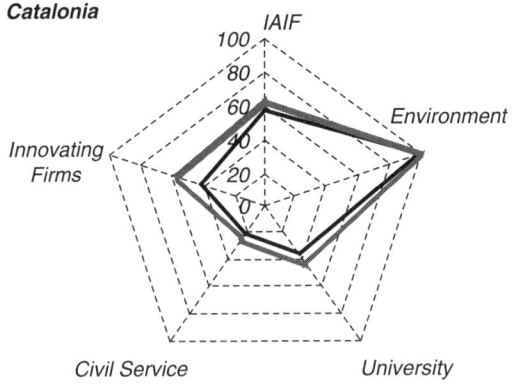

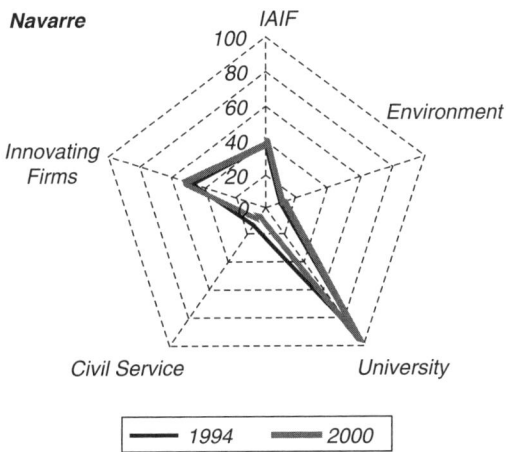

first group is formed by Madrid (the leading region) and Catalonia, which we might consider highly innovative, as both obtain the highest score in one of the partial indexes but also present scores above the average in the other three partial indexes. The second group (innovative regions) includes the Basque Country, Navarre and Valencia, which (with the exception of the latter)[19] lead one of the partial indexes, but do not stand out in any of the others. Finally, the rest of the regions, which we may consider not innovative, all present scores below 30.

As we can observe in Figure 7.3, from the four regions that lead one of the partial indexes, only two – Madrid and Catalonia – present a certain equilibrium between the partial indexes, what we could consider *symmetric* innovation systems,[20] while the others – Navarre and the Basque

Table 7.2 IAIF-index of regional innovation

Region	1994	1995	1996	1997	1998	1999	2000
Andalusia	25.75	26.13	27.87	29.31	26.50	26.02	26.21
Aragon	22.99	24.94	20.57	22.86	22.02	21.58	22.06
Asturias	15.48	19.44	15.69	17.16	15.35	15.35	20.76
Balearic Islands	3.11	5.10	4.59	3.92	4.16	4.05	3.81
Canaries	14.28	14.04	12.83	13.09	15.20	13.26	13.86
Cantabria	12.98	14.32	13.22	12.88	16.30	12.30	10.86
Castilla-La Mancha	5.98	6.33	7.12	9.52	7.19	6.34	7.48
Castilla y León	23.51	23.44	22.20	25.67	25.32	24.87	24.87
Catalonia	57.37	61.29	58.14	60.33	61.27	60.96	62.89
Valencia	37.52	37.64	35.79	38.14	36.20	35.49	35.93
Extremadura	9.88	8.03	5.95	9.37	8.91	7.72	9.98
Galicia	15.07	17.29	16.41	20.67	19.13	18.95	20.84
La Rioja	5.32	7.71	8.06	7.82	7.73	9.60	10.11
Madrid	69.51	72.01	67.00	70.19	66.75	66.26	67.02
Murcia	14.52	16.51	14.10	16.31	15.48	15.52	16.17
Navarre	36.15	36.57	36.48	37.36	36.40	37.22	37.57
Basque Country	35.51	37.73	37.16	39.02	40.13	37.16	36.97

Source: Own elaboration with the IAIF-RIS (Spain) Database.

Country – have to be considered as *asymmetric* innovation systems. Note that over the period studied, Catalonia has experienced a noticeable expansion of its innovation capacity, while Madrid's has slightly decreased.

According to these results, we may conclude that the Spanish regional innovation system presents a very heterogeneous structure, with strong asymmetries between the strengths and weaknesses of each region. Simultaneously, while the distance between the leading region of the composed index (Madrid), and the second one (Catalonia) has shortened over the period studied, the partial indexes show a differentiated behaviour over time.[21] The scores for the partial and the composite index for the year 2000 are presented in Appendix 7.1 at the end of the chapter.

7.5   THE INNOVATION SYSTEM AND KNOWLEDGE-GENERATING PROCESSES

Once the factors inherent to the regional innovation system have been established, we take a further step, using the corresponding factorial scores as independent variables in a *knowledge production function*.[22] As our output variables are the number of patents, we have taken them out of the corresponding factor, recalculating the factorial scores. Although there is a certain debate about the convenience of using patents as a measurement of innovation,[23] we may conclude that, up to now, and though recognizing its limitations, it is the best innovation output available.[24]

The output indicator we use takes into account the patents requested and published by both the Spanish and European Patents Office (EPO). We have deemed it necessary to reflect the greater value of European patents, which have higher registration costs both in time and money, using a factor of 5 to weight them in comparison with the Spanish ones, since European patents are registered on average for five countries.

As our aim is to detect which of the above-mentioned factors enable innovation flow to be estimated and to what extent, the generation of fresh knowledge function is fixed by the following equation:

$$PAT^{ES}_{r,t} + 5 \times PAT^{EU}_{r,t} = \delta_{ENV} W^{ENV}_{r,t} + \delta_{CIV} X^{CIV}_{r,t} + \delta_{INN} Y^{INN}_{r,t} + \delta_{UNI} Z^{UNI}_{r,t}$$

(7.1)

Where PAT^{ES} and PAT^{EU} are respectively the patents registered at the Spanish and European Patent Office,[25] W^{ENV} designates the Environment factor, X^{CIV} measures the Civil Service factor, Y^{INN} indicates the Innovating Firms factor and Z^{UNI} records the value of the University factor, and in which the sub-indices r and t designate, respectively, the region and the year. Note that we have estimated the model without a lag between input and output, considering that in Spain the relationship between R&D and patents is almost simultaneous.[26]

From the findings in table 7.3 it is confirmed that the four factors turn out to be statistically significant and also have a positive sign, which confirms the validity of the evolutionary, holistic approach in arguing that knowledge creation is the result of the interaction – remember that each factor is calculated taking into account all variables included in the model, thus reflecting the relationship between them[27] – of different elements considered to be under the concept of regional innovation systems. Now, it is also of interest to interpret the relative weight of those factors in the model. That will be done by taking into account the values of the standard BETA coefficients,[28] which enables us to compare the importance of the factors in the model.

Within the economic interpretation, we will be able to highlight that for the Spanish case there is a strong influence of Environment variables in the quantified innovation flows across the weighted sum of patents. Specifically, a larger-sized productive structure plays a key role in achieving results related to technological innovation, which ratifies the importance of a certain critical mass and a minimum market size. In this way, the hypothesis that states the importance of the business segment within innovation systems

Table 7.3 Regression results

	Non-standardized Coefficients	Standardized Coefficients	Parametric Contrasts	
	B	BETA	t	Sig.
(Constant)	201.506		28.428	0.000
Environment	267.463	0.874	37.510	0.000
Civil Service	106.291	0.347	14.907	0.000
Innovating Firms	68.356	0.223	9.587	0.000
University	45.104	0.147	6.326	0.000
R	R^2		Durbin Watson	
0.978	0.957		2.02	

Notes:
Dependent variable: weighted sum patents.
Heteroskedasticity robust coefficients.

Source: Own elaboration with the IAIF-RIS (Spain) Database.

is verified. If we also bear in mind the relative weight of the factor related to Innovating Firms, this hypothesis is reinforced. Moreover, the Civil Service and the University, albeit with a significant, positive role, are reduced to a secondary role, which is not an obstacle to their interaction with the other factors contributing to obtaining greater innovation results.

The findings obtained via the use of factors corresponding to regional innovation systems are in accordance with those of preceding studies where the work was carried out with a set of non-hypothetical indicators instead of factors,[29] for the same time period and using the same dependent variable (weighted sum of patents) and, at the same time, they are in keeping with those that have been highlighted in international literature, both for regional and national cases.[30]

7.6 ANALYSIS OF THE EFFICIENCY OF INNOVATION SYSTEMS

Until now we analysed the structure of the regional innovation systems (input side) and the determinants of the innovative capacity (output side). The only question left, which we will analyse in this section, is: do the regions use their resources in an efficient manner? In this section we combine both perspectives – input versus output – analysing whether the regions use a minimum of resources to reach a maximum of output. In this way it is

Table 7.4 Level of efficiency of the Spanish regional innovation system (frontier of efficiency = 100)

	1994	2000
Madrid	100	100
Catalonia	100	100
Valencia	*58.62*	*53.55*
Basque Country	*46.48*	*42.0*
Navarre	*26.65*	*19.93*
Andalusia	22.32	26.08
Aragon	12.98	15.96
Castilla y León	9.47	12.80
Galicia	4.25	8.49
Cantabria	3.3	3.93
Asturias	*8.58*	*7.68*
Murcia	5.6	8.64
Canaries	4.03	8.35
Castilla-La Mancha	2.92	6.60
Balearic Islands	3.01	7.89
Extremadura	1.17	1.95
La Rioja	*3.64*	*1.78*

Note: In italics, the regions with a declining relative efficiency level.

Source: Own elaboration with the IAIF-RIS (Spain) Database.

possible to establish the efficiency in the assignation of resources in the regional innovation systems. The methodology used is the data envelopment analysis (DEA).[31]

The methodology to measure or quantify the efficiency distinguishes between two types of models. The parametric model requires the specification of a certain production function and a specific distribution of the residuals. The second type – non-parametrical models[32] – do not require a specific production function.[33] The DEA is an outstanding model within the latter ones, and we may distinguish between two main types of DEA analysis: while the CCH model[34] assumes constant scale returns of scale, the BCC model[35] admits other types of returns, including variable ones.

Anyway, both models analyse the relative efficiency of each unit, relating it to the most efficient ones included in the sample, which are supposed to form the technological frontier. Consequently, the (relative) efficiency is expressed as the percentage related to this frontier. The application of this methodology to the Spanish regional innovation system generates the results shown in Table 7.4.

Concluding, it can be stated that in the period 1994–2000 we observe a modest improvement in the innovative efficiency of the non-leading regions in relation to the most efficient ones. These results confirm the already mentioned existing heterogeneity of the Spanish regional innovation systems. As seen before, Spain has two leading regions – Madrid and Catalonia – in terms of efficiency. These are the same regional innovation systems that in the former sections were defined as the ones with a higher level of development and also with a more balanced relationship between the four main factors of the system.[36]

7.7 CONCLUSIONS AND FINAL REMARKS

This study can be considered as an initial approach to using combined indicators (factors) to analyse the structure, development, determinants and efficiency of a regional innovation system. We developed some new ways to measure innovation (systems) considering this concept as non-directly observable. Factor analysis allowed us to reduce the set of existing variables to a lower set of non-observable hypothetical variables. These variables we used to do further empirical analysis.

The four presented analyses are complementary because they correspond to each of the perspectives of an economic analysis that tries to evaluate the innovation system. The *typology of regional innovation systems* describes the structure of configuration of the regional innovation system, the *IAIF-index of regional innovation* summarizes these typologies and offers the possibility of quantifying and analysing their development over time. The ideas production function establishes the relationship between the 'structural aspects' indicating the *determinants of knowledge creation* and their impact in boosting innovation, while the data envelopment analysis evaluates the *efficiency* of the innovative activities on a regional level.

As we did not find any other study that uses this methodology, we controlled our results comparing the outcome of four different analyses in this chapter. Although we propose some further analysis, especially in the case of the efficiency index, the outcome seems reliable. The results confirm each other and are the expected ones, taking into account the literature on technological change, economic growth and innovation systems.

NOTES

1. For a discussion about the concept of innovation systems see Lundvall, 1992; Nelson, 1993; Edquist, 1997.

2. The study is part of a large research project, carried out since 1999 by the Instituto de Análisis Industrial y Financiero (IAIF), aimed at the collection and development of indicators to analyse the regional innovation activities in Spain. In this project, we collected and elaborated over 70 variables related to different aspects of the Spanish regional innovation systems.
3. For example, the technological level of Spain (in 2001 in comparison to the European Union = 100) is 45 per cent, taking into account the R&D expenditures by GNP and 62 per cent in the case of employment in R&D by total employment. However, if we use the number of patents per capita as an indicator this level is only 15 per cent.
4. Heijs (2001b).
5. A more detailed analysis of the variables can be found in Martínez Pellitero and Baumert (2003).
6. The CDTI is a public institution managing credit funding of business projects involving technological innovation. It is probably one of the most important instruments of Spanish technological policy. See Molero and Buesa (1998) and Heijs (2001a).
7. In previous studies (Martínez Pellitero, 2002; Buesa, Martínez Pellitero, Heijs, Baumert, 2002) patents were also used as an indicator of accumulated know-how. However, given that in the following section they are used as a measure of output – in statistical terms as a dependent variable of regression – they are omitted from this first part of the analysis.
8. Due to a lack of space we do not consider variables that have not been included in the final model.
9. Both, Barlett's test of sphericity and the KMO (Kaiser-Meyer-Olkin) measurement of sample adequacy verify the convenience and suitability of factorial analysis for the variables given.
10. After the extraction of the four factors, 73 per cent of the variables show communality qualities over 0.800.
11. The exclusion barrier for variables has been placed in saturations below 0.5. This is only done in order to facilitate the visual interpretation of the factors. In any case, the factors take into account the relations between all variables and their saturations with each factor, even if this saturation is below 0.5. In doing so, the factor scores calculated do not only consider the variables included in that specific factor, but also all the other variables that conform to the other factors, thus measuring the relationship and, somehow, the interaction between them.
12. We have also tested models with a reduced number of variables conforming to the first factor. In any case, the factorial loadings proved to be very robust. The first factor is composed of scalar variables, reflecting both the economic and human size of the system, the importance of which was already pointed out by Adam Smith (1776).
13. To use the technique it is necessary to fix a difference and a method of group building. Distance is an index reflecting the greater or lesser similarity among individuals, so the greater it is the lesser the similarity between the defined systems of innovation. The distance used here, *Euclid squared*, can be seen to be affected by the types of unit being handled, so this problem has been corrected by standardizing the variables according to the Z-score method. With regard to the group-forming method, two *agglomeration* procedures have been used – *the nearest neighbour and the most distant neighbour* – that is, all the individuals are considered to belong to isolated groups and they become members of the cluster consecutively. In the case of the nearest neighbour method the groups are formed on the basis of lesser distance, and in that of the most distant neighbour, the nearest groups of individuals join together within the most distant ones.
14. The deficiency of most of these studies lies in the small number of variables used – especially at the regional level – and in determining a priori, relying on theoretical proposals the composition and weightings of the (sub) indices. As has been conveniently pointed out by Grupp (2003), these subjective criteria are not always disinterested, as they seem to be in some cases 'country friendly', optimizing the results of a certain country or

region by what he calls 'country-tuning'. See also Grupp and Mogee (2004). For a further discussion on this topic, see European Commission (2005).
15. Grupp (2003).
16. Zabala (2005) has compared the results obtained for the Spanish regions by the European Innovation Scoreboard 2002 with the IAIF-index, and also the IAIF methodology with alternative forms of index calculation, concluding that our procedure (IAIF methodology) has proved to be quite robust (p. 9).
17. For a detailed description on how to calculate the weighting, see Martínez Pellitero and Baumert (2003) and Buesa et al. (2003).
18. In this research we have attempted to reduce the number of scalar variables in Factor 1. However the reduction did not imply that the weight of the partial index would be lower, but the total variance explained by the model decreased considerably. This is also the case in the other factors.
19. The position of Valencia is singular, and though it does not lead any of the partial indexes, it presents a notable equilibrium between each of the partial indexes, which has important consequences on the innovative efficiency of the region, as will be shown later on.
20. See also note 7.
21. Due to a lack of space, we are not able to present in detail the evolution of each of the sub-indexes, which may be found in Martínez Pellitero and Baumert (2003).
22. Our approach is similar to the one by Furman, Porter and Stern (2002).
23. Already pointed out by Griliches (1990).
24. OECD (2004).
25. The patents of the EPO have been assigned according to where the inventor lived, thus avoiding the 'headquarters effect'. Anyway, this does not occur with the Spanish patents, but is minimized by the higher weighting of the former.
26. Buesa and Molero (1992). For a broad discussion about patents being an adequate measurement of innovation, see Baumert (2006).
27. See note 11 on this topic.
28. This coefficient represents, in terms of elasticity, the increase in the dependent variable – in typical deviations – produced when the typical deviation increases by one unit the value of the dependent variable under the ceteris paribus hypothesis.
29. Buesa, Baumert, Heijs and Martínez Pellitero (2002).
30. See Baumert (2006); Furman, Porter and Stern (2002) and, to a less extent, also Faber and Hesen (2004).
31. The mathematical background of the DEA combines techniques of the linear programming and non-parametric models. This methodology is frequently used in microeconomic studies whose main objective is the control and evaluation of the efficiency of different agents and activities from the public and the private sectors. See among others Martínez Cabrera (2003).
32. The parametric perspective distinguishes between two models: the deterministic model of the frontier (DMF) and the stochastic model of the frontier (MEF). For a revision of those models see Silkman (1986).
33. Although in this methodology they do not specify a certain production function it requires the accomplishment of some assumptions: free availability of inputs and outputs, convexity and constant scale return.
34. Developed by Charnes, Cooper and Rhodes (1978).
35. See Banker, Charnes and Cooper (1984).
36. Although the European Innovation Scoreboard 2005 has made an attempt to calculate the relative innovative efficiency of the EU members, they are not really calculating efficiency, but (overall) performance. This becomes clear in an article published in *European Innovation* (January 2006) p. 25. Consequently, they conclude, that 'investing in areas of greater weakness has a greater impact on overall performance' while a true efficiency (DEA) analysis might point out just the opposite: that greater efficiency might be the result of reinforcing the strengths.

REFERENCES

Baumert, T. (2006), 'Los Determinantes de la Innovación. Un Análisis Aplicado Sobre las Regiones de la Unión Europea', PhD Thesis, Universidad Complutense de Madrid (Spain), www.ucm.es/BUCM/cee/iaif.
Banker, R., A. Charnes and W. Cooper (1984), 'Some models for estimating technical and scale efficiencies in Data Envelopment Analysis', *Management Science*, **30**(9), 1078–92.
Buesa, M. and J. Molero (1992), 'Capacidad tecnológica y ventajas competitivas en la industria española: análisis a partir de las patentes', *Ekonomiaz*, 22, 220–47.
Buesa, M., T. Baumert, J. Heijs and M. Martínez Pellitero (2002), 'Los factores determinantes de la innovación. Un análisis econométrico sobre las regiones españolas', *Economía Industrial*, 347, 2002/V, 67–84.
Buesa, M., T. Baumert, J. Heijs and M. Martinez Pellitero (2003), 'Metodología y resultados del índice IAIF de la Innovación Regional', *Madri+d*, 16, Abril-Mayo 2003, www.madrimasd.org.
Buesa, M., M. Martínez Pellitero, J. Heijs and T. Baumert (2002), 'Los sistemas regionales de innovación en España: tipología basada en indicadores económicos e institucionales de las Comunidades Autónomas', *Economía Industrial*, 347, 2002/V, 15–32.
Charnes, A., W. Cooper and E. Rhodes (1978), 'Measuring the efficiency of decision-making units', *European Journal of Operational Research*, 2, 429–44.
Edquist, C. (1997), *Systems of Innovation. Technologies, Institutions and Organizations*, London: Pinter.
European Commission (2005), *Methodology Report on European Innovation Scoreboard*, www.cordis.lu/trendchart.
Faber, J. and A.B. Hesen (2004), 'Innovation capabilities of European nations. Cross-national analyses of patents and sales of product innovations', *Research Policy*, **33**, 193–207.
Furman, J.L., M.E. Porter and S. Stern (2002), 'The determinants of national innovative capacity', *Research Policy*, 31, 899–933.
Griliches, Z. (1990), 'Patent statistics as economic indicators: a survey', *Journal of Economic Literature*, 28, 1661–703.
Grupp, H. (2003), 'National Innovation Measurement between Scoreboarding, Metrics Making and Mapping', paper presented at SPRU Conference *What Do We Know About Innovation?* 13–15 November, 2003, University of Sussex.
Grupp, H. and M.E. Mogee (2004), 'Indicators for national science and technology policy: how robust are composite indicators?', *Research Policy*, 33, 1373–84.
Heijs, J. (2001a), *Política Tecnológica e Innovación. Evaluación de la Financiación Pública de I+D en España*, Madrid: Consejo Económico y Social.
Heijs, J. (2001b), 'Sistemas Nacionales y Regionales de Innovación y Política Tecnológica', Documento de Trabajo No. 24, Madrid: Instituto de Análisis Industrial y Financiero, Universidad Complutens, www.ucm.es/BUCM/cee/iaif.
Lundvall, B.A. (1992), *National Systems of Innovation: Towards a Theory of Innovation and Interactive Learning*, London: Pinter.
Martínez Cabrera, M. (2003), *La Medición de la Eficiencia en las Instituciones de Educación Superior*, Bilbao: Fundación BBVA.
Martínez Pellitero, M. (2002), 'Recursos y Resultados de los Sistemas de Innovación: Elaboración de una Tipología de Sistemas Regionales de Innovación

en España', Documento de Trabajo No. 34, Madrid: Instituto de Análisis Industrial y Financiero, Universidad Complutense, www.ucm.es/BUCM/cee/iaif.

Martínez Pellitero, M. and T. Baumert (2003), 'Medida de la Capacidad Innovadora de las Comunidades Autónomas Españolas: Construcción de un Índice Regional de la Innovación', Documento de Trabajo No. 35, Madrid: Instituto de Análisis Industrial y Financiero, Universidad Complutense, www.ucm.es/BUCM/cee/iaif.

Molero, J. and M. Buesa (1998), 'Les partenariats de technologie industrielle en Espagne', *OCDE-STI Revue*, 23.

Nelson, R.R. (ed.) (1993), *National Innovation Systems: A Comparative Study*, New York: Oxford University Press.

OECD (2004), *Compendium of Patent Statistics*, Paris.

Silkman, R.H. (ed.) (1986), *Measuring Efficiency. An Assessment of Data Envelopment Analysis*, San Francisco, Jossey-Bass Publishers.

Smith A. (1776), *An Inquiry into the Nature and Causes of the Wealth of Nations*.

Zabala, J.M. (2005), 'Debilidades Metodológicas en la Medición de la Capacidad Innovadora de los Sistemas Regionales de Innovación', paper presented at the International Complutense Seminary *Innovation Systems: A Regional Perspective*, 6–7 June, 2005, Universidad Complutense, Madrid, http://ideas.repec.org.

APPENDIX 7.1

Table A7.1 *Index scores, year 2000*

Region	Partial Index 1 Regional Environment	Partial Index 2 Universities	Partial Index 3 Civil Service	Partial Index 4 Innovating Firms	Composed Index IAIF-index
Andalusia	29.67	38.07	16.84	14.23	26.21
Aragon	12.73	28.63	19.47	35.39	22.06
Asturias	5.63	49.37	14.39	21.56	20.76
Balearic Islands	2.21	5.03	5.93	3.14	3.81
Canaries	3.57	36.78	15.79	2.98	13.86
Cantabria	2.24	23.03	12.52	10.78	10.86
Castilla-La Mancha	8.58	3.39	1.70	16.97	7.48
Castilla y León	17.28	50.16	8.46	25.77	24.87
Catalonia	100.00	43.63	24.74	54.70	62.89
Valencia	44.31	41.77	10.31	39.74	35.93
Extremadura	1.16	27.14	10.87	4.72	9.98
Galicia	16.70	39.33	13.63	13.35	20.84
La Rioja	2.59	16.70	6.62	20.75	10.11
Madrid	53.19	61.27	100.00	65.99	67.02
Murcia	5.70	34.72	14.07	15.75	16.17
Navarre	10.10	96.50	7.40	50.65	37.57
Basque Country	31.84	25.77	5.71	96.57	36.97

Source: Own elaboration with the IAIF-RIS (Spain) Database.

8. Over-embeddedness and under-exploration issues in cohesive networks: an application to territorial clusters

Francesc Xavier Molina-Morales and María Teresa Martínez-Fernández

8.1 INTRODUCTION

It is frequently argued that the context of geographical proximity of the industrial district and cluster provides some characteristic features of the internal social networks of firms, namely, their being a cohesive network with strong ties through redundant and frequent relationships. Authors have devoted a lot of attention to analyzing potential benefits of these social networks. It has been concluded that social interactions and trust facilitate the exchange and combination of knowledge resources and as a result improve the innovation capacity of firms (Uzzi, 1996).

However, a cohesive network also presents certain limitations that have been analyzed to a lesser extent and, in our opinion, still need to be properly addressed. Critics have claimed that the same mechanisms that constitute the basis for efficient continuous improvements of clustered firms are also considered as being restraints and limitations to coping with other strategic proposals (Glasmeier, 1991; Harrison, 1991; Grabher, 1993).

First, according to the *over-embeddedness* argument, the positive impact of embedded relationships on the performance of firms (i.e., innovation) is eroded with an intensive use of ties. Beyond a certain point, additional increases in intensity or strength produce no additional benefits and may even decrease returns for the firms involved (Langfred, 2004).

A second concern refers to the *under-exploring* capacity of clustered firms because of the lack of *bridging ties* (Burt, 1992). It is argued that cohesive networks may have serious limitations when it comes to facing radical external changes, for example, technological shocks that require *exploring* abilities to detect and acquire new and exclusive resources (Gargiulo and Benassi, 2000; Rowley, Behrens and Krackhardt, 2000).

The research outlined in this chapter deals essentially with exploring the advantages and disadvantages of cohesive networks and how they affect a firm's innovation performance in industrial clusters. In particular, we examine how the lack of bridging ties (i.e., over-embeddedness) in cohesive networks can become a hindrance to a firm's innovation in response to radical changes from outside (Ahuja, 2000). Although the general line of argument has been explained by previous research, the contribution of this study is the formal testing of the hypotheses.

We have structured the chapter as follows: first, we have developed our theoretical framework, including the explanation of the cohesive argument within the social capital perspective. We then argue the issues of over-embeddedness and under-exploring, and our hypotheses are formulated. In the second part of the chapter we have developed the empirical research that was conducted in order to test our hypotheses. This research was based on a sample of clustered manufacturing firms in the Valencia Region in Spain.

8.2 THEORETICAL FRAMEWORK

8.2.1 Social Capital as a Source of Innovation

Social capital is defined as the sum of resources accumulated by the firm because it has a stable network of interfirm relationships (Bourdieu and Wacquant, 1992, p. 119). Organizations import knowledge into the firm by means of social capital. This knowledge can be exchanged and combined with internal knowledge and, thus, by comparing the two types of knowledge, the organization can observe inconsistencies that enable it to identify weaknesses in the existing internal knowledge. By so doing it becomes possible to determine the benefits that a firm can derive from social capital (Anand, Glick and Manz, 2002). Access to external sources of innovation is associated with the characteristics of the interactions of the firm within the social networks and is regulated by the amount of social capital it possesses (Yli-Renko, Autio and Sapienza, 2001).

Coleman (1990) stressed the positive effect exerted by the cohesive or dense structure of networks on the production of social norms and sanctions that facilitate trust and cooperative exchanges. In the same vein, the *strong tie argument* (i.e., Krackhardt, 1992) suggests that it provides organizations with two primary advantages, namely, exchanges of high-quality information and tacit knowledge, and it serves as a mechanism of social control that governs the interdependencies in partnerships (Uzzi, 1996; 1997).

Another, and contradictory, point of view has been offered by the *structural holes approach* (Burt, 1992), which proposes a *disperse characterization* as an alternative perspective and defines social capital in terms of the information diversity and control advantages of being the broker in relations between otherwise disconnected people within social structures. In other words, the causal agent determining whether a tie will provide access to new information and opportunities is the extent to which it is non-redundant (McEvily and Zaheer, 1999). Moreover, Granovetter (1973) argues in favor of the *strength of the weak tie*, emphasizing how weak ties enable an actor to access new, exclusive information.

8.2.2 Industrial District as a Cohesive Network

Previous research has explained how industrial districts represent local configurations that are high in social capital because they are characterized by mutual trust, cooperation and an entrepreneurial spirit as well as by the existence of a multitude of small local firms with complementary specialized competencies (Saxenian, 1994; Dakhli and De Clercq, 2004).

Generally speaking, proximity provides frequent, repeated, non-marked, informal contacts, all of which facilitate the strong ties and the density of the network of ties. These interactions stimulate exchanges of information about competitors, production technologies, recent developments, and so on (Decarolis and Deeds, 1999). These authors have pointed out a number of particular mechanisms present in districts by which social capital can be enhanced. Interactions among employees of firms located in the same area can be facilitated through belonging to different kinds of local associations or clubs linked with diverse fields of interest and that belong to the same neighborhood. Likewise, human resources mobility across district firms is another opportunity for information and knowledge exchange.

8.2.3 The Role of Local Institutions

The interorganizational network represented by the district includes not only specialized firms but also a broad range of local institutions that support the whole system. For the purposes of this research, we define local institutions as locally-oriented organizations that provide firms in the local area with a host of collective support services. Examples of local institutions include universities, research institutes, vocational training centers, technical assistance centers and trade and professional associations.

A number of authors have provided evidence of the impact of local institutions on firm performance in territorial agglomerations (e.g., Decarolis and Deeds, 1999; McEvily and Zaheer, 1999). Other authors have analyzed the effects of specific local institutions. Swan and Newell (1995) found evidence for the positive effect of the role played by professional associations in the diffusion of knowledge. The notion of 'innovation community' was put forward as an institutional arrangement fostering innovation (Lynn, Reddy and Aram, 1996; Haake, 2002). Likewise, Allison and Long (1987) offered evidence that institutional affiliation has a significant stimulating effect on productivity. Finally, Almeida and Kogut (1999) investigated how the relationships among firms, universities, scientists and engineers strongly affect the extent to which knowledge spillover occurs.

8.2.4 Limitations of the Cohesive Industrial District Network

The potential of the previous characterization of the cohesive network and strong ties has received some criticism, which can be classified into three groups: (1) costs of maintaining strong ties; (2) lack of autonomy, and (3) obligations derived from norms and values. A good review article on social capital, and more particularly about its negative effects, is the one published by Portes (1998).

The first group means that strong ties imply interaction among firms and these are costly to maintain (Boorman, 1975; Hansen, 1999), both in terms of the costs associated with maintaining ongoing relationships and the norms and costs involved in maintaining slack resources (Leana and Van Buren III, 1999). In the second case, firms engaged in strong ties adapt to each other and develop a similarity of knowledge base (Rogers, 1986). In contrast, firms engaged in weak ties, which are in a better position to search for new knowledge, enjoy greater autonomy and will find it easier to adapt (Sharma and Blomstermo, 2003). In addition, the obligations deriving from the cohesive networks also include some restraints. Strong ties are associated on a *reciprocal* basis in which advice and help flow in both directions (Marsden and Campbell, 1984). Firms that provide information will also expect to receive similar information, if needed. Finally, if strong exit barriers exist, the feasibility of opportunistic behavior increases (Blumberg, 2001).

Although few studies have explored crises in industrial districts, some do provide evidence of cases in which an excessive interaction among the same actors (Soda and Usai, 1999) can undermine the efficiency of economic actions and sometimes lead an industrial district to crisis and decline. In his example, Glasmeier (1991; 1994) attributed part of the responsibility for the Swiss watch industry's crisis to the limited information flows in the area, which suffocated advances in the business (Alberti, 2004).

8.3 HYPOTHESES

We have conceptualized the limitations of the cohesive network in the district using the notions of over-embeddedness and under-exploring. The former could occur when all firms in a network are connected through embedded ties (Burt, 1992; Uzzi, 1996, 1997). When the impact of social capital decreases beyond a certain level of social interactions and trust, the result will be parochialism and inertia (Adler and Kwon, 2002). Under-exploring refers to the absence of autonomous relationships that develop exploring strategies in order to capture new and exclusive resources (Woolcock, 1998; Yli-Renko et al., 2001), which means that there are few or no links to outside members who can potentially contribute innovative ideas.

We formulated our hypotheses based on prior arguments and evidence supporting a non-monotonic relationship between social capital indicators and performance (innovation).

8.3.1 Social Interactions and Innovation

The intensity of the social interactions of an organization can be used as an indicator of the strength of the ties and its social capital (Nahapiet and Ghoshal, 1998). Social interactions are channels through which information and resources flow and enable an actor to gain access to other actors' resources (Kanter, 1988). Social interactions dissolve the boundaries between organizations and stimulate the formation of a common interest, which offers advantages such as obtaining information and access to specific resources (Powell, Koput and Smith-Doer, 1996). Through social interactions, firms may increase the depth, breadth and efficiency of the mutual exchange of knowledge (Lane and Lubatkin, 1998). Thus, social interactions exert an influence on the future capabilities of firms and constitute a factor explaining their performance (Andersson, Forsgren and Holm, 2002).

However, as the over-embeddedness issue suggests, the positive effect of social interactions on innovation is not linear and positive. Initially, newly formed contacts are expected to benefit from significant effects, but diminishing returns are also expected and, ultimately, these diminishing returns could become negative returns (Berman, Down and Hill, 2002). It is argued that, as the number of interactions between two firms increases, additional interaction provides less information about the counterpart and consequently the chances of value creation are reduced (Chung, Singh and Lee, 2000). Contacts begin to crystallize and additional benefits from shared experience become increasingly difficult to attain (Berman et al., 2002).

Likewise, another adverse consequence can be described, since the relational ties of the firm are, to some degree, substitutes for one another. A firm might be better off establishing other ties with non-redundant actors rather than investing the time and resources required to form and maintain strong ties (Rowley et al., 2000). The power benefits of social capital may, in some cases, trade off its information benefits (Adler and Kwon, 2002). McEvily and Zaheer (1999) found that the interfirm information networks of firms in geographical clusters with greater redundancy tend to acquire fewer competitive capabilities. Building social capital requires a considerable investment in establishing and maintaining relationships and, as with any costly investment, social capital investment may not be cost-efficient in certain situations (Adler and Kwon, 2002). This dysfunctional effect of this dimension arises when firms get locked into their current networks, thus inhibiting their flexibility in creating new ties. Such networks could have an adverse effect on firm performance when the environment changes, as they may not have the capabilities or the information necessary to compete in the new environment (Pouder and St. John, 1996).

Consequently, we find support for a predicted positive relationship between social capital and performance that declines as social interactions increase and eventually becomes negative. The non-linear inverted U-shaped relationship is the one that best captures expectations based on the hypothesis:

H1:   As a consequence of over-embeddedness, the effect of social interactions will have a non-linear (inverted U-shaped) relationship with innovation.

8.3.2   Trust and Innovation

Previous researchers have argued that trust in interorganizational settings may foster innovation (Gemser and Wijnberg, 2001; Dakhli and De Clercq, 2004). Trust acts as a governance mechanism for embedded relationships (Uzzi, 1996), thus facilitating innovation and learning (Meeus, Oerlemans and Hage, 2001). Trust among organizations facilitates the exchange of confidential information by diminishing the risk that one party will opportunistically exploit this information to the other's disadvantage (Knack and Keefer, 1997). Trust also facilitates social exchange by reducing the need for time-consuming and costly monitoring, and therefore makes it possible for people and organizations to devote additional time to beneficial actions and endeavors (Blau, 1986).

Although it can be argued that trust exerts a positive effect on innovation, the over-embeddedness issue states that this positive effect is moderated by the level of trust. Portes and Sensenbrenner (1993) argued that, in some cases, benefits from the support and resources provided by cohesive networks are important, but the obligations (in terms of trust, reciprocity, solidarity, and so on) that resulted from those benefits and the difficulties firms experienced in trying to extricate themselves from those obligations curtailed their subsequent capacity to pursue new opportunities. The solidarity benefits of social capital may have negative effects since the resulting obligations can also be considered as a form of cost. Due to the norms of reciprocity, asking contacts for significant amounts of help may place a person in their debt (Blau, 1986; Coleman, 1988, 1990; Fiske, 1991). How much debt is incurred will vary from contact to contact depending on such factors as relative status and attitude (Borgatti and Cross, 2003).

Firms may devote too much time and effort to maintaining trusting relationships and thus affect performance in a negative manner. The higher the level of trust, the more likely the local firm is to be subjected to a boomerang effect, which can take several different shapes. Such over-embeddedness reduces the flow of new ideas into the group, resulting in lock-in and inertia (Adler and Kwon, 2002).

Hence, it can be argued that the relationship between the level of trust and innovation will take on a non-linear inverted U-shape. We formulated the following hypothesis in order to capture the relationship argued above.

H2: *As a consequence of over-embeddedness, the effect exerted by the level of trust will have a non-linear (inverted U-shaped) relationship with innovation.*

8.3.3 Local Institutions and Innovation

Local institutions are relevant actors in territorial networks that provide specific knowledge as a consequence of their position as intermediaries. This argument is backed by previous research such as Galaskiewicz (1985); Baum and Oliver (1992); Suchman (1994) and McEvily and Zaheer (1999).

Because local institutions interact with a large number of firms in the geographical cluster, they are exposed to a wide variety of solutions to organizational challenges. Based on broad experience gained from observing others who have dealt with similar problems, local institutions, acting as go-betweens, compile and disseminate summaries about capabilities and routines (Suchman, 1994). Indeed, local institutions facilitate managerial innovation by providing access to information and resources, which in turn enable firms to acquire new (and to extend existing) innovation capabilities (McEvily and Zaheer, 1999), thus reducing the under-exploring effect in the industrial district.

Local institutions also diminish the search costs associated with locating external sources of the knowledge and specialized expertise that is critical for district firms. By maintaining an extensive network of ties, these intermediaries generate search economies (Molina and Martínez, 2003).

Hence, it can be argued that local institutions involvement has a direct effect on the capacity of district firms to innovate. The above discussion can be stated more formally through the following hypothesis:

H3:   The extent to which a firm is involved with local institutions will be positively associated with its level of innovation.

8.4   RESEARCH METHODOLOGY

8.4.1   The Empirical Setting

The empirical research drew upon a sample of Spanish industrial firms located along the east coast of the country (Valencia Region), where there is a predominance of SMEs in the industrial structure. The use of a public database (ARDAN, 2000)[1] enabled us to identify the address and four-digit Standard Industrial Classification (SIC) of the companies involved in the study.

Data needed to operationalize variables were collected using a questionnaire distributed among firms and addressed to the general manager in each case. We collected complete data for 154 firms, whose basic characteristics are shown in Table 8.1 (see Results later on in the chapter). Since few precedents were available to guide the development of indicators, fieldwork helped to refine the choice of constructs and identify the most relevant items. Item selection was also based on the feedback obtained from a pilot questionnaire. For the sake of simplicity, we employed a five-point Likert scale. The fieldwork was carried out during fall and winter of 2002.

We checked for possible differences between sample and non-respondent firms in order to determine the possible bias due to the latter, and no significant differences were observed in terms of size and technological attributes.

8.4.2   Research Design

8.4.2.1   Independent variables[2]
Social interactions   To operationalize this variable we based our work on prior research, in particular Tsai and Ghoshal (1998), and took the frequency and intimacy of contact as a reference (Marsden and Campbell,

1984; Brown and Konrad, 2001). Other items were also incorporated in accordance with the territorial context of our sample. The expression 'other firms' was included to refer to all the firms in contact with one individual firm including, for instance, customers, competitors or suppliers. Items used in the questionnaire were:

1. People from your company spend a considerable amount of time on social occasions with people from other firms.
2. People from your company spend a considerable amount of time on social events organized by the local community.
3. A local origin and common academic background of the employees at local firms allow social interactions to take place.
4. There is an informal network among customers, suppliers and competitors.
5. You talk to an external contact person very often (more than once a week).
6. You feel comfortable talking to the contact person responsible for getting you the information that allowed your company's performance to be improved.

Trust   To operationalize this variable we based our work on prior research, in particular by combining indicators used in Tsai and Ghoshal (1998); Knack and Keefer (1997); Blumberg (2001) or Dakhli and De Clercq (2004). We also incorporated other items in accordance with the territorial context of our sample:

1. Other firms can rely on your company without any fear that you will take advantage of them, even if the opportunity arises to do so.
2. In general, your company will always keep the promises it makes to others.
3. Suppose your company is seeking to be a business partner in a joint project. You are confident that you will do what is required in the agreement (i.e., what partners believe you should do) even without a written contract that clearly specifies your obligations.
4. You consider that other firms feel a special duty to stand by you in times of trouble, so you consider it only fair that your company should also give support to other firms.
5. Generally speaking, there is a trusting climate among suppliers and customers in the local area, that is to say, a feeling that most people can be trusted or that you can deal with people easily.
6. You have confidence in a variety of organizations or institutions, such as the legal system, the government or major companies.

Involvement of local institutions While the conceptual foundations of this measure are drawn from Burt's (1992) notion of structural holes, like Zaheer and Zaheer (2001) we used a simpler approximation of the concept due to the large network in our study. To operationalize this variable we based our work on McEvily and Zaheer's (1999) definition and we adapted the items to our specific case:

1. Your company has received significant support for R&D activities from local institutions.
2. You or your employees have received specific training by local academic institutions.
3. Your company has received considerable information about products and markets from local institutions.
4. You consider that you cannot receive support from external firms directly instead of through local institutions.
5. You can obtain on-site assistance at your company from any local institutions.
6. You can select/install new equipment or systems with the help of local institutions.

8.4.2.2 Dependent variables

Innovation[3] Prior research has measured innovation by combining several dimensions related to the level of technology activities and output generated in a given firm, and self-reported data has been suggested as one of the valid indicators (Keeble, 1997). To measure this variable, two groups of items were included in the questionnaire that asked respondents to report the number of product and process innovations that had been produced in their field of activity over the last three years. This measurement of innovation is based on Tsai and Ghoshal (1998) and Meeus et al. (2001):

1. number of developments or introductions of new materials;
2. number of developments or introductions of new intermediate products;
3. number of developments or introductions of new components;
4. number of developments or introductions of new attributes of the products;
5. number of developments or introductions of new equipment;
6. improvements in the level of automation;
7. number of new organizational methods of the productive activities;
8. use of new energy sources.

8.4.2.3 Control variables

We assumed that the size of the firm can affect its capacity for innovation, thus allowing us to control for economies and diseconomies of scale at firm level (Grant, Jammine and Thomas, 1988; Hitt, Hoskisson and Kim, 1997). Large organizations tend to have more resources with which to enhance their innovation and performance (Tsai, 2001). They are also usually more powerful than small ones and have some advantages in gaining support for their business operations and innovation activities from other organizations (public institutions). Size was operationalized as the number of employees using a conventional classification. In addition, industry was a necessary control variable, given the systematic differences between innovation factors, and it was controlled by assigning different scores to firms. We used industrial segments or SIC epigraphs (food, textiles, furniture, ceramics, leather, chemical products, machinery and paper) and, in order to define the sample, we employed a random stratified process to select firms with proportional assignation according to size and product segments.

8.4.2.4 Analysis techniques

To test our first two hypotheses we ran a non-linear, inverted U-shaped (quadratic) regression analysis for each independent variable against the dependent variable. Accordingly, we ran a model with one turning point following the equation:

$$Y = b_0 + b_1 X_1 + b_2 X^2_1$$

where:

b_0 = constant
$b_1 X_1$ = linear effect of X_1
$b_2 X^2_1$ = non-linear effect of X_1.

Finally, in order to measure the effect of the involvement of local institutions on firms' innovation (H3), we used the estimated model of multiple linear regression analysis (for a similar selection see Hagedoorn and Duysters, 2002). In this case we included the two control variables.

8.4.2.5 Validity

Regarding construct validity, since a measure of a construct is valid to the extent that it actually measures what it purports to measure (Carmine and Zeller, 1979), we controlled different aspects. In the first step, the logic of construct validity suggests that multiple indicators of the same theoretical construct should be positively and strongly related. In particular, *convergent validity* refers to 'the degree to which multiple attempts to measure the same concept by different methods are in agreement' (Campbell and Fiske, 1959; Phillips, 1981, p. 399). We included Cronbach's alpha here as a test of the *reliability* of the measurement. For district firms the least favorable Cronbach's alpha value corresponded to the multiple-item scale measuring innovation, with a score of 0.64. Bearing in mind precedents, the value of the alpha was within the suggested limits of tolerance (Malhotra, 1997). Second, we added the correlation matrix since the *discriminant validity* of two constructs can be assessed by demonstrating that the correlation between a pair of constructs is significantly different. Finally, we evaluated the *validity of answers* using data gathered from a second knowledgeable respondent who was able to provide an accurate report. Drawing on these analyses it is reasonable to conclude that the validity of the measures is acceptable, since no significant mean differences were found. This indicated that our self-report measure provided a reasonably valid proxy of original responses.

8.5 RESULTS

Table 8.1 shows descriptive statistics, Cronbach's alpha for the multiple-item variables, and Pearson's correlation for all pairs of variables. Regarding the latter, the only point worth highlighting refers to the significant correlation

Table 8.1 Descriptive statistics, mean, standard deviation, Cronbach's alpha and bivariate correlation for all pairs of variables

Variables	Mean	S.D.	α	1	2	3	4	5	6
(1) *Innovation*	3.87	1.99	0.64	1.000					
(2) *Size*	1.26	0.47	–	0.067	1.000				
(3) *Activity*	–	–	–	–0.002	–0.038	1.000			
(4) *Social interactions*	3.98	0.68	0.78	0.298**	0.129	–0.073	1.000		
(5) *Trust*	3.57	0.96	0.82	0.095*	–0.023	0.039	0.208*	1.000	
(6) *Involvement of local institutions*	3.75	0.74	0.89	0.185*	0.083	0.193**	0.148*	0.206*	1.000

Notes:
N = 154.
Pearson's correlation is significant at levels: * $p < 0.10$; and ** $p < 0.05$.
α = Cronbach's alpha for all multiple-item variables.

Table 8.2 Results of inverted U-shaped function analysis: quadratic method

Variable	Innovation		
	Inverted U-shaped	R² Adjusted	F Statistic
Social interactions	1.249* (0.701)	0.111	8.993****
*Social interactions**2*	−0.134 (0.104)		
Constant	0.169 (1.162)		
Trust	0.899*** (0.375)	0.079	6.530***
*Trust**2*	−0.109** (0.059)		
Constant	1.063* (0.590)		

Notes:
N = 154.
* $p < 0.10$; ** $p < 0.05$; *** $p < 0.01$ and **** $p < 0.001$.
Non-standardized regression coefficients (errors in brackets).

between the local institutions variable and the other social capital variables. Moreover, social capital variables are correlated with each other. Likewise, as hypothesized, social interactions, trust and local institutions are associated with innovation. Finally, control variables, size and activity were not associated with either dependent or independent variables, except for activity with local institutions. This means that social capital did not rely on industry characteristics.

Table 8.2 shows the results of a non-linear (inverted U-shaped) regression analysis carried out to determine the effect of over-embeddedness. We can say that H1 and H2 were supported, since significant correlations were obtained for the variables. Both social interactions and trust affect positively up to a certain point, where the positive effect is not only reduced but in fact becomes negative (see Figure 8.1 and Figure 8.2). Thus, the positive effect of the social capital factors was eroded by their intensive use. Although hypotheses are supported by empirical findings, over-embeddedness is far more significant for the case of trust, which can be understood to mean that the cost of an excess of trust in relationships is more expensive than an excess of social interactions.

Table 8.3 shows the results of the regression analysis conducted in order to estimate the effects of the involvement of local institutions on innovation. The coefficient was positive and significant, thus indicating that local institutions do indeed contribute to innovation. Hence, H3 is supported. As regards the control variables, neither size nor activity was significant, which suggests that economies of scale are not so important and the industry does not play a substantial role in determining the innovative behavior of firms.

Over-embeddedness and under-exploration issues in cohesive networks   189

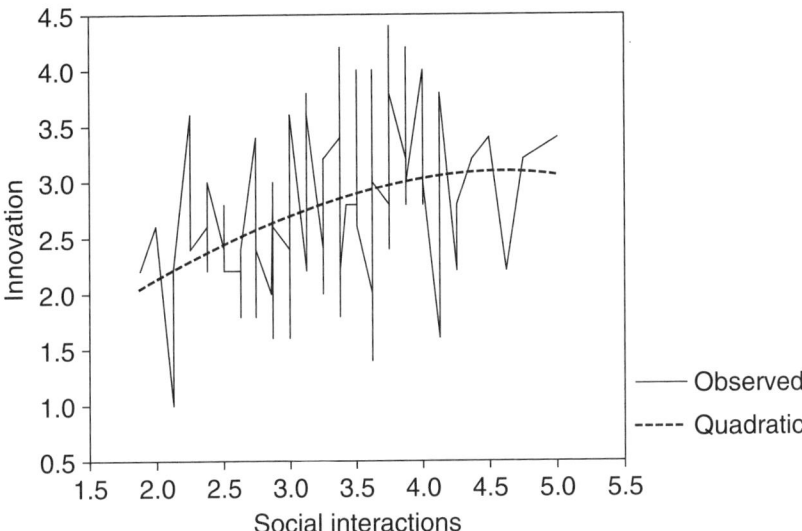

Figure 8.1   Inverted U-shaped function analysis: social interactions

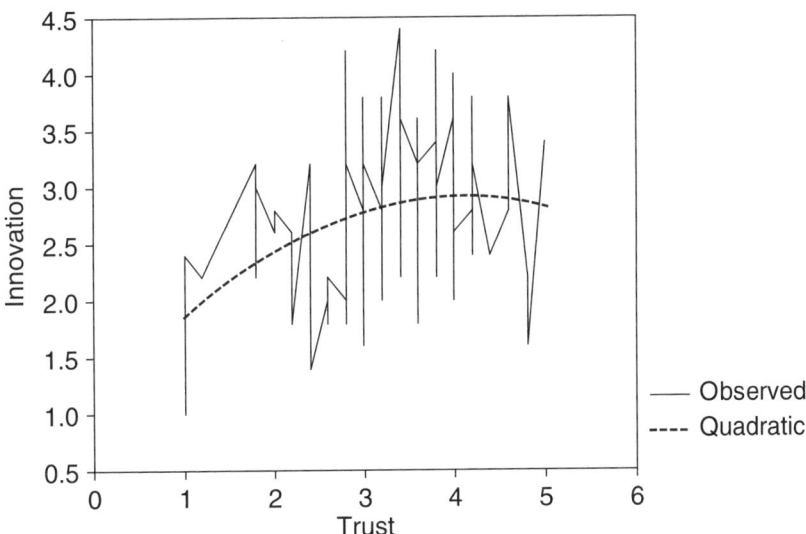

Figure 8.2   Inverted U-shaped function analysis: trust

Table 8.3 Results of regression analysis: effects of local institutions on firm innovation

Variable	Firm Innovation
Constant	1.886**** (0.211)
Size	0.023 (0.083)
Activity	0.008 (0.009)
Involvement of local institutions	0.273*** (0.060)
R^2 Adjusted	0.226
F	7.241***

Notes:
N = 154.
*** $p < 0.01$, and **** $p < 0.001$.
Non-standardized regression coefficients (errors within brackets).

8.6 DISCUSSION AND CONCLUSION

The aim of this study was to provide a better understanding of the effect of social networks on innovation through the analysis of territorial agglomerations of firms. Territorial agglomerations can shape the social relationships of firms, giving rise to a cohesive structure with frequent and redundant ties among members. Although as a result of this characterization industrial districts enjoy a number of advantages, a number of relevant limitations are also produced. We have identified the over-embeddedness issue and the difficulties involved in the exploring activities. To address these issues, first we suggested that the impact of social capital decreased beyond some tipping point. In fact, the effect of social interactions and trust on innovation can be described as an inverted U-shaped curve. On the other hand, local institutions have been considered as intermediary agents that allow districts to escape from exploring restrictions, since they can monitor what is happening outside the district and, in consequence, the involvement of local institutions has a linear correlation effect on innovation.

8.6.1 Comparison with Previous Research

First, the extent to which the main conclusions reached in this chapter coincide with those of previous research is quite striking. Just as examples, a positive association between involvement in regional institutions and the assimilation of competitive capabilities by clustered firms, as put forward in McEvily and Zaheer (1999), is largely supported. Moreover, Decarolis and Deeds's (1999) research offered evidence of a causal relationship between localization and firm performance. Capello (1999a; 1999b) also provided some evidence for the relationship between relational capital and innovation.

What differentiates our study and can be considered to be its main contribution lies in its initial premises, that is, the limitations of the industrial district in terms of innovation capacity and value creation. The findings of the study give support to the existence of a number of specific conditions in the industrial district under which innovations are produced in collective processes. District firms need to maintain a balanced portfolio of ties between internal and cohesive networks and more autonomous contacts with external networks (Baker, 1990; Uzzi, 1997).

In consequence, we are in line with the new approach (i.e., Rowley et al., 2000), which has recently suggested that, rather than being contradictory perspectives, both views (dense and disperse) are useful in explaining benefits, albeit for different strategic purposes. Learning processes have to cope with the complicated problem of balancing the competing goals of developing new knowledge (i.e., exploring) and exploiting current competencies in the face of dynamics that tend to emphasize one or the other (Levinthal and March, 1993). While exploitation involves using existing information to improve efficiency and returns from present strategies, competencies and procedures, exploration entails searching and experimenting to find emerging innovations that will produce future profits (Hite and Hesterly, 1999).

8.6.2 Prescriptions

In our opinion, the findings of our study are not only relevant from a theoretical point of view, but are also fundamental when it comes to formulating useful and effective policies. Our proposition supported a number of prescriptions for firms' strategies. We argue that firms should interact with local institutions and other cluster participants in order to improve environmental conditions (Molina and Martínez, 2004). Dynamics between the formation of tacit and codified knowledge and other elements of the innovation processes call for a reassessment of institutional arrangements. Firms may pursue diverse strategies for knowledge and skills resourcing (Lam, 1997), including, among others, strategic partnerships with key institutions so as to be able to influence the education and training of future researchers; research collaboration with individual academics or departments in universities in order to gain early access to research; or, finally, the creation of hybrid research organizations between firms and institutions to allow common research programs to be developed. On the other hand, since the findings of our research underline the crucial role played by the entrepreneur and employees as a mechanism of knowledge transmission, it is desirable to implement policies that both improve the quality of local labor and foster the internal mobility of employees and creation of new ventures. Finally, there is a need for policies to encourage cooperation among different members of the districts and to build social capital, since both of these are important for the innovative capacity of firms. Therefore, our study is consistent with previous research dealing with the role of government and policy-makers in enhancing overall national growth by stimulating the innovation capability of individual regions (Camagni, 1992).

8.6.3 Limitations and Future Research

Finally, this line of thought can be carried a bit further. In fact, the following points can also be viewed as possible limitations of this study:

1. The fine-grained process through which network structures are created or modified is an interesting and important area for future research. Another fruitful area of inquiry is the dynamics of how firms' networks evolve and change in response to external challenges and opportunities. In other words, to what extent does inertia constrain a firm's ability to reconfigure its pattern of network ties?
2. On the other hand, the processes of cooperative competition in geographical clusters could benefit greatly from a more detailed analysis of the mixture of cooperation and competition in networks. The balance between interfirm cooperation and competition, while a popular idea, warrants greater research attention, particularly in the network context; and
3. A final question may be raised as to the diversity of local institutions because, since they may be predominantly from the same industry, the information accessed by local firms could be less diverse. A deeper analysis is therefore needed of how local institutions vary in terms of the scope of the activities they carry out.

ACKNOWLEDGEMENT

This research was financially supported by Bancaixa-Universitat Jaume I, project number P1.1B2004-11 (2004–06).

NOTES

1. The ARDAN is a public database published by IMPIVA, a regional industrial policy agency, and it provides productive and financial information about all manufacturing firms except those that have an annual revenue below €240 000 (40 million pesetas). We used firms from up to 18 different industrial segments or Standard Industrial Classification (SIC) epigraphs and, in order to define the sample, we used a random stratified selection process to choose firms with assignation in proportion to their size and product segments.
2. Responses were scored on a five-point Likert scale where 1 = fully disagree and 5 = fully agree. To measure each variable we obtained an average of all the items for each firm and Cronbach's alpha was run to validate the aggregation of items.
3. To measure the variable, we added up the number of innovations reported for each item over the period of time under consideration and Cronbach's alpha was run to validate the aggregation of items.

REFERENCES

Adler, P.S. and S.-W. Kwon (2002), 'Social capital: prospects for a new concept', *Academy of Management Review*, **27**(1), 17–40.
Ahuja, G. (2000), 'Collaboration networks, structural holes, and innovation: a longitudinal study', *Administrative Science Quarterly*, **45**(3), 425–55.
Alberti, F. (2004), 'The Crisis of the Industrial District of Como: A Longitudinal Analysis of its Evolution', *20th EGOS Colloquium*, Ljubljana.
Allison, P. and S. Long (1987), 'Interuniversity mobility of academic scientists', *American Sociological Review*, 52, 643–52.
Almeida, P. and B. Kogut (1999), 'Localization of knowledge and the mobility of engineers in regional networks', *Management Science*, **45**(7), 905–17.
Anand, V., W.H. Glick and C.C. Manz (2002), 'Thriving on the knowledge of outsiders: tapping organizational social capital', *Academy of Management Executive*, **16**(1), 87–101.
Andersson, U., M. Forsgren and U. Holm (2002), 'The strategic impact of external networks: subsidiary performance and competence development in the multinational corporation', *Strategic Management Journal*, 23, 979–96.
ARDAN (2000), *Comunidad Valenciana 2000. Directorio e Informe Económico-Financiero*, Vigo: Consorcio de la Zona Franca de Vigo.
Baker, W.E. (1990), 'Market networks and corporate behavior', *American Journal of Sociology*, 6, 589–625.
Baum, J.A.C. and C. Oliver (1992), 'Institutional embeddedness and dynamics of organizational populations', *American Sociological Review*, 57, 540–59.
Berman, S.L., J. Down and C.W.L. Hill (2002), 'Tacit knowledge as a source of competitive advantage in the National Basketball Association', *Academy of Management Journal*, **45**(1), 13–31.
Blau, P. (1986), *Exchange and Power in Social Life*, New Brunswick, NJ: Transaction Publishers.
Blumberg, B.F. (2001), 'Cooperation contracts between embedded firms', *Organization Studies*, **22**(5), 825–52.
Boorman, A.S. (1975), 'A combination optimization model for transmission of job information through contact networks', *Bell Journal of Economics*, 6, 216–49.

Borgatti, S.P. and R. Cross (2003), 'A relational view of information seeking and learning in social networks', *Management Science*, **49**(4), 432–45.

Bourdieu, P. and L. Wacquant (1992), *An Invitation to Reflexive Sociology*, Chicago, IL: University of Chicago Press.

Brown, D.W. and A.M. Konrad (2001), 'Granovetter was right. The importance of weak ties to a contemporary job search', *Group & Organization Management*, **26**(4), 434–62.

Burt, R.S. (1992), 'Social structure of competition', in N. Nohria and R.G. Eccles (eds), *Networks and Organizations: Structure, Form and Action*, Boston, MA: Harvard Business School Press.

Camagni, R.P. (1992), 'Development scenarios and policy guidelines for the lagging regions in the 1990', *Regional Studies*, 26, 361–74.

Campbell, D.T. and D.W. Fiske (1959), 'Convergent and discriminant validation by multitraitmultimethod matrix', *Psychological Bulletin*, 56, 81–105.

Capello, R. (1999a), 'Spatial transfer of knowledge in high-technology mileux: learning versus collective learning processes', *Regional Studies*, **33**(4): 353–68.

Capello, R. (1999b), 'A measurement of collective learning effects in Italian high-tech milieux', *Réveu d'Economie Régionale et Urbaine*, 3, 449–68.

Carmine, E.G. and R.A. Zeller (1979), *Reliability and Validity Assessment*, Newbury Park, CA: Sage.

Chung, S., H. Singh and K. Lee (2000), 'Complementarity, status similarity and social capital as drivers of alliance formation', *Strategic Management Journal*, 21, 1–22.

Coleman, J.S. (1988), 'Social capital in the creation of human capital', *American Journal of Sociology*, 94, 95–120.

Coleman, J.S. (1990), *Foundation of Social Theory*, Cambridge, MA: Harvard University Press.

Dakhli, M. and D. De Clercq (2004), 'Human capital, social capital, and innovation: a multicountry study', *Entrepreneurship & Regional Development*, 16, 107–28.

Decarolis, D.M. and D.L. Deeds (1999), 'The impact of stocks and flows of organizational knowledge on firm performance: an empirical investigation of the biotechnology industry', *Strategic Management Journal*, 20, 953–68.

Fiske, A. (1991), *Structures of Social Life: The Four Elementary Forms of Human Relations*, New York: Free Press.

Galaskiewicz, J. (1985), *Social Organization of an Urban Grants Economy*, Orlando, FL: Academic Press.

Gargiulo, M. and M. Benassi (2000), 'Trapped in your own net? Network cohesion, structural holes, and the adaptation of social capital', *Organization Science*, 11, 183–96.

Gemser, G. and N.M. Wijnberg (2001), 'Effects of reputational sanctions on the competitive imitation of design innovations', *Organization Studies*, **22**(4), 563–91.

Glasmeier, A. (1991), 'Technological discontinuities and flexible production networks: the case of Switzerland and the world watch industry', *Research Policy*, 20, 469–85.

Glasmeier, A. (1994), 'Flexible regions? The institutional and cultural limits to districts in an era of globalization and technological paradigm shifts', in A. Amin and N. Thrift (eds), *Globalization, Institutions and Regional Development in Europe*, Oxford University Press.

Grabher, G. (1993), *The Embedded Firm*, London: Routledge.

Granovetter, M. (1973), 'The strength of weak ties', *American Journal of Sociology*, 78, 1360–80.
Grant, R.M., A.P. Jammine and H. Thomas (1988), 'Diversity, diversification and profitability among British Manufacturing Companies, 1972–1984', *Academy of Management Journal*, 31, 771–801.
Haake, S. (2002), 'National business systems and industry-specific competitiveness', *Organization Studies*, **23**(5), 711–36.
Hagedoorn, J. and G. Duysters (2002), 'Learning in dynamic inter-firm networks: the efficacy of multiple contacts', *Organization Studies*, **23**(4), 525–48.
Hansen, M.T. (1999), 'The search-transfer problem: the role of weak ties in sharing knowledge across organization subunits', *Administrative Science Quarterly*, 44, 82–111.
Harrison, B. (1991), 'Industrial districts: old wine in new bottles?', *Regional Studies*, 26, 469–83.
Hite, J.M. and W.S. Hersterly (1999), 'The influence of the firm life cycle on the evolution of entrepreneurial dyadic network ties', *Strategic Management Journal*, Special Issue–Conference on Strategic Networks, Northwestern University.
Hitt, M.A., R.E. Hoskisson and H. Kim (1997), 'International diversification: effects on innovation and firm performance in product-diversified firms', *Academy of Management Journal*, 40, 767–98.
Kanter, R.M. (1988), 'When a thousand flowers bloom: structural, collective, and social conditions for innovation in organizations', in B.M. Straw and L.L. Cummings (eds), *Research in Organizational Behavior*, Greenwich, CT: JAI Press. Vol. 10, pp. 169–211.
Keeble, D. (1997), 'Small firms, innovation and regional development in Britain in the 1990s', *Regional Studies*, 31, 281–93.
Knack, S. and P. Keefer (1997), 'Does social capital have an economic payoff? A cross-country investigation', *The Quarterly Journal of Economics*, November, 1252–88.
Krackhardt, D. (1992), 'The strength of strong ties: the importance of philos in organizations', in N. Nohria and R. Eccles (eds), *Networks and Organizations: Structures, Form and Action*, Boston, MA: Harvard Business Press, pp. 216–39.
Lam, A. (1997), 'Embedded firms, embedded knowledge: problems of collaboration and knowledge transfer in global cooperative ventures', *Organization Studies*, **18**(6), 973–96.
Lane, P.J. and M. Lubatkin (1998), 'Relative absorptive capacity and interorganizational learning', *Strategic Management Journal*, 19, 461–77.
Langfred, W. (2004), 'Too much of a good thing? Negative effects of high trust and individual autonomy in self-managing teams', *Academy of Management Journal*, 47, 385–399.
Leana, C.R. and H.J. Van Buren III (1999), 'Organizational social capital and employment practices', *Academy of Management Review*, **24**(3), 538–55.
Levinthal, D.A. and J.G. March (1993), 'The myopia of learning', *Strategic Management Journal*, 14, 95–112.
Lynn, L.H., M.N. Reddy and J.D. Aram (1996), 'Linking technology and institutions: the innovation community framework', *Research Policy*, 25, 91–106.
Malhotra, N.K. (1997), *Investigación de Mercados: Un Enfoque Práctico*, Mexico: Prentice Hall Hispanoamericana.
Marsden, P. and K. Campbell (1984), 'Measuring tie strength', *Social Forces*, 8, 482–501.

McEvily, B. and A. Zaheer (1999), 'Bridging ties: a source of firm heterogeneity in competitive capabilities', *Strategic Management Journal*, 20, 1133–56.

Meeus, M.T.H., L.A.G. Oerlemans and J. Hage (2001), 'Patterns of interactive learning in a high-tech region', *Organization Studies*, **22**(1), 145–72.

Molina, F.X. and M.T. Martínez (2003), 'The impact of the industrial district affiliation on firm value creation', *European Planning Studies*, **11**(2), 155–70.

Molina, F.X. and M.T. Martínez (2004), 'Factors that identify industrial districts. An application in Spanish manufacturing firms', *Environment & Planning A* (EPA), 36, 111–26.

Nahapiet, J. and Ghoshal, S. (1998), 'Social capital, intellectual capital, and the organizational advantage', *Academy of Management Review*, **23**(2), 242–66.

Phillips, L.W. (1981), 'Assessing measurement error in key informant reports: a methodological note on organizational analysis in marketing', *Journal of Marketing Research*, 18, 395–415.

Portes, A. (1998), 'Social capital: its origins and applications in modern sociology', *Annual Review of Sociology*, 24, 1–24.

Portes, A. and J. Sensenbrenner (1993), 'Embeddedness and immigration: notes on the social determinants of economic action', *American Journal of Sociology*, 98, 1320–50.

Pouder, R. and C. St. John (1996), 'Hot spots and blind spots: geographic clusters of firms and innovation', *Academy of Management Review*, **21**(4), 1192–1225.

Powell, W.W., K.W. Koput and L. Smith-Doer (1996), 'Interorganizational collaboration and the locus of innovation: networks of learning in biotechnology', *Administrative Science Quarterly*, **41**(1), 116–45.

Rogers, E. (1986), *Diffusion of Innovations*, Third Edition, New York: Free Press.

Rowley, T., D. Behrens and D. Krackhardt (2000), 'Redundant governance structures: an analysis of structural and relational embeddedness in the steel and semiconductor industries', *Strategic Management Journal*, 21, 369–86.

Saxenian, A. (1994), *Regional Advantage: Culture and Competition in Silicon Valley and Route 128*, Cambridge, MA: Harvard University Press.

Sharma, D.D. and A. Blomstermo (2003), 'The internationalization process of Born Globals: a network view', *International Business Review*, 12, 739–53.

Soda, G. and A. Usai (1999), 'The dark side of dense networks: from embeddedness to indebtedness', in A. Grandori (ed.), *Interfirm Networks*, London: Routledge, pp. 276–302.

Suchman, M.C. (1994), 'On Advice of Counsel: Law Firms and Venture Capital Funds as Information Intermediaries in the Structuration of Silicon Valley', Doctoral Dissertation, Stanford University.

Swan, J.A. and S. Newell (1995), 'The role of professional associations in technology diffusion', *Organization Studies*, **16**(4), 847–74.

Tsai, W. (2001), 'Knowledge transfer in intraorganizational networks: effects of network position and absorptive capacity on business unit innovation and performance', *Academy of Management Journal*, 44, 996–1004.

Tsai, W. and S. Ghoshal (1998), 'Social capital and value creation: the role of intrafirm networks', *Academy of Management Journal*, **41**(4), 464–74.

Uzzi, B. (1996), 'The sources and consequences of embeddedness for the economic performance of organizations', *American Sociological Review*, 61, 674–98.

Uzzi, B. (1997), 'Social structure and competition in interfirm networks: the paradox of embeddedness', *Administrative Science Quarterly*, 42, 35–67.

Woolcock, M. (1998), 'Social capital and economic development: toward a theoretical synthesis and policy framework', *Theory and Society*, 27, 151–208.

Yli-Renko, H., E. Autio and H.J. Sapienza (2001), 'Social capital, knowledge acquisition, and knowledge exploitation in young technology-based firms', *Strategic Management Journal*, 22, 587–613.

Zaheer, S. and A. Zaheer (2001), 'Market microstructure in a global B2B network', *Strategic Management Journal*, 22, 859–73.

9. The regional dimension of university–industry interaction

Joaquín M. Azagra Caro

9.1 INTRODUCTION

It is commonplace for scientific policy-makers and university managers to promote university–industry interaction (UII) in order to increase technological innovation. Not so common is for them to clarify if they are referring to interaction *inside* or *outside* the region. Implicitly, they are assuming that incentives and possibilities for all firm managers and faculty members to interact *inside* the region are homogeneous. Nevertheless, there is no a priori reason to assume that interaction will not take place *outside* the region.

The aim of this study is to analyse what type of firm managers and faculty members interact more often inside and/or outside the region. For this purpose, it is useful to decompose this aim into three target questions: (1) What type of firm manager interacts more often with universities? (2) What type of faculty member interacts more often with firms? (3) Does the answer to these two questions vary according to whether the actors are inside or outside the same region? To find some answers, the rest of the chapter follows the usual structure. Section 9.2 explores the literature and formulates testable hypotheses. Section 9.3 explains the methodology and data used to test the hypotheses. Section 9.4 presents the results. Section 9.5 concludes.

9.2 THE DECISION TO INTERACT AND THE FREQUENCY OF INTERACTION INSIDE AND OUTSIDE THE REGION

This section explores the existing literature on the determinants of UII according to our target questions. Sub-section 9.2.1 focuses on firm managers and sub-section 9.2.2 on faculty members. Sub-section 9.2.3 treats them jointly in order to argue whether they will tend to interact more frequently inside or outside the region.

9.2.1 Interaction with University by Type of Firm Manager

Since the empirical part of this study will follow an econometric methodology, the literature review has focused on other econometric studies, although it has widened the scope of possibilities as necessary. Sub-section 9.2.1.1 raises hypotheses on the relation between firm managers' institutional and input factors and their decision to interact with universities. Sub-section 9.2.1.2 analyses firm managers' personal characteristics.

9.2.1.1 Firm managers' institutional and input factors

By institutional factors, we do not mean 'organizations' but 'things that print character' (Edquist, 1997) or, more concretely, the type of firm in which the firm manager works. Several statistical and econometric works exist on the relation between the characteristics of the firm and the degree of interaction with universities. We focus on firm size, technological level, belonging to a group and geographic location.[1]

We found six studies that test the relationship between different measures of size and UII. Beise and Stahl (1999) find a positive significant effect of firm size, measured by the number of employees, on the generation of innovations that could not have been developed without public research by universities. Caloghirou, Vonortas and Tsakanikas (2000) do not find evidence that the number of employees at firms that have participated in research joint ventures (RJVs) of the European Union Framework Programmes (EU-FP) influences the degree of participation in R&D cooperative agreements with universities, but the firms' sales revenue does. Acosta Ballesteros and Modrego Rico (2001) do not find a significant effect of the combined factor number of employees–sales revenue, on the participation in publicly funded concerted projects. Bayona, García-Marco and Huerto (2001) find a significant positive effect of dummy variables for large firms on R&D cooperation. Schartinger et al. (2002) find a significant negative effect of the proportion of large firms in an economic sector on the frequency of the resource to contract research. Laursen and Salter (2003) find a significant positive effect of the number of employees on the degree of use of knowledge created at universities. In summary, four out of these six studies that incorporate variables with firm size find some evidence of the latter's positive relation with the degree of UII.

There are two ways to study the technological level of the firm: one, through the firm's R&D intensity, and another through the specific economic sector of the firm. Beise and Stahl (1999) do not find a significant effect of firm R&D intensity on the generation of innovations that could not have been developed without public research by universities, nor a significant effect of belonging to high-tech sectors. However, they do find a significant effect of belonging to capital goods sectors. Caloghirou et al. (2000) do not find evidence that the intensity of R&D expenditure of firms that have participated in EU-FP RJVs influences the degree of participation in R&D cooperative agreements with universities, but their number of scientists over total staff does. Acosta Ballesteros and Modrego Rico (2001) find significant positive effects of several combined variables relative to R&D intensity on participation in publicly funded concerted projects. Bayona et al. (2001) find positive significant effects of most of their variables for R&D capacity on R&D cooperation, as well as of belonging to high-tech intensity sectors. Schartinger et al. (2002) find a significant positive effect of the average R&D intensity of an economic sector on the frequency of contract research, although the influence of specific sectors is not significant. Laursen and Salter (2003) find a significant positive effect of the ratio of R&D expenditure to sales revenue, on the degree of use of knowledge created at universities, as well as of belonging to chemical and machinery sectors. In general, we can find evidence of a positive relation between technological level and degree of UII.

We have not found evidence with regard to belonging to a group of firms. Nevertheless, Patel and Pavitt (1995) show that firms in a group are more prone to performing technological activities, although parent companies tend to decentralize these to a lesser extent than their production activities. It is possible that a greater financial potential lies behind the investment that R&D requires. It seems reasonable to assume that these groups can also spend more money on technology surveillance to lower the marginal cost of externalizing their R&D, so we depart from the idea that a positive relation between the fact of belonging to a group and the degree of UII may exist.

Spatial proximity may affect UII, at least along two dimensions. First, through knowledge spillovers and formal collaboration, studied in subsection 9.2.3. Second, through neighbourhood effects (Malmberg and Maskell, 2005), a factor that is studied next. The geographic context mentioned in the studies is not homogeneous; there exist differences inside a country or a region between its sub-divisions regarding per capita income, agglomeration of economic activities, provision of infrastructures, legal and institutional settings, cooperative culture, etc. The regional innovation systems or the innovative milieu approaches would give grounds to support the idea that a richer endowment provides regions with higher possibilities of making UII fluent. On this issue though, Beise and Stahl (1999) do not find significant to UII that the firm belongs to less favoured regions (in their case study for East Germany). However, since this is the only, sparse evidence found, we prefer to go back to the assumption of expecting a positive relation between belonging to the richest sub-division of a region and the degree of UII.

9.2.1.2 Firm managers' personal characteristics

Additional reflection becomes necessary to formulate a number of hypotheses on some other interesting variables: years of professional activity, academic degree and position within the firm.

Years of professional activity denote experience in the firm and, therefore, greater probability that the individual has faced the decision to interact outside the firm and, if so, that he/she has received some feedback, which would reduce the marginal cost of later attempts. In addition, he/she will have had more time to develop confidence, on which UII often relies (Rappert, Webster and Charles 1999). On the other hand, age may lie behind years of professional activity, and if the manager comes from a tradition of rare interaction, age will probably impose resistance to change and the status quo will continue. These two opposite effects suggest that the relation between years of professional activity and UII is theoretically uncertain.

In every interactive event, at least two parties get involved. Both choose their respective interlocutors, who will settle into a process of communication, subject to their own code. In the context of UII, academic and commercial elements will makeup this code, the conjunction of which requires learning from both interlocutors. It is easy to assume that the greater the starting knowledge of this code, the more fluent communication will be. In addition, we can assume that an interlocutor with higher starting knowledge is the one who has spent more time and gained a higher reputation in the other's environment. From the point of view of faculty members, their interlocutor in the firm will fulfil those conditions the greater is his or her level of academic training.

Another bridge between the codes of academic and commercial communication that may enhance UII refers to the position of the firm manager. If this position involves responsibilities in similar activities to those demanded from universities, for example, R&D, it is probable that faculty members and firm managers reduce the cost of interacting. For that reason, the hypothesis that arises is that holding a position of responsibility in R&D activities increases the propensity of the firm manager to interact with universities.

9.2.2 Interaction With Industry by Type of Faculty Member

In parallel with the previous section, sub-sections 9.2.2.1 and 9.2.2.2 deal with the type of faculty member who interacts with firms; the former section focuses on institutional and input factors and the latter on personal characteristics.

9.2.2.1 Faculty members' institutional and input factors

We focus on the influence of type of university, type of discipline and dedication to R&D activities.[2]

Lee (1996) finds a negative relation between university prestige and the support for the objectives of collaboration with firms, which he considers a proxy for actual UII.[3] However, and although using the firm as the observation unit, Mora-Valentin, Montoro-Sanchez and Guerras-Martin (2004) find a significant effect of the perceived reputation of research organizations (mostly universities) on the perceived success of participation in cooperative agreements. To add complexity to this issue, D'Este and Patel (2005) show that their university dummy variables are not significant in determining the variety of interaction. Taking into account these considerations, it is recommended that an a priori vision of the relation between university prestige and degree of UII should not be imposed.

Lee (1996) also finds a positive relation between being a faculty member in engineering and technological disciplines and the support for collaboration with firms. However, Schartinger et al. (2002), using panel data by scientific discipline and economic sector, find a greater propensity to interact in natural, technical, farming and economic sciences than in medicine, other social sciences and humanities. That is to say, unlike Lee's study, neither does engineering stand out alone at the top nor do social sciences stand out alone at the bottom. D'Este and Patel (2005) find their disciplinary dummy variables significant in determining the variety of interaction, but they do not report the econometric effect of each dummy variable. In any case, caution is recommended before raising possible relations between variables.

Finally, Lee (1996) finds some evidence through Pearson tests that the higher the dedication to R&D activities, the higher the support for collaboration with firms; however, this is not the case if R&D dedication is included as an explanatory variable in an econometric model together with prior ones (type of university, disciplines). It is possible to argue that the difference between Lee's proxy for UII and actual UII is sensitive to R&D dedication, since the latter raises the possibility of having something to offer to firms. Thus, before the inconclusive evidence presented by Lee, we prefer to assume that the higher the dedication to R&D activities, the higher the degree of UII.

9.2.2.2 Faculty members' personal characteristics

The literature has long studied the idea that some personal characteristics matter in the process of scientific production. There are grounds to support the fact that they can be related to UII, because scientific production and UII are linked in two ways. First, pecuniary opportunities arising from UII may modify the incentive structure in the process of scientific production (Dasgupta and David, 1994). Second, even for the sake of academic prestige or social recognition, willingness to engage in UII may divert time from scientific production to scientific diffusion.

Stephan (1996) sums up some findings about the influence of age. For example, age is inversely related to research productivity and the acceptance of new ideas, but it is a weak relation. In their bibliographical review, Kotrlick et al. (2002) find evidence that the relation between age and research productivity, if any, is negative, but their results are not conclusive and their own finding is that it is not determinant. However, since individual research productivity has cumulative features (Merton, 1968), we believe that a better explanatory factor than age should include other features of seniority, for example, teaching rank, research awards, etc. Actually, when age and some of these features are both included in an estimation, results for age may change. For example, D'Este and Patel (2005) find that age has a negative impact on the variety of interactions, whereas academic status has a positive impact on this variety.

Regarding sex, Kotrlick et al. (2002) reach similar conclusions as for age. Traditional evidence points to higher research productivity in male faculty members, but not conclusively. Xie and Shauman (1998) find that with enough control variables (time between a Bachelor's Degree and a PhD, marital status, time in classroom teaching, likelihood of securing research funding and research assistance) differences in research productivity between males and female members disappear.

In addition to variables explored by the literature on scientific production, two other personal characteristics may deserve some attention. These are holding a managerial position and having done research abroad. Let us assume that if most faculty members support UII, they will choose managers who lead them to that goal. Let us also assume that faculty members who do research abroad do so to improve their scientific knowledge. Hence, they will tend to travel to leading scientific countries with more to offer, especially if they are from regions with low absorptive capacity. Some of these leading countries also interact more with industry (e.g., the United States). Therefore, faculty members who do research abroad may meet a more interactive culture.

9.2.3 Interaction Inside and Outside the Region

Having listed the characteristics of firm managers that may explain UII, it is possible to clarify which type of UII is more common, that is, if individuals who show a greater propensity to interact are those who interact more often inside or outside the region. An indication in favour is the existence of a lot of literature justifying that geographic proximity of firms to universities enhances technological innovation (Jaffe, 1989; Acs, Audretsch and Feldman, 1990). In order to confirm if it exerts the same effect on UII, we resorted again to some of the studies mentioned in sub-section 9.2.1.1, plus others.

Finally, we found four papers that test the relationship between different measures of geographical distance and UII. Beise and Stahl (1999) do not find a significant effect of the percentage of scientists employed by universities in municipalities less than 100 kilometres from the municipality of the firm, on the generation of innovations that could not have been developed without public research by universities. Arundel and Geuna (2001) find that compared with four other information sources, proximity effects are greatest for public research organizations. Schartinger et al. (2002) find a (weak) significant negative effect of the average of the spatial distance between the departments of a scientific discipline and firms of an economic sector on the frequency of the resource to contract research.[4] Mora-Valentin et al. (2004) do not find a significant effect of the perception of distance in kilometres and the perception of the time wasted travelling to the partner's address, on the success of the participation in cooperative agreements, so much for firms as for public research organizations.

So, according to our bibliographic review of these four studies that have raised the question, only two find a positive relation between spatial proximity and UII, and it is weak. If proximity does not influence UII, it is possible to argue that the determinants of the propensity of firms to interact will cause the same effect whether interacting inside or outside the region. Nevertheless, from the fact that the other two studies do not find evidence against, but simply non-significant, and from the positive association between proximity and innovation, we raise the hypothesis that firm managers who interact with universities do so more often with universities inside the region than outside the region.

In the absence of studies analysing this question for faculty members, we assume that faculty members who interact with industry do so more often with firms inside the region than outside the region.

9.3 DATA AND METHODOLOGY

We have data from the Valencian Community, a Spanish region with a per capita GDP of about the national average. However, it has a number of technological weaknesses, for example, a low expenditure on R&D (0.70 per cent of GDP in 2001), mainly on the part of firms (31 per cent of total R&D funds in 2001), few financial organizations that provide funds for innovation, and little articulation of institutional links (Fernandez et al., 2001). For these reasons, we define it as a region with low absorptive capacity.[5]

We gathered data on firm managers from the Valencian Community through a survey done in 2001. The population consisted of firms belonging to the manufacturing and telecommunications sectors. The distribution by sector was proportional to the number of firms with ten or more employees. We contacted 1843 firms and obtained a response rate of 38 per cent, which allowed us to form a database with 700 observations.

The survey included questions regarding the cooperation in R&D with universities, according to their geographical location. It resulted in the following dependent variables, whose descriptive statistics appear in Table 9.1:

- *Cooperation*: usual R&D cooperation with universities – 1 if 'yes', 0 if 'no'. Ten per cent of firm managers declare to be involved in such cooperation.
- *Region*: frequency of R&D cooperation with universities of the Valencian Community – 0 ('never'), 1 ('not often'), 2 ('often') and 3 ('very often'). The frequency distribution is strongly biased to the left, with most respondents in the first category (91 per cent), followed by the second and third categories (3 per cent and 4 per cent, respectively), and finally the fourth one (2 per cent).
- *Non-region*: highest frequency value of R&D cooperation with Spanish universities outside the Valencian Community or with foreign universities – 0 ('never'), 1 ('not often') and 2 ('often').[6] Almost none of the respondents cooperate outside the region (96 per cent), a few do but not often (3 per cent) and very few do more frequently (1 per cent).

We gathered data on faculty members from the five public universities of the Valencian Community through a survey made in 2001. We stratified the population in three categories: full-time professors, assistant professors and associate professors.[7] The sample accounted for 10 per cent of the

Table 9.1 *Firm managers' sample. Descriptive statistics of dependent variables*

Variable	Mean	Standard Deviation	Minimum	Maximum	No. of Observations
Cooperation	0.0974212	0.296743	0	1	698
Region	0.183381	0.638919	0	3	698
Non-region	0.0415473	0.226619	0	2	698

population, or 872 individuals. We obtained a response rate of 44 per cent, so we could build a database with 380 observations.

The survey included questions regarding participation in contracts with firms, according to their geographical location. It gave rise to the following dependent variables, whose descriptive statistics are shown in Table 9.2:

- *Contracts*: usual participation in contracts with firms – 0 ('no') and 1 ('yes'). Twenty-nine per cent of faculty members declare to have participated in such contracts.
- *Region*: frequency of participation in contracts with firms of the Valencian Community – 0 ('never'), 1 ('not often'), 2 ('often') and 3 ('very often'). Respondents predominate in the first category (71 per cent), have the same share in the two following categories (12 per cent each) and a few belong to the fourth one (5 per cent).
- *Non-region*: highest frequency value of participation in contracts with Spanish firms outside the Valencian Community or with foreign firms. It presents the same values as for *Region*. Most respondents belong to the category 'never' (81 per cent), some do not often participate (11 per cent) or often participate (6 per cent) and few do very often (2 per cent).

Next, we explain the variables that are of qualitative and indexed nature. *Cooperation* and *Contracts* are binary, so we will estimate them through a probit model. *Region* and *Non-region*, as defined for each sample, take more than two values, so we start by regressing them through an ordered probit model.

However, we may consider that first, individuals make their decision of whether to interact or not depending on their preferences and possibilities, and then they engage in more or less frequent interaction. Therefore, the appropriate technique of estimation must take into account that the equations for *Cooperation* or *Contracts* act as selection equations for *Region* and

Table 9.2 Faculty members' sample. Descriptive statistics of dependent variables

Variable	Mean	Standard Deviation	Minimum	Maximum	No. of Observations
Contracts	0.293134	0.45581	0	1	375
Region	0.493609	0.88608	0	3	370
Non-region	0.289216	0.65744	0	3	357

Note: Weighting variable: teaching scale.

Non-region, which should therefore be estimated through an ordered probit model with sample selection.

Finally, we may also consider that the determinants of interaction frequency are relevant for individuals who interact, thus those who report no interaction are removed from the sample. In this case, we would have a sub-sample of individuals from a larger population and the appropriate estimation technique would be a truncated model.

Next, we explain how we built the independent variables on firm managers from the survey, as well as their descriptive statistics shown in Table 9.3:

- *Labour*: number of employees in the firm – up to 10 employees (8 per cent), 11–50 employees (69 per cent), 51–250 employees (18 per cent), more than 250 employees (3 per cent).
- *Sales*: firm's revenue – up to 0.6 million euros (11 per cent), 0.6–1.5 million euros (25 per cent), 1.5–3 million euros (20 per cent), 3–6 million euros (14 per cent), more than 6 million euros (15 per cent). Notice the high number of 'don't know' answers for this variable (15 per cent).
- *Science*: 1 for science-based sectors ('chemicals' and 'telecommunications', 12 per cent), 0 otherwise (88 per cent).
- *Group*: 1 for firms within a group (20 per cent), 0 otherwise (80 per cent).
- *Province*: 1 for firms in the province with the highest per capita GDP, Valencia (48 per cent), 0 otherwise (52 per cent).
- *Experience*: years of professional activity in current and previous firms: less than 5 years (11 per cent), between 5 and 9 years (16 per cent), between 10 and 14 years (18 per cent) and more than 14 years (55 per cent).

Table 9.3 *Firm managers' sample. Descriptive statistics of independent variables*

Variable	Mean	Standard Deviation	Minimum	Maximum	No. of Observations
Labour	2.1611	0.608942	1	4	689
Sales	2.97315	1.29613	1	5	596
Science	0.117143	0.32182	0	1	700
Group	0.200288	0.400505	0	1	694
Province	0.48	0.499957	0	1	700
Experience	3.1763	1.05732	1	4	692
Training	0.345428	0.475853	0	1	689
Position	0.0243902	0.154368	0	1	697

- *Training*: 1 if the individual has a graduate or post-graduate (e.g., PhD) university degree (35 per cent), 0 otherwise (65 per cent).
- *Position*: 1 for directors or heads of R&D in the firm (2 per cent), 0 otherwise (98 per cent).

We will estimate starting econometric models on faculty members as a function of the following independent variables, also based on the survey data, whose descriptive statistics are shown in Table 9.4:

- *University*: *Univ1*, the oldest university (500 years old) with the highest scientific prestige, (traditionally) the culture most opposed to UII with the largest number of professors (31 per cent); *Univ2*, a younger university (35 years old), with technological orientation, some reputation of active involvement in UII and next in size (29 per cent); and *Univ3*, a group of the three youngest universities (created during the last 20 years), the least prestigious and smallest (40 per cent).
- *Disciplines*: *Ens* (exact and natural sciences), *Et* (engineering and technology) and *Ssh* (social sciences and humanities, benchmark). The distribution of the three groups is homogeneous, around one-third of the faculty members in each group.
- *RDt*: time devoted to R&D activities (30 per cent) and not to other academic activities (teaching, other educational activities, management and other activities).
- *Senior*: 1 if the faculty member is older than 40 years, his/her teaching experience has lasted at least ten years, his/her teaching scale is

Table 9.4 Faculty members' sample. Descriptive statistics of independent variables

Variable	Mean	Standard Deviation	Minimum	Maximum	No. of Observations
Univ1	0.310921	0.463481	0	1	380
Univ2	0.284886	0.451955	0	1	380
Ens	0.35209	0.478258	0	1	376
Et	0.326234	0.469459	0	1	376
RDt	0.298841	0.192734	0	0.9	376
Senior	0.215161	0.411509	0	1	361
Sex	0.723726	0.447743	0	1	380
Management	0.155714	0.363068	0	1	376
Abroad	1.28506	1.37666	0	4	373

Note: Weighting variable: teaching scale.

the highest (full professor) and he/she has received at least one Spanish six-year term research award (so-called sexenium). Twenty-two per cent of the respondents fit our definition of senior faculty member.
- *Sex*: 1 if the respondent is a man (72 per cent), 0 if it is a woman (28 per cent).
- *Management*: 1 if the respondent holds a managerial position within the university (16 per cent), 0 otherwise (84 per cent).
- *Abroad*: length of research abroad: ranging from 0 (the shortest) to 4 (the longest). The average length is between our categories 1 (0–5 months) and 2 (6–11 months).

9.4 RESULTS

The following tables show the results of the models simplified after a selection strategy based on minimizing the Bayesian information criterion (BIC).[8] Table 9.5 gathers the estimations on firm managers' R&D cooperation with universities. On the one hand, neither belonging to a firm located in Valencia nor to a firm that forms part of a group has a significant effect on the propensity to cooperate in R&D with universities. On the other hand, belonging to larger firms (measured by both number of employees and sales revenue), and in science-based sectors, has a significant positive influence on the probability of R&D cooperation with universities.

Regarding personal characteristics, there is no evidence that experience in industry or being head of R&D units are causes of R&D cooperation. Conversely, there is some evidence that having a high academic degree is a significant cause.

Our hypothesis on the regional dimension of the firm manager's interaction with universities can now be reformulated to include the previous results. The expectation is that firm managers who belong to large firms in science-based sectors, and who have a high academic degree, cooperate more frequently in R&D with universities inside the region and less frequently with universities outside the region.

Columns 2 and 3 in Table 9.5 offer a first test of the hypothesis, regarding R&D cooperation with universities inside the region. The significant variables in the ordered probit model (column 2) are the same as for the decision to cooperate, indicating that firm managers interact inside the region. Nevertheless, notice that the threshold parameters are not ordered, so the model is not satisfactory. Even more, it is not possible to generate a significant model using the decision equation in column 1 for the selection. In column 3, the truncated model includes only one significant effect, firm size,

Table 9.5 Firm managers' decisions to cooperate in R&D with universities and of their frequency of such cooperation with universities inside and outside the region

	(1) Binomial Probit Model	(2) Ordered Probit Model	(3) Truncated Model	(4) Ordered Probit Model	(5) Ordered Probit with Selection
Dependent variable	Cooperation	Region	Region	Non-region	Non-region
No. of observations	594	594	62	595	595
Log likelihood	−147.73	−190.86	−76.55	−80.57	−188.22
Prob[χ^2 > value]	0.00	0.00		0.00	0.01
	Coeff. (t-ratio)	Coeff. (t-ratio)	Coeff. (t-ratio)	Coeff. (t-ratio)	Coeff. (t-ratio)
Constant	−3.56 (−10.95)**	−3.81 (−11.24)**	0.98 (1.93)*	−3.69 (−8.52)**	−0.36 (−0.19)
Labour	0.45 (2.81)**	0.49 (3.08)**	0.36 (2.06)*	0.44 (2.08)*	
Sales	0.26 (2.94)**	0.27 (3)**		0.12 (1)	−0.18 (−0.66)
Science	0.59 (3.03)**	0.57 (2.96)**			
Group				0.92 (3.89)**	1.53 (3.28)**
Training	0.39 (2.33)*	0.45 (2.67)**			
μ_1		0.32 (4.79)**		1 (4.52)**	1.58 (5.11)**
μ_2		0.62 (6.28)**			
ρ_{12}					0.06 (0.09)
σ			0.88 (9.67)**		

Note: ** Significant at 1%; * significant at 5%.

measured by the number of employees. It is difficult, then, to assure that we fully understand the analysed phenomenon. In any case, it looks as if there was no relation between the decision to cooperate and the frequency to do so inside the region, but if there is any, it relies on the same type of firm manager.

Columns 4 and 5 in Table 9.5 offer the other side of the coin since they explain R&D cooperation with universities outside the Valencian Community. In the ordered probit model (column 4), there are two other significant variables: size and belonging to a group. In Column 5, the model with sample selection shows that the coefficient of firm size is no longer significant, but belonging to a group is. However, the correlation parameter of the model in column 5 is only significant at 10 per cent, which suggests that the relation between the decision to cooperate with universities and the frequency to do so outside the region is limited. For that reason, there is no clear preference for the model without sample selection. It was not possible to fit a significant truncated model to find more evidence. In any case, the fact that the majority of significant variables for the decision to cooperate (sales revenue, science-based sector, training level) is not significant for the frequency of cooperation outside the region provides additional evidence to support the fact that that firm managers interact more often inside the region.

Estimations for the faculty members' sample are shown in Table 9.6. The model of the decision to participate in contracts with firms is shown in column 1. Beginning with institutional and input variables, we can observe that the type of university does not significantly affect the probability that faculty members contract with firms. On the contrary, the effect of the type of discipline is significant, since the propensity to contract with firms is larger for faculty members in engineering and technology and, to a lesser extent, exact and natural sciences. In addition, more time devoted to R&D activities increases the probability for faculty members to contract with firms.

Regarding personal characteristics, being a senior, being male and holding a managerial position are factors that increase the probability of contracting with firms. On the other hand, spending more years researching abroad does not cause any significant effect.

Given the previous results, the expectation now is that faculty members who are senior, male and hold a managerial position, who belong to engineering and technology disciplines (and to a lesser degree those working at exact and natural sciences) and who devote more time to R&D activities, participate more frequently in contracts with firms inside the region and less frequently with firms outside the region.

Columns 2 to 4 in Table 9.6 show the estimations for the variables relative to firms inside the Valencian Community. As expected, the type of university does not exert a significant influence. Unexpectedly, the type of discipline and dedication to R&D activities do not show any influence either in most cases.[9] That is to say, for faculty members, institutional and input variables are more important for the decision to interact than for the interaction

Table 9.6 Faculty members' decisions to participate in contracts with industry and of their frequency of such cooperation with firms inside and outside the region

Dependent variable	(1) Binomial Probit Model	(2) Ordered Probit Model	(3) Ordered Probit with Selection	(4) Truncated Model	(5) Ordered Probit Model	(6) Ordered Probit with Selection	(7) Truncated Model
	Contracts	Region	Region	Region	Non-region	Non-region	Non-region
No. of observations	347	341	340	93	335	334	62
Log likelihood	−173.72	−259.95	−262.15	−100.67	−192.16	−250.32	−56.47
Prob[χ²>value]	0.00	0.00	0.04		0.00	0.01	
	Coeff. (t-ratio)	Coeff. (t-ratio)	Coeff. (t-ratio)	Coeff. (t-ratio)	Coeff. (t-ratio)	Coeff. (t-ratio)	Coeff. (t-ratio)
Constant	−2.24 (−8.61)**	−2.66 (−8.51)**	3.35 (7.51)**	1.88 (18.18)**	−2.67 (−8.31)**	2.17 (3.91)**	0.56 (1.62)
Univ1		0.53 (2.73)**					
Univ2		0.13 (0.67)					
Ens	0.65 (3.11)**	0.41 (1.97)*	−0.68 (−2.15)*		0.76 (3.09)**	−0.5 (−1.16)	
Et	0.95 (4.47)**	0.91 (3.99)**	−0.44 (−1.26)		0.87 (3.48)**	−0.95 (−2.41)*	
RDt	1.44 (3.28)**	1.54 (3.63)**			1.36 (2.97)**		
Senior	0.51 (2.68)**	0.28 (1.53)	−0.39 (−1.71)	−0.13 (−0.73)	0.29 (1.49)	−0.29 (−1.03)	−0.3 (−1.6)

Sex	0.54 (2.77)**	0.53 (2.73)**	−0.37 (−1.39)		0.79 (3.19)**	0.7 (2.18)*
Management	0.45 (2.2)*		−0.62 (−2.47)**			
Abroad		0.16 (2.66)**	0.15 (1.91)	−0.39 (−2.01)*		0.16 (2.49)**
μ_1		0.48 (7.01)**	1.6 (4.21)**		0.58 (6.54)**	−0.6 (−2.13)*
μ_2		1.18	2.29		1.36	0.94 (3.43)**
ρ_{12}		(9.91)**	(4.54)**		(7.94)**	1.78 (2.97)**
			−0.93 (−8.2)**			−0.7 (−1.81)
σ				0.75 (11.97)**		0.63 (9.9)**

Note: ** Significant at 1%; * significant at 5%. Weighting variable: teaching scale.

frequency. About personal characteristics, many unexpected effects occur. Being a senior is not significant anymore, and being male loses significance. More important, holding a managerial position has a significant negative sign, which means that these faculty members, although showing greater propensity to interact, do so less frequently inside the region. On the contrary, doing research abroad for longer periods becomes positive and significant for some of the estimations. All this suggests little correlation between the decision to interact and the frequency of doing so inside the region. The negative, significant correlation parameter in column 3 shows evidence in favour of this assertion. Therefore, in general, there exists evidence against our assumption that faculty members who interact with industry do so more often inside the region.

Columns 5 to 7 in Table 9.6 provide evidence on faculty interaction with firms outside the Valencian Community. As expected, the type of university has no influence. The type of discipline and dedication to R&D activities are significant only in the ordered probit model without selection. Hence, once again, institutional and input factors seem less important than the decision to participate in contracts with industry. With respect to personal characteristics, being a senior is no longer significant, but being male still is, at least in two of the models. Holding a managerial position has a significant negative effect, but only in one model. The length of research abroad has a significant positive effect, but only in one model. There is no clear preference for ordered probit with selection over that without selection, because the correlation parameter is significant only at 10 per cent. In general, evidence on personal characteristics is scattered, but some unexpected effects are worth mentioning: men do not fulfil the expectation of being less prone to interact outside the region, whereas having done research abroad does not fulfil the expectation of causing no effect.

9.5 CONCLUSIONS, LIMITATIONS AND FUTURE RESEARCH LINES

Three questions have guided the research developed throughout this work: (1) What type of firm manager interacts more often with universities? (2) What type of faculty member interacts more often with firms? (3) Does the answer to these two questions vary according to whether the actors are inside or outside the same region?

Concerning the first question, data from the Valencian Community shows evidence to support that belonging to large firms in science-based sectors has a significant positive effect. This constitutes a limit to UII given the abundance of micro-firms in supplier-dominated sectors in regions alike. Perhaps it should be recommended not to promote R&D contracts as much as other indirect routes to benefit from the results of academic R&D. On the other hand, certain personal characteristics of firm managers, like a higher academic degree, positively influence their propensity to interact with universities. Therefore, a policy designed to facilitate the placement of university graduates and doctors in industry would seem appropriate to increase UII.

Concerning the second question ('What type of faculty member interacts more often with firms?'), in the case of the Valencian Region, promoting engineering and technology and exact and natural sciences will have a positive effect on contracts with firms, although we may query the cost of taking resources from social sciences and humanities, which can offer other benefits. Similarly, to increase the time devoted to R&D acts positively, justifying policies to alleviate the teaching and management load or to harness possible synergies between these and R&D activities. On the other hand, senior, male faculty members who hold a managerial position present a higher propensity to contract with firms. We may wonder whether this situation is optimal, for example, are sex differences due to preferences or to discrimination? Do seniority and holding a managerial position constitute an opportunity or a barrier for involvement in UII?

We approached the third question ('Does the answer to the previous two questions vary according to whether the actors are inside or outside the same region?') from the point of view of both firm managers and faculty members.

With regard to firm managers, since the managers in our sample rarely cooperate in R&D with universities outside the region, the previous results on the decision to interact apply here. Beyond that, trying to explain the frequency of cooperation inside the region is arduous and seems to depend solely on firm size. Yet it is clear that the frequency of R&D cooperation with universities outside the region depends on the fact of belonging to a group of firms, which indicates that UII is not very decentralized, as increasing globalization in the production of goods and services suggests.

Concerning faculty members, those with a higher propensity to contract do not stand out for their frequency of interaction; some even interact less often than the rest (those who hold a managerial position) or do so more often outside the region (males). On the contrary, faculty members who do not stand out for their propensity to contract, those who have done research abroad for longer periods, interact as frequently with firms inside the region as with firms outside the region.[10]

As issues for discussion, let us recall that improving human capital in firms becomes crucial, since it enhances UII, and seems a more suitable way of policy-making than trying to change the sticky economic structure. On the other hand, faculty members' propensity to interact relies on personal characteristics that do not ensure that they will interact more often inside the region than outside the region, since firms in regions like the Valencian Community may not be able to absorb academic R&D. This is not necessarily a caveat, because the region may benefit indirectly from interaction taking place outside it. Rather, it implies that policy-makers and university managers should design conscious strategies to find equilibrium between UII inside and outside the region. In any case, our results aim to be valid only for regions with low absorptive capacity.

One important limitation of the study is that, in the absence of a well-founded theoretical approach with the specification of a model, the statistical associations do not provide enough evidence of dependent relationships. Therefore, we should build a theory to introduce optimality criteria in order to provide more robust policy recommendations, along the lines of Azagra-Caro, Aznar-Márquez and Blanco (forthcoming).

There are several ways to widen the scope of this research. First, the surveys allow us to discriminate firm managers as well as faculty members who devote more than 0 per cent of their academic time to R&D activities, and the analysis of these sub-samples would raise new hypotheses on the influence of different types of R&D, R&D budget and share of external funding. Second, our results on firm managers who cooperate outside the region rely on a small proportion of positive observations, so a deeper look into these firms should be useful. Third, our results on faculty members' sex, managerial position and research experience abroad require additional evidence, perhaps through interviews.

ACKNOWLEDGEMENTS

To the Valencian High Consultancy Council in R&D, for providing funds to develop this research. To Ignacio Fernandez de Lucio for providing the author with the elaboration of the report on which this work relies. Once again to him, plus to Antonio Gutiérrez Gracia and Fragiskos Archontakis for working with the author on previous analyses of the same survey. To Fernando Jiménez Sáez, for the application of techniques in preliminary analyses that were not necessary to develop.

NOTES

1. There are some other characteristics related to firm managers linkable to UII, for example, amplitude of the range of products (Beise and Stahl, 1999), cognitive proximity

(Schartinger et al., 2002) or motivational factors (Caloghirou, Vonortas and Tsakanikas, 2000; Bayona, García-Marco and Huerta, 2001; Mora-Valentin, Montoro-Sanchez and Guerras-Martin, 2004). We have not considered the latter subjective factors, since we understand that they could be caused by the objective characteristics introduced in the following sub-sections, thus preventing problems of endogeneity.
2. There are some other characteristics related to faculty members linkable to UII. Lee (1996) finds significant the perceived support of the university and the fear of four possible disadvantages of UII. We do not include these subjective variables for the reasons given in note 1. D'Este and Patel (2005) also include 'number of joint publications with industry' and 'involvement in patenting activities' in their regressions on the variety of interaction. We consider these to be outputs of academic research that should be explained simultaneously with the degree of UII.
3. Lee implicitly assumes that support for the objectives of UII is a necessary condition for actual UII to take place. Azagra-Caro, Archontakis, et al. (2006) find that it is not a sufficient condition.
4. Schartinger et al. (2002) highlight that contract research is the only type of interaction on which geographic distance matters (p. 324). However, this result relies on a low significant effect, at 10 per cent.
5. For further information on the Valencian Community and its university system, see Azagra-Caro, Archontakis et al. (2006), Section 9.3.
6. Although the possibility existed, nobody answered 'very often'.
7. The equivalence between the Spanish original categories and the three categories that we mention is not exact, but the latter are more popular terms and capture the intuition behind the original categories.
8. BIC tends to penalize the entrance of new observations. Hence, final reduced models admit some non-significant variables that, if deleted, incorporate a large number of 'don't knows'.
9. There are some significant effects of some universities and disciplines, but together they are not significantly different from their respective benchmarks. If they appear in the ordered probit models it is because the BIC indicates a better fit this way. In the truncated model they are finally eliminated.
10. Exploratory evidence suggests that the former need firms with greater technological level to contract with, and they do not find them inside the region, while the latter compensate the lower technological level of the firm, if they find an interlocutor with a high academic degree.

REFERENCES

Acosta Ballesteros, J., A. Modrego Rico (2001), 'Public financing of cooperative R&D projects in Spain: the concerted projects under the National R&D Plan', *Research Policy*, 30, 625–41.

Acs, Z.J., D.B. Audretsch and M.P. Feldman (1991), 'Real effects of academic research: comment', *American Economic Review*, **82**(1), 363–67.

Arundel, A. and A. Geuna (2001), 'Does Proximity Matter for Knowledge Transfer from Public Institutes and Universities to Firms?', *SPRU Electronic Working Paper*, No. 73.

Azagra-Caro, J., J. Aznar-Márquez and J.M. Blanco (forthcoming), 'Interactive vs. non-interactive knowledge production by faculty members', *Applied Economics*, accepted for publication.

Azagra-Caro, J., F. Archontakis, I. Fernández-de-Lucio, A. Gutiérrez-Gracia (2006), 'Faculty support for the objectives of university–industry relations versus degree of R&D cooperation: the importance of regional absorptive capacity', *Research Policy*, 35, 37–55.

Bayona, C., T. García-Marco and E. Huerta (2001), 'Firms' motivation for cooperative R&D: an empirical analysis of Spanish firms', *Research Policy*, 30, 1289–1307.
Beise, M. and H. Stahl (1999), 'Public research and industrial innovations in Germany', *Research Policy*, **28**(4), 397–422.
Caloghirou, Y., N.S. Vonortas and A. Tsakanikas (2000), 'University–industry cooperation in research and development', *Organizational Issues in University Technology Transfer*, Indianapolis (US), 9–11 June.
Dasgupta, P. and P. David (1994), 'Towards a new economics of science', *Research Policy*, **23**(5), 487–521.
D'Este, P. and P. Patel (2005), 'University–industry linkages in the UK: what are the factors determining the variety of interactions with industry', *5th Triple Helix Conference*, Turin, Italy, 18–21 May.
Edquist, C. (1997), 'Introduction', in C. Edquist (ed.), *Systems of Innovation: Technologies, Institutions and Organizations*, London: Pinter, Ch. 1.
Fernández de Lucio, I., A. Gutiérrez Gracia, J. Azagra Caro and F. Jiménez Sáez (2001), 'Las debilidades y fortalezas del sistema valenciano de innovación', in M. Olazarán and M. Gómez Uranga (ed.), *Sistemas Regionales de Innovación*, Bilbao: UPV.
Jaffe, A.B. (1989), 'Real effects of academic research', *American Economic Review*, **79**(5), 957–70.
Kotrlick, J.W., J.E. Bertlett II, C.C. Higgins and H.A. Williams (2002), 'Factors associated with research productivity of agricultural education faculty', *Journal of Agricultural Education*, **43**(3), 1–10.
Laursen, K. and A. Salter (2003), 'Searching low and high: what types of firms use universities as a source of innovation?', *Research Policy*, 33, 1201–15.
Lee, Y.S. (1996), 'Technology transfer and the research university: a search for the boundaries of university–industry collaboration', *Research Policy*, 25, 843–63.
Malmberg, A. and Maskell, P. (2005), 'Localized Learning Revisited', *Druid Working Paper*, No. 05–19.
Merton, R.K. (1968), 'The Matthew effect in science', *Science*, 159, 56–63.
Mora-Valentin, E.M., A. Montoro-Sanchez and L.A. Guerras-Martin (2004), 'Determining factors in the success of R&D cooperative agreements between firms and research organizations', *Research Policy*, **33**(1), 17–40.
Patel, P. and P. Pavitt (1995), 'Patterns of technological activity', in P. Stoneman (ed.), *Handbook of the Economics of Innovation and Technical Change*, Oxford and Cambridge: Blackwell.
Rappert, B., A. Webster and D. Charles (1999), 'Making sense of diversity and reluctance: academic–industrial relations and intellectual property', *Research Policy*, 28, 873–90.
Schartinger, D., C. Rammer, M.M. Fischer and J. Frölich (2002), 'Knowledge interactions between universities and industry in Austria: sectoral patterns and determinants', *Research Policy*, 31, 303–28.
Stephan, P. (1996), 'The economics of science', *Journal of Economic Literature*, **34**(3), 1199–1235.
Xie, Y. and K.A. Shauman (1998), 'Sex differences in research productivity revisited: new evidence about an old puzzle', *American Sociological Review*, 63, 847–70.

10. Which factors underlie public selection of R&D cooperative projects?

Lluís Santamaría Sánchez, Andrés Barge Gil and Aurelia Modrego Rico

10.1 INTRODUCTION

The importance of research and development (R&D) as one of the main contributors to sustainable growth in highly industrialized economies is undisputed among economists, and especially in the context of modern knowledge-based economies. Therefore, in contrast to the criticisms of the public support given to firms in production or commercial areas, government financing of R&D activities is widely accepted. In the OECD countries, public funding accounts for some 30 per cent of total R&D expenditure (OECD, 2001) and in the EU countries reaches 36 per cent. In the case of Spain the share of public funding is near to 40 per cent (OECD, 2001). Thus, public investment in R&D, similar to all other areas of public decision-making, should be subject to review.

From a neoclassical point of view, science and technology (S&T) activities involve market failures, which lead to inadequate resource allocations for these activities (Arrow, 1962). Appropriability problems, indivisibilities, uncertainty due to information imperfections, among other factors, mean that firms are unable to allocate optimal resources to S&T. Their investment and production decisions become entwined with decisions about risk strategies, which leads to lower investment and, consequently less than efficient output (Geroski, 1995).

In a bid to correct for these market failures, we distinguish two different types of public support: selective and non-selective (Heijs, 2001). Non-selective support includes fiscal incentives and generic financing of public research organizations (PROs) budgets; selective support implies some discrimination among agents, mainly through the support of research projects using competitive calls. These types of initiative, which are implemented by regional, national and supranational governments, have been increasing since the mid-1980s (OECD, 2003). It is therefore important to understand the factors underlying the public sector's selection of R&D projects.

Research funding is an uncertain business, and the outputs of R&D are equally uncertain and also skewed (Molas-Gallart and Salter, 2002). The problem for research policy is how to distribute research funds under these conditions. According to Bozeman and Rogers (2001), it seems that public R&D management tends to be discrete and ad hoc, focusing on generating maximum output through individual projects. As Teece (1992) points out, technology alliances can facilitate innovation, and thus, the greatest challenge to public policy is to acknowledge the importance of cooperation and to encourage the private sector to build technological agreements. As a result, government is paying more attention to these aspects, particularly through the provision of funding (Bozeman, 2000).

However, there are few studies that analyse the criteria adopted in choosing which R&D projects will be accepted. In this study we aim to improve the knowledge about the underlying factors influencing the decision-making related to project proposals. In analysing the selection of R&D cooperative projects among firms and other organizations such as universities and technology institutes, we try to underline the formative role of evaluation as a learning process in which the funding research decision plays a part.

Existing studies (Blanes and Busom, 2004) use firm-level data, whereas our analysis is based on project-level data, taken from cooperative R&D project calls under the Spanish PROFIT initiative in the period 2000–03. PROFIT is the Spanish government's main technical innovation support programme and aims to foster innovation in all sectors (industry, government, and research) and technological areas. The period 2000–03 was the first time that support was explicitly given to both individual and cooperative projects and to implement measures designed to encourage the participation of technology institutes and the first to design a special tool – Technology Institutes Plan – for technology institutes to participate in the initiative.[1]

The chapter is organized as follows. First, we review the existing literature to enable us to develop arguments about the public selection of R&D cooperative projects. We go on to describe the data, the variables and the empirical specification. Finally, we discuss the results and draw some conclusions.

10.2 PREVIOUS LITERATURE

The main trend in innovation policies during the 1990s has been characterized by what is termed the 'cooperative paradigm', or fostering cooperation among sectors – industry, government and research – and among rival or vertically related firms (Bozeman, 2000). There is a range of R&D funding programmes designed to finance this type of cooperation at regional, national and supranational level. However, some of these programmes may fail to reach the targeted population and the selection criteria in some are not well defined (Blanes and Busom, 2004; Heijs, 2005). Therefore, it is important that the public sector evaluation criteria and procedures for selecting R&D cooperative projects are clearly set out.

Some studies have looked at the evaluation of the effectiveness of R&D programmes (Meyer-Krahmer and Montigny, 1989; Ormala, 1989; Roessner, 1989) and their influence on private R&D efforts (David, Hall and Toole, 2000; Klette, Moen and Griliches, 2000). However, few works have examined the criteria used by government evaluators to select projects (Lee and Om, 1996, 1997; Hsu, Tzeng and Shyu, 2003). These criteria are very important because they reflect the objectives of policy-makers and affect the characteristics of those projects that are actually implemented or developed. Moreover, these criteria will affect future replies to public calls because researchers will get to know which types of projects are more likely to be selected (Lee and Om, 1996) and, consequently, they will adapt their proposals to fit the criteria being applied by public evaluators.

The fact that government-sponsored projects differ from those in the private sector must be taken into account (Hsu et al., 2003): (1) government-sponsored R&D is a strategic and long-term investment; (2) the allocation of public sector R&D resources is influenced by political considerations. Bozeman and Rogers (2001) point out that systematic and strategic R&D programme management is difficult to achieve in the public sector for several reasons:

1. government-funded R&D generally does not have commercial products and processes as a near-term objective;
2. public agencies are subject to annual budget cycles;
3. the various goals of different government agencies produce conflict; and
4. time horizons are different.

Thus, public selection of R&D projects is no easy task, and it is important to explore the factors that influence project selection. We would expect project size (Heijs, 2005) and type of cooperation partners (Hayashi, 2003) to be significant.

Acosta Ballesteros and Modrego Rico (2001) found that government evaluators favour large projects. Thus, we would conjecture that the amount of inputs could be an important factor in project selection. More specifically, we expect that more inputs – larger projects – will increase the probability of project acceptance. In addition to the traditional dimensions of size (like money or workers) and owing to the fact that we are analysing only cooperative projects, we explore the effect of the number of organizations involved in the project. One of the explicit aims of PROFIT was to encourage cooperation among organizations, so we expect this measure to be positively correlated with the probability of project acceptance.

The fact that technological cooperations very often have the underlying purpose of finding a partner that will provide easier access to public funding for the development of technological activities is well documented in the literature (Hagedoorn, 1993; Cassiman, 1999; Hagedoorn, Link and Vonortas, 2000; Caloghirou, Ioannides and Vonortas, 2003). In this sense, research organizations (universities or technology institutes) are the preferred partners in terms of gaining access to public funding (Bonaccorsi and Piccaluga, 1994; Ham and Mowery, 1998; Cassiman and Veugelers, 2002; Miotti and Sachwald, 2003). An acknowledged objective of technology policy since the 1980s has been the strengthening of relationships between firms and non-profit knowledge organizations (Bozeman, 2000). Sometimes, the proposal criteria specify the inclusion of both industry and university partners (Hayashi, 2003). Thus, we consider it relevant to analyse entrepreneurial collaborations with Spanish universities and technology institutes in terms of probability of acceptance. This allows us to discover whether PROFIT has encouraged firms' utilization of the knowledge embedded in these organizations and fostered the cooperation with them.

10.3 METHODOLOGY

10.3.1 Data

Our analysis draws on data from cooperative R&D project calls within the Spanish PROFIT initiative in the period 2000–03. PROFIT has some novelty compared with earlier programmes. As mentioned above, in this period for the first time, support was explicitly targeted to cooperative projects as well as individual ones (Castro, 2001).

Two modes of funding were implemented: straightforward, non-refundable grants and advance payments, one of the main novelties of the programme. In the period 2000–03 the total number of cooperative project proposals received was 2867, from which 1289 were accepted (44.96 per cent). The average value of the grants awarded was €448 108 per project and the average advance payment was €214 299. Median values demonstrate that the distribution among projects was highly skewed ranging from €52 394 to €0.[2]

The variables in the analysis[3] are derived from the Science and Technology Office administrative database of both accepted and rejected projects.

10.3.2 Variables and Descriptive Statistics

The objective is to analyse the factors on which the selection or rejection of cooperative projects is based. We constructed an endogenous variable (*Selected project*) as a dichotomous variable that takes the value 1 if the project was selected and 0 if it was rejected.

In the empirical analysis we consider five groups of independent variables:

1. project input characteristics;
2. the presence of universities and/or technology institutes;
3. the area to which the project belongs;
4. the region of the applicant; and
5. the year of the proposal.

A description of all the variables is provided in Table A10.1 in the Appendix at the end of the chapter.

10.3.2.1 Project inputs

We employ three measures of project inputs simultaneously: total amount of project budget (*Budget*), total planned number of working hours by qualified personnel (*Hours*) and number of organizations involved in the project (*Partners*). All are indicators of project size, but refer to different dimensions and, in fact, there are no strong correlations among them (Table 10.6).

Table 10.1 shows that all input variables show mean values highly above the median, reflecting the existence of some very large projects. With independence of the measure employed, both budget and hours of accepted projects are shown to be higher in successful projects than those that were rejected, demonstrating the preference for big projects.

10.3.2.2 Research organizations

To develop our empirical analysis and check the influence of research organizations in the project selection process, we constructed two dichotomous

Table 10.1   Input project variables

	Accepted Projects		Rejected Projects	
	Mean	Median	Mean	Median
Total budget (€)	1 827 073.3	613 250	1 527 397.2	412 294
Total hours by qualified workers	20 053	13 075	12 051.9	8 750
Number of organizations	3	2	3.1	2

Table 10.2   Participation of technology institutes and universities

	Number of Proposals	Share %	Number of Accepted Projects	Share %	% of Accepted Projects
Only technology institutes	702	24.49	316	24.52	45.01
Only universities	913	31.85	407	31.57	44.58
Technology institutes and universities	107	3.73	51	3.96	47.66
Neither technology institutes nor universities	1145	39.93	515	39.95	44.98
Total	2867	100.00	1289	100.00	44.96

variables reflecting whether *Universities* or *Technology Institutes* are project partners.

Table 10.2 presents a count of the projects that have technology institutes and/or universities as collaborators, and indicates the importance of these organizations as partners. At least one of these types of organizations is involved in more than half of the projects. It should be noted, however, cooperation among them is rather limited, since only 4 per cent of projects involve cooperation between at least one university and one technology institute (with or without other organizations). The rate of acceptance is similar to that for projects with no university or technology institute as partners.

10.3.2.3   Project area

PROFIT consists of 17 programmes, which represent the priorities of Spanish technology policy. However, in order to improve information processing, we aggregated these programmes into four main areas:

1. *NEW*, which includes Biotechnology, Materials, Natural Resources, Agro-food Industry, Biomedicine and Environment;
2. *ICT*, which includes Information and Communication Technologies and Information Society;
3. *CLASSICAL*, which includes Industrial Design and Production, Chemical Products and Processes, Aeronautics, Automobile Industry, Energy, Space and Transports and Territory Arrangement; and
4. *OTHER*, which includes Socioeconomic, Horizontal Actions to Support Technology Institutes – Technology Institutes Plan[4] – and Horizontal Actions to Support the Project Guarantee System.

We capture the effect of these four areas by means of dichotomous variables. The objective of this grouping is to try to obtain evidence of

Table 10.3 Technological area distribution

	Number of Proposals	Share %	Number of Accepted Projects	Share %	% of Accepted Projects
NEW	810	28.25	266	20.64	32.84
ICT	950	33.14	479	37.16	50.42
CLASSICAL	964	33.62	487	37.78	50.52
OTHER	143	4.99	57	4.42	39.86
Total	2867	100.00	1289	100.00	44.96

whether there is a political preference for a particular type or types of technologies.

The distribution of projects across the four areas is presented in Table 10.3. A preliminary examination shows that while the percentage of approved proposals belonging to *ICT* and *CLASSICAL* groups was 50.42 per cent and 50.52 per cent respectively, only 32.84 per cent of proposals in *NEW* were positively evaluated.

10.3.2.4 Applicant region
We employ a dummy for each Spanish region, in the case of at least one organization from the region being involved in the project.[5]

Concerning the regional distribution of projects, we found that three regions stood out: Madrid, País Vasco and Cataluña (see Table 10.4). At least one organization from Madrid is involved in 42.8 per cent of initial proposals and in 47.5 per cent of successful proposals. País Vasco and Cataluña were involved in more than 30 per cent and 25 per cent respectively of both presented and selected projects, which had at least one organization from these regions. These figures, to some extent, reflect the distribution of Spanish production and economic activity. We can also see that acceptance rates differ greatly by region. While for some (C. Valenciana, Madrid, País Vasco) acceptance rates are around 50 per cent, for others (Baleares, Extremadura, Galicia) they fall to around 35 per cent.

10.3.2.5 Yearly control
Finally, we want to control for the probability of a project acceptance by the year in which it was proposed. The reason for this is to analyse whether the characteristics of this programme induce trust and confidence in target organizations such that acceptance of proposals is not conditional on the year (Shapira, Roessner and Barke, 1995).

Table 10.4 Regional distribution

Region	Number of Proposals	Share %	Number of Accepted Projects	Share %	% of Accepted Projects
Andalucía	403	14.06	164	12.72	40.69
Aragón	222	7.74	97	7.53	43.69
Baleares	79	2.76	27	2.09	34.18
C. Valenciana	335	11.68	168	13.03	50.15
Canarias	74	2.58	29	2.25	39.19
Cantabria	47	1.64	20	1.55	42.55
Castilla L.M.	59	2.06	24	1.86	40.68
Castilla León	194	6.77	77	5.97	39.69
Cataluña	757	26.40	323	25.06	42.67
Extremadura	57	1.99	21	1.63	36.84
Galicia	150	5.23	55	4.27	36.67
La Rioja	36	1.26	15	1.16	41.67
Madrid	1227	42.80	612	47.48	49.88
Murcia	116	4.05	50	3.88	43.10
Navarra	176	6.14	79	6.13	44.89
País Vasco	867	30.24	440	34.13	50.75
Pdo. Asturias	70	2.44	29	2.25	41.43
Unassigned projects	47	1.64	10	0.78	21.28
Total	2867	100.00	1289	100.00	44.96

Table 10.5 Yearly distribution

Year	Number of Proposals	Share %	Number of Accepted Projects	Share %	% of Accepted Projects
2000	560	19.53	265	20.56	47.32
2001	756	26.37	323	25.06	42.72
2002	789	27.52	316	24.52	40.05
2003	762	26.58	385	29.87	50.52
Total	2867	100.00	1289	100.00	44.96

Project distribution across years is presented in Table 10.5. Year one has the least number of proposals, while the number of applications in the three following years is fairly stable. However, there are sharp differences in acceptance rates probably related to the availability of resources and the duration of projects. The first and last years show acceptance rates of

47.32 per cent and 50.52 per cent respectively while 2002 and 2003 are both below 43 per cent.

10.3.3 Empirical Specification

The existing literature and the discussion above lead to several conjectures about the factors involved in the public selection of R&D cooperative projects. First, we expect that the inputs of the project – as a proxy for project size – exert a positive effect on the probability of project acceptance. Second, with regard to inclusion of a scientific partner we expect this to have a positive effect on the probability of project acceptance. Third, as we also include some proxies for political factors using control variables such as technological area, applicant region and year of the call, we expect these variables to have significant effects. However, the sign cannot be predicted because it is related to political preferences.

To explore the criteria used by public evaluators in assessing whether or not to finance cooperative projects, we estimate a probit model.[6] The full probit equation is estimated as follows:

$$Project\_Selection = \beta_1\ Project\_Inputs + \beta_2\ Research\_Organizations + \beta_3\ Project\_Area + \beta_4\ Applicant\_Regions + \beta_5\ Year + U$$

Table 10.6 presents the descriptive statistics and correlations of the variables used in the study.

10.4 RESULTS

Table 10.7 summarizes the probit analyses of the factors affecting acceptance or rejection of cooperative R&D projects. The coefficients in this table show the marginal effect of the independent variables on the probability of project acceptance, everything else remaining constant. Robust standard errors are in brackets.

First, we can see that input characteristics are very important. More precisely, evaluators prefer projects with a high numbers of working hours (p-value = 0.000) and low budgets (p-value = 0.070). That is to say, when controlling for all variables, we discover that total project budget negatively affects the probability of acceptance.[7] This reflects a preference for human-capital-intensive projects and raises questions about the strategy of public evaluators: do they prefer a large number of small projects or do they prefer to concentrate their economic resources in fewer, more expensive projects? According to the descriptive analysis we can see that, despite the inclusion

Table 10.6 Means, standard deviations and correlations

Variables	Mean	Std. Dev.	1	2	3	4	5	6	7	8	9	10	11	12	13	14
1 Budget	1,662,131	21,700,000														
2 Hours	1,569,114	2,271,647	0.160													
3 Partners	3.04	2.99	−0.007	0.053												
4 Technology institutes	0.244	0.430	−0.026	−0.018	0.154											
5 Universities	0.318	0.465	0.013	−0.027	−0.041	−0.205										
6 NEW	0.282	0.450	−0.022	−0.071	−0.025	−0.073	0.066									
7 ICTs	0.331	0.470	0.017	0.093	0.035	−0.031	−0.074	−0.445								
8 CLASSIC	0.336	0.472	0.009	−0.001	−0.052	0.014	0.043	−0.439	−0.504							
9 OTHER	0.049	0.217	−0.012	−0.053	0.089	0.185	−0.069	−0.143	−0.164	−0.162						
10 Region 1	0.140	0.347	0.011	0.043	0.204	−0.020	0.071	0.007	−0.040	0.002	0.068					
11 Region 2	0.077	0.267	−0.012	−0.030	0.153	−0.027	0.174	0.004	−0.066	0.074	−0.023	−0.011				
12 Region 3	0.027	0.163	−0.007	0.026	0.067	0.022	−0.005	−0.031	0.085	−0.085	0.062	0.033	0.001			
13 Region 4	0.116	0.321	−0.012	−0.008	0.192	0.208	−0.019	−0.034	0.032	−0.049	0.106	0.021	0.026	0.022		
14 Region 5	0.025	0.158	−0.006	0.028	0.099	−0.046	0.093	−0.021	0.037	−0.029	0.025	0.005	−0.013	0.084	0.005	
15 Region 6	0.016	0.127	−0.006	−0.017	0.110	−0.035	0.033	0.001	−0.003	−0.002	0.009	−0.019	−0.006	−0.022	−0.038	−0.003
16 Region 7	0.020	0.141	−0.006	−0.015	0.184	0.006	0.010	−0.011	0.020	−0.005	−0.010	−0.014	0.054	0.038	0.035	−0.008
17 Region 8	0.067	0.251	−0.010	−0.005	0.268	0.106	−0.029	−0.007	−0.004	−0.031	0.088	0.095	0.050	0.016	0.142	0.046
18 Region 9	0.264	0.440	0.032	0.015	0.130	0.034	−0.008	−0.049	0.071	−0.034	0.019	−0.057	−0.035	0.024	0.003	−0.016
19 Region 10	0.019	0.139	−0.007	−0.036	0.137	0.022	−0.023	0.081	−0.007	−0.077	0.015	0.055	0.018	−0.024	0.022	0.043
20 Region 11	0.052	0.222	−0.009	0.010	0.211	−0.041	0.037	−0.024	0.067	−0.050	0.012	0.062	0.023	0.050	0.061	0.043
21 Region 12	0.012	0.111	−0.005	−0.015	0.023	−0.023	0.021	0.046	−0.027	−0.012	−0.009	−0.033	0.020	0.003	−0.029	0.004
22 Region 13	0.427	0.494	−0.003	0.107	0.047	−0.143	0.015	−0.030	0.000	0.010	0.039	0.051	−0.063	0.024	−0.067	−0.032
23 Region 14	0.040	0.197	−0.008	0.006	0.073	0.024	0.103	0.060	−0.011	−0.066	0.043	0.004	−0.012	0.032	0.071	0.012
24 Region 15	0.061	0.240	−0.009	−0.012	0.227	0.060	−0.067	0.039	−0.064	0.005	0.050	0.007	0.032	−0.007	0.014	0.014
25 Region 16	0.302	0.459	−0.019	0.050	0.169	0.319	−0.162	−0.066	−0.002	0.034	0.066	−0.061	0.006	−0.063	−0.035	−0.073
26 Region 17	0.024	0.154	−0.005	−0.004	0.314	−0.019	−0.037	−0.004	0.007	−0.016	0.028	0.098	0.052	0.060	0.060	0.019
27 Region 18	0.016	0.127	−0.005	−0.016	0.128	−0.028	−0.010	0.064	−0.075	0.028	−0.030	0.045	0.016	−0.022	0.006	0.014
28 Year 2000	0.195	0.396	0.003	0.022	0.072	0.060	−0.070	−0.023	0.047	−0.071	0.098	−0.011	−0.016	−0.009	0.029	−0.023
29 Year 2001	0.263	0.440	−0.014	0.020	0.030	−0.011	0.026	0.077	−0.077	0.007	−0.006	0.002	0.029	−0.022	−0.005	0.009
30 Year 2002	0.275	0.446	0.030	0.001	−0.050	−0.001	0.053	−0.021	0.020	0.022	−0.049	−0.022	−0.003	0.028	0.010	0.024
31 Year 2003	0.265	0.441	−0.019	−0.040	−0.042	−0.040	−0.019	−0.036	0.016	0.032	−0.029	0.030	−0.012	0.002	−0.030	−0.013

	15	16	17	18	19	20	21	22	23	24	25	26	27	28	29	30
16 Region 7	0.001															
17 Region 8	0.021	0.052														
18 Region 9	−0.039	−0.029	−0.011													
19 Region 10	0.064	0.053	0.107	−0.025												
20 Region 11	0.033	0.012	0.128	−0.006	0.084											
21 Region 12	0.013	0.080	0.011	−0.019	0.009	0.005										
22 Region 13	−0.033	0.074	0.004	−0.155	0.030	0.036	−0.060									
23 Region 14	0.030	0.021	0.044	−0.022	0.023	0.016	−0.022	−0.027								
24 Region 15	0.025	0.015	0.113	−0.013	0.061	0.053	0.098	−0.083	0.044							
25 Region 16	0.006	−0.007	0.020	−0.109	−0.025	−0.001	−0.020	−0.177	−0.102	0.102						
26 Region 17	0.108	0.093	0.134	0.023	0.131	0.173	0.071	0.058	0.026	0.105	0.029					
27 Region 18	0.005	0.001	−0.013	−0.020	−0.018	0.020	0.013	−0.022	0.030	0.013	−0.049	0.017				
28 Year 2000	−0.002	−0.015	0.044	0.016	−0.005	0.016	0.002	0.038	−0.008	0.000	0.008	0.030	−0.046			
29 Year 2001	0.030	0.033	−0.006	0.033	0.021	0.003	0.049	0.003	0.013	0.009	−0.023	0.021	0.042	−0.283		
30 Year 2002	−0.025	0.011	−0.008	0.017	−0.001	−0.029	−0.015	−0.001	0.015	0.018	−0.041	−0.020	0.019	−0.293	−0.379	
31 Year 2003	−0.003	−0.031	−0.024	−0.064	−0.015	0.013	−0.035	−0.035	−0.021	−0.026	0.058	−0.027	−0.022	−0.285	−0.369	−0.381

Table 10.7 Explanatory model for the public selection of R&D cooperative projects

Variables	Project Selection			
	MODEL A		MODEL B	
Project inputs				
Budget	−6.94e−10*	(4.03e−10)		
Hours	6.56e−06***	(7.89e−07)	6.45e−06***	(7.82e−07)
Partners	−0.0062	(0.0069)	−0.0062	(0.0069)
Science partner				
Technology institutes	−0.0279	(0.0253)	−0.0274	(0.0253)
Universities	0.0222	(0.0225)	0.0219	(0.0225)
Technological area				
NEW	**−0.1671****	**(0.0240)**	**−0.1665****	**(0.0241)**
ICT	−0.0249	(0.0241)	−0.0246	(0.0241)
OTHER	**−0.0922***	**(0.0451)**	**−0.0922****	**(0.0451)**
Applicant region				
Region 1	**−0.0515***	**(0.0300)**	**−0.0519***	**(0.0300)**
Region 2	0.0125	(0.0385)	0.0129	(0.0385)
Region 3	**−0.1265****	**(0.0582)**	**−0.1255****	**(0.0581)**
Region 4	**0.1048****	**(0.0332)**	**0.1050****	**(0.0332)**
Region 5	−0.0372	(0.0649)	−0.0362	(0.0648)
Region 6	0.0000	(0.0785)	0.0004	(0.0784)
Region 7	−0.0393	(0.0678)	−0.0393	(0.0678)
Region 8	−0.0444	(0.0396)	−0.0442	(0.0395)
Region 9	−0.0167	(0.0242)	−0.0173	(0.0241)
Region 10	−0.0173	(0.0744)	−0.0178	(0.0744)
Region 11	**−0.0972****	**(0.0458)**	**−0.0968****	**(0.0458)**
Region 12	0.0621	(0.0935)	0.0625	(0.0934)
Region 13	**0.0850****	**(0.0217)**	**0.0855****	**(0.0217)**
Region 14	0.0265	(0.0499)	0.0272	(0.0499)
Region 15	0.0454	(0.0428)	0.0455	(0.0428)
Region 16	**0.0894****	**(0.0254)**	**0.0899****	**(0.0253)**
Region 17	0.0175	(0.0736)	0.0174	(0.0736)
Region 18	**−0.1883****	**(0.0727)**	**−0.1880****	**(0.0727)**
Year of call				
Year 2001	**−0.0648****	**(0.0300)**	**−0.0645****	**(0.0300)**
Year 2002	**−0.1052****	**(0.0296)**	**−0.1056****	**(0.0296)**
Year 2003	0.0133	(0.0303)	0.0136	(0.0303)
Chi-squared	212.53***		210.72***	
Log-likelihood	−1788.1875		−1788.9001	

Notes: $N = 2790$; * $p \leq 0.10$; ** $p \leq 0.05$; *** $p \leq 0.01$.
Use of bold type indicates coefficients are significant.

of some very big projects (mean budget is €1 827 073), the median project has a budget of €613 250.

On the other hand, the number of entities involved in the project, is not only non-significant but also has a negative sign. This result is quite surprising because it does not fit with the aim of the PROFIT programme concerning cooperation.

Second, we can see that neither the presence of technology institutes nor universities is significant in explaining the evaluation of projects. That is to say, the PROFIT initiative is not fostering relationships among these knowledge sources and firms. This result is in line with that obtained by Acosta Ballesteros and Modrego Rico (2001) who analysed the financing of Spanish concerted projects. In the case of technology institutes, despite a special tool (the Technology Institutes Plan) having been implemented to foster cooperation; the coefficient is negative, showing that projects with technology institutes as partners were not favoured at all. On the other hand, university partners show a positive coefficient, which is not significant.

Third, although government selected several areas ex ante, the analysis shows that some ex post decisions were made that favoured some of these. Thus, we find *NEW* projects are rejected much more frequently than *CLASSICAL* projects (p-value = 0.000). This latter group is the most preferred, while *ICT* and *OTHER* show negative, but non-significant, coefficients. This is a very important result and can be interpreted in various ways. On the one hand, it may be evidence of the poor public commitment to new technologies; on the other, it might reflect the fact that it is more difficult both to design and evaluate projects in areas that involve processes of rapid technological change.

Fourth, in the analysis of the regional preferences of central government we found that the applicants' region was relevant. Three regions where projects were more likely to receive finance are Madrid (p-value = 0.000), País Vasco (p-value = 0.000) and C. Valenciana (p-value = 0.002). We interpret this to mean that organizations in Madrid benefit from an administrative capital effect and from proximity to the location of decision-making. The other two regions have some common features: both have a regional technology policy focused on the role of technology institutes and in fact are the two regions with the highest number of technology institutes. To check for an interaction between their presence in the projects and the two regional dummies we ran two separate regressions for each region, in which technology institutes had a negative coefficient in both cases.[8] However, the historical presence of such organizations in these regions could have contributed to improving firms' abilities to meet the requirements in public calls.

On the other hand, projects involving organizations from Andalucía, Baleares and Galicia are more likely to be rejected (p-values equal to 0.082, 0.042 and 0.042, respectively). All these are less developed regions from an industrial viewpoint. These results are in line with those in other analyses. For example, Vence (1998) found that European technology policy is focused more on encouraging technological capacity and competitiveness of successful firms than on increasing regional cohesion through the reduction of disparities.

Finally, we control for the year of the proposals to check the stability of the programme, which is necessary to build confidence in the targeted organizations. We found that similar projects had different probabilities of being approved, depending on the year of application. Project proposals sent in 2001 and 2002 received more frequent rejections. The number of proposals increased by 34.64 per cent between 2000 and 2001. This, together with the amount of funding committed in the first year might have negatively affected the probability of being accepted in the subsequent two years. Strong year to year variations in public financing are not new to Spanish technology policy; it occurred in the funding of concerted projects (Acosta Ballesteros and Modrego Rico, 2001).

10.5 CONCLUSIONS

Despite the growing importance of public funding for R&D cooperation, few studies have examined the criteria used by public sector evaluators when selecting which projects to finance. This study aimed to shed some light on this topic.

We analysed the factors underlying the selection of projects in the PROFIT programme, the main Spanish technology policy initiative in the period 2000–03. We found input variables to be very important in explaining the selection or rejection of a project. More precisely, human-capital-intensive projects, with large numbers of working hours and low budgets are preferred while the presence of universities or technology institutes seems to have little effect on whether a project will be accepted. This is in line with other studies (Acosta Ballesteros and Modrego Rico, 2001), but questions the literature that emphasizes the importance of access to public support for firms that cooperate with research organizations (Hagedoorn, 1993; Cassiman, 1999; Hagedoorn et al., 2000; or Caloghirou et al., 2003). Moreover this result also questions one of the declared objectives of PROFIT, which is to encourage relationships among firms and the science base: a special, horizontal, action was implemented to facilitate technology institutes' participation.

According to Lee and Om (1996) political factors, captured by area, region and year of proposal, are relevant. We found that not all the areas were considered equally. Projects from *NEW* (Biotechnology, Materials, Natural Resources, Agro-food Industry, Biomedicine and Environment) were not favoured by evaluators. This calls into question public commitment to the new technologies. On the other hand, some regions, especially País Vasco, C. Valenciana and Madrid, were relatively favoured, while others (Andalucía, Baleares and Galicia) were underprivileged. This biased regional distribution of funded projects may be explained in part by the preference in R&D public initiatives for encouraging technological capacity to the detriment of regional cohesion (Vence, 1998).

Finally, we found great instability in acceptance rates, which reduced radically in 2001 and 2002. This is an important shortcoming of PROFIT, since initiative stability is very important to build confidence in the target organizations (Shapira et al., 1995).

In summary, our findings shed some light on the criteria used by the public sector to select which projects to support. The use of project-level data allows us to observe some project effects, which are not captured by firm-level data. However, the absence of certain data impeded the full analysis of the effects of both projects and firms together. Future research should further explore this.

ACKNOWLEDGEMENTS

This project was financed by Spanish Science and Technology Office. We want to thank Íñigo Segura and Juan Carlos Castro for their insights and contribution to this work.

NOTES

1. Technology institutes are legally defined as non-profit innovation and technology organizations aiming to enhance the competitive capacity of firms in Spain, through the provision of a wide range of technological activities, like training, technical services, consultancy and R&D contracting. They are very active agents in the Spanish National System of Innovation (NSI).
2. This means that less than half of the projects received advance payments.
3. Unfortunately we were not allowed full access to the data and some relevant information, such as the characteristics of applicant firms, could not be included in the analysis.
4. It should be noted that a project belongs to this area only if it is a Technology Institutes Plan project and it cannot be classified in another technological area. As a consequence it is a residual area. Only 22.5 per cent of projects belonging to the Technology Institutes Plan are classified in this group.

5. Note that several organizations are involved in each project. In particular, 48.48 per cent of projects involve organizations from at least two different regions and 11.47 per cent of projects involve organizations from at least three different regions. As a consequence there is no multicollinearity problem.
6. Logit estimations give similar results.
7. The results of the regression without total budget are also provided in Table 10.7.
8. Results are available upon request.

REFERENCES

Acosta Ballesteros, J. and A. Modrego Rico (2001), 'Public financing of cooperative R&D projects in Spain: the concerted projects under the National R&D Plan', *Research Policy*, 30, 625–41.

Arrow, K.J. (1962), 'Economic welfare and the allocation of resources for invention', in R.R. Nelson (ed.), *The Rate and Direction of Inventive Activity*, Princeton, NJ, Princeton University Press.

Blanes, J.V. and I. Busom (2004), 'Who participates in R&D subsidy programs? The case of Spanish manufacturing firms', *Research Policy*, 33, 1459–76.

Bonaccorsi, A. and A. Piccaluga (1994), 'A theoretical framework for the evaluation of university–industry relationships', *R&D Management*, **24**(3), 229–47.

Bozeman, B. (2000), 'Technology transfer and public policy: a review of research and theory', *Research Policy*, 29, 627–55.

Bozeman, B. and J. Rogers (2001), 'Strategic management of government-sponsored R&D portfolios', *Environment & Planning C: Government and Policy*, 19, 413–42.

Caloghirou, Y., S. Ioannides and N. Vonortas (2003), 'Research joint ventures', *Journal of Economic Surveys*, **17**(4), 541–70.

Cassiman, B. (1999), 'Cooperación en Investigación y Desarrollo. Evidencia para la Industria Manufacturera Española', *Papeles de Economía Española*, No. 81, 143–54.

Cassiman, B. and R. Veugelers (2002), 'R&D cooperation and spillovers: some empirical evidence from Belgium', *The American Economic Review*, **92**(4), 1169–85.

Castro, J.C. (2001), 'Dos años de PROFIT: algunos datos para un balance provisional', *Economía Industrial*, 340, 179–83.

David, P.A., B.H. Hall and A.A. Toole (2000), 'Is public R&D a complement or substitute for private R&D? A review of the econometric evidence', *Research Policy*, 29, 497–529.

Geroski, P. (1995), 'Markets for technology, knowledge, innovation and appropriability', in P. Stoneman (ed.), *Handbook of the Economics of Innovation and Technological Change*, Blackwell, Oxford.

Hagedoorn, J. (1993), 'Understanding the rationale of strategic technology partnering: interorganizational modes of cooperation and sectoral differences', *Strategic Management Journal*, 14, 371–85.

Hagedoorn, J., A. Link and N. Vonortas (2000), 'Research partnerships', *Research Policy*, 29, 567–86.

Ham, R.M. and D.C. Mowery (1998), 'Improving the effectiveness of public–private R&D collaboration: case studies at a US weapons laboratory', *Research Policy*, 26, 661–75.

Hayashi, T. (2003), 'Effect of R&D programmes on the formation of university–industry–government networks: comparative analysis of Japanese R&D programmes', *Research Policy*, 32, 1421–42.

Heijs, J. (2001), 'Sistemas Nacionales y Regionales de Innovación y Política Tecnológica: una Aproximación Teórica', Documento de trabajo, No. 24, Madrid: Instituto de Análisis Industrial y Financiero, Universidad Complutense de Madrid.

Heijs, J. (2005), 'Identification of firms supported by technology policies: the case of Spanish low interest credits', *Science and Public Policy*, **32**(3), 219–30.

Hsu, Y.G., G.H. Tzeng and J.Z. Shyu (2003), 'Fuzzy multiple criteria selection of government-sponsored frontier technology R&D projects', *R&D Management*, **33**(5), 539–51.

Klette, T.J., J. Moen and Z. Griliches (2000), 'Do subsidies to commercial R&D reduce market failures? Microeconometric evaluation studies', *Research Policy*, 29, 471–95.

Lee, M. and K. Om (1996), 'Different factors considered in project selection at public and private R&D institutes', *Technovation*, **16**(6), 271–5.

Lee, M. and K. Om (1997), 'The concept of effectiveness in R&D project selection', *International Journal of Technology Management*, **13**(5–6), 511–24.

Meyer-Krahmer, F. and P. Montigny (1989), 'Evaluations of innovation programmes in selected European countries', *Research Policy*, 18, 313–32.

Miotti, L. and F. Sachwald (2003), 'Co-operative R&D: why and with whom? An integrated framework of analysis', *Research Policy*, 32, 1481–99.

Molas-Gallart, J. and A. Salter (2002), 'Diversidad y Excelencia: Consideraciones sobre Política Científica', *IPTS Report*, No. 66.

OECD (2001), *OECD Science, Technology and Industry Scoreboard. Towards a Knowledge-based Economy*, OECD, Paris.

OECD (2003), *Main Science and Technology Indicators*, OECD, Paris.

Ormala, E. (1989), 'Nordic experiences of the evaluation of technical research and development, *Research Policy*, 18, 333–42.

Roessner, D. (1989), 'Evaluating government innovation programmes: lessons from the U.S. experience', *Research Policy*, 18, 343–59.

Shapira, P., D. Roessner and R. Barke (1995), 'New public infrastructures for small firm industrial modernization in the USA', *Entrepeneurship & Regional Development*, 7, 63–84.

Teece, D.J. (1992), 'Competition, cooperation and innovation. Organizational arrangements for regimes of rapid technological progress', *Journal of Economic Behavior and Organization*, 18, 1–25.

Vence, X. (ed.) (1998), *La Política Tecnológica Comunitaria y la Cohesión Regional*, Madrid: Civitas.

APPENDIX 10.1

Table A10.1   Description of variables

Variable	Definition
Selected project	Dichotomous variable, it takes value 1 if the project was accepted
Budget	Quantitative variable, it measures the total amount of project budget
Hours	Quantitative variable, it measures the total number of hours planned
Partners	Quantitative variable, it measures the number of organizations cooperating in the project
Technology institutes	Dichotomous variable, it takes value 1 if a technology institute participated in the project
Universities	Dichotomous variable, it takes value 1 if a university participated in the project
NEW	Dichotomous variable, it takes value 1 if the project belongs to the following programmes: Biotechnology, Materials, Natural Resources, Agro-food Industry, Biomedicine and Environment
ICT	Dichotomous variable, it takes value 1 if the project belongs to the following programmes: Information and Communication Technologies and Information Society
CLASSIC	Dichotomous variable, it takes value 1 if the project belongs to the following programmes: Industrial Design and Production, Chemical Products and Processes, Aeronautics, Automobile Industry, Energy, Space and Transports and Territory Arrangement
OTHER	Dichotomous variable, it takes value 1 if the project belongs to the following programmes: Socioeconomic, Horizontal Action to Support Technology Institutes Horizontal Action to Support the Project Guarantee System
Region 1	Dichotomous variable, it takes value 1 if there is an applicant organization from Andalucía
Region 2	Dichotomous variable, it takes value 1 if there is an applicant organization from Aragón
Region 3	Dichotomous variable, it takes value 1 if there is an applicant organization from Baleares
Region 4	Dichotomous variable, it takes value 1 if there is an applicant organization from Comunidad Valenciana
Region 5	Dichotomous variable, it takes value 1 if there is an applicant organization from Canarias
Region 6	Dichotomous variable, it takes value 1 if there is an applicant organization from Cantabria

Table A10.1 (continued)

Variable	Definition
Region 7	Dichotomous variable, it takes value 1 if there is an applicant organization from Castilla-La Mancha
Region 8	Dichotomous variable, it takes value 1 if there is an applicant organization from Castilla León
Region 9	Dichotomous variable, it takes value 1 if there is an applicant organization from Cataluña
Region 10	Dichotomous variable, it takes value 1 if there is an applicant organization from Extremadura
Region 11	Dichotomous variable, it takes value 1 if there is an applicant organization from Galicia
Region 12	Dichotomous variable, it takes value 1 if there is an applicant organization from La Rioja
Region 13	Dichotomous variable, it takes value 1 if there is an applicant organization from Madrid
Region 14	Dichotomous variable, it takes value 1 if there is an applicant organization from Murcia
Region 15	Dichotomous variable, it takes value 1 if the region of the applicant organization was Navarra
Region 16	Dichotomous variable, it takes value 1 if there is an applicant organization from País Vasco
Region 17	Dichotomous variable, it takes value 1 if there is an applicant organization from Asturias
Region 18	Dichotomous variable, it takes value 1 if an applicant organization was unassigned
Year 2000	Dichotomous variable, it takes value 1 if the year of the call was 2000
Year 2001	Dichotomous variable, it takes value 1 if the year of the call was 2001
Year 2002	Dichotomous variable, it takes value 1 if the year of the call was 2002
Year 2003	Dichotomous variable, it takes value 1 if the year of the call was 2003

PART III

Regional economic growth and knowledge

11. Convergence clubs and the role of education in Spanish regional growth
Adriana Di Liberto

11.1 INTRODUCTION

Differences in human capital endowments and their rates of investment are recognized by the theoretical growth literature as an important element in explaining growth and observed GDP gaps. Despite this, cross-country studies of aggregate returns to education typically using the standard growth-regression approach usually find that education is not strongly associated with per capita income growth. This study investigates the returns to education among Spanish regions using measures of the stock of regional human capital and examines if these have been different in different regional clubs. Indeed, as observed for cross-country studies, previous empirical evidence on returns to education in Spain reveals puzzling, non-homogeneous results. Many studies have found that education has not positively influenced Spanish regional development processes,[1] while we identify few studies where the role of human capital on growth is unambiguously positive.[2]

In particular, this study examines if, dealing with the typical problems arising in a standard macro analysis of returns to education, we are able to find significant results. In general, it has been claimed[3] that the main problem causing the observed lack of empirical support is that most growth regressions that use large international datasets, incorrectly impose a single coefficient and thus equal returns on schooling among different countries. This problem is likely to arise when the quality of education is influenced by differences in educational institutions. However, this is not (or less) the case when we analyze a regional sample. The Spanish regions have common institutions so that, in large part, the data represent a controlled experiment in *ceteris paribus* variation of labor force educational endowments in a developed economy. Second, it may well be that the quantity of education affects its quality: returns to education may be higher in more educated areas as usually predicted by growth models.⁴ In all these cases, standard regressions would produce distorted estimates on education due to the presence of parameter heterogeneity and measurement error problems.

The use of a regional dataset does not eliminate this problem since inequalities and, thus, different returns may arise even at regional level. Indeed, Spanish poorer regions are also the least educated areas, and this suggests the existence of a clear duality in the Spanish economy between the developed North (or Northeast) and the less developed South (or Southwest), and thus the presence of two convergence clubs. In this case, allowing the different Spanish clubs to converge separately may test the previous hypothesis. In sum, this is an ideal sample to test the relationship between quantity and returns to education: allowing for parameter heterogeneity in the two clubs, we analyze if returns to education have been different in these two areas of the country considered separately.

Further, we have data on average years of schooling together with data on primary, secondary and tertiary school attainments. Thus, we ask if different levels of education produce different impacts on growth. In fact, due to their emphasis on the role of technology, most of the theoretical growth models expect that higher levels of educational attainments act more powerfully on growth than, say, primary school. This prediction contradicts microeconometric evidence, where returns to investments in primary education are usually estimated as the largest.⁵ Moreover, we may expect that the different levels of education have varying impacts on growth depending on the level of development of an economy. In particular, the so called Nelson and Phelps models⁶ stress the importance of a catch-up mechanism where technological improvement is the combination of two distinct types of activities, innovation and imitation. The first role is generally related to technologically advanced economies or economies that may be considered at the technology frontier, and can be thought of as pure research. The second role identifies a growth mechanism resulting from technology transfers among economies and, thus, should be important for less developed economies. In this case, stocks of human capital increase the capacity to adopt and implement innovations or new technologies from more advanced countries, implying the possibility of a process of growth/catch-up occurring among countries. In this case, we expect that the three standard levels of educational attainment (primary, secondary and tertiary education) perform differently in the poor and rich clubs.

A final source of distortions when we estimate returns to schooling arises from the fact that in some cases acquisition of educational skills is not obviously linked with productivity. As noted by Schultz (1962), education may represent not only an investment for individuals but can also be considered as a consumption good and, thus, be privately valued for its own sake.

Moreover, in Spain, as in many other countries, the public sector is the chief employer of most of the skilled labor force.[7] As emphasized by Griliches (1997), this may be a factor that produces distorted results when we estimate returns to schooling since the output of the public sector is certainly badly measured in National Accounts and, possibly, underestimated. Moreover, the public sector, while employing most of the skilled labor force, is not obviously an innovative sector while, as predicted by many theoretical growth models, especially Schumpeterian models, educational capital is growth-enhancing only when allocated in innovative sectors.[8] Given the quality and the level of disaggregation of data, it is possible to deal with the problem of the link between acquisition of educational skills and productivity. Opportunely, regional Spanish data on human capital endowments include a disaggregation by sector. Examining the different levels of educational attainment in the labor force disaggregated by sector enables us to estimate whether or not excluding the public sector from the analysis significantly changes our results on returns to schooling.

11.2 REGIONAL INEQUALITIES: GDP TRENDS

In terms of regional GDP patterns, Spain has high levels of regional economic disparities but has seen these disparities decrease, mainly during the 1960s and 1970s. In Spain we identify 17 regions defined at NUTS 2 level[9] and data on regional GDP in Spain are computed every two years. Table 11.1 shows the logarithm of per capita GDP for each region (or Comunidad Autónoma) together with the percentage of people with the corresponding maximum educational qualification. Years included are 1964 and 1997, the initial and final year in our dataset. To facilitate the reading, regions are ordered starting from the poorest region in 1964 (Extremadura) in terms of per capita GDP.

Table 11.1 shows seven regions in 1964 with (the logarithm of) per capita GDP lower than the national average: Extremadura, Castilla-La Mancha, Galicia, Andalucía, Castilla y León, Murcia and Canarias. Among these regions there is only one group that may well form a geographical cluster of Southern regions: Extremadura, Andalucía, Murcia and Castilla-La Mancha. In other words, in terms of per capita GDP, the group of relatively poor regions is partly formed by Southern regions together with the inclusion of Galicia and Castilla y León (both Northwest), and the Canaries.

Standard σ-convergence analysis, as in Figure 11.1, would identify a significant decrease in the dispersion of regional per capita GDP during the 1960s and mid-1970s.

Table 11.1 GDP and educational levels (initial and final year)

	Per Capita GDP		Primary School		Secondary School		Tertiary Education		Average Years	
	1964	1997	1964	1997	1964	1997	1964	1997	1964	1997
Extremadura	5.57	6.77	82.2	37.9	1.7	46.5	2.2	13.7	3.42	8.68
Castilla-La Mancha	5.72	6.87	85.4	37.5	1.6	48.7	2.1	12.5	3.51	8.73
Galicia	5.84	6.91	87.7	43.4	2.2	43.8	2.3	12.3	3.68	8.37
Andalucía	5.86	6.78	80.1	37.1	2.6	48.2	2.6	13.2	3.52	8.77
Castilla y Léon	5.96	7.01	90.8	34.7	3.3	47.7	3.5	17.4	4.11	9.32
Murcia	5.99	6.93	81.2	33.0	3.9	50.9	3.2	15.0	3.79	9.22
Canarias	6.02	7.03	77.7	34.6	3.9	50.3	3.4	13.8	3.70	9.01
Asturias	6.24	6.95	91.0	34.0	3.7	51.6	3.2	14.4	4.12	9.23
Aragón	6.24	7.20	89.4	30.8	3.7	52.2	3.6	16.6	4.12	9.56
Rioja	6.28	7.29	89.9	37.1	4.2	45.5	3.8	17.3	4.23	9.16
Com. Valenciana	6.28	7.11	86.9	31.3	3.8	54.3	3.0	13.7	3.95	9.33
Cantabria	6.29	7.05	90.0	28.5	4.8	56.8	3.6	14.7	4.26	9.66
Navarra	6.32	7.30	89.4	30.4	4.2	50.6	3.9	18.7	4.23	9.72
Baleares	6.56	7.46	84.8	29.1	3.8	59.3	3.3	10.8	3.91	9.32
Cataluña	6.58	7.34	87.3	28.7	5.2	56.0	3.5	14.9	4.20	9.62
País Vasco	6.62	7.26	89.0	25.5	5.3	53.9	3.8	20.3	4.33	10.19
Madrid	6.75	7.32	80.2	24.5	9.7	51.2	6.6	24.1	4.96	10.49
Average Spain	6.18	7.09	86.1	32.8	4.0	51.0	3.4	15.5	4.00	9.32

Notes:
a. Per capita GDP is the logarithm of the corresponding variable.
b. Numbers for primary, secondary, tertiary and average years represent the percentage of people in each Comunidad Autónoma with the corresponding maximum educational qualification.
c. Tertiary education includes data from the two different attainment levels ('ciclo corto', three years and 'ciclo largo', two years) offered by the Spanish university system.

Sources:
a. Fundación BBV (various years).
b. Mas et al. (various years).

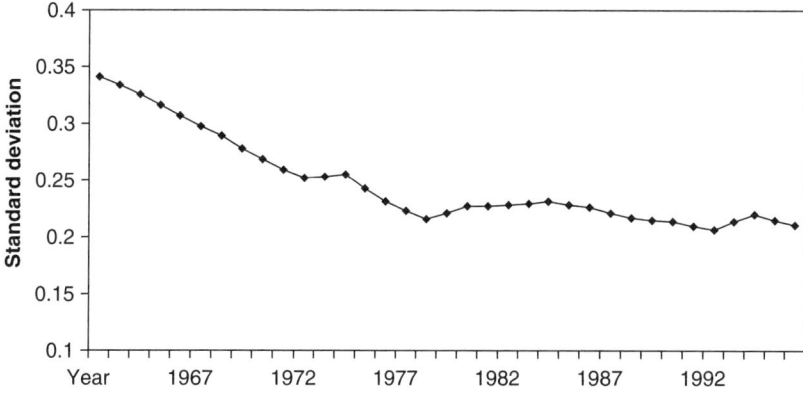

Figure 11.1 Sigma convergence: per capita GDP

This process ended after that period. Thus, stylized facts on Spanish regional convergence are similar to those observed in many other countries.[10] Table 11.1 shows that, even if Spain has experienced a decrease in regional inequalities, the regional per capita GDP distribution is characterized by persistency or low regional mobility: poor regions in 1964 are still the lagging regions in 1997. Thus, the pattern of σ-convergence may hide both the presence of a non-homogeneous process of convergence or the existence of convergence clubs.

11.3 HUMAN CAPITAL DATA: SOME NOTES OF CAUTION

We claim that Spanish data are most suitable for a macro study of returns to education: different from most regional datasets, the Spanish regions are quite diverse in their endowments of human capital and, since the 1960s, have experienced vast increases in the average duration of education at all three levels. This study uses the human capital dataset developed by the IVIE.[11] This dataset includes variables at regional (NUTS 2) level for the different levels of educational attainment of the labor force.[12] These different levels of education include: illiterate, primary school, secondary, lower tertiary and higher tertiary education. As stressed by De la Fuente (2002), this dataset is highly informative, and it enables us to investigate the effects of education on growth and convergence in considerable detail and to control for many possible distortions arising in the empirical literature on human capital and growth.

If we focus on educational levels we see that despite there being a law on compulsory schooling dating back to 1945, the proportion of illiterate people in Spanish regions has been high until relatively recently. We do not explicitly show data on illiteracy rates. With 15 percent of illiterates in 1964, the Canaries used to be the 'least educated' region and during the 1960s and 1970s regional percentages of illiterate labor force were far from zero even in more developed areas. This phenomenon has currently disappeared almost everywhere.[13]

Further, Table 11.1 shows that the proportion of people completing only primary education decreased from an average of 86 percent in 1964 to approximately 33 percent in 1997. However, in this dataset it is not possible to distinguish between the active population that has finished primary school from primary education dropouts and this may cause an upward bias for poorer (in terms of human capital) regions and so reduce the observed regional inequalities, since it is usually the case that the proportion of active population that did not complete primary school is higher in 'less educated' regions.[14]

Conversely, even if data show that, among OECD countries, Spain has a low percentage of people with a secondary school qualification, there was a significant expansion in numbers completing secondary school: the proportion of people with this level of education dramatically increased from 4 percent to 51 percent. However, this is not surprising, since this variable includes also (part of) compulsory schooling and the length of compulsory studies in Spain increased during the period analyzed.[15] Note that Spanish data on secondary schooling covers a variety of school curricula, embracing the range from compulsory schooling to upper secondary education and the length of these curricula may vary significantly. In general, this non-homogeneity of curricula implies that the secondary school indicator implicitly assumes that workers with very diverse levels of education (such as compulsory schooling only and upper secondary education) are perfectly substitutable and does not enable us to distinguish returns to secondary schooling from returns to lower levels of education.[16]

In addition to secondary education we also observe a significant increase in terms of higher educational attainments.[17] However, at the same time there was an increase in regional dispersion. For example, we observe that the proportion of people with tertiary education varied in 1997, from 10 percent in Baleares to 24 percent in Madrid, a significant difference indeed.

Finally, using these data we compute the average years of education, a synthetic measure of the regional stock of human capital.[18] From Figure 11.2 we observe that in Spain the stock of human capital has rapidly increased during the last 30 years, in particular during the 1980s.

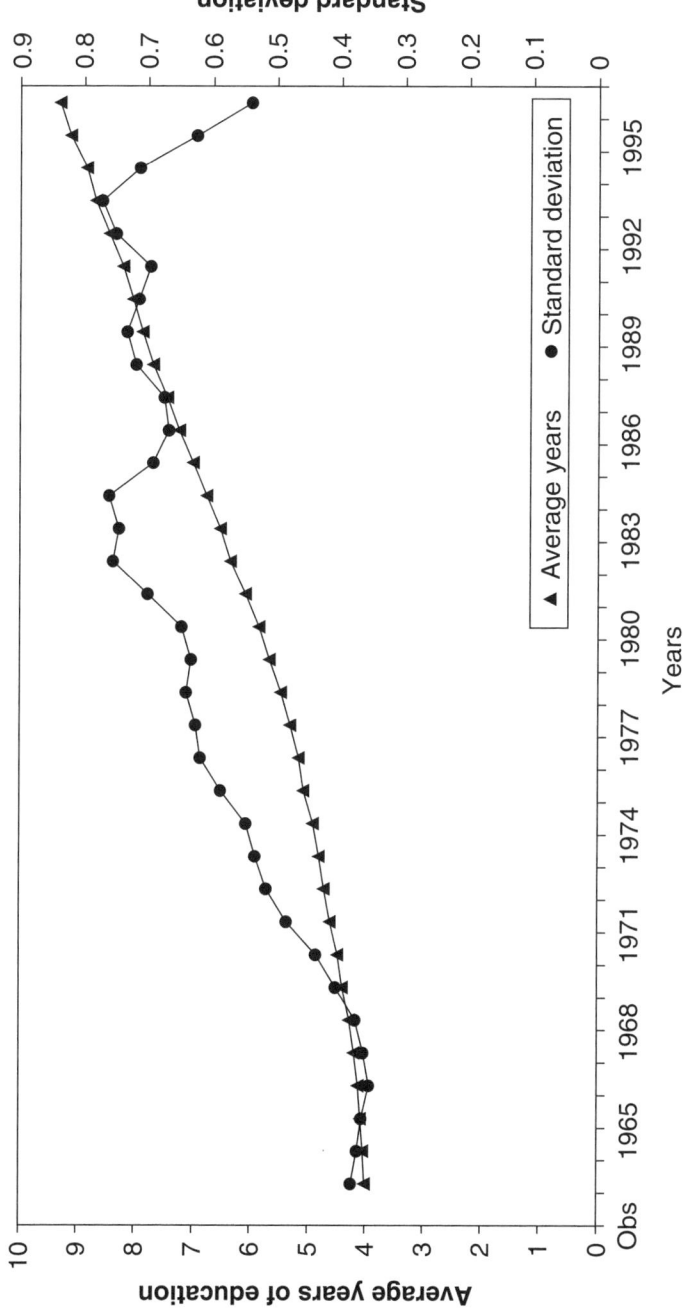

Figure 11.2 Trends in human capital: inequalities and levels

In the same figure we also investigate if the process of increase in regional educational levels brought about a commensurate decrease in regional inequalities. To this aim, we examine the pattern of regional inequalities in educational levels computing the σ-convergence process of the average years of schooling over time. It seems that in Spain, differences among regions increased for almost 30 years while decreasing significantly only very recently. This result is surprising, since policies directed at promoting education will usually also promote equality in educational standards. Apparently, this has not been the case in Spain for very long.[19]

Moreover, Table 11.1 shows that the regional distribution of this synthetic measure of human capital is characterized by persistency or low regional mobility. Again, if we focus on the first and last year of our sample, we see that the poor (in terms of human capital) regions in 1964 are still the lagging regions in 1997. Overall, we observe a similar correspondence between poor (in terms of per capita GDP) regions and uneducated regions.

11.4 ESTIMATION ISSUES AND CONVERGENCE CLUBS

Unlike previous studies, we identify two clubs of poor and rich (in terms of both per capita GDP and human capital endowment) Spanish regions.[20] As stressed above, in Table 11.1 we have seen that seven regions show a level of per capita GDP below the national average both in the initial and final year. Moreover, these regions also share another characteristic, since they all have low human capital levels, lower than the national average. The main exception to the rule are the Balearic Islands, which exhibit a very high level of per capita GDP but a relatively low level (less than the Spanish average) of human capital throughout the period analyzed. Although not as extreme as the Balearic Islands, Cataluña is a comparable (opposite) case.

Thus, in our empirical analysis we will consider two different clubs. The first group is the poor regions group and includes Extremadura, Castilla-La Mancha, Andalucía, Galicia, Murcia and Castilla y León. Accordingly, Comunidad Valenciana, Asturias, Aragón, Rioja, Cantabria, Navarra, Cataluña, País Vasco and Madrid form the second group of rich/educated regions. We eliminate the Canaries and Balearic Islands from the regression analysis as these regions clearly represent outliers: their (small island) economies are highly dependent on the tourism sector. Note that groups of regions sharing the same characteristics in terms of either per capita GDP or human capital levels do not form a geographical cluster. Nevertheless, even though this definition may certainly be disputed, from now on we will define these groups in terms of their geographical location: that is, we shall call the group of relatively poor regions Southwest, while the remaining regions will form the rich club called Northeast.

The use of a regional sample convinces us to estimate a system of regional equations with an unrestricted variance–covariance matrix, thus allowing for cross-sectional correlation of the disturbances (maximum likelihood).[21] In particular, this estimator is more efficient than the standard estimator used in this literature when three conditions are satisfied. First of all, we need a panel in which the time length is greater than the number of individuals. Second, shocks must be correlated among regions. Finally, errors must be non-autocorrelated. Thus, the ML estimator may be confidently applied when we investigate if returns to education are different in our two convergence clubs since our three conditions are met. First, in the following analysis we estimate two systems of equations separately where $T=16$[22] and where one system is formed by the Southwest group ($N=6$), and the other by Northeast regions ($N=9$). Second, when we check for the possible presence of (second order) autocorrelation, our standard Durbin tests largely do not reject the null hypothesis of absence of serial correlation.[23] Finally, it is very likely that macroeconomic factors that affect regions affect all of them to varying degrees.

The system of equations is described by:

$$gry_{it} = \alpha + \beta y_{it-\tau} + \gamma H_{it-\tau} + \lambda_t + \varepsilon_{it} \qquad (11.1)$$

where y_{it} is the logarithm of per capita GDP in period t for region i, gry_{it} is the growth rate of y, H_{it} is the of stock of human capital (or a vector of stocks), λ_t is an index of technology, assumed constant across the Spanish regions, and $\tau=2$. In particular, the variable H represents our four different educational attainment indices: primary, secondary and tertiary education plus the total stock, where these indicators are estimates of the average years of schooling in the given category. For each club equation (11.1) is transformed to:

$$gry^*_{it} = \beta y^*_{it-\tau} + \gamma H^*_{i,t-\tau} + \varepsilon^*_{i,t} \qquad (11.2)$$

with

$$y^*_{it} = y_{it} - \bar{y}_t \qquad H^*_{it} = H_{it} - \bar{H}_t \qquad (11.3)$$

where $\bar{y}_t$ and $\bar{H}_t$ represent the clubs average of y and H in period t. Data are taken in difference from the clubs' mean, in order to control for the presence of a time trend component η_t and of a likely common stochastic trend (the common component of technology) across regions.

In sum, unlike most studies on Spanish regions, we define two Spanish convergence clubs and allow for some heterogeneity in the slope coefficients. In particular, previous studies, while controlling for the possibility of unobserved regional heterogeneity using popular fixed effects estimators,[24] do not allow for parameter heterogeneity; that is, they have ruled out by assumption the possibility of different returns to education in different areas.[25]

11.5 RETURNS TO EDUCATION IN THE TWO CLUBS

In this section, we investigate how far returns to education in Spain have differed in the Southwest and Northeast clubs. As stressed above, various considerations suggest a possible role of the public sector when we investigate returns to schooling.

Table 11.2 shows how the proportion of highly educated labor employed in the public sector in Spain is significant in all regions. Data represent the average 1964–97.

On average, in Spain 53 percent of people with tertiary education are employed in the public sector. In the poorest regions this percentage is very high, and reaches 70 percent in Extremadura, while we observe significantly lower percentages in the more developed areas, especially País Vasco (35 percent) and Cataluña (38 percent). The Madrid area, which represents the region with the highest proportion of highly educated labor force, absorbs 46 percent of its graduates in the public sector. With regard to other levels of education, we observe that the public sector absorbs a relatively low percentage of people with secondary schooling (the Spanish average is 15 percent), and marginal percentages of people with very basic levels of education (only 5 percent). These observations confirm our idea that when we investigate returns to schooling we have to probe the public sector, especially with regard to tertiary education.

In order to test if returns to education are affected by the sectoral allocation of the labor force, we adopt two strategies. First, we introduce a measure of the proportion of the public sector in our regression.[26] These results are shown in Tables 11.3 and 11.4. Second, since Spanish regional data includes sectoral disaggregation, we compute a new set of human capital indicators (total stock of human capital plus primary, secondary and tertiary schooling) excluding the individuals employed in the public sector: that is, we effectively compute measures of average years of schooling for the private sector.[27] These results are shown in Table 11.5.

Table 11.2 Percentage of the labor force with different educational attainments employed in the public sector

	Tertiary Education	Secondary Education	Primary Education
Andalucía	60	18	6
Aragón	53	15	5
Asturias	48	12	3
Baleares	44	11	4
Canarias	60	17	6
Cantabria	50	14	4
Castilla-La Mancha	69	15	5
Castilla y León	60	16	4
Cataluña	38	9	3
Com. Valenciana	53	11	4
Extremadura	70	21	6
Galicia	55	14	3
Madrid	46	19	10
Murcia	62	18	5
Navarra	49	11	5
País Vasco	35	10	3
Rioja	50	15	4
Average Spain	53	15	5

Notes:
a. Numbers in the table represent the percentage of people employed in the public sector within each educational category in each region. That is, 60% of tertiary education in Andalucía, means that the 60% of the Andalusian labor force with a degree is employed in the public sector. Each percentage is an average 1964–97.

Source: Mas et al. (various years).

Table 11.3 shows the results for the Southwest club. In Model 1 we estimate the standard (absolute) β-convergence equation. The β-convergence parameter is negative and significant in all specifications. In Model 2 we introduce the total stock of human capital as a regressor and find a negative but non-significant coefficient. Introducing the proportion of the public sector in Model 3 does change the sign of our human capital indicator but does not enable the coefficient to become significant. The public sector indicator is itself negative and significant. Models 4 and 5 include the different levels of education estimated as average years of primary, secondary and tertiary education. In this case, only primary schooling seems to have been beneficial for growth. Both the coefficients on secondary and tertiary education are never significant, with the latter even showing a

Table 11.3 Southwest as convergence club (sample: 1964–97)

Dependent Variable: Average Regional Growth Rates	Model				
	1	2	3	4	5
Beta-convergence: y_{it-2}	−0.027*	−0.027**	−0.042*	−0.048*	−0.052*
	(0.009)	(0.014)	(0.014)	(0.015)	(0.015)
Total stock of human capital		−0.001	0.006		
		(0.004)	(0.005)		
Average years of tertiary studies				−0.086	−0.070
				(0.055)	(0.060)
Average years of secondary studies				0.006	0.010
				(0.008)	(0.008)
Average years of primary studies				0.069*	0.054*
				(0.017)	(0.018)
Proportion of the public sector			−0.021*		−0.010
			(0.005)		(0.007)
Log likelihood	299.4	279.9	282.5	284.0	284.5
Obs	102	96	96	96	96

Notes:
a. Standard errors in brackets. * Significant at 1% level, ** Significant at 5%.
b. y_{it} is the logarithm of per capita GDP in region i in period t.
c. Proportion of the public sector means public sector employment as a proportion of the total employment.
d. Variables are expressed as deviations from the Southwest average.
e. Total stock of human capital means the average years of schooling in the labor force.
f. Average years means the average years of each level of schooling in the labor force.
g. Region excluded: Canaries.

negative sign although considerably smaller and less significant once we control for the share of the public sector. Thus, our estimates indicate high returns to basic education in the poorest areas of the country.

In Table 11.4 we have replicated the same analysis using the Northeast club. In Model 1 the β-convergence coefficient is significant at the 9 percent level, but its value and significance increases when we introduce our human capital indicators. In particular, Models 2 and 3 show that, unlike the poor regions club, the average years of education coefficient is now positive and significant.[28] The public sector coefficient is never significant and the use of this indicator never affects other results. Comparing this result with that obtained for the Southwest club, we are thus induced to interpret our negative coefficient in poor areas as a spurious result. In other words, the estimate of this coefficient may be plagued by reverse causality, since it is

Table 11.4 Northeast as convergence club (sample: 1964–97)

Dependent Variable: Average Regional Growth Rates	Model				
	1	2	3	4	5
Beta-convergence: y_{it-2}	−0.014	−0.086*	−0.085*	−0.079*	−0.077*
	(0.008)	(0.011)	(0.011)	(0.009)	(0.010)
Total stock of human capital		0.022*	0.023*		
		(0.002)	(0.003)		
Average years of tertiary studies				−0.055*	−0.058*
				(0.020)	(0.022)
Average years of secondary studies				0.031*	0.030*
				(0.003)	(0.003)
Average years of primary studies				−0.067	−0.078**
				(0.038)	(0.039)
Proportion of the public sector			−0.001		0.004
			(0.003)		(0.003)
Log likelihood	442.5	425.4	425.4	425.1	425.3
Obs	153	144	144	144	144

Notes:
a. Standard errors in brackets. * Significant at 1% level, ** Significant at 5%.
b. y_{it} is the logarithm of per capita GDP in region i in period t.
c. Proportion of the public sector means public sector employment as a proportion of the total employment.
d. Variables are expressed as deviations from the Northeast average.
e. Total stock of human capital means the average years of schooling in the labor force.
f. Average years means the average years of each level of schooling in the labor force.
g. Region excluded: Balearic Islands.

possible that the expansion of public administration has been one of the policies adopted to reduce the very high unemployment levels in the poorest areas of the country. When we distinguish among the different levels of education (Models 4 and 5) only secondary school seems to affect growth positively, while we may explain the non-significant result on primary education observing that, among developed regions, there is a very low variance in terms of primary school endowments, and this may imply that this coefficient is more difficult to be estimated precisely. Moreover, the coefficient on tertiary education is negative in both clubs.

Remember that this result of the negative sign on tertiary education is not new in this literature, as similar results have been found not only with international datasets but also in the specific literature on Spanish regions.[29] We will briefly summarize some possible explanations of this result. First, we have already seen that university-educated workers have a greater tendency to be employed in the public sector and that this fact may influence our empirical analysis on returns to education. Second, the screening model is considered more relevant in case of higher education analysis. In this case, education does not directly add to productivity. Rather it confers credentials used in the labor market to select able workers: private returns to schooling can be high at the same time as social returns are nugatory.[30] Further, note that Spain has low percentages of students with scientific and technical background and it may be claimed that with the exception of these technical, vocational studies, the experience of university does not necessarily increase productivity in the market place. Finally, even if the use of the initial stocks instead of enrollment rates of education should help to mitigate problems of endogeneity, remember that the opportunity cost of education, especially for tertiary education may act countercyclically.[31]

In Table 11.5 we introduce our alternative human capital indicators and exclude the labor force employed in the public sector. The average years of

Table 11.5 Exclusion of the public sector. Northeast and Southwest as convergence clubs (sample: 1964–97)

Dependent variable: Average Regional Growth Rates	Convergence Club			
	Northeast 1a	Northeast 2a	Southwest 1b	Southwest 2b
Beta-convergence:	−0.072*	−0.07*	−0.030*	−0.046*
y_{it-2}	(0.012)	(0.011)	(0.014)	(0.013)
Total stock of human capital	0.020* (0.003)		−0.0005 (0.004)	
Average years of tertiary studies		−0.131* (0.027)		−0.220* (0.078)
Average years of secondary studies		0.033* (0.003)		0.015** (0.008)
Average years of primary studies		−0.015 (0.032)		0.071* (0.015)
Log likelihood	422.3	424.7	279.8	285.4
Obs	144	144	96	96

Notes:
a. Standard errors in brackets. * Significant at 1% level, ** Significant at 5%.
b. Total stock of human capital means the average years of schooling in the labor force excluding the public sector.
c. Average years means the average years of each level of schooling in the labor force excluding the public sector.

schooling coefficient remains positive and significant only in the Northeast area and primary school is positive and significant only in the Southwest club. The only exception is represented by secondary school in the Southwest club, whose coefficient is positive and significant at the 6 percent level even in poorer regions. Therefore, our results do not indicate that the public sector plays a significant role in the analysis of returns to schooling.

Overall, these results seem to suggest that the level of development of an economy influences the estimation of returns of schooling in growth regressions. In particular, our evidence is consistent with the idea that there exist complementarities between skills and proximity to the frontier. In the so-called Nelson and Phelps approach to growth[32] technological progress represents the engine of growth, where technology is a dual phenomenon including both innovation and imitation activities. The latter activities do not necessarily involve the use of the highly educated. In other words, when a country is far from the frontier, growth may be mainly caused by imitation activities that do not require a highly skilled labor force. Conversely, growth in economies that are close to the frontier is mainly driven by innovation activities that rely more on the most educated. Vandenbussche, Aghion and Meghir (2006) show evidence confirming this hypothesis with a sample of OECD countries, but similar results have also been obtained with other regional samples.[33] On the whole, our results seem to be consistent with this hypothesis since they suggest that skilled human capital has a stronger growth-enhancing effect in more developed regions.

Finally, even if our emphasis is on clubs, we have also replicated the previous analysis using the whole sample and assuming parameter homogeneity. We do not explicitly introduce these results here[34] but, in general, this analysis proves that the results obtained assuming common coefficients across Spanish regions are different from those obtained in our club analysis. In particular, in this case we are not able to identify the different impact that educational levels have on different groups of homogeneous regions. Thus, we claim that failing to take this heterogeneity into account in empirical analysis may produce misleading results.

11.6 CONCLUSION

This study estimates the social returns to education at Spanish regional level. Different from other studies, we allow for some parameter heterogeneity and analyze separately the effect of education in two clubs of poor and rich Spanish regions. We find that the coefficients on human capital variables do not change significantly when we take the public sector into account. Moreover, we find that returns to education are different in the two areas. In particular, human capital computed as average years of education is positive and significant only in the more developed regions club. Further, when we divide human capital into the three different levels of education we find significant differences in the two clubs. Among poor regions, only primary schooling seems to affect growth rates positively: our estimates indicate high returns to basic education in the poorest areas of the country. Conversely, for rich regions we find a positive result only for secondary schooling.

In general, our results on Spanish regions stress the importance of the relationship existing between the level of development of an economy and returns to different levels of education and are supportive of the so-called Nelson and Phelps approach that emphasizes the importance of technological progress for catching up and growth. In particular, the Spanish evidence suggests that, while primary schooling seems to contribute to growth in poorly developed areas, more skilled human capital has a stronger growth-enhancing effect in more developed economies. In other words, our evidence emphasizes that there is likely to be heterogeneity in rates of returns to education across economies since the effect of schooling in growth regressions is influenced by the level of development of an economy. Failing to take this heterogeneity into account in empirical analysis may produce misleading results. Moreover, overall, our results suggest that educational policies should take into account the link between stages of development and growth and coherently expand human capital, taking into account its composition as much as its level.

NOTES

1. Among them we include Dolado, Gonzalez and Roldan (1994); Gorostiaga (1999); Serrano Martínez (1999).
2. See De la Fuente and Vives (1995) and López-Bazo and Moreno (2006). Both studies use a different approach with respect to the standard convergence literature with datasets starting from the 1980s.
3. See Krueger and Lindhal (2001).
4. For example, Azariadis and Drazen (1990) and Benhabib and Spiegel (2004) describe models in which the presence of threshold externalities to education cause the investments in human capital to have different returns depending on the existing level of human capital. In particular, these models introduce the presence of threshold effects on returns to education that depend on human capital endowments. See also Kyriacou (1991).
5. See Psacharopoulos (1994); Pritchett (1996) and Krueger and Lindhal (2001).
6. See Nelson and Phelps (1964) and Aghion and Howitt (1998).
7. See for example Griliches and Regev (1995) for Israel, and Funkhouser (1998) for Costa Rica.
8. For an exhaustive survey of these models see Aghion and Howitt (1998).
9. We are excluding Ceuta y Melilla for which data were not available.

10. Instituto Valenciano de Investigaciones Económicas. See Sala-i-Martin (1996) for OECD economies and Di Liberto (2001) for Italy.
11. See Mas et al. (various years).
12. More precisely, the exact definition is not labor force but active population.
13. We observe that in 1993 (in absolute terms) more than six million people had no school qualifications (no completed studies), but, as expected, more than half of these were people over 64 years of age, and 25.7 percent were in the 55–64 age group.
14. For example, the percentage of the population that completed primary studies in Andalucía in 1993 was only 29 percent. In our dataset, primary studies (which includes both the percentage of people that completed primary studies plus people that only have some schooling) shows a percentage of 50.6 percent in the same region, same year. That is, 20 percent of individuals only have some schooling.
15. Spanish compulsory schooling embraced five years only between 1945 and 1964. Thus, only during this period (not included in our sample) did the definition 'primary schooling' coincide with compulsory schooling. After 1964, compulsory schooling was increased by two years and, again, by a further two years in 1990. See Serrano Martínez (1997).
16. The average years of schooling indicator attracts the same criticism. See Serrano Martínez (1997), Mulligan and Sala-i-Martin (2000) and López-Bazo and Moreno (2007).
17. In this case we prefer to use the sum of lower and higher tertiary education, which approximately corresponds to the OECD tertiary education level. Moreover, these indicators are so similar that we would incur serious problems of multicollinearity during our regression analysis.
18. Following Serrano Martínez (1996), we assume for each level of schooling the following average years of attendance: illiterate, 0 years; primary school and some school, 3.5 years; average schooling, 11 years; lower tertiary, 16 years; tertiary and more (higher tertiary), 17 years.
19. De la Fuente and Vives (1995) find the opposite result but use a different dataset and concentrate their analysis on the 1980s only.
20. As far as we know, there has been just one previous attempt to distinguish different groups of Spanish regions or clubs, Dolado et al. (1994), but they do not perform any regression analysis on clubs.
21. This is obtained by iterating a feasible generalized least squares (FGLS) procedure. ML enjoys no advantage over FGLS procedure in its asymptotic properties; however, it may be preferable in small samples. See Di Liberto and Symons (2003).
22. Note that the use of a two-year time span represents a sensible choice in order to control for problems of short-term disturbances (certainly exacerbated in a single year setting) and the use of a long (in the time dimension) panel.
23. We apply Durbin's (1970) standard alternative test. See Wooldridge (2003).
24. As least squares dummy variable (LSDV) or the Arellano and Bond (1991) estimators.
25. Moreover, these estimators have been recently criticized for the presence of small sample bias. See Kiviet (1995); Judson and Owen (1996) and Bond, Hoeffler and Temple (2001).
26. This variable is defined as the ratio between the numbers of workers employed in the public sector over total employment.
27. In this case the definition is not active but employed population in the various sectors.
28. To report all details, the results of Models 2 and 3 in Table 11.4 on human capital are not robust to the inclusion of the beta-shift, while that obtained in Models 4 and 5 on primary, secondary and tertiary education are robust to the use of different possible specifications.
29. For example, Wolff and Gittelman (1993) find ambiguous evidence on the role of university education as a source of growth. See also Dolado et al. (1994), Di Liberto (2001) and Vandenbussche, Aghion and Meghir (2003) for the case of Spanish regions.
30. See Spence (1974).
31. On these issues, see Wolff and Gittelmann (1993); Bils and Klenow (1995) and Sakellaris and Spilimbergo (1999) among others.
32. See Aghion and Howitt (1998).
33. See Di Liberto (2001) for Italian regions.
34. These results may be found in Di Liberto (2004).

REFERENCES

Aghion, Philippe and Peter Howitt (1998), *Endogenous Growth Theory*, Cambridge: MIT Press.

Arellano, M. and S. Bond (1991), 'Some tests of specification for panel data: Monte Carlo evidence and an application to employment equations', *Review of Economic Studies*, 58, 277–97.

Azariadis, C. and A. Drazen (1990), 'Threshold externalities in economic development', *Quarterly Journal of Economics*, 105, 501–26.

Benhabib, J. and M.M. Spiegel (2004), 'Human capital and technology diffusion', in P. Aghion and S. Durlauf (eds), *Handbook of Economic Growth*, North-Holland/Elsevier.

Bils, M. and P. Klenow (1995), 'Does Human Capital Drive Growth or the Other Way Around?', Mimeo, Department of Economics, Rochester University.

Bond, S., A. Hoeffler and J. Temple (2001), 'GMM Estimation of Empirical Growth Models', Mimeo, Institute for Fiscal Studies, London.

De la Fuente, A. (2001), 'Regional Convergence in Spain: 1965–95', Discussion Paper, EEE 120, Fundacion de Estudios de Economia Aplicada.

De la Fuente, A. (2002), 'On the sources of convergence: a close look at the Spanish regions', *European Economic Review*, 46, 569–99.

De la Fuente, A. and X. Vives (1995), 'Infrastructure and education as instruments of regional policy: evidence from Spain', *Economic Policy*, 20, 13–51.

Di Liberto, A. (2001), 'Stock di capitale umano e crescita delle regioni Italiane: un approccio panel', *Politica Economica*, Il Mulino, 17, 159–84.

Di Liberto, A. (2004), 'Convergence Clubs and the Role of Human Capital in Spanish Regional Growth', *Crenos Working Paper*, No. 18, Università di Cagliari.

Di Liberto, A. and J. Symons (2003), 'Some econometric issues in convergence regressions', *The Manchester School*, 71, 293–307.

Dolado, J.J., J. Gonzalez-Paramo and J.M. Roldan (1994), 'Convergencia economica entre las provincias Espanolas: evidenzia empirica', *Moneda y Credito*, 198, 81–110.

Fundación BBV (various years), *Renta Nacional de España y su Distribución Provincial*, Fundación BBV, Bilbao.

Funkhouser, E. (1998), 'Changes in the returns to education in Costa Rica', *Journal of Development Economics*, 57, 289–317.

Gorostiaga, A. (1999), 'Como afectan el capital publico y el capital humano al crescimiento? Un analisis para las regiones espanolas en el marco neoclasico', *Investigationes Economicas*, 23, 95–114.

Griliches, Z. (1997), 'Education, human capital and growth: a personal perspective', *Journal of Labor Economics*, 15, S330–S344.

Griliches, Z. and H. Regev (1995), 'Firm productivity in Israeli industry 1979–1988', *Journal of Econometrics*, 65, 175–203.

Judson, R. and A. Owen (1996), 'Estimating DPD Models: a Practical Guide for Macroeconomists', Mimeo, Federal Reserve Board of Governors.

Kiviet, J. (1995), 'On bias, inconsistency, and efficiency of various estimators in dynamic panel data models', *Journal of Econometrics*, 68, 53–78.

Krueger, A.B. and M. Lindhal (2001), 'Education for growth: why and for whom?', *Journal of Economic Literature*, 39, 1101–36.

Kyriacou, G.A. (1991), 'Level and Growth Effects of Human Capital: A Cross-country Study of the Convergence Hypothesis', *Economic Research Reports*, No. 91-26, New York University, New York.

López-Bazo E. and R. Moreno (2007), 'Regional heterogeneity in the private and social returns to human capital', *Spatial Economic Analysis* (forthcoming).

Mankiw, N.G., D. Romer and D. Weil (1992), 'A contribution to the empirics of economic growth', *Quarterly Journal of Economics*, 107, 407–37.

Mas, M., F. Pérez, E. Uriel and L. Serrano (various years), *Capital Humano, Series Históricas*, Fundació Bancaixa, Valencia.

Mulligan, C.B. and X. Sala-i-Martin (2000), 'Measuring aggregate human capital', *Journal of Economic Growth*, 5, 215–52.

Nelson, R. and E. Phelps (1966), 'Investments in humans, technological diffusion, and economic growth', *American Economic Review*, 56, 69–75.

Palafox, J., J.G. Mora and F. Perez (1995), *Capital Humano, Educacion y Empleo*, Fundación Bancaja, Valencia.

Pritchett, L. (1996), 'Where Has All the Education Gone?', *World Bank Policy Research Working Paper*, No. 1581, Washington DC.

Psacharopoulos, G. (1994), 'Returns to investments in education: a global update', *World Development*, 22, 1325–43.

Sakellaris, P. and A. Spilimbergo (1999), 'Business Cycles and Investment in Human Capital: International Evidence on Higher Education', SSRN Electronic Library, http://papers.ssrn.com/paper.taf?abstract_id=188048.

Sala-i-Martin, X. (1996), 'The classical approach to convergence analysis', *The Economic Journal*, 106, 1019–36.

Schultz, T.W. (1962), 'Reflection on investment in Man', *Journal of Political Economy*, 70, S1–S8.

Serrano Martínez, L. (1996), 'Indicatores del capital humano y productividad', *Revista de Economia Aplicada*, 11, 177–90.

Serrano Martínez, L. (1997), 'Productividad y capital humano en la economia Espanola', *Moneda y Credito*, 205, 79–101.

Serrano Martínez, L. (1999), 'Capital humano, estrucrura sectorial y crescimiento en la regiones Espanolas', *Investigaciones Economicas*, 23, 225–49.

Spence, M. (1974), *Market Signalling*, Cambridge, MA: Harvard University Press.

Vandenbussche, J., P. Aghion and C. Meghir (2006), 'Growth, distance to frontier and composition of human capital', *Journal of Economic Growth*, 11, 97–127.

Wolff, E.N. and M. Gittleman (1993), 'The role of education in productivity convergence: does higher education matter?', in A. Szirmai, B. Van Ark and D. Pilat (eds), *Explaining Economic Growth*, Elsevier.

Wooldridge, J.M. (2003), *Introductory Econometrics*, Thomson.

12. Non-linearities, spatial dependence and regional economic growth in Europe: a semiparametric approach
Roberto Basile

12.1 INTRODUCTION

Many empirical studies have emphasized the role of spatial effects (that is, spatial dependence and spatial heterogeneity) in regional economic growth (see Magrini, 2004 for a review of the literature on regional convergence). First, per-capita GDP growth rates of an economy seem to depend critically on the growth and initial (and structural) conditions of nearby economies, rather than just on its own initial (and structural) conditions. López-Bazo, Vayá and Artís (2004) have recently demonstrated that spatial technological externalities (or spatial spillovers) between economies can be explicitly modelled within a neoclassical framework in order to take account of the effect of neighbours on growth and convergence processes. These authors have tested the prediction of their model on a sample of 108 NUTS 2 European regions. The empirical results strongly suggest that spillovers are far from negligible.

Second, the assumption that all economies obey a common linear specification of the growth model (spatial homogeneity), disregarding the possibility of nonlinearities and of parameter heterogeneity in growth behaviour, has been strongly criticized. Initially, this issue has been raised in some cross-country growth studies that make use of nonparametric or semiparametric approaches to model the regression function (see, for example, Liu and Stengos, 1999 and Banerjee and Duflo, 2003). According to these studies, the evidence of nonlinearities is coherent with the theoretical prediction of multiple, locally stable, steady-state equilibria as in Azariadis and Drazen (1990). In these studies, however, spatial dependence is rarely taken into account, although even in cross-country growth studies spatial autocorrelation can be very important. Very recently, however, Ertur and Koch (2006), following the same lines of reasoning of

López-Bazo et al. (2004), have proposed a neoclassical growth model with technological externalities and spatial spillovers that yields a conditional convergence equation, which is also characterized by parameter heterogeneity. Using a sample of 89 countries, these authors have estimated a locally linear spatial Durbin model that provides a different convergence speed for each economy in the sample.

In the same vein as Ertur and Koch (2006), in this study, a semiparametric spatial Durbin model is employed to analyse the growth behaviour of European regions in the period 1988–2000. This specification, originally proposed by Gress (2004) and Basile and Gress (2005), combines the semiparametric approach with the usual parametric spatial econometric technique, to accommodate both spatial dependence and nonlinearities. The aim is to test for the presence of spatial externalities on the process of economic growth of European regions, maintaining the functional form as flexible as possible to detect the existence of heterogeneity in convergence speed and growth behaviour. The econometric results provide strong evidence of nonlinearities in the effect of initial per-capita incomes and schooling attainment levels. Specifically, the negative marginal effect of initial conditions increases with the level of initial per-capita income and a threshold effect in secondary school enrolment ratio has been found so that the proxy for human capital investment is only associated with a positive impact on growth if it exceeds the European average rate of schooling. Moreover, the specification used allows identifying the effect of interactions between the characteristics (initial conditions and human capital investment) of each region and those of its neighbours. Thus, also those regions with schooling rates lower than the EU average seem to benefit from externalities generated by accumulation of human capital in nearby regions and, thus, have the opportunity to grow faster than other regions. Finally, the effect of the interaction between the initial per-capita income and the corresponding spatial lag suggests that regions surrounded by richer regions have higher expected growth rates than regions surrounded by poorer regions.

The rest of the chapter is organized as follows. Section 12.2 provides a brief review of the recent literature on conditional β-convergence that has generalized the basic growth regression proposed by Mankiw, Romer and Weil (1992) to take account of parameter heterogeneity (or nonlinearities) and spatial dependence, as well as a combination of them. Section 12.3 reports the results of the econometric analysis of regional convergence based on a dataset of 155 European NUTS 2 regions for the period 1988–2000. Some conclusions are reported in Section 12.4.

12.2 CONDITIONAL CONVERGENCE, NONLINEARITIES AND SPATIAL EXTERNALITIES

The notion of conditional β-convergence arises from the neoclassical growth model based on the assumptions of a convex production function with constant returns to scale, a closed economic system and labour market clearing. The basic idea is that the long-run economic growth can be described by a steady-state balanced path. In the short run, economies that have not yet reached their steady state show higher growth rates than economies closer to the steady state. If steady states are similar between economies, convergence is unconditional; when the steady states differ, convergence becomes conditional upon a set of structural variables.[1] Since the famous contribution of Mankiw et al. (1992; MRW thereafter), the conditional β-convergence hypothesis is tested by estimating the following model:

$$\gamma_y = \beta \ln y_0 + \psi X + \pi Z + \varepsilon \qquad (12.1)$$

where $\gamma_y = T^{-1}(\ln y_T - \ln y_0)$ is the per-capita GDP growth rate between periods 0 and T, $\ln y_0$ is the initial per-capita GDP, X is a vector of structural variables that includes physical and human capital accumulation rates, population growth rate and a constant term, Z is a vector of additional control variables not directly derived from MRW, but allowing for predictable heterogeneity in the steady-state growth path and/or initial technology and ε is a vector of normally identically and independently distributed errors. The unknown parameters β, ψ and π are generally assumed to be constant across regions and are estimated by OLS, GLS (to account for heteroskedasticity problems), IV and GMM (to accommodate problems of endogeneity and measurement errors). Conditional convergence is said to be favoured by the data if the estimated coefficient on the initial per-capita GDP, $\beta = -T^{-1}(1-e^{-\lambda t})$ (with λ measuring the rate of convergence), is negative and statistically significant.

Equation (12.1) represents the baseline for much of growth econometrics. Recently, this regression has been generalized in a number of dimensions (see Durlauf, Johnson and Temple, 2005). First, the assumption of a common linear model for a set of very different economies (and, thus, of parameter constancy across units of observation) has appeared as particularly unappealing. This concern has been addressed by estimating more general models that allow for multiple regimes, parameter heterogeneity and nonlinearities. The hypothesis of multiple regimes has been tested in different ways.[2] Some authors have simply included interactions between variables in the right-hand side of equation (12.1) and dummy variables that indicate the membership of a region to a specific – arbitrarily identified – sub-sample, so that the marginal effect of a given explanatory variable can differ across sub-samples (see, for example, Le Gallo, Ertur and Baumont, 2003). Some other authors have used statistical methods (such as classification and regression trees) to identify properly the presence of 'convergence clubs', that is sub-groups of economies that obey a common linear growth model (see Durlauf et al., 2005, for a review). All these studies, therefore, assume a common data-generating process for all economies within each sub-sample.[3] More flexible methods have been proposed to allow for complete parameter heterogeneity and nonlinearities. Thus, a group of studies have produced evidence of parameter heterogeneity by imposing a functional relationship between parameters and initial conditions (see, for example, Durlauf, Kourtellos and Minkin, 2001). Finally, some authors have used semiparametric methods that properly allow identifying nonlinearities in the growth model without the imposition of a functional relationship between parameters and various observable variables (see, for example, Liu and Stengos, 1999; Banerjee and Duflo, 2003). An important limitation of this last group of studies is that, usually, they only allow for nonlinearity for a subset of growth determinants (Durlauf et al., 2005). Moreover, rarely do they look for interactions between explanatory variables. However, such limitations can be easily overcome by using modern semiparametric techniques.

Second, a broad strand of literature has criticized the closed-economy assumption of the Solow–MRW neoclassical growth model, especially when regional convergence has been the object of the analysis (Magrini, 2004).[4] The closed economy model leaves out aspects of interdependence that are surely important. As suggested by Durlauf et al. (2005), empirical growth frameworks must acknowledge that economies interact among each other through factor mobility (capital and labour migration), trade relations, technological diffusion and knowledge spillovers. It must be recognized, in particular, that there is a strong technological interdependence among countries and regions and that this interdependence affects the levels and the rate of productivity growth of all economies. However, it is also very important to acknowledge that the spatial diffusion of technological knowledge may be geographically bounded, which means that productivity effects of R&D decline with the geographic distance between economies (the so-called 'spatial friction').

Recently, López-Bazo et al. (2004) and Ertur and Koch (2006) have proposed modified versions of the neoclassical MRW growth model that include spatial externalities between economies in order to take account of the neighbourhood effects (that is, 'spatial diffusion with frictions') on growth and convergence processes. López-Bazo et al. (2004) consider an economy composed by N regions denoted by $i = 1, \ldots, N$. Each region produces a homogeneous good (Y_{it}). Following MRW, the aggregate Cobb-Douglas production function for region i at time t exhibits constant returns to scale in labour (L_{it}) and reproducible physical (K_{it}) and human capital (H_{it}):

$$Y_{it} = A_{it} K_{it}^{\tau_k} H_{it}^{\tau_h} L_{it}^{1-\tau_k-\tau_h} \qquad (12.2)$$

The two parameters (τ_k and τ_h) denote internal returns to physical and human capital, respectively. The aggregate level of technology in region i at time t, A_{it}, is assumed to depend on the technological level of the neighbours, which in turn is related to their stock of both types of capital per unit of labour:

$$A_{it} = \Omega_t (\breve{k}_{it}^{\tau_k} \breve{h}_{it}^{\tau_h})^\rho \qquad (12.3)$$

where $\Omega(t)$ is exogenous technological progress, identical for all regions, $\breve{k}_{it}$ and $\breve{h}_{it}$ denote the physical and human-capital–labour ratios in the neighbouring regions, and ρ measures the (positive) externalities across economies. Thus, differently from MRW, who adopt the closed-economy assumption, López-Bazo et al. (2004) explicitly assume that technological knowledge spreads across economies so that a region benefits from investments made by its neighbours.

As in MRW, the population growth rate (n), the technological growth rate (g), the depreciation rate (δ) and the rates of accumulation of physical (s_k) and human capital (s_h) are assumed to be exogenous. The sum ($n + g + \delta$) represents the effective rate of depreciation, assumed equal across types of capital and economies. Under the assumption of decreasing returns to capital within each economy, the following empirical growth equation is derived:

$$\gamma_y = \beta \ln y_0 + \chi W \ln y_0 + \psi X + \rho W \gamma_y + \varepsilon \qquad (12.4)$$

where $X = [const \ln s_k \ln s_h \ln(n+g+\delta)]$. As in MRW, the model predicts convergence, $\beta < 0$, a positive relation between growth and reproducible factors accumulation rates, $\ln s_k$ and $\ln s_h$, and a negative relation between growth and the effective rate of depreciation, $\ln(n+g+\delta)$. Compared with equation (12.1), model (12.4) includes two spatially lagged terms, $W \ln y_0$ and $W \gamma_y$, computed by multiplying the vectors of initial per-capita incomes and of growth rates by a $N \times N$ standardized spatial weight matrix, W. The characteristic element of this matrix, $w_{ij} \leq 0$, summarizes the interaction between regions i and j.

The reduced form of this model can be easily derived:

$$\gamma_y = (I-\rho W)^{-1}\ln y_0\beta + (I-\rho W)^{-1}W\ln y_0\chi$$
$$+ (I-\rho W)^{-1}X\psi + (I-\rho W)^{-1}\varepsilon \qquad (12.5)$$

This expression clearly suggests that the growth rate in a region i is affected negatively by the initial income of that region and positively by those in all other locations through the inverse spatial transformation $(I-\rho W)^{-1}$, the so-called 'spatial multiplier effect' (Anselin, 2004). Thus, every location is correlated with every other location in the system. However, given the characteristics of the standardized spatial weight matrix, the strength of spatial dependence between observed regions declines with the distance between them. In other words, neighbouring units exhibit a higher degree of spatial dependence than units located far apart. This is in line with the notion of 'spatial diffusion with friction' described above. Thus, for any two regions with the same preferences and technological conditions and starting from similar initial levels, growth rates will be higher for those economies that have neighbours with large initial per-capita GDP. Equation (12.5) also suggests that there are spatial externalities in un-modelled effects: a random shock (or disturbance) in a specific location i does not only affect the outcome in that region, but also has an impact on the outcome in all other locations through $(I-\rho W)^{-1}$ ('spatial diffusion process of random shocks').

Following the same lines of reasoning, Ertur and Koch (2006) propose a growth model with physical and human capital externalities and technological interdependence, which leads to a spatial autoregressive reduced form of the convergence equation different from that proposed by López-Bazo et al. (2004). Even though they start from a production function specified as in equation (12.2), they suggest a different specification for the technology function A_{it}:

$$A_{it} = \Omega_t\, k_{it}^{\phi_k} h_{it}^{\phi_h} \prod_{j\neq i}^{N} A_{jt}^{\rho w_{ij}} \qquad (12.6)$$

According to equation (12.6), technological knowledge in region i at time t is in part exogenous Ω_t, in part it depends on the level of accumulated factors k_{it} and h_{it} (with parameters ϕ_k and ϕ_h reflecting the strength of physical and human capital externalities among firms within the region) and, in part, it depends positively on the technology accumulated in all other regions, $\prod_{j\neq i}^{N} A_{jt}^{\rho w_{ij}}$. Again the parameter ρ reflects the degree of spatial externalities.

This model predicts conditional convergence, but the speed of convergence is specific to each economy, since it is a function of the spatial weights w_{ij} reflecting the links between regions. Moreover, the speed of convergence of a region i is a function of the speed of convergence of its neighbours. In particular, when the neighbours of region i are close to their own steady states, the convergence speed of region i is high. Thus, the conditional convergence equation is characterized by parameter heterogeneity:

$$\gamma_y = D \ln y_0 \beta + DW \ln y_0 \chi + DX\psi + DWX\theta + \rho D\Gamma W\gamma_y + \varepsilon \quad (12.7)$$

where $X = [const \ \ln s_k \ \ln s_h \ \ln(n+g+\delta)]$, D is a diagonal matrix reflecting the specific effects of the convergence speed in each region, Γ is a diagonal matrix containing scale heterogeneous parameters reflecting the effects of the speeds of convergence in the neighbouring economies. The growth rate is a negative function of the initial level of per-capita income and a positive function of the initial conditions of its neighbours. It is also a positive function of reproducible factors accumulation rates observed within the region and in its neighbours ($\ln s_k$, $W \ln s_k$) and ($\ln s_h$, $W \ln s_h$), and a negative function of the effective rate of depreciation within the region and in the neighbours [$\ln (n+g+\delta)$, $W \ln (n+g+\delta)$]. The last term in equation (12.7) represents the rate of growth in the neighbouring regions.

Ertur and Koch (2006) refer to equation (12.7) as the local spatial Durbin model (SDM) with heterogeneous parameters, as opposed to the global SDM with homogeneous parameters obtained if all speeds of convergence are identical across regions:

$$\gamma_y = \beta \ln y_0 + \chi W \ln y_0 + \psi X + \theta WX + \rho W\gamma_y + \varepsilon \quad (12.8)$$

The reduced form of equation (12.8) can be easily derived:

$$\gamma_y = (I - \rho W)^{-1} \ln y_0 \beta + (I - \rho W)^{-1} W \ln y_0 \chi$$
$$+ (I - \rho W)^{-1} X\psi + (I - \rho W)^{-1} WX\theta + (I - \rho W)^{-1} \varepsilon \quad (12.9)$$

Thus, the outcome in a location i is influenced not only by the exogenous characteristics of i, but also by those in all other locations through the inverse spatial transformation $(I - \rho W)^{-1}$. A spatial diffusion process of random shocks appears also in this case.

In sum, the local SDM (equation 12.7) proposed by Ertur and Koch (2006) is a general and flexible specification, since it allows us to identify both spatial-interaction effects and parameter heterogeneity (and, thus, nonlinearities). The global SDM (equation 12.8) represents a less general specification, because it imposes the restriction of parameter homogeneity in the cross-section growth regression. The model proposed by Lòpez-Bazo et al. (2004) (equation 12.4) imposes a further restriction on the parameters since the spatial lags of the structural characteristics of the regions are not included. Finally, the linear model without spatial dependence represents the most restricted model. A critical point of all these approaches is that they model growth rates by using a sum of univariate terms, while there are strong arguments for modelling $\ln y_0$ and $W \ln y_0$ as well as X and WX as interaction terms (see Section 12.3.3, below).

12.3 NONLINEARITIES AND SPATIAL DEPENDENCE IN GROWTH BEHAVIOUR OF EUROPEAN REGIONS

In this section, a semiparametric SDM is used to analyse the growth behaviour of European regions in the period 1988–2000. As in Ertur and Koch (2006), spatial autocorrelation is included in the form of spatial lags of exogenous and endogenous variables. Nonlinearities, however, are identified by using semiparametric techniques, rather than by imposing a functional relationship between parameters and spatial weights w_{ij}.

12.3.1 Data and Variables

The empirical analysis is based on the dataset compiled by Cambridge Econometrics on total value-added (computed at 1995 prices and converted in the PPP of the same year), population, employment and physical capital investments and on data collected by Eurostat on levels of education attainment for the European NUTS 2 regions. The dataset consists of 155 regions.[5]

The dependent variable is the growth rate of the per-capita GDP of the region (γ_y), while the predictors are:

1. $\ln y_0$, initial per-capita GDP;
2. $\ln s_k$, average share of gross investment in value-added;
3. $\ln s_h$, average percentage of working-age population in secondary school (data available only for the period 1993–97);
4. $\ln (n + g + \delta)$, effective rate of depreciation with n the average growth rate of the population and, as in previous studies $(g + \delta)$ equal to 0.05; and
5. $\ln (agr)$, percentage of workers employed in agriculture.

All of the variables are scaled to the total sample average. The model is estimated for the period 1988–2000, which covers the first two programming periods of EU Structural Funds. Variables 1–4 are those included in the MRW specification of the growth regression (vector X in equation 12.1), while ln (agr) is included to control for the effect of the regional economic structure (vector Z in equation 12.1).[6] Finally, the spatial weights matrix chosen is a 15-nearest-neighbours weight matrix.

12.3.2 Results for the Linear Parametric Models

Before assessing the prediction for conditional convergence of the semi-parametric SDM, this section focuses on the results of parametric linear models with and without spatial dependence. The first column of Table 12.1 shows the OLS results of the estimation of the MRW equation (12.1) augmented with ln (agr). All the coefficients are significant and with the expected sign, except for the effective rate of depreciation, ln $(n+g+\delta)$, which turns to be positive. The coefficient on the initial level of income is negative and significant, corroborating the hypothesis of conditional convergence. The implied speed of convergence (1 per cent) is below the traditional figure of 2 per cent. The results also show that both human and physical capital accumulation rates have a positive and significant effect on growth.

There are no signs of heteroskedasticity, as the result of the Studentized Breusch-Pagan test reveals, while spatial autocorrelation in the residuals is clearly detected, as deduced from the results of the Lagrange multiplier (LM) tests. Thus, the traditional MRW model is mis-specified in the case of our sample and spatial dependence must be taken into account. In particular, the value of the LM-error is larger than that of LM-lag. Moreover, the robust LM-error test rejects its null, while the robust LM-lag test does not. In this case, the spatial error model (SEM) should be the preferred specification (Anselin and Rey, 1991). The SEM is specified as:

$$\gamma_y = \beta \ln y_0 + \psi X + \varepsilon \qquad (12.10)$$

$$\varepsilon = \varphi W \varepsilon + v \qquad v \sim \text{NID}(0, \sigma_v^2 I)$$

Its reduced form is:

$$\gamma_y = \beta \ln y_0 + \psi X + \theta W X + (I - \rho W)^{-1} v \qquad (12.11)$$

From equation (12.11), it appears clear that the choice of the error growth model based on the prevalence of the LM-error test might lead to the conclusion that only random shocks diffuse across economies, while there are no substantive spatial externalities. However, the reduced form of the SEM can also be written as:

Table 12.1 Regression results

	MRW	SDM	SDM
$\ln y_0$	−0.934	−1.167	
	(0.000)	(0.000)	see Fig. 12.1
$W \ln y_0$		1.029	
		(0.016)	
$\ln s_h$	0.588	−0.337	
	(0.032)	(0.253)	see Fig. 12.2
$W \ln s_h$		1.795	
		(0.002)	
$\ln s_k$	1.588	1.198	1.696
	(0.000)	(0.009)	(0.000)
$W \ln s_k$		0.134	−0.104
		(0.834)	(0.880)
$\ln(n+0.05)$	0.426	0.101	0.162
	(0.004)	(0.441)	(0.217)
$W \ln(n+0.05)$		1.286	1.656
		(0.000)	(0.000)
$\ln(agr)$	−0.230	−0.280	−0.245
	(0.000)	(0.000)	(0.000)
$W \ln(agr)$		0.216	0.178
		(0.100)	(0.199)
Const	−0.235	−0.716	−1.314
	(0.078)	(0.019)	(0.000)
$W\gamma_y$		0.479	0.297
		(0.000)	(0.000)
Implied speed of convergence	0.010	0.012	
Log-likelihood	−136.680	−113.491	
Akaike information criterion	287.360	252.98	
Studentized Breusch-Pagan test	3.167	19.235	
	(0.674)	(0.037)	
LM-error	37.124		
	(0.000)		
LM-lag	32.196		
	(0.000)		
R-LM-error	5.918		
	(0.015)		
R-LM-lag	0.989		
	(0.320)		
Common factor test (SDM vs. SEM)		21.349	
		(0.000)	
LM test for residual autocorrelation		0.203	
		(0.652)	

$$\gamma_y = \beta \ln y_0 - \varphi \beta W \ln y_0 + \psi X - \varphi \psi W X + \rho W \gamma_y + v \quad (12.12)$$

This model represents a constrained version of equation (12.8), whose reduced form (equation 12.9) implies the existence of substantive spatial externalities. This restriction can be assessed through the so-called 'common factor' test (at the bottom of column 2 in Table 12.1). In the case of the sample used here, the result of this test clearly suggests that the null hypothesis of restriction can be rejected at 1 per cent level of probability and, thus, the unconstrained SDM is an appropriate specification (equation 12.8).

Therefore, the second column of Table 12.1 reports the results of the SDM estimations. The LM test for residual spatial autocorrelation does not reject the null hypothesis of absence of dependence. However, the null hypothesis of absence of heteroskedasticity is rejected at 5 per cent, according to the result of the spatial version of the Studentized Breusch-Pagan test.

The spatial autocorrelation coefficient ρ is 0.48 and statistically significant, confirming the presence of strong spatial externalities among regions in Europe. A direct comparison with the results reported in López-Bazo et al. (2004) may be misleading, since both the sample of regions (EU12 regions vs. EU15 regions) and the time period (1980–96 vs. 1988–2000) are different. These caveats notwithstanding, it is worthwhile mentioning that the estimated magnitude of spatial externalities in the López-Bazo et al. (2004) is much higher (between 0.6 and 0.9). Such a difference might partially depend on the specification of the model. López-Bazo et al. (2004), in fact, do not control for the effect of physical and human capital accumulation rates, because of the lack of data for the period under analysis. Omission of relevant variables can indeed strongly influence the magnitude of the coefficient of spatial externalities.

The coefficient of the initial per-capita income is -1.167 confirming the existence of conditional convergence. The implied rate of convergence (1.2 per cent per year) is much lower than the 3 per cent estimated by López-Bazo et al. (2004) for the case of EU12 regions. As predicted by the neoclassical growth models with spatial externalities reviewed in Section 12.2, the growth rate in a region is also positively affected by the initial income of the neighbours.

The coefficient on the population growth rate is not significant, while the parameter on its spatial lag is positive and significant. The effect of the share of agriculture on employment is negative and its spatial externalities are positive and weakly significant. Finally, the expected growth rate is a positive function of the accumulation rate of physical capital in that region and of the human capital in the neighbours. This means that growth is higher in those economies surrounded by areas with high rates of human capital accumulation, because externalities across those economies will increase the returns of these investments.

In conclusion, the results of the parametric linear SDM give only partial evidence in favour of equation (12.8) and against equation (12.4), since not all the parameters turn out to be significant, although five out of six spatial lag parameters are significant, confirming the existence of spatial externalities. However, one should also be conscious that the non-significance of a parameter (such as, for example, the non-significance of coefficient on $\ln s_h$) might mask the existence of nonlinearities, which should be identified. Moreover, the effect of each variable and its correspondent spatial lag does not necessarily have to be an additive one. Rather, a multiplicative effect can be expected. These issues are fully clarified in the following section where a semiparametric SDM with interaction terms is proposed.

12.3.3 Results for the Semiparametric Model

This section reports the results of a semiparametric spatial Durbin model (SP-SDM). The methodology for the estimation of this model is described in the Appendix 12.1 at the end of the chapter. As mentioned above, in the context of the present analysis interest must focus also on testing for terms of interaction between initial conditions (as well as structural characteristics) within the region and in the neighbours. Thus, the starting point was to estimate a general specification where all bivariate (interaction) terms entered the model as smoothed nonparametric terms. Only the spatial lag of the dependent variable entered the model linearly. Then, the results of likelihood ratio tests suggested to allow only $s\,(\ln y_0, W \ln y_0)$ and $s\,(\ln s_h, W \ln s_h)$ to make up the nonlinear components of the model and to leave all other terms entering the model linearly. Therefore, the final specification is a mixture of parametric linear terms and bivariate thin plate regression splines:

$$\gamma_y = s\,(\ln y_0, W \ln y_0) + s\,(\ln s_h, W \ln s_h)$$
$$+ \ln s_k + W \ln s_k + \ln(n + g + \delta) + W \ln(n + g + \delta)$$
$$+ \ln(agr) + W \ln(agr) + \rho W \gamma_y + \varepsilon \qquad (12.13)$$

Figures 12.1 and 12.2 show the estimated smooth functions. The vertical axis reports the scale of per-capita growth rates; the axes on the plane report the scale of each independent variable and of its correspondent spatial lag.

Figure 12.1 shows the estimated effect of the interaction between initial conditions and the correspondent spatial lag on the growth of per-capita

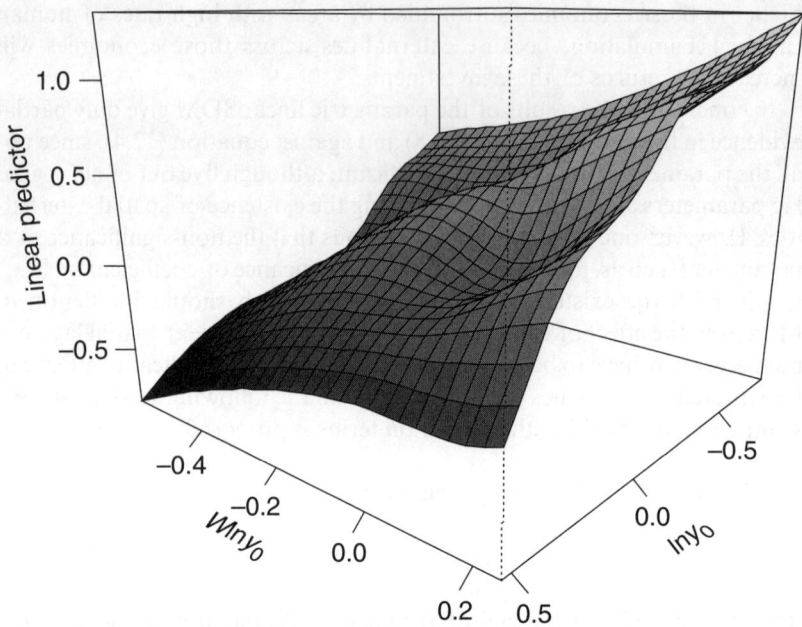

Figure 12.1 SP-SDM. GDP growth versus the interaction between ln y_0 and $W \ln y_0$

income. It clearly suggests that regions surrounded by richer regions have higher expected growth rates than regions surrounded by poorer regions. Thus, while very poor regions have generally higher expected growth rates, as it is usual, those with rich neighbours have the highest rates of growth. Moreover, even very rich regions (which are closer to their steady state and, thus, have lower margins for catching up) have chance to grow faster when other rich regions surround them.

As expected, the effect of the interaction between initial conditions with the region and initial conditions in the neighbours is also characterized by strong nonlinearities. It is particularly interesting to analyse the marginal effect of ln y_0. As already observed, when a region is initially very poor, its growth rate is expected to be high; for higher initial levels, the expected growth rates decreases, but the speed of convergence increases (the curve becomes steeper). One can identify at least three groups of regions with different speeds of convergence (see Appendix 12.2 at the end of the chapter).

Figure 12.2 shows the effect of the interaction between ln s_h and $W \ln s_h$. First, some nonlinearities in the effect of secondary school enrolment ratio

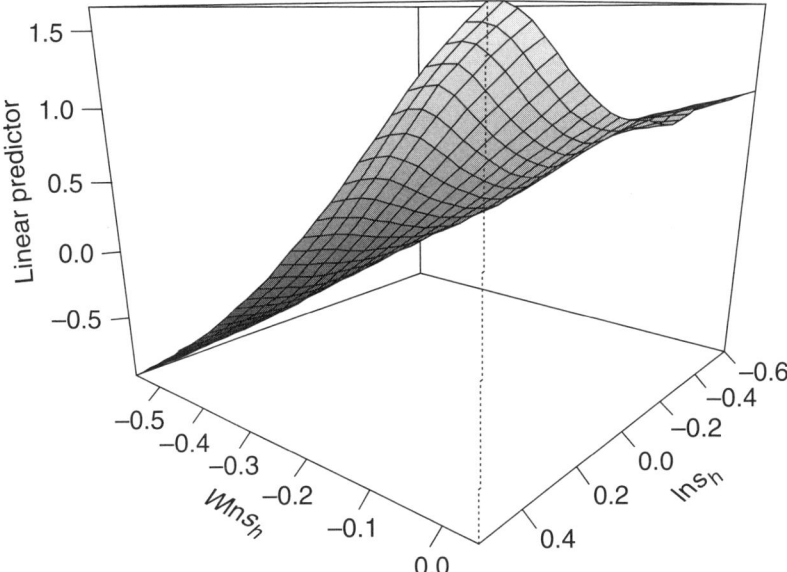

Figure 12.2 SP-SDM. GDP growth versus the interaction between $\ln s_h$ and $W \ln s_h$

are clearly detected: an increase in the rate of schooling is associated with an increase in growth rate only when $\ln s_h$ is above the EU average. The existence of a threshold in the effect of $\ln s_h$ was also found by Liu and Stengos (1999) for the case of OECD countries. However, as clearly shown in Figure 12.2, the growth rate of a region is also a positive function of the schooling rate in the neighbours. Thus, even those regions with schooling rates lower than the EU average benefit from externalities generated by accumulation of human capital in nearby regions and, thus, have a chance to grow faster than other regions.

The evidence for the linear terms included in the semiparametric model confirms the results obtained for the parametric SDM. The coefficient of spatial externalities still appears positive and statistically significant, but its value (0.297) is lower than that found in the case of the parametric SDM, suggesting that spatial dependence can partly absorb nonlinearities. This result is in line with Basile and Gress (2005) who show the existence of a trade-off between the smoothness of the estimated function and the estimation of the spatial parameter: as the estimated function is forced to be smoother (with a larger bandwidth parameter) the estimated spatial parameter becomes larger as it 'absorbs' the nonlinearity of the true function.

Thus, the estimates of the spatial parameters in the semiparametric model can be considered more reliable than its parametric counterpart.

12.4 CONCLUSIONS

In the most recent literature on convergence, two main extensions of the 'standard' MRW growth regression have been proposed (among others): the first one allows for parameter heterogeneity, nonlinearities and multiple regimes and is often based on nonparametric and semiparametric techniques (Durlauf et al., 2005); the second one addresses the issues of technological externalities and spatial dependence (López-Bazo et al., 2004). More recently, Ertur and Koch (2006) have used a local linear spatial autoregressive model to accommodate both spatial dependence and parameter heterogeneity.

In the same vein, here a semiparametric spatial Durbin model is employed to analyse the growth behaviour of European regions in the period 1988–2000. This specification combines the semiparametric approach with the usual parametric spatial econometric technique. By using Monte Carlo simulations, Gress (2004) has already shown that the semiparametric spatial autocovariance estimator has better statistical properties than its parametric counterparts.

The results provide strong evidence of nonlinearities in the effect of initial per-capita incomes and of schooling levels in line with Liu and Stengos (1999). In particular, European regional data reveal that the negative marginal effect of initial conditions increases with the level of initial per-capita income and it is possible to identify at least three groups of regions with different speeds of convergence. A threshold in the effect of secondary school enrolment ratio is also clearly detected: an increase in the rate of schooling is associated with an increase in the growth rate only when the level of schooling investment is above the EU average. These results confirm that assuming a common linear model for a set of very different economies is misleading: nonlinearities are important in regional growth in Europe even when spatial dependence is taken into account.

Moreover, different from the approaches used by López-Bazo et al. (2004) and Ertur and Koch (2006), the specification employed here allows also identifying the effect of the interactions between the characteristics of each region and those of its neighbours. Thus, for example, it emerges that even those regions with schooling levels lower that the EU average benefit from externalities generated by accumulation of human capital in nearby regions. Furthermore, European data suggest that very poor regions with very rich neighbours have the highest rates of growth and that even very rich regions (which are close to their steady state) have the possibility to grow, when other very rich regions surround them. This evidence is in line with the argument that spillovers from nearby regions can compensate the mechanisms of decreasing returns to scale to capital accumulation and allow rich economies to grow (López-Bazo et al., 2004).

Further research is oriented towards the development of semiparametric spatial autocorrelation models for panel data. In fact, the limited number of regions available can limit the robustness of semiparametric estimators. By working with a number of time series observations in a panel of N regions, the precision of the estimations increases significantly. Moreover, panel data allow the estimation of region- and time-specific effects and, thus, to control for unobserved heterogeneity in growth behaviour.

NOTES

1. The hypothesis of conditional convergence is often understood to mean that regions converge to parallel growth paths, the levels of which are a function of a set of variables. Regions that start out below their balanced growth path must grow relatively quickly if they are to catch up with other regions that have the same levels of steady-state per-capita income and initial efficiency. The concept of conditional convergence is therefore consistent with persistent interregional income inequalities.
2. The concept of multiple regimes (or 'convergence clubs') is often based on endogenous growth models characterized by the possibility of multiple, locally stable, steady-state equilibria as in Azariadis and Drazen (1990). In this model, there is a discontinuity in the aggregate production function for aggregate economies. This discontinuity means that the steady-state behaviour of a given economy depends on whether its initial capital stock is above or below a certain threshold. As in the case of conditional convergence, the rejection of absolute convergence in favour of multiple regimes implies the existence of permanent cross-region differences in per-capita income levels although for very different reasons. In the case of conditional convergence the differences reflect cross-region heterogeneity in variables such as rates of capital accumulation and the appropriate econometric response is the introduction of 'control variables' into the growth regression. In the case of multiple regimes, the differences reflect regions lying in different basins of attraction defined by initial conditions and the appropriate econometric response is dividing the regions into groups using variables measuring initial conditions referred to as 'split variables'.
3. Very recently, however, Canova (2004) has proposed a method to identify multiple regimes that also allows for parameter heterogeneity across regions within a given sub-group.
4. Other extensions of equation (12.1) reflect its application to time series and panel data settings. Further problems with the canonical regression equation (12.1) are robustness with respect of choice of control variables (model uncertainty), endogeneity and measurement errors (Durlauf et al., 2005).
5. For various reasons, some regions have been excluded from the dataset. Specifically, for the region of Bruxelles extremely low levels of agricultural employment have been observed. Other regions, namely Berlin, Luxembourg, Ireland, Sterea Ellada and Flevoland turned out to be outliers in growth behaviour.
6. The choice concerning which Z variables to include varies greatly in the literature. The range of potential factors is indeed very large. This raises the problem of model uncertainty that should be properly taken into account using Bayesian approaches to data

analysis. This issue goes beyond the scope of the present study. However, in the case of European regions, many studies have already demonstrated that the share of employment in agriculture represents a good proxy for predicting differences in technological efficiency (see, for example, Paci and Pigliaru, 1999).

REFERENCES

Anselin, L. (1988), *Spatial Econometrics*, Dordrecht: Kluwer Academic Publishers.
Anselin, L. (2004), 'Spatial externalities, spatial multipliers and spatial econometrics', *International Regional Science Review*, 26, 153–66.
Anselin, L. and S. Rey (1991), 'Properties of tests for spatial dependence in linear regression models', *Geographical Analysis*, 23, 112–31.
Azariadis, C. and A. Drazen (1990), 'Threshold externalities in economic development', *Quarterly Journal of Economics*, **105**(2), 501–26.
Banerjee, A. and E. Duflo (2003), 'Inequality and growth: what can the data say?', *Journal of Economic Growth*, **8**(3), 267–300.
Basile, R. and B. Gress (2005), 'Semi-parametric spatial auto-covariance models of regional growth in Europe', *Région et Développement*, 21, 93–118.
Canova, F. (2004), 'Testing for convergence clubs in income per capita: a predictive density approach', *International Economic Review*, **45**(1), 49–77.
Durlauf, S.N., P.A. Johnson and J.R.W. Temple (2005), 'Growth econometrics', in P. Aghion and S.N. Durlauf (ed.), *Handbook of Economic Growth*, Volume 1A, Amsterdam: North-Holland, pp. 555–677.
Durlauf, S., A. Kourtellos and A. Minkin (2001), 'The local Solow growth model', *European Economic Review*, **45**(4–6), 928–40.
Ertur, C. and W. Koch (2006), 'Convergence, Human Capital and International Spillovers', mimeo, Université de Bourgogne.
Gress, B. (2004), 'Semiparametric Spatial Autocovariance Models', University of California at Riverside, PhD Dissertation.
Le Gallo, J., C. Ertur and C. Baumont (2003), 'A spatial econometric analysis of convergence across European regions, 1980–1995', in B. Fingleton (ed.), *European Regional Growth*, Berlin: Springer-Verlag.
Liu, Z. and T. Stengos (1999), 'Non-linearities in cross-country growth regressions: a semiparametric approach', *Journal of Applied Econometrics*, 14, 527–38.
López-Bazo, E., E. Vayá and M. Artís (2004), 'Regional externalities and growth: evidence from European regions', *Journal of Regional Science*, **44**(1), 43–73.
Magrini, S. (2004), 'Regional (di) convergence', in V. Henderson and J.F. Thisse (eds), *Handbook of Regional and Urban Economics*, 4, 2741–96.
Mankiw, N.G., D. Romer and D.N. Weil (1992), 'A contribution to the empirics of economic growth', *Quarterly Journal of Economics*, May, 407–37.
Paci, R. and F. Pigliaru (1999), 'European regional growth: do sectors matter?', in J. Adams and F. Pigliaru (eds), *Economic Growth and Change. National and Regional Patterns of Convergence and Divergence*, Cheltenham, UK and Northampton, MA, USA: Edward Elgar.
Wood, S.N. (2006), *Generalized Additive Models. An Introduction with R*, Boca Raton: Chapman & Hall/CRC.

APPENDIX 12.1 MAXIMUM LIKELIHOOD ESTIMATION OF SDM AND SP-SDM

This appendix is dedicated to the explanation of the estimation procedure for the semiparametric spatial Durbin model (SP-SDM). The original methodology was proposed by Gress (2004) and Basile and Gress (2005) and labelled SP-SAR.[1] Here, this specification is implemented and called SP-SDM. As is well known the parametric SDM is specified as:

$$y = \rho W y + X\phi + \lambda W X + \varepsilon \qquad \varepsilon \sim N(0, \sigma^2 I) \qquad (12.1A)$$

Denoting $\tilde{X} = [X \; WX]$, equation (12.1A) can be written as:

$$y = \rho W y + \tilde{X}\theta + \varepsilon \qquad (12.2A)$$

There are no closed-form solutions for ρ in terms of the observations and all estimates of parameters must be obtained by numerical maximization of the log-likelihood function. Anselin (1988) derives the (concentrated) log-likelihood function in (12.2A):

$$\ell(y|\rho) = -\frac{N}{2} ln[2\pi + 1] - \frac{N}{2} ln\left[\frac{(\hat{e}_0 - \rho \hat{e}_L)'(\hat{e}_0 - \rho \hat{e}_L)}{N}\right] + ln|I - \rho W| \qquad (12.3A)$$

where e_0 and e_L are the residuals from the OLS regressions of y on $\tilde{X}$ and of W_y on $\tilde{X}$, respectively. Maximizing (12.3A) is equivalent to minimizing:

$$\min_{\{\rho\}} \left\{ \frac{e_0' e_0 - 2\rho e_0' e_L + \rho^2 e_L' e_L}{\sum_i ln(1 - \rho \omega_i)} \right\} \qquad (12.4A)$$

This time-saving simplification utilizes the eigenvalues of the weights matrix, $\omega_i = Eigenvalues[W]$. The estimator $\hat{\rho}$ is then substituted into the solution for θ to yield $\hat{\theta}$:

$$\begin{aligned}
\hat{\theta}_{ML} &= (\tilde{X}'\tilde{X})^{-1}\tilde{X}'(I - \hat{\rho}W)y \\
&= (\tilde{X}'\tilde{X})^{-1}\tilde{X}'y - \hat{\rho}(\tilde{X}'\tilde{X})^{-1}\tilde{X}'Wy \qquad (12.5A) \\
&= b - \hat{\rho} b_L
\end{aligned}$$

where

$$b = (\tilde{X}'\tilde{X})^{-1}\tilde{X}'y \text{ and } b_L = (\tilde{X}'\tilde{X})^{-1}\tilde{X}'y_L.$$

The SP-SDM extends the SMD to allow for flexible functional forms in the exogenous variables. An unknown functional form, $s(\tilde{X})$, replaces the linear form $\tilde{X}\theta$ of the parametric SDM:

$$y = \rho W y + s(\tilde{X}) + \varepsilon \quad (12.6A)$$

Estimators for $s(\tilde{X})$ and ρ within the semi-parametric model use a similar procedure, minimizing (12.5A), except using the residuals e_0 and e_L from nonparametric (or semiparametric) regressions of y on $\tilde{X}$, and y_L on $\tilde{X}$, respectively, and then running a final nonparametric (or a semiparametric) regression of the 'de-spatialized' y values on $\tilde{X}$:

$$y - \hat{\rho} W y = y^* = s(\tilde{X}) + \varepsilon \quad (12.7A)$$

Equation (12.7A) can also be written as an additive model as follows:

$$y^* = s(x_1, Wx_1) + s(x_2, Wx_2) + \ldots + s(x_k, Wx_k) + \varepsilon \quad (12.8A)$$

In the study, bivariate (interaction) smoothed terms, $s(X, WX)$, are estimated using conventional thin plate splines with smoothing parameters selected by generalized cross-validation (Wood, 2006).

APPENDIX 12.2   GROUPS OF REGIONS WITH DIFFERENT SPEEDS OF CONVERGENCE

As discussed in Section 12.3.3, the marginal effect of $\ln y_0$ allows us to identify at least three groups of regions with different speeds of convergence. The group with the highest expected growth rate, but with the lowest speed of convergence, includes regions with a relative per-capita GDP in 1988 lower than -0.25: Greece, Portugal except Lisboa, five regions of the Mezzogiorno of Italy (Campania, Puglia, Calabria, Sicilia, Basilicata), ten Spanish regions, three Belgian regions (Hainaut, Luxembourg, Namur), three UK regions (Northern Ireland, West Wales and the Welsh Valleys), Burgenland (Austria) and Lunenburg (Germany).

The group with intermediate rates of growth and convergence comprises regions with a relative per-capita GDP between -0.25 and $+0.25$: 17

French regions (Champagne-Ardenne, Picardie, Centre, Basse-Normandie, Bourgogne, Nord-Pas-de-Calais, Lorraine, Franche-Comte, Pays de la Loire, Bretagne, Poitou-Charentes, Aquitaine, Midi-Pyrénées, Limousin, Auvergne, Languedoc-Roussillon, Corse), five Spanish regions (País Vasco, Comunidad Foral de Navarra, La Rioja, Comunidad de Madrid, Cataluña), three regions of the Mezzogiorno of Italy (Abruzzo, Molise and Sardinia), four Austrian regions (Niederösterreich, Karnten, Steiermark, Oberösterreich), 13 German regions (Niederbayern, Oberpfalz, Oberfranken, Unterfranken, Giessen, Kassel, Braunschweig, Weser-Ems, Münster, Koblenz, Trier, Saarland, Schleswig-Holstein), six Belgian regions (Limburg, Oost-Vlaanderen, Vlaams-Brabant, West-Vlaanderen, Brabant Wallon, Liège), six Dutch regions (Friesland, Drenthe, Overijssel, Gelderland, Noord-Brabant, Limburg), eight UK regions (Tees Valley and Durham, Cumbria, East Riding and North Lincolnshire, Derbyshire and Nottinghamshire, Herefordshire, Worcestershire and Warwickshire, Berkshire, Buckinghamshire and Oxfordshire) and Lisboa.

The last group with the lowest expected growth rate and with the highest speed of convergence includes regions with a level of per-capita GDP higher than 0.25: Centre-North of Italy, Sweden, Denmark, four French regions (Ille de France, Haute-Normandie, Rhône-Alpes, Provence-Alpes-Côte d'Azur), 16 German regions (Stuttgart, Karlsruhe, Freiburg, Tübingen, Oberbayern, Mittelfranken, Schwaben, Bremen, Hamburg, Darmstadt, Hannover, Düsseldorf, Koln, Detmold, Arnsberg, Rheinhessen-Pfalz), four Austrian regions (Wien, Salzburg, Tirol, Vorarlberg), five Dutch regions (Groningen, Utrecht, Noord-Holland, Zuid-Holland, Zeeland), two UK regions (East Anglia, Inner London) and Antwerpen (Belgium).

Note

1. Gress (2004) has demonstrated through some Monte Carlo simulations that the SP-SAR has better statistical properties than the parametric SAR model.

13. Urban heterogeneity in knowledge-related economic growth
Frank G. van Oort and Otto Raspe

13.1 INTRODUCTION

How can cities and metropolitan regions remain prosperous and competitive in a rapidly changing economy? The spatial-economic literature suggests that 'the knowledge economy' offers perspectives for growth and value-added creation. Especially, the role of agglomeration economies in the economic growth processes of firms and sectors has been studied intensively in the recent urban economic literature. It has shown the value of agglomeration economies in explaining differences in knowledge intensity of firms and knowledge diffusion between firms (Rosenthal and Strange, 2003; Capello and Nijkamp, 2004; Cheshire and Duranton, 2004). This relates to the endogenous growth theory as formulated by Romer (1986) and Lucas (1988), which states that investment in knowledge is likely to be associated with spillovers to other agents in the economy. These knowledge spillovers, an important source of agglomeration economies, play a fundamental role in determining the rate of technological progress. As such, the efficiency of transmitting knowledge to economic applications is seen as a crucial factor in explaining economic growth. These spillovers from knowledge institutions or high-tech firms are subject to geographic constraints, especially when they relate to relatively new (tacit) knowledge (Acs, 2002; Howells, 2002). There exist a variety of definitions of the knowledge economy in the literature. In an earlier paper (Raspe and van Oort, 2006) a broad definition of the knowledge economy was proposed. Knowledge is conceptualized as the adding up of abilities (capabilities, creativity and persistency) to recognize and solve problems, by collecting, selecting and interpreting information. 'Change' is an essential element in this. The knowledge economy then is the use of knowledge in interactive relations between market actors and others, while producing and using goods and services, from the first idea to final products. This definition does not focus solely on technological renewal as the goal of a knowledge economy, but on all factors that contribute to productivity and employment growth of firms by means of knowledge relations. The Dutch economy – like many other Western economies – consists mainly of service- and distribution-based specializations, and hence a focus on technical innovation (predominantly measured by R&D, see OECD, 2004) does not seem to encompass all opportunities in the knowledge economy. In this study therefore, using the broad definition and eight indicators that are related to it (see Raspe and van Oort, 2006), we analyze economic performances of localized firms on various urban scales of analyses and controlling for proximate concentrations of knowledge-intensive firm characteristics.

The current embedding of knowledge externalities in endogenous economic growth theory has led to important contributions that stress the urban character of knowledge transmission in particular. The reasoning is that if knowledge spillovers and externalities are important to growth and innovation, they should be more easily identified in cities where many people are concentrated into a relatively small geographic space so that knowledge can be transmitted between them more easily. A general hypothesis in the literature states that the largest cities have the biggest opportunities for economic growth in a knowledge economy (Acs 2002; Drennan 2002). But although there is growing evidence concerning the role of the urban condition (agglomeration economies) in the knowledge economy, the scales of urban economies tend to be ill defined and ambiguously measured. In this study we aim to improve the conceptualization and measurement of the knowledge economy in relation to urban economic growth. Independent and complementary indicators of the knowledge economy are analyzed in clearly defined urban regimes along three spatial scales in the Netherlands – those of national zoning, labor market connectedness and urban size.

Much of the research sacrifices greater precision in the operational definition in order to relate the interesting story of the knowledge and information sector in metropolitan economies (Drennan, 2002, p. 18). Because we are able to measure knowledge economy indicators at the municipal level in the Netherlands ($n = 469$) our analyses are not subject to these restrictions. At the same time it means that spatial dependence should be dealt with explicitly, because spatial interdependences on this low spatial scale are obvious. These models explicitly take into account that neighboring clusters of knowledge-intensive firms can cause benefits for other nearby cities. They also test whether a location within one of the defined urban regimes matters for growth performances. We use data for the period 1996–2003 for testing. Good 'performances' of firms in relation to knowledge economy indicators in one municipality are hypothesized to be related to performances in municipalities nearby (spatial lag/error estimation) or to performances in functionally related municipalities – in, for instance, municipalities of the same urban size, municipalities in larger urban regions or in municipalities that are employment (central cities) or population (suburban) dominated.

This chapter is organized as follows. Section 13.2 briefly reviews the literature in order to identify knowledge economy indicators that are hypothesized to be connected to economic growth. Eight indicators are distinguished and, by means of factor analysis, subsequently synthesized into three distinctive factors. Section 13.3 defines the urban regimes that are central in empirical testing. Section 13.4 presents the results of spatial econometric models that link the three factors to economic (employment) growth and value-added creation. Section 13.5 concludes.

13.2 KNOWLEDGE ECONOMY INDICATORS

The recent attention paid to the knowledge economy is embedded in a longer tradition. During the 1960s the term 'knowledge economy' was introduced in Drucker (1959) and Machlup (1962). The concept was central in much OECD-based research, being 'an economy in which the production factors labor and capital are aimed at the development and application of new technologies' (Godin, 2004). This definition seems to fail on two aspects. First, it does not define knowledge, while we have to know what knowledge is before applying it to an economy. Second, the ultimate goal of the knowledge economy appears to be the application of new technologies. Meanwhile, the theoretical and empirical literature has broadened the concept. We will discuss this literature shortly, using the broader definition provided in the previous section, and distill eight measurable indicators from it. In Table 13.1 and Raspe and van Oort (2006) the details of the data used are given.

The first aspect that is central in many studies is the role of education and professional capabilities. Many studies focus on these forms of human capital as crucial conditions for a knowledge-based economy (Lucas, 1988; Mathur, 1999). A capable and highly educated workforce has more opportunities to absorb and use information. Firms with such a workforce are more competitive, since search costs are lower. In spatial-economic terms it is good to have a highly educated and capable workforce in the firm's area – a labor market characteristic. This is often the case in larger urban agglomerations. Recently, Florida (2002) replaced human capital as the source of entrepreneurship and economic growth with creative capital. From his analyses it becomes clear that creativity (measured by occupations rather than sectors) spatially coincides with positive urban growth potentials. Different from human capital theory, the creative class (as Florida labels knowledge workers and artists) does not necessarily need to have a high educational level in order to create more than average added-value. Because his research shows that creativity as motor for local economic potential can be considerable, we added the presence of creative industries (distinguished, as Florida does, with Dutch labor force data) in our analysis as second knowledge economy indicator.

The literature distinguishes two more conceptualizations that focus on the communicative aspects of knowledge and knowledge transfer. A large literature focuses on the growth potentials of firms due to an increased accessibility of information through information and communication technology (ICT) in their entrepreneurial operations, especially in urban areas (Drennan, 2002). In theory, ICT as a general-purpose technology can accelerate organizational processes in terms of productivity. Contrary to other communicative indicators, ICT functions as an optimal vehicle of knowledge transfer when information is codified. We take this aspect (measured by computer usage per employee per five-digit industry, localized in municipalities) as the third indicator in our research. Furthermore, much socioeconomic research focuses on social, cultural and communicative capital as sources for productivity gains in economic sectors (Cooke and Morgan, 1998). This conceptualization looks at trustworthy connections between economic actors as sources of social and economic networks. Communicative skills are particularly required in that sense, and for the ability to persuade and convince others. An indicator based on communicative skills in network relations (first developed in McCloskey and Klamer, 1995) is applied to the detailed municipal industry structure in the Netherlands, and functions as the fourth indicator.

The broad definition of the knowledge economy also addresses more technical- and production-oriented aspects of economic renewal that can (endogenously) lead to economic growth of firms. By tradition, the largest amount of literature focuses on these aspects (which are also central to the dictionary definition of knowledge economy). Attention is predominantly paid to research and development (R&D) as a source of growth, because this input factor can be stimulated by subsidies (Acs, 2002; Foray 2004). Although not all R&D activities lead automatically to innovative output and growth (Black, 2004), we use the number of R&D employees in firms as the fifth indicator in our analysis. A special, and according to many, independent indicator of R&D activity, occurs when R&D-intensive firms cooperate in international networks, and their export is also technology-driven. In those cases the literature speaks of high- and medium-tech economic activities, whose overrepresentation functions as a source of internalizing macroeconomic growth (Cortright and Mayer, 2001). An indicator of relative overrepresentation of high- and medium-tech industries is the sixth indicator in our analysis.

Innovation is generally regarded as the most important knowledge economy key source for economic growth. R&D is an input indicator of innovation (intentions); it does not measure actual innovative output of firms. Several sources for innovative output exist (Jaffe and Trajtenberg, 2002): patents and patent citations, copyrights, new product announcements and questionnaires in which firms are asked in great detail about their innovative behavior (new products and processes for the market and the industry in which one operates). It is important to distinguish between technological and non-technological innovations. Both aspects are introduced in our analyses, by focusing on innovations in the third Community Innovation Survey (CIS3) of Statistics Netherlands and EUROSTAT. They are the seventh and eighth indicators in our analyses.

Table 13.1 gives descriptive statistics of the eight indicators used in our analysis. Individual maps of all indicators can be found in Raspe and van Oort (2006).

The spatial repercussion of these eight indicators differs a lot. Many indicators show spatial association. We carried out a factor analysis[1] to group the municipal scores of the eight indicators of the local knowledge economy into spatially independent underlying factors. Often, this also means sectoral (in)dependence. For example, the spatial correlation between the level of education and the use of ICT seems obvious: highly educated employees often use computers in their business processes (on the sectoral level the correlation is 0.36). The spatial patterns show an even stronger correlation: a regional overrepresentation of highly educated employees coincides with strong specializations in ICT use (on the regional level the correlation is 0.58). Of course, the previous section made clear that there are also theoretical motives that clarify why the eight indicators are different.

The result of the factor analysis is a three-factor structure. Table 13.2 shows the factor scores: the correlation between the eight individual indicators and the three remaining factors. The three factors are relatively straightforward to interpret. The third factor, labeled 'R&D', is usually most identified with the knowledge economy. The factor is closely related to the indicators research and development and the relative presence of high-tech and medium-tech enterprises. Concerning their content, there is a large overlap between these two indicators. The factor labeled 'innovation' is built up by the indicators of innovation output, both technological and non-technological in character. Regions that have high scores on this factor contain relatively many enterprises that introduced new products or services to the market or carried out new business processes in the recent

Table 13.1 Descriptive statistics of eight indicators of the knowledge economy

Indicator	Mean	Standard Deviation	Minimum	Maximum
1. Education level[a]	1.92	0.08	1.76	2.21
2. Creative economy[b]	2.03	1.58	0.26	20.84
3. ICT-sensitivity[c]	0.75	0.11	0.53	1.27
4. Communicative skills[d]	0.53	0.08	0.33	0.80
5. R&D[e]	1.20	1.12	0.08	12.00
6. High-tech & medium-tech[f]	7.70	4.69	0.00	27.00
7. Tech. innovation[g]	50.44	9.71	20.88	81.95
8. Non-tech. innovation[g]	61.06	7.67	39.38	83.11

Notes: $N = 496$ (Dutch municipalities).
[a] The education level is the weighted average (with the weights: 1 for low, 2 for medium, 3 for high) of the employment in three educational levels: high (university – WO – and higher vocational education – HBO), middle (intermediate vocational education – MBO, higher general secondary education – HAVO – and pre-university education – VWO) and low (lower general secondary education – MAVO – and lower vocational education – LBO).
[b] Based on Raspe and van Oort (2006).
[c] The number of computers and terminals per sector (National Statistics; Computerization Survey) is linked to the population of firm establishments at the level of municipalities (LISA database): the indicator measures the number of computers and terminals per employee on a municipal level.
[d] Based on a classification by McCloskey and Klamer (1995).
[e] The R&D intensity per sector per Dutch province form the third Community Innovation Survey (CIS3, Statistics Netherlands) is allocated to municipalities (based on LISA data base). See De Bruijn (2004). Units: number of R&D jobs in the total number of jobs in a region.
[f] High-tech and medium-tech firms are classified by their (detailed) SIC codes by their extent of research and export orientation, see OECD (2003). Units: number of jobs in high- and medium-tech sectors in the total number of jobs in a region.
[g] The innovation intensity per sector per Dutch province form the third Community Innovation Survey (CIS3, Statistics Netherlands) is allocated to municipalities (based on LISA database). See De Bruijn (2004). Innovations are registered as products and services, which are new in the market of sector. Units: number of jobs of innovative firms in the total number of jobs in a region.

years. Remarkably, the number of employees that carry out research and development is sectorally and spatially clearly a different indicator from the outcome of research, innovation. After all, not every bit of research leads to new products or services. The factor 'knowledge workers' finally, shows high scores on ICT sensitivity, education level, employment specialized in communicative skills and the number of creative economic sectors. These knowledge workers are important in the diffusion process of knowledge, not only codified knowledge but also the more difficult transferable tacit

Table 13.2   Factor scores of the 8 variables

Indicators	Factors		
	Factor 1 'Knowledge workers'	Factor 2 'Innovation'	Factor 3 'R&D'
ICT-sensitivity	*0.764*	0.369	0.233
Education level	*0.960*	0.120	0.037
Creative economy	*0.473*	0.114	−0.350
Communicative skills	*0.933*	−0.003	−0.070
High-tech and medium-tech	−0.169	0.239	*0.790*
Research and development	0.176	0.102	*0.832*
Innovation (technological)	0.129	*0.899*	0.217
Innovation (non-technological)	0.155	*0.911*	0.071

knowledge (van Oort, Weterings and Verlinde, 2003). It is important to consider this (difficult to measure and therefore often neglected) dimension simultaneously with the (technical) industrial factors R&D and technological innovation. After all, they qualify equally as conditions or sources for innovation and hence embody economic renewal.

The spatial patterns of the factor scores are presented in Figures 13.1, 13.2 and 13.3. From Figure 13.1 it becomes clear that large cities like Amsterdam and Utrecht as well as their suburban surroundings have high scores on the factor 'knowledge workers'. Hilversum, with specialization in media activities, has a top position. But also, The Hague, Delft and Leiden have economies highly driven by knowledge workers. Also, a number of medium-sized cities outside the Randstad region specialize in economies that are characterized by knowledge workers. The rural regions and the regions in the national periphery of the Netherlands are lagging behind in intensity of this employment. The map of the second factor, 'innovation' (Figure 13.2), shows a different spatial pattern from that of the knowledge workers. Especially, regions in the western part (the Randstad), and the eastern part of the Netherlands show a higher degree of innovative businesses. The region Amsterdam, and the areas nearby this big city are very innovative in character. Also, several smaller cities and regions are connected and show high scores; the chemical industrial clusters in Sittard-Geleen (DSM) and Terneuzen (DOW Chemicals) form innovative hotspots. Additionally, the spatial pattern of the third factor, 'R&D' (Figure 13.3), differs from the 'knowledge workers' and 'innovation' regional patterns. The regions in the western part of the Netherlands, which showed strong orientations to the

Urban heterogeneity in knowledge-related economic growth 287

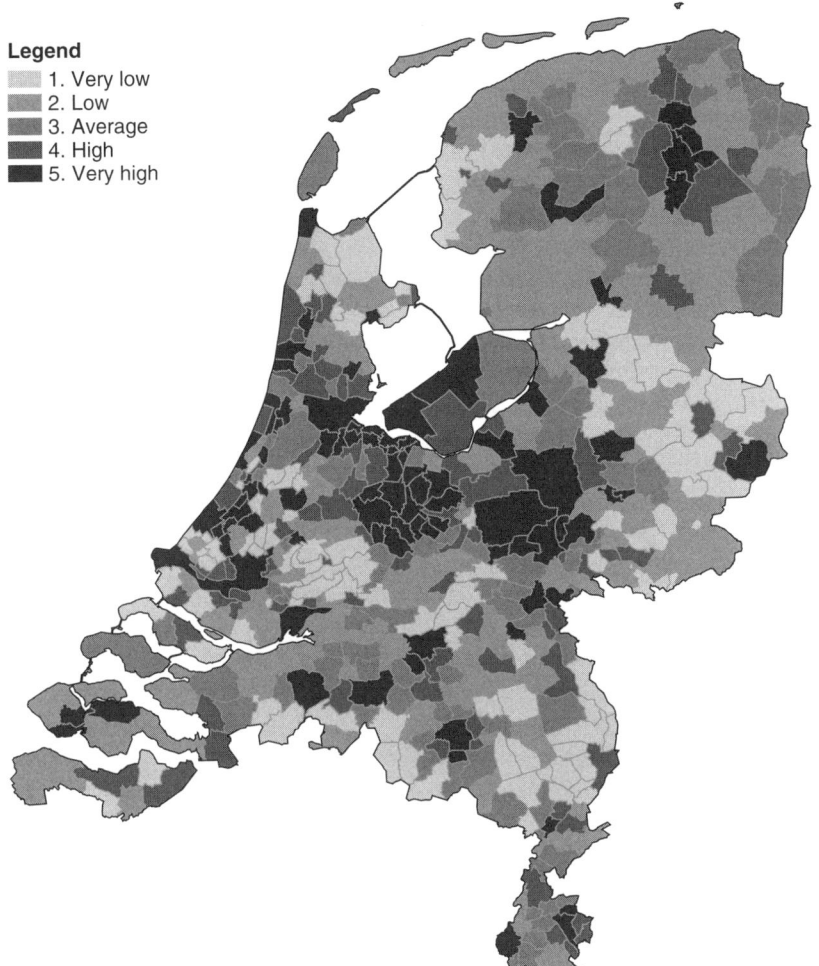

Figure 13.1 The 'knowledge workers' dimension (factor 1)

'Knowledge workers' and 'Innovation' dimensions, are characterized by relatively low degrees of R&D activities. Instead, the regions in the southern and eastern national periphery are ahead in (relative) R&D employment specialization. These are the regions that have a stronger industrial orientation. The Eindhoven region (with Philips and ASML), Wageningen, De Bilt, Delft and Terneuzen (with universities or technologically oriented multinational firms) are the R&D hotspots in the Netherlands.

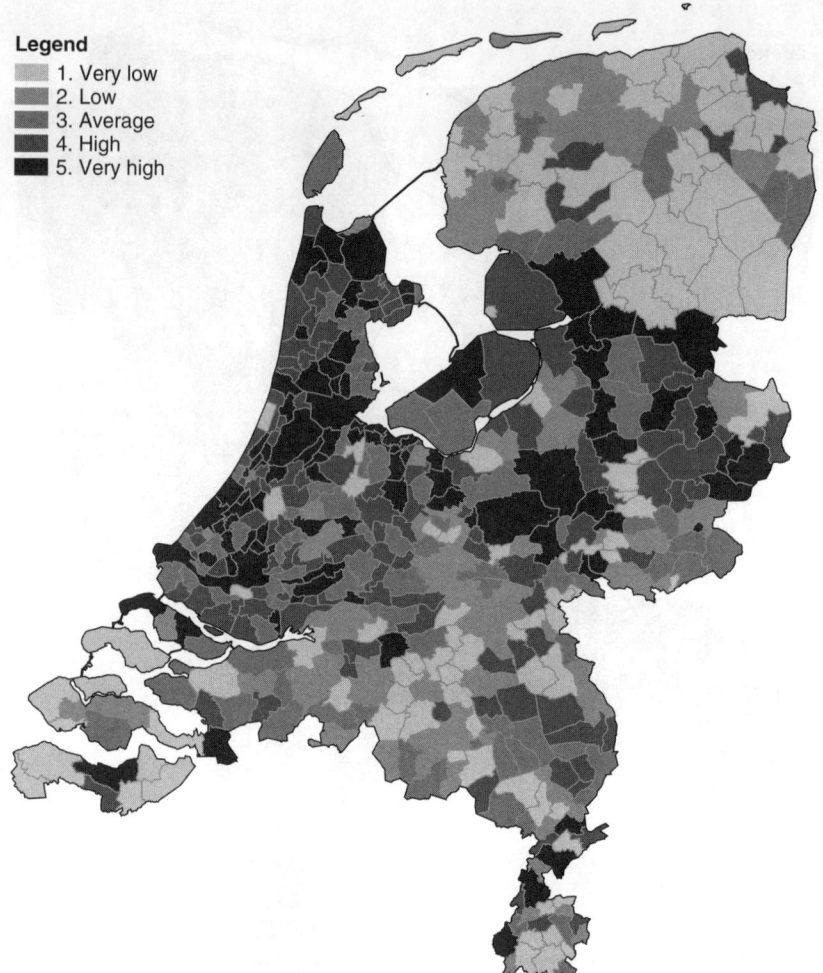

Figure 13.2   The 'innovation' dimension (factor 2)

13.3   THE URBAN DIMENSIONS

Research and development, innovation and knowledge availability are unambiguously believed to be good for economic growth. The current embedding of knowledge externalities in endogenous economic growth theory leads to several important contributions that stress the *urban* character of knowledge transmission in particular (van Oort, 2004). Most of the relevant empirical literature focuses on American states as the spatial

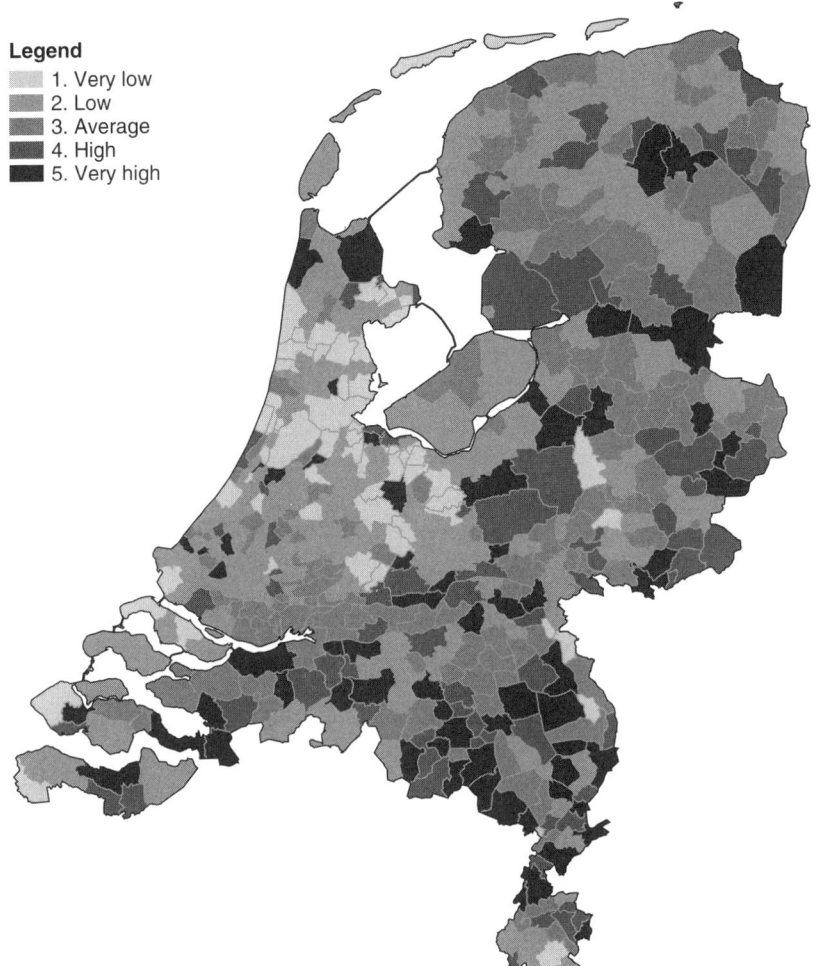

Figure 13.3 The 'R&D' dimension (factor 3)

unit of analysis. Some research, however, focuses on lower scales of analysis. Wallsten (2001), Anselin, Varga and Acs (2000) and Black (2004), for instance, use metropolitan statistical areas in the US context to analyze the spatial extent of R&D, innovation (patent) and growth externalities and find that local spatial externalities are present and important. Proximity matters in the transmission of innovation- and growth-based knowledge of dynamic firms, while distance decays tend to be rather steep (Jaffe, Trajtenberg and Henderson, 1993). As hypothesized in our study, many of these 'stylized conclusions' depend heavily on the definitions of innovation and knowledge intensity, on the research population and on the hypothesized functional relations over space.

The (geographic) literature also provides clues for non-contiguous (regime) types of spatial dependence. Quality of life aspects, regional labor markets, specialized urban networks and city size appear to be significant locational considerations for knowledge-intensive firms (van Oort, 2004). The spatial structures of proximity – contiguous nearness at the municipal level – and heterogeneity – urban hierarchical and regional, not necessarily contiguous, spatial dependence – have been tested for in this study by spatial dependence (spatial lag and spatial error) tests and spatial regimes respectively. When appropriate, the spatial coefficient in spatial lag estimation shows whether the dependent variable in a model (in our case localized firm growth or value-added creation) is dependent on neighboring values of this dependent variable. If so, conclusions can be drawn on the significance and magnitude of this spatial dependence (Anselin, 1988). Spatial heterogeneity on the other hand is modeled by spatial regimes, involving change-of-slope regression estimation over various types of locations that theoretically 'perform' differently. Three sets of spatial regimes are distinguished, each indicating aspects of urban structures at different spatial scales:

1. On the macro-level, three national zoning regimes have been distinguished: the Randstad core region, the so-called intermediate zone and the national periphery (Figure 13.4). Distinguishing between macro-economic zones in the Netherlands is based on a gravity model of total employment concerning data from 1996. The Randstad region in the Netherlands historically comprises the economic core provinces of Noord-Holland, Zuid-Holland and Utrecht; the intermediate zone mainly comprises the growth regions of Gelderland and Noord-Brabant; while the national periphery is built up by the northern and southern regions of the country. This zoning distinction is hypothesized as important in many studies on endogenous growth in the Netherlands, in the sense that the Randstad region traditionally has better economic potential for development (cf. van Oort, 2004).
2. On the meso-level we distinguish a labor-market-induced connectedness regime from a non-connectedness regime (Figure 13.5). This spatial regime concerns commuting-based labor market relations. In the figure, core and suburban municipalities together comprise the connected regime, as opposed to the other types of locations that are characterized as non-connected. The three types of locations have been distinguished, initially based on municipal data for 1990–99. The

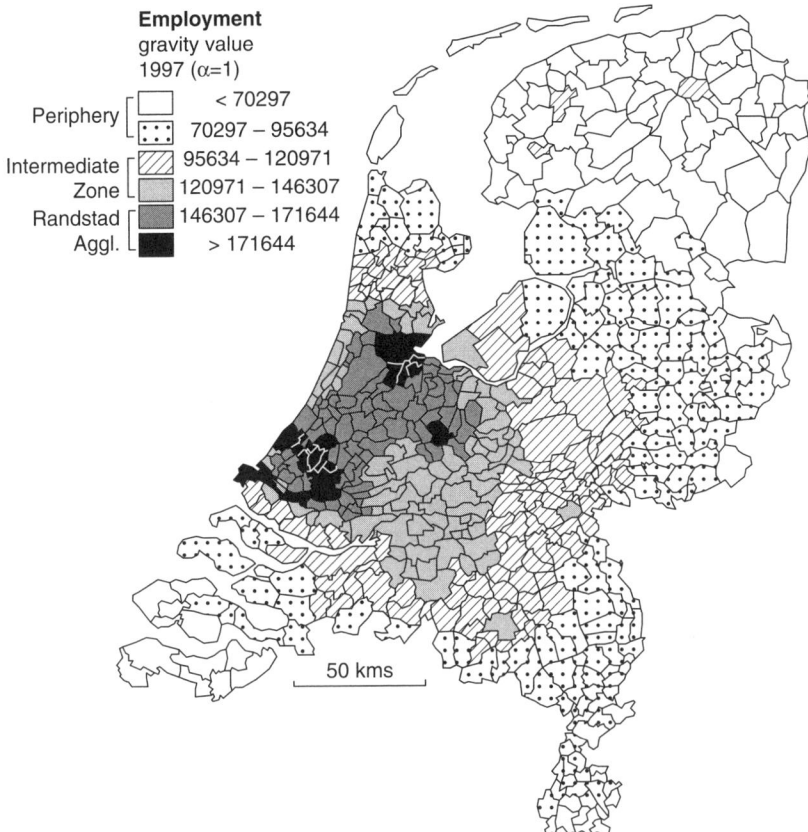

Figure 13.4   National zoning spatial regimes

classification is based on the dependency of a municipality's population upon employment and services proximity and accessibility. Urban core areas have an important employment function. More than 15 000 people commute into these municipalities (while living somewhere else) on a daily basis. Municipalities where more than 20 percent of residents commute to central core locations are labeled suburban. The literature finds in general that urban areas in the connected regime show higher economic growth and innovation rates than areas in the non-connected regime (e.g., Anselin et al., 2000). As becomes clear from Figure 13.5, locations in the connected regime are not necessarily adjacent to each other.

3. The third set of spatial regimes is constructed using the degree of urbanization of municipalities (Figure 13.6). Following Dutch standards of

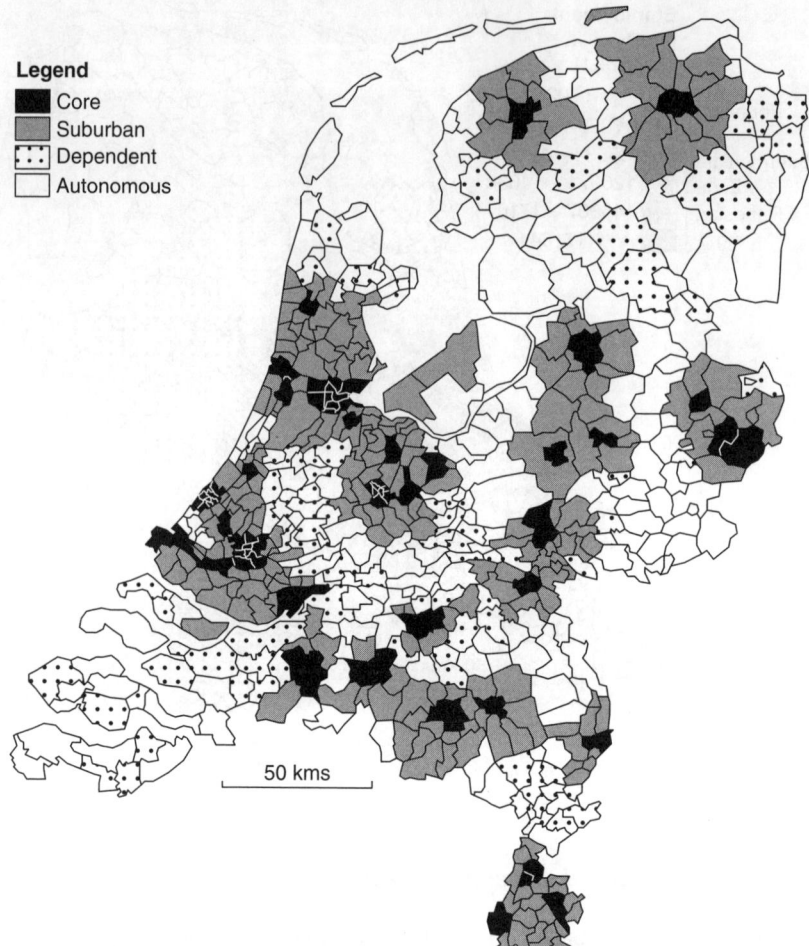

Figure 13.5   The labor market spatial regimes

urbanization, cut-off population thresholds of 200 000 and 45 000 inhabitants distinguish large and medium-sized cities in the Netherlands from small cities and rural municipalities.

In sum, these three aspects of spatial heterogeneity constitute three spatial levels of urban constellation: the urban level itself, the functional (commuting) region and the meso-level 'agglomerative fields' of the Randstad core region compared with its adjacent intermediate zone and the national periphery.

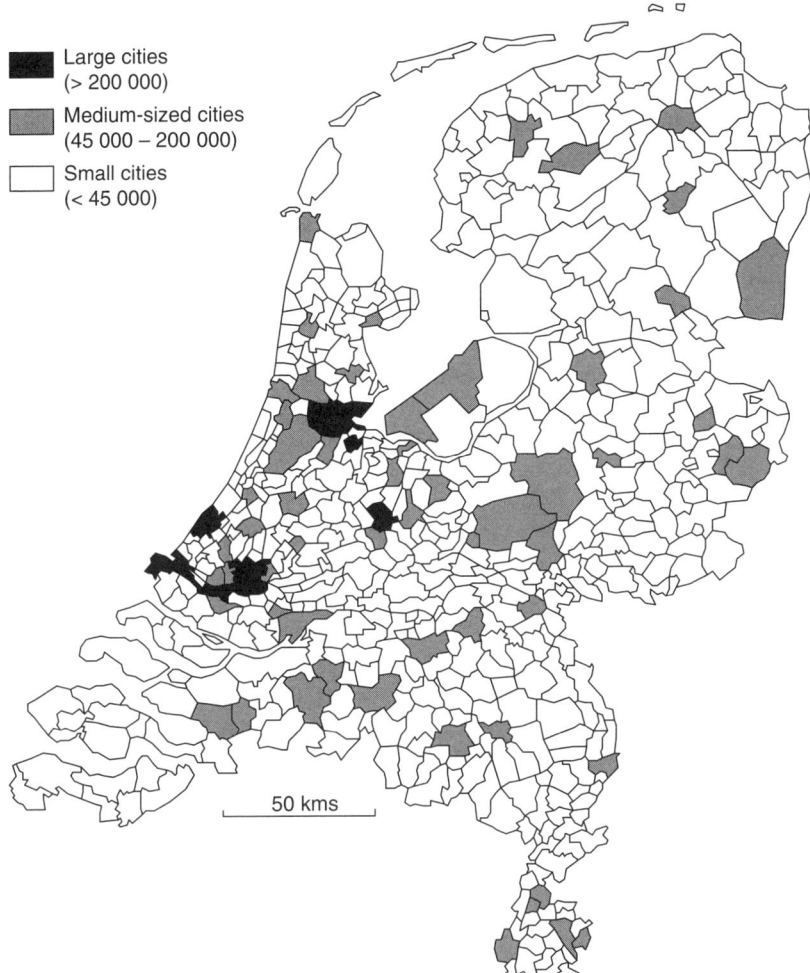

Figure 13.6   Urban size (municipal) spatial regimes

13.4   SPATIAL ECONOMETRIC ANALYSES OF GROWTH AND VALUE-ADDED

In Tables 13.3 and 13.4, the econometric models that we ran are summarized. Below the tables technical explanation on the models is provided. The models are numbered over the two tables – Models (1) to (5) on employment growth in the period 1996–2002 in Table 13.3 and Models (6) and (10)

Table 13.3 Econometric models on employment growth (1996–2002) in municipalities in the Netherlands (n = 496, t-values in parentheses)

	(1) Basic Model (OLS)	(2) Spatial Lag Model	(3) Spatial Lag Model with Urban Size Regimes			(4) Spatial Lag Model with National Zoning Regimes			(5) Spatial Lag Model with Labor Market Regimes		
			Large	Medium	Small	Randstad	Interm. zone	Nat. periphery	Central city	Suburban	Other
Explanatory Variables											
Constant	89.819 (30.311)	50.586 (4.701)	136.686 (0.637)*	119.789 (6.058)*	45.677 (5.185)*	70.842 (4.761)	54.220 (5.253)	52.518 (5.749)	97.644 (2.456)	47.318 (4.971)	53.531 (5.744)
Factor 1: Knowledge workers	14.737 (4.968)	13.634 (4.700)	−5.395 (−0.065)*	−21.527 (−1.937)*	10.674 (3.107)*	2.471 (0.441)	14.342 (2.943)	15.665 (3.052)	0.077 (0.004)	8.735 (1.945)	20.014 (3.894)
Factor 2: Innovation output	15.431 (5.206)	13.504 (4.613)	−81.096 (−0.516)	8.398 (0.905)	10.638 (3.392)	20.827 (2.569)	13.242 (2.165)	9.633 (2.300)	−10.910 (−0.730)	16.825 (3.915)	12.869 (2.969)
Factor 3: R&D	−0.801 (−0.270)	0.076 (0.026)	−60.091 (−0.475)*	24.834 (3.058)*	2.325 (0.754)*	−8.835 (−1.227)*	9.045 (1.986)*	−3.225 (−0.688)*	−9.990 (−0.905)	1.814 (0.359)	−2.633 (−0.665)
Spatial Coefficient (ρ)	—	0.430 (4.701)	0.445 (4.950)			0.356 (3.688)			0.442 (4.815)		
Test statistics											
R^2	0.095	0.118	0.157			0.156			0.131		
Max. likelihood	−2779.80	−2769.37	−2757.78			−2759.77			−2765.52		
LM (BP)	8.28 (0.004)	6.84 (0.077)	6.07 (0.087)			5.27 (0.093)			5.81 (0.071)		

LM (ρ)	30.284	—	—	—
	(0.000)			
LM (λ)	26.225	0.139	—	—
	(0.000)	(0.708)		
LR (ρ)	—	20.865	22.876	12.489
		(0.000)	(0.000)	(0.000)
Chow-Wald	—	—	23.755	19.116
			(0.003)	(0.014)
				21.741
				(0.000)
				7.756
				(0.457)

Notes:
Following Anselin (1995), LM (ρ) and LM (λ) are statistics for the presence of a spatial lag in the dependent variable and in the residual respectively, with a critical value of 3.84 at the 5 percent level of significance.
LM (BP) tests for homoscedasticity of regression errors using the Breusch-Pagan Lagrange multiplier test for normal distributed errors.
The spatial weight matrix used is w_2 (row standardized, distance-squared), probability levels (p-values) are presented in the tables. Significant p-levels are printed in italic. Models with w_1 (single) distance weight matrices and w_3 (triple) distance weight matrices have a less significant model fit.
The spatial Chow-Wald test is distributed as an F-variate and tests for structural instability of the regression coefficients over regimes (Anselin 1995, p. 32). Significant results (95 percent confidence interval) of the spatial Chow-Wald in general and on individual coefficients (rejection of H_0 of joint equality of coefficients over regimes) are marked (*).
All variables are log transformed and corrected for extreme values.

Table 13.4 Econometric models on value-added per km^2 (2002, log) in municipalities in the Netherlands (n = 496, t-values in parentheses)

Explanatory Variables	(6) Basic Model (OLS)	(7) Spatial Lag Model	(8) Spatial Lag Model with Urban Size Regimes			(9) Spatial Lag Model with National Zoning Regimes			(10) Spatial Lag Model with Labor Market Regimes		
			Large	Medium	Small	Randstad	Interm. zone	Nat. Periphery	Central city	Suburban	Other
Constant	0.031 (−0.001)	1.079 (6.486)*	−0.435 (−0.902)*	2.524 (6.038)*	3.929 (2.816)*	2.981 (8.463)	1.252 (6.006)	1.336 (6.767)	2.892 (2.819)	0.625 (3.238)	0.649 (3.956)
Factor 1: Knowledge workers	1.364 (15.693)	1.285 (14.399)	0.497 (2.200)*	0.846 (7.977)*	1.194 (6.166)*	2.169 (13.337)*	0.909 (6.399)*	1.133 (7.885)*	2.190 (2.318)*	0.784 (6.423)*	0.907 (6.733)*
Factor 2: Innovation output	0.793 (9.134)	0.682 (7.757)	0.463 (1.305)	0.068 (0.327)	1.534 (4.892)	0.681 (3.086)	0.708 (3.968)	0.529 (4.378)	−0.285 (−0.729)*	0.639 (5.622)*	0.386 (3.388)*
Factor 3: R&D	0.002 (0.028)	0.066 (0.769)	0.325 (−1.138)	−0.093 (−0.512)	1.352 (1.926)	0.144 (0.740)*	0.415 (3.207)*	−0.156 (−1.197)*	−0.254 (−0.880)	0.212 (1.595)	0.016 (0.161)
Spatial Coefficient (ρ, λ)	–	0.340 (4.216)	0.445 (6.315)			0.372 (3.714)			0.460 (5.824)		
Test statistics											
R^2	0.401	(0.417)	(0.669)			(0.590)			(0.539)		
Max. likelihood	−9023.46	−9014.39	−8871.93			−8969.38			−8953.86		

LM (BP)	3.998	2.15	1.83	1.604	1.60
	(0.000)	(0.200)	(0.093)	(0.063)	(0.081)
LM (ρ)	43.277	–	–	19.532	–
	(0.000)			(0.202)	
LM (λ)	22.811	1.682	–	–	–
	(0.000)	(0.194)			
LR (ρ)	–	18.152	45.784	14.543	35.506
		(0.000)	(0.000)	(0.000)	(0.000)
Chow-Wald	–	–	86.061	87.108	137.688
			(0.003)	(0.000)	(0.000)

Note: For technical explanation see notes to Table 13.3.

on value-added patterns per square kilometer (log) in Table 13.4. In order to correct for high growth rates when growing from a low base, employment growth is defined as the growth in employment from 1996 to 2002 relative to the average potential labor force (people in the range 15–65 of age) in municipalities. For the same reason, value-added is measured relative to municipalities' physical sizes (relative to employment density gave the same model results). The three factors 'knowledge workers', 'innovation' and 'R&D' are introduced according to the definitions given in Section 13.2. The three factors are uncorrelated to each other, which therefore solves possible multicollinearity problems.

Four remarks should be made beforehand. First, the three factors are measured in standardized values (z-scores with average 0 and standard deviation 1). We are interested in which knowledge economy factors are *relatively* more profoundly attached to economic growth and value-added. Second, and in line with the first remark, the weighting of different factors in terms of policy measures is not up to researchers. We treat all three factors equally in the models in order to determine their simultaneous relationship with growth and value-added. Third, many control variables influencing employment growth and value-added should ideally be included, like size and specializations of a region's and municipality's economy, agglomeration factors and accessibility factors (van Oort, 2004). But, indirectly these factors are already present in the eight indicators that form the basis of the three knowledge economy factors. There, the size and specializations of all industries are weighted in their build-up of ICT usage, innovation intensity, educational level of the employees, etc. Fourth, all models turned out to be best fit by spatial models using w_2 (distance squared) spatial weight model, in which distances are measured in kilometers (all models were also tested for w_1 and w_3 distance weights relevance). This already leads us to conclude that the indicators of economic performance are clustered, but in a very localized way (very proximate to each other).

The ordinary least squares (OLS) model for employment growth (column 1 in table 13.3) shows the significance of the factors 'knowledge workers' and 'innovation'. The third knowledge economy factor ('R&D') turns out to be not significantly attached to local economic performances. The test statistics of LM (ρ) and LM (λ) in column (1) reveal the presence of spatial autocorelation dependency of the model. In column (2) in Table 13.3, therefore, the model is estimated using a spatial lag specification. Spatial lag models make use of maximum likelihood estimation techniques, in which the explained variance is no longer an adequate measure for model fitting. The spatial coefficient indeed turns out to be significant. Introducing spatial dependency in the model alters the coefficients slightly when compared with the OLS base model. Relative high values of R&D specialization, in particular, hampers growth dynamics, while high values of innovation and knowledge workers characteristics remain unambiguously connected to employment growth. The likelihood-based measure (LM in the summary statistics of the tables) can be used to compare the model fit with that of the basic OLS model. It turns out that for the employment growth model, the fit considerably improves when the spatial lag is added to the model, as indicated by an increase in the log likelihood. Heteroscedasticity emerges as a problem in the OLS model, but less so in the spatial lag models (see the LM [BP] statistics in the table). The interpretation of the model outcomes does not change when the spatial lag specification is applied.

Columns (3a–c), (4a–c) and (5a–c) present spatial lag estimations, but with the allowance of structural change of coefficient estimates between spatial regimes. Column (3) shows that the 'knowledge workers' and 'innovation' dimension works out more favorably in connection with employment growth in small municipalities, as opposed to large and medium-sized ones. The model fit again improves when compared with the OLS and spatial lag model without the urbanization regimes, and the spatial Chow-Wald test confirms the significance of the spatial regimes (especially because of the different signs and levels of significance of the 'knowledge workers' dimension). The relations found thus work out most profoundly in medium-sized and smaller urban environments. This conclusion questions the large-city urban focus of urban-economic theory and Dutch policy: highest potentials for growth connected to the knowledge economy are in smaller cities (that theoretically do not suffer from congestion).

Column (4) in Table 13.3 shows that the intermediate zone region most notably 'exhibits' the significant set of knowledge economy factors related to growth, as opposed to the Randstad region and (to a much lesser extent) the national periphery. This is remarkable, since most agglomeration indicators are attached to the Randstad region (van Oort, 2004). The model fit is slightly less than in the urban regimes model, but still considerably better than the OLS and spatial lag (SEC) model. The regime of macroeconomic zoning is significant, especially due to diverging scores on R&D factor.

Column (5a–c) shows the significance of the connected spatial regimes (central cities and suburbs), as opposed to the unconnected regime. Central cities in the Netherlands are, contrary to the theoretical literature, not the central foci of knowledge economy circumstances that are related to employment growth. Suburban municipalities in general have better cards to play in this respect.

Table 13.4 shows the results of the econometric models made for (log) value-added per square kilometer. Note that this indicator does not reflect growth, as the models in Table 13.3 did. The results are in magnitude and significance comparable to the employment growth models, except for the 'knowledge workers' dimension. In Table 13.4, this factor shows considerably more significant attachment to the explained variable than in that of Table 13.3. Large and medium-sized cities, the Randstad municipalities and central city and suburban municipalities now all have significant positive signs for the 'knowledge workers' variable. When value-added is a policy goal alongside employment creation and growth, the attention shifts more to larger cities as potential investment areas for knowledge-intensive economic activities. The factor 'knowledge workers', attached to the service economy of larger metropolitan areas, comes to the fore as a good 'predictor' of localized growth and value-added concentrations in the Netherlands. Regions and locations with R&D overrepresentation though are little attached to good economic performances, even when corrected for spatial dependency. This might also be the case in other Western countries. The analyses show that urbanization matters for employment growth in relation to knowledge economy characteristics at different scales of urban analyses in the Netherlands, both defined by contiguous proximity (as envisaged by the spatial lag significance) and by the spatial heterogeneous regimes. No large city paradigm emerges. This gives a more balanced insight in the working of urbanization and localization externalities in relation to the knowledge economy. It adds to the current debate on external economies that mainly focuses on proximity-based spillovers and knowledge transfer in R&D-intensive sectors in the largest cities.

13.5 CONCLUSION

In this study we tested the hypothesis that larger cities have the biggest opportunities for economic growth in a knowledge economy, since these cities offer the best opportunities for interaction, variety and specializations. The Dutch government, as well as policy-makers in other Western countries, have indicated that they want to stimulate urban economies by focusing on knowledge economy potentials, especially indicated by R&D intensity. We improved the conceptualization and measurement of the knowledge economy and urban heterogeneity. In the study we used eight indicators of the knowledge economy on the municipal level of the Netherlands ($n=469$) that the literature indicated to be related to good (urban) economic performances:

1. innovative industrial firms;
2. innovative non-industrial firms;

3. employment in research and development;
4. representation of high- and medium-tech industries;
5. educational level of the working population;
6. ICT adaptation in firms and industries;
7. an industry-specific indicator for communicative skills and
8. an indicator for the creative labor force.

Three independent and complementary indicators of the knowledge economy – labeled 'R&D', 'innovation' and 'knowledge workers' – were distilled from these indicators and analyzed in clearly defined urban regimes along three spatial scales in the Netherlands – those of national zoning, labor market connectedness and urban size. The extent of spatial spillover of growth externalities appeared limited, but we found that firms in smaller cities, suburban municipalities and cities outside the Randstad core region of the Netherlands – but still near the largest agglomerations – are more attached to employment growth in relation to the knowledge economy than the largest cities. Especially, the 'knowledge worker' dimension that captures service-based economic activities with a highly educated and creative workforce and the innovation dimension are positively related to localized economic growth and value-added outside the largest urban concentrations. The R&D dimension is not per se positively related to economic growth, not even after controlling for proximate concentrations of R&D and municipal functional heterogeneity. We recommend a more careful treatment in the knowledge economy and economic growth debate of spatial heterogeneity within larger urban regions instead of cities per se.

ACKNOWLEDGEMENTS

We thank Hans van Amsterdam for technical assistance and Koen Frenken and an anonymous referee for useful comments on an earlier version of this chapter.

NOTE

1. Factor analyses (including VARIMAX rotation) identifies the underlying variables (named factors) in a dataset in which multiple characteristics are included that show mutual correlation. This technique is often used to remove the overlap between different indicators and reduce these characteristics to independent factors: the similarity within a factor is high, while low between the factors.

REFERENCES

Acs, Z.J. (2002), *Innovation and the Growth of Cities*, Cheltenham, UK and Northampton, MA, USA: Edward Elgar.
Anselin, L. (1988), *Spatial Econometrics: Methods and Models*, Dordrecht: Kluwer.
Anselin, L. (1995), *SpaceStat. A Software Program for the Analysis of Spatial Data (Version 1.80)*, Morgantown: Regional Research Institute, West Virginia University.
Anselin, L., A. Varga and Z.J. Acs (2000), 'Geographical and sectoral characteristics of academic knowledge externalities', *Papers in Regional Science*, 79, 435–43.
Black, G. (2004), *The Geography of Small Firm Innovation*, Dordrecht: Kluwer.
Capello, R. and P. Nijkamp (2004), *Urban Dynamics and Growth. Advances in Urban Economics*, Amsterdam: Elsevier.
Cheshire, P. and G. Duranton (2004), *Recent Developments in Urban and Regional Economics*, Cheltenham, UK and Northampton, MA, USA: Edward Elgar.
Cooke, P. and K. Morgan (1998), *The Associational Economy. Firms, Regions and Innovation*, Oxford: University Press.
Cortright, J. and H. Mayer (2001), 'High-tech specialization: a comparison of high-tech centers', *The Brookings Survey Papers*, 1–18.
De Bruijn, P. (2004), 'Mapping innovation: regional dimensions of innovation and networking in the Netherlands', *Journal of Economic and Social Geography (TESG)*, 95, 433–40.
Drennan, M.P. (2002), *The Information Economy and American Cities*, Baltimore: The Johns Hopkins University Press.
Drucker P. (1959), *Landmarks of Tomorrow: A Report on the New Post-modern World*, New York: Harper.
Florida, R. (2002), *The Rise of the Creative Class*, New York: Basic Books.
Foray, D. (2004), *The Economics of Knowledge*, Cambridge, MA: The MIT Press.
Godin, B. (2004), 'The new economy: what the concept owes to the OECD', *Research Policy*, 23, 679–90.
Howells, J.R. (2002), 'Tacit knowledge, innovation and economic geography', *Urban Studies*, 39, 871–84.
Jaffe, A. and M. Trajtenberg (2002), *Patents, Citations and Innovation. A Window on the Knowledge Economy*, Cambridge, MA: The MIT Press.
Jaffe, A.B., M. Trajtenberg and R. Henderson (1993), 'Geographic localization of knowledge spillovers as evidenced by patent citations', *The Quarterly Journal of Economics*, 36, 577–98.
Lucas, R.E. (1988), 'On the mechanism of economic development', *Journal of Monetary Economics*, XXII, 3–42.
Machlup, F. (1962), *The Production and Distribution of Knowledge in the United States*, Princeton: University Press.
Mathur, V.K. (1999), 'Human-capital-based strategy for regional economic development', *Economic Development Quarterly*, XIII, 203–16.
McCloskey, D.N. and A. Klamer (1995), 'One quarter of GDP is persuasion', *American Economic Review*, 85, 191–5.
OECD (2003), *Science, Technology and Industry Scoreboard*, Paris: OECD.
OECD (2004), *Global Knowledge Flows and Economic Development*, Paris: OECD.
Raspe, O. and F.G. van Oort (2006), 'The knowledge economy and urban economic growth', *European Planning Studies*, 14, 1209–34.

Romer, P.M. (1986), 'Increasing returns and long-run growth', *Journal of Political Economy*, 94, 1002–37.
Rosenthal, S.S. and W.C. Strange (2003), 'Geography, industrial organization, and agglomeration', *Review of Economics and Statistics*, 85, 377–93.
van Oort, F.G. (2004), *Urban Growth and Innovation*, Aldershot: Ashgate.
van Oort, F.G., A. Weterings and H. Verlinde (2003), 'Residential amenities of knowledge workers and the location of ICT-firms in the Netherlands', *Journal of Economic and Social Geography* (TESG), 94, 516–23.
Wallsten, S.J. (2001), 'An empirical test of geographic knowledge spillovers using geographic information systems and firm-level data', *Regional Science and Urban Economics*, 31, 571–99.

Index

absorptive capacity 8, 11, 139, 145–6, 149, 154, 195–6, 203, 205, 216–17
adoption of new technologies 149
AEG 5, 45, 48–50, 55, 58
agglomeration
  agglomeration economies 3, 4, 6–7, 92, 135, 280–81
  agglomeration forces 7, 112, 132–3
  agglomeration and industrial structure 112
anticipations 69

bioRegio competition 52
biotechnology 4–5, 25–6, 29, 41, 43–5, 51–7, 59, 60, 106, 151, 194, 196, 224, 233, 236
bridging ties 176–7, 196

Centre for the Development of Industrial technology (CDTI) 157
circular causation 6, 92
cities 14, 34, 48–50, 56, 84, 95, 106, 132, 134–5, 138, 143, 151–2, 157, 280–82, 286, 292, 293, 299, 300–302
cluster
  cluster analysis 160–62
  cluster life cycle 84
cognitive proximity 6, 65–8, 75–6, 81, 83–6, 216
collective identity 74, 76, 78, 81, 82
collective learning 67, 77, 85, 88, 194
communicative skills 283, 285, 286, 301
computer industry 54, 57, 104
convergence
  beta (or ß)convergence 251–4
  conditional convergence 261–2, 266, 268, 270, 275
  convergence clubs 13, 241–2, 245, 248–50, 253–4, 258–9, 263, 275–6

convergence equation 261, 265–6
sigma (or σ) convergence 243, 245, 248
speed of convergence 14, 266, 268–9, 272, 278–9
cooperation R&D 200, 205, 209, 215, 217, 232, 234
coordination failures 6, 92, 103–4
creation of value 180, 191, 196
creative capital 282

data envelopment analysis 9, 156, 169, 170, 173–4
death of the distance 137, 151
demand complementarities 92, 104, 106
digital divide
  global digital divide 8, 152
  local digital divide 8, 138
domain name registrations 140
dyestuff industry 47, 56

economic geography 4, 6–7, 19, 21, 23, 61, 69, 88–9, 92, 97, 104–5, 107, 111–16, 126, 133, 135
education
  primary 13, 242, 246, 251, 253
  secondary 175, 246, 285
  stocks of 242, 246, 249
  tertiary 163, 242, 245–6, 249–51, 253–4, 257
efficiency (of the innovative activities) 156, 170
employment growth 280, 282, 293, 298–9, 300–301
endogeneity 132, 217, 254, 262, 275
endogenous growth theory 258, 280
entrepreneurial spirit 10, 178
entrepreneurship 29, 43, 48, 55, 57, 59, 194, 282
epidemic models 136
equilibrium models 8, 136

305

Index

Europe 2–3, 13–14, 39, 41, 44, 48, 53, 57–9, 61, 64, 93–5, 106–7, 119, 136–7, 150, 152–3, 194, 260, 270, 274, 276
European patent office 167
externalities
  geographical scope externalities 115
  Jacobs externalities 114, 126
  knowledge externalities 3, 5, 7–8, 42–3, 55, 111–17, 121–3, 131–3, 281, 288, 302
  MAR externalities 114
  network externalities 72, 75, 77, 85, 89, 90, 107
  pecuniary externalities 6–8, 92, 99, 104, 106, 111–18, 123, 126, 131–3
  sectoral scope externalities 115

factor analysis 9, 155–6, 158, 170, 282, 284
faculty members 11–12, 198, 201–6, 208, 211, 214–17
fashion leader 74
firm-level databases 95
firm managers 198, 199, 201, 203–5, 207, 209–11, 215, 216
fixed costs 96, 98, 102–6
flow 4, 21–3, 25, 29–30, 167, 179, 180, 182

geography of innovation 39, 57–8, 63, 88, 112, 115, 123, 126, 131, 134
growth 1–3, 6–7, 12–15, 32, 39, 41, 56, 59, 62, 72, 75, 77, 84, 87, 92–9, 100, 104–7, 111–14, 126, 134–5, 137, 150–52, 170, 192, 219, 238, 241–3, 245, 251–76, 278–84, 287–303
growth accounting exercises 93

high technology 5, 55, 88, 134, 159, 194
human capital
  accumulation rate 260–61, 271
  level 248, 256

IAIF index of regional innovation 9, 156, 162–6, 170, 172
increasing returns 27, 28, 43, 59, 71, 72, 76, 85, 87–8, 92, 98, 106, 135, 303

industry
  industrial district 10, 62, 88, 176, 178–9, 182, 190–91, 193, 195–6
  industrial structure 6, 7, 92–3, 112, 114–15, 126, 132, 134, 183
information and communications technologies (ICTs)
  ICTs adoption 136, 138–40, 142–3, 145–6, 148–51
  ICT cluster 62, 77, 79, 85, 89
information technology (IT)
  IT adoption 6, 92, 95–6, 104–5
  IT clusters 107
  IT intermediate inputs 6, 96, 98–9
  IT producing sectors 6, 92, 94–5, 104–5
  IT using sectors 94
informational cascade 69, 71, 73, 80, 85, 87–8
infrastructure for innovation 156–7
innovation
  innovation geography 39, 57–8, 63, 88, 112, 115, 123, 126, 131, 134
  innovation diffusion 136
  innovation system 2–4, 19, 24–30, 32–4, 36–40, 57, 88, 155–62, 165–9
  organizational innovation 5, 34, 36, 44, 46–7, 49–52, 55, 57, 139
innovative capacity 11, 162, 168, 173, 192
interaction 1, 4–6, 10–14, 20–21, 24–5, 29, 31–2, 34–5, 37, 61–4, 66, 68–78, 80–81, 83–8, 111–12, 131, 167–8, 171, 176–81, 183–4, 187–90, 198–9, 201–3, 206–7, 209, 211, 214–18, 231, 261–4, 266–7, 271–4, 278, 300
internet domain names 140
inverted U-shaped 10, 181–2, 186, 188, 189, 190

knowledge
  acquisition 13, 197
  economy 280–85, 298–302
  externalities 3, 5, 7–8, 42–3, 55, 111–17, 121, 123, 131–3, 281, 288, 302
  production function 9, 126, 133, 156, 166

Index

spillovers 3–5, 7, 27–8, 42–52, 54–9, 61, 88, 112, 115, 126, 133–5, 149, 200, 263, 280–81, 302–3
workers 283, 285–7, 198–301, 303

labour market 3, 7, 8, 100, 118, 126, 131–3, 262
learning 19–24, 29–31, 33–4, 36–8, 40, 49–50, 54, 57–9, 69, 71–3, 77, 80, 85, 88, 139, 151, 157, 173, 181, 191, 194–6, 201, 218, 220
legitimacy 5–6, 62, 70, 72–8, 81, 83–4, 86–7
local institutions 10–11, 178–9, 182–3, 185–92
location economies 120–23
locational
 locational norm 62, 86
 locational cascade 76, 84

main components 158
managerial position 11, 203, 209, 211, 214–6
maximum likelihood 249, 277, 298
mimetic interactions 6, 69, 71–6, 78, 80, 84–6
monopolistic competition 69, 98, 100, 105–6, 114
multiple equilibria 93, 101

Nelson and Phelps approach 255–6
network externalities 72, 75, 77, 85, 89–90, 107
no-growth trap 100
nonlinearities 13, 260–63, 266–7, 271–4
North–South divide 106, 146, 149

observational learning 69, 71, 73, 80
ordered probit 11, 206–7, 209–11, 214, 217
organic chemicals 4, 5, 43–6, 48, 51, 55
over-embeddedness 10, 176–82, 188–90

panel data
 and FGLS procedures 257
 and parameter heterogeneity 242
parameter heterogeneity 260–61, 263, 266, 274–5

patents 4, 8–9, 24, 42, 45, 49, 52, 68, 145–8, 154–5, 163, 166–8, 171–3, 284, 302
physical capital 267–8, 270
policy-makers 2, 5, 43, 52, 192, 198, 216, 221, 300
population (growth rate) 262, 264, 270
probit 11, 206–7, 209–12, 214, 217, 227
production function 7, 9, 20, 111, 116–17, 126, 133, 156, 169–70, 172, 262, 264–5, 275
productive environment 9, 158, 161
productivity 2, 33, 58, 93–6, 100, 104–7, 112, 114–15, 132–5, 138, 150, 152, 179, 203, 218, 242–3, 254, 258–9, 263, 280, 283
PROFIT 220–22, 224, 231–2, 233, 234
project selection 221–3, 227, 230, 235
public
 public funding 52, 219, 222, 232
 public research bodies 157
 public sector 12, 13, 31, 52, 59, 157, 220–21, 232–3, 243, 250–55, 257

redundant 178, 181, 190, 196
regional absorptive capacity 217
regional innovation index 3–4, 9, 19, 25, 27, 29–30, 32–4, 36–40, 155, 156, 158–61, 166–71, 200
regional innovation system 3, 4, 9, 19, 25, 27, 29–30, 32–4, 36–40, 155–6, 158–61, 166–71, 200
relational dimension 65
relational proximity 6, 67–8, 75–8, 82–3, 85–6
research abroad 12, 203, 209, 214–15
research and development (R&D)
 R&D expenditures 155, 163, 171
 private (R&D) 221, 234–5
 public (R&D) 220, 233–4
research organizations 191, 202, 204, 218–9, 222–3, 227, 232
returns to education
 private 254, 258
 social 267

scientific publications 145, 154
sectoral composition 8, 95, 138, 145–6, 154
sectoral differences 44, 234

self-defeating process 85–6, 90
self-fulfilling process 85–6
semiparametrics 13, 260–61, 263, 267–8, 271, 273–8
Siemens 5, 45, 48–51, 53–6, 58
Silicon Sentier 5, 61–3, 65, 67–8, 79, 81–6, 88
small Open Economy 6, 92, 96
social capital 10, 11, 34, 177–82, 188, 190, 192–7
social interactions 10, 37, 71, 83, 88, 176, 180–81, 183–4, 188
spatial
  spatial autocorrelation 7, 121, 150, 260, 267–8, 270, 275
  spatial dependence 8, 13–4, 120–22, 142–3, 260–61, 265, 267–8, 273–6, 281, 290
  spatial diffusion 138, 149, 263, 265–6
  spatial Durbin model 261, 266, 271, 274, 277
  spatial externalities 14, 106, 135, 151, 261–3, 265, 268, 270–71, 273, 276, 289
  spatial heterogeneity 8, 142, 143, 146, 149, 260, 290, 292, 301
  spatial lag 14, 148, 261, 267, 270–71, 281, 290, 298–300
  spatial multiplier 265, 276
  spatial regimes 146, 290–93, 299
spatial econometrics 134, 152, 276, 302
specialization 1, 8, 14, 26–7, 95, 97, 113–15, 126, 131–2, 134, 145, 281, 284, 286–7, 298–300, 302
spillover (Molina)
  information spillovers 136, 139
  knowledge spillovers 3–5, 7, 27–8, 42–52, 54–9, 61, 88, 112, 115, 126, 131, 133–5, 149, 200, 263, 280–81, 302–3
spline
  regression spline 271
  with smoothing parameters 278

stability 5, 62, 66, 70, 84–7, 89, 90, 232–3, 295
steady state 260, 262, 266, 272, 275
stock of scientific capital 157, 163

tacit knowledge 30, 33, 39, 69, 77, 83, 177, 193, 280, 286, 302
tacitness 4, 42–3, 54, 56–7
technological
  area 220, 225, 227, 230, 233
  frontier 13, 169
  progress 105, 235, 255–6, 264, 280
technology
  institutes 24, 220, 222–4, 230–33, 236
  policy 57–9, 173, 222, 224, 231–2
truncated model 207–9, 211, 217
trust 10, 15, 63, 66, 82–3, 85–6, 176–8, 180–84, 187–90, 195, 225, 283

uncertainty 2, 5–6, 39, 62, 70–78, 80, 84, 86, 219, 275
under-exploration 10, 176, 185, 187–9, 191, 193, 195, 197
universities 1, 4, 9, 10–12, 25–6, 31, 34–5, 40, 46–7, 64, 66, 140, 157, 163, 175, 178–9, 191, 198–205, 208–18, 220, 222, 223–4, 228, 230–32, 236, 287
urban
  urban heterogeneity 14, 280, 285, 300
  urban regimes 281–2, 299, 301
  urban/rural gap 138
urbanization economies 120–22, 126

venture capital 1, 27, 35–6, 56, 81, 83, 87, 157, 159, 160, 196
vertical integration 53

zoning
  labour market connectedness 281, 301